| *exploring* |

Adobe Flash CS4

| *exploring* |

Adobe Flash CS4

Annesa Hartman

Exploring Adobe Flash CS4
Annesa Hartman

Vice President, Career and Professional Editorial: Dave Garza

Director of Learning Solutions: Sandy Clark

Senior Acquisitions Editor: Jim Gish

Managing Editor: Larry Main

Product Manager: Nicole Calisi

Editorial Assistant: Sarah Timm

Vice President Marketing, Career and Professional: Jennifer McAvey

Executive Marketing Manager: Deborah S. Yarnell

Marketing Manager: Erin Brennan

Marketing Coordinator: Jonathan Sheehan

Production Director: Wendy Troeger

Senior Content Project Manager: Kathryn B. Kucharek

Art Directors: Bruce Bond and Joy Kocsis

Technology Project Manager: Christopher Catalina

Production Technology Analyst: Tom Stover

Library of Congress Control Number: 2008939781

ISBN-13: 978-1-4354-8555-6

ISBN-10: 1-4354-8555-6

Delmar
5 Maxwell Drive
Clifton Park, NY 12065-2919
USA

Cengage Learning is a leading provider of customized learning solutions with office locations around the globe, including Singapore, the United Kingdom, Australia, Mexico, Brazil, and Japan. Locate your local office at:
international.cengage.com/region

Cengage Learning products are represented in Canada by Nelson Education, Ltd.

To learn more about Delmar, visit **www.cengage.com/delmar**
Purchase any of our products at your local college store or at our preferred online store **www.ichapters.com**

Printed in Canada
1 2 3 4 5 6 7 13 12 11 10 09

With love, for Dave Marx

contents

contents

contents

contents

| *preface* |

INTENDED AUDIENCE

The intended audience for this book is most likely . . . you! If you have found this book in your hands, then you probably have some inkling of what Flash is all about and its important role in today's animation, interactive design and development industries.

Flash is a multi-faced program with features and tool sets that attract people of many different talents—designers, developers, animators, educators, students, even the creative dabbler or hobbyist. That being said, it's a challenging program to master all the parts, but its creative results for online distribution of content, Web sites, interactive experiences, and animated movies, makes it a win-win program for someone at any level of its learning.

FLASH IN CONTEXT

Often it's a challenging task to decipher the big picture view of the graphic design and development processes. We are inundated with an abundance of innovative technologies, techniques, and "wow" features that it's difficult, especially for the newcomer, to really comprehend how all the pieces—creative methods, tools, and skills—fit together to produce the inspirational digital content we digest most everyday. How does it all come together? In part, it comes together with a lot of practice and planning, tweaking and testing, deletes and do over's. But from a broader context it's important to ask and eventually be able to answer the following:

- What programs, tools, features, and furthermore strategies, best practices, theories and trends are best for creating content? From a graphics application standpoint, examples might include Photoshop and Illustrator for digital image creation, Microsoft Word for textual content, Audacity for audio content, and TechSmith's Jing (*http://www.jingproject.com/*) for screen captured video.

- What programs, tools, and features best optimize, compress, encode, and covert digital content? For example, Adobe Acrobat for PDF's, Adobe's Media Encoder, or Photoshop's Save for Web & Devices command.
- What programs best layout and assemble content? Examples include Adobe InDesign, Quark, Microsoft Publisher for print layouts, and Dreamweaver or Flash for online content.

Understanding the broad perspective of this interrelationship with tools, processes, and programs can be a turning point in the success of anyone venturing into the field of computer graphic design. While I tend to categorize Flash as a layout program, overall I find Flash to be one of the best programs to give someone a snapshot of all the different skill sets required in the graphic and Web design and development industries—it offers hands-on with vector graphics, animation, object oriented programming, audio and video. Each aspect of Flash can continue to be explored to such an extent as to launch someone into a full-on career as an animator, a Web designer, or a programmer/developer (all of which are related to digital technologies, yet require distinctly different disciplines with unique skill sets). The talented someone who is well versed in all the aspects of Flash is a rare find.

BACKGROUND OF THIS TEXT

Explaining at a basic level the various aspects of the Flash program—graphics, animation, interactive authoring, audio and video—is what makes teaching this program such a challenge, but that's the result of the instructional design of this book. This book focuses on Flash through the eyes of a designer. It's a thorough introduction to the main aspects of the program, offering a good dose of the visual design features and the behind the scenes development of online experiences.

Each aspect of the book is clearly and visually explained to cater to the designer intellect and any new recruits to the program. The lessons build slowly but purposefully a readers understanding of all that Flash has to offer—with opportunity to explore each aspect individually and also within the context of a complete project or interactive experience. By the end of the book a reader has the ability to make his/her own basic Flash Web sites, movies, and presentations replete with graphics, animation, text, and interactive events such as buttons and video and audio playback, and all along getting an ample introduction of design concepts and real world advice from professionals in the field. No other book offers this extensive, yet approachable and practical outlook to learning Flash; it comes from an author who has been teaching Flash to designers and newcomers since its inception. And, many lessons in the book have been successfully taught to high school and college level students in introductory Flash courses for over 7 years.

This full-color book:

- Offers clear explanations and hands-on experiences to explore each of the major aspects of Flash—graphics, animation, interactive authoring, and audio and video integration.

- Contains industry advice, tips, strategies, and intermediate explorations for further study of the program and the field of graphic design in general.
- Is visually enhanced; featuring numerous screen shots of interface elements, Flash movie examples, and diagrams to scaffold one's comprehension of unfamiliar or complex concepts.
- Is written by a graphic designer and an instructional designer. Information provided is not random and disjointed as often seen in other books. It's purposeful in its attempt to get to the heart of what users can do with Flash—presenting a focused view, but within the context of the larger construct and intention of the program.

A Word about ActionScript

ActionScript 2.0 and ActionScript 3.0 are the two current scripting languages supported by Adobe Flash CS4 and the latest version of the Flash Player (the engine that runs Flash movies within the Web environment, or as independent presentations). Each new version of ActionScript aims to be more compliant with ECMAScript. The result of this has made the language less intuitive for designers and more in line with what programmers want and need to make their coding more streamlined and flexible. This book sticks with ActionScript 2.0. As a novice to Flash, ActionScript 2.0 syntax and usage is easier to grasp until one gets enough understanding under the belt to venture into ActionScript 3.0. If there is any program that provides a somewhat comfortable foray for designers to dabble in left-brain activity (i.e., coding), Flash is it.

TEXTBOOK ORGANIZATION

In this book, and in purpose all the books in Cengage Delmar Learning's Design Exploration series, the objective is to be clear and no-nonsense in approach, never negating the practical—yet vastly experiential—aspects of the program.

Each chapter builds upon itself, and material is presented in a linear fashion, introducing Flash tools and features on a "need-to-know" basis. This approach streamlines the amount of information a reader must know to successfully render a task. However, it's encouraged to jump around to get certain facts when you need them, especially if you are already somewhat familiar with the program. As well, to accommodate those who appreciate alternative methods of learning information, both textually and visually succinct explanations of the important concepts to grasp in each chapter are provided. For those who prefer structured, hands-on experiences, step-by-step lessons are provided; for those who prefer to wander around a bit, final project files, samples, and suggestions for further exploration are available for deconstruction.

The following is a brief overview of the concepts and skills covered in each chapter.

Chapter 1: **A Discovery Tour** In this chapter explore the process of interactive design, some of the current trends in Web design and development, what makes Flash so special, and making a Flash animation.

Chapter 2: **Getting Around** Practice navigating through the Flash interface, and develop a fundamental understanding of bitmaps and vectors.

Chapter 3: **Object and Drawing Fundamentals** Master the drawing tools, and effective importing and manipulating of shape and group objects in the program.

Chapter 4: **Symbols** Discover the power of symbol objects, and their importance in more advanced application of the program.

Chapter 5: **Animation Basics** Learn how to make things move and develop a thorough understanding of how to use the Flash timeline, tweening, and frame-by-frame animation techniques.

Chapter 6: **Introduction to Interactivity** The basis of Flash interactivity is ActionScript, an object oriented programming language. Get an overview of the object oriented programming structure. Dissect basic ActionScripts and their syntax, create actions in the Actions panel, add some simple interactivity to a movie and construct a click-through presentation.

Module 7: **Putting It All Together** This chapter addresses the architecture and development of a Flash site using multiple SWFs, enhanced integration of movie clips, and movie output and optimization options. Also an overview of the Web site design process is presented.

Chapter 8: **Working with Text** Discover the many attributes of text in Flash—static, dynamic and input, and its interactive functionality and features, such as embedded vs. device fonts, anti-aliasing, font mapping, forms, scrolling, and accessibility.

Chapter 9: **Working with Sound** In this chapter explore the use of sound in Flash, covering an overview of sound reproduction, basic audio terminology and concepts, the sound options available in Flash, and practice working with sound within a movie.

Chapter 10: **Working with Video** In this chapter explore the use of video in Flash, including an overview of video characteristics, and the conversion, optimization, and publishing of video within a Flash movie.

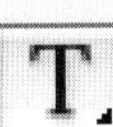

FEATURES

The following list provides some of the salient features of the text:

- Learning goals are clearly stated at the beginning of each chapter.
- Instructional focus is on a visually oriented introduction to the basic functions and tools of Flash, meeting the needs of design students and professionals alike.
- Client projects highlighted in the "Adventures in Design" sections share processes and techniques that a designer might encounter on the job.
- "Explorer Pages" sections provide an inside look at how artists' working in the field come up with their ideas and inspirations.
- "Exploring on Your Own" sections offer suggestions and sample lessons for further study of content covered in each chapter.
- "In Review" sections are provided at the end of each chapter to test reader understanding and retention of the material covered.
- A CD-ROM at the back of the book contains support files to complete the book's exercises.

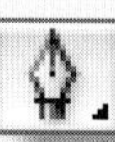

INSTRUCTOR RESOURCES

This CD was developed to assist instructors in planning and implementing their instructional programs. It includes sample syllabi for using this book in either an 11- or 15-week semester. It also provides answers to the "In Review" questions, PowerPoint slides highlighting the main topics, and additional instructor resources.

To order, please call 1-800-347-7707.

ISBN: 1435485556

FILE SETUP

Located in the back of this book is a CD-ROM containing all files for completing the lessons in this book. These lesson files are compatible with Adobe Flash CS4. For a trial version of Adobe Flash CS4, visit *http://www.adobe.com/downloads/*.

Before starting any of the lessons, create a folder on your local computer named My Lessons (or whatever name you prefer). From the CD, drag a copy of the lesson files to the folder. As you work on the lessons, open the lessons, assets, and sample files from this location. You can then also save your work at the same place.

        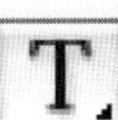

HOW TO USE THIS TEXT

The features discussed in the following sections are found in the book.

▶ Charting Your Course and Goals

The introduction and chapter objectives start off each chapter. They describe the competencies the reader should achieve upon understanding the chapter.

charting your course

OK, now we get into the fun part—the moving experience of animation! This chapter takes you on a whirlwind overview of tweening and frame-by-frame animation, the animation-specific features of Flash, and hands-on practice with various animation techniques. In conclusion, use the animation skills learned to animate the sailboat scene introduced in the last module.

goals

In this chapter you will:

- **Get an overview of Flash animation types—tweening and frame-by-frame**
- **Learn the parts of the Timeline, and identify animation types on the Timeline**
- **Get hands-on practice with tweening the motion, position, color, rotation, scale, and shape of objects**
- **Explore techniques for editing a tween's path**
- **Complete a frame-by-frame animation**
- **Discover the power of the movie clip Timeline**
- **Practice animation skills learned on the sailboat scene you created in the last chapter**

▶ Explorer Pages

These sections showcase the imagery, insights, and work flow processes of successful graphic artists.

166 | Ellis Neder |

Explorer pages

ELLIS NEDER

"View the Process" Flash presentation for TimeSlips Creative Storytelling Project (*http://www.timeslips.org/*). Designed and developed by Ellis Neder, Sway Design.

About Ellis Neder

Along with many graphic designers, Ellis began creating Web sites in the late 1990s completely unaware that this new medium we were all suddenly involved in would turn out to be such an ideal teaching tool. In 1999, he started his design studio, Sway Design (along with Annesa who moved on three years after), when he moved back to New York after living in Seattle for two years where he was the director of a children's art school and taught drawing and painting classes to teenagers. Ellis had done some marketing and graphic design for the school, including working with a design firm to launch the school's first Web site, and when he returned to New York, a number of his artist friends asked for help moving their film and theater projects online.

A year later he was asked by a Madison Avenue advertising firm to create branding projects in Flash and HTML for Sony and Sprint, so he quickly learned everything he could about how large companies were using interactive technologies. United Way saw his work and asked him to redesign their Web templates and also create an online manual that taught their local partner organizations how to build successful Web sites while correctly using the United Way brand. The project was a huge challenge and a great way to learn about the importance of Web standards because it forced him to explain everything he had learned up to that point about online content development "best practices".

Since 2000 Ellis has designed projects for non-profits, universities, and *Fortune 500* companies, and using the Web as an educational tool has been a constant theme throughout. The Web sites he has created teach people a variety of skills including how to use technology in the classroom, how to engage in the voting process, how artists go about creating their work, and how to be socially responsible when purchasing products online.

The two years Ellis spent in the classroom struggling to explain the mysteries of drawing and painting to a room full of restless teenagers honed his communication skills and, in a hands-on way, taught him the importance of clear, direct communication. Today he uses these same skills to help his clients educate the public about their brands, the products they sell, and the services they offer that make them unique.

Enjoy more of Ellis's work at *http://www.swaydesign.com*.

| EXPLORER PAGES | 167

About the Work of Ellis Neder

"The first move in any creative process is to introduce constraints."
Alan Fletcher, *The Art of Looking Sideways*

In his own words, Ellis shares his work process . . . "We all begin a web design project with a few constraints; typography, the browsers and the tools we use like Flash and Photoshop to design with all limit us in some way at the outset. If you're creating work for a client, their initial content and their ideas about how a website should look also begin to constrain us. But there's one more constraint that plays a key role and it's one that often gets forgotten by younger designers. You aren't really designing for yourself and you aren't even designing for your client. You're designing for the client's audience and it's your job to define that audience and develop a visual language that connects with them."

"When people ask me what I do as a web designer I tell them—'I get paid to think like someone else.' This usually throws them off a little but I explain that, over the years, I've developed a solid understanding of the grid and the rules of typography and the roles they both play in creating a good design, but it's my ability to think outside of my own head that adds the most value to a project. It's key to imagine what the viewers of your sites will experience as they begin clicking links and scanning pages of text, and it's important to make that experience both easy and engaging, especially as faster and faster web technologies like mobile platforms become important. In his classic work on typography, *The Elements of Typographic Style*, the designer Robert Bringhurst called this 'the task of creative non-interference.' In all of my projects I strive for this approach of 'non-interference' with simple, clear design that lets my client's content say what it needs to say and connect with the audience as quickly as it can."

"The Journey Across 90 Miles" is a Flash mini-site for the documentary *90 Miles* that aired on P.O.V., a PBS showcase for independent non-fiction films (*http://www.pbs.org/pov/pov2003/90miles/*). Created by Ellis Neder, Sway Design.

A Flash portfolio for Peace Design (*http://www.peacedesign.org*). Site designed and developed by Ellis Neder, Sway Design.

▶ In Review and Exploring on Your Own

Review questions are located at the end of each chapter and allow the reader to assess his or her understanding of the chapter. The section "Exploring on Your Own" contains exercises that reinforce chapter material through practical application.

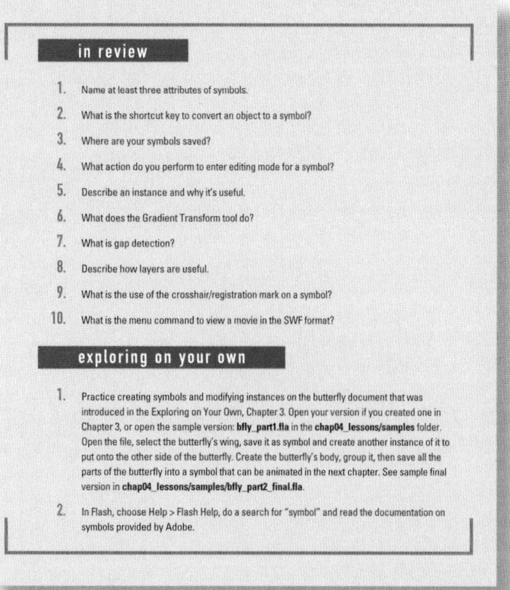

in review

1. Name at least three attributes of symbols.
2. What is the shortcut key to convert an object to a symbol?
3. Where are your symbols saved?
4. What action do you perform to enter editing mode for a symbol?
5. Describe an instance and why it's useful.
6. What does the Gradient Transform tool do?
7. What is gap detection?
8. Describe how layers are useful.
9. What is the use of the crosshair/registration mark on a symbol?
10. What is the menu command to view a movie in the SWF format?

exploring on your own

1. Practice creating symbols and modifying instances on the butterfly document that was introduced in the Exploring on Your Own, Chapter 3. Open your version if you created one in Chapter 3, or open the sample version: **bfly_part1.fla** in the **chap04_lessons/samples** folder. Open the file, select the butterfly's wing, save it as symbol and create another instance of it to put onto the other side of the butterfly. Create the butterfly's body, group it, then save all the parts of the butterfly into a symbol that can be animated in the next chapter. See sample final version in **chap04_lessons/samples/bfly_part2_final.fla**.
2. In Flash, choose Help > Flash Help, do a search for "symbol" and read the documentation on symbols provided by Adobe.

▶ Adventures in Design

These spreads contain client assignments showing readers how to approach a design project using the tools and design concepts taught in the book.

128 | masking | | ADVENTURES IN DESIGN | 129

ADVENTURES IN DESIGN

Masking

Masks are one of the most common effects used in computer graphics; to mask is to hide or reveal an object(s) or part of an object(s). In the instance of Flash any filled shape can be a mask. The filled area, when placed on a mask layer, represents a completely transparent window in which other shapes, graphics, etc., can be revealed behind it. Creating masks is easy, but how you use them is up to your imagination.

PROFESSIONAL PROJECT EXAMPLE

For the last few years, I have been asked by The Roxbury Latin School, an independent boys school in West Roxbury, Massachusetts, to create a Flash presentation for their annual online giving appeal. The presentations are always full of attractive photographs that I'm challenged to find the most appealing way to subtly transition one photo into another with text and music included. My favorite way to do this is to frame the photos within a mask shaped as the school's logo or design elements found on their Web site (*http://www.roxburylatin.org*). Figure A-1 is a screen shot of The Roxbury Latin School's presentation I designed in 2006, which shows an example of a photo framed by a mask in the shape of the school's shield. Photos are animated fading in and out within the mask shape.

Figure A-2 shows The Roxbury Latin School's presentation for 2007—another example of a mask, but one that swoops horizontally across the screen with photos that pass within the curved shape.

YOUR TURN

Now, it's your turn to make a mask and animate it.

Setting up the Mask

1. Open Flash and create a new Flash File (ActionScript 2.0).
2. Set the workspace to Classic.

figure A-1 Example of a mask effect in a presentation for The Roxbury Latin School. The mask is in the shape of the school's logo.

figure A-2 Another example of a mask effect in a presentation for The Roxbury Latin School. Photos are animated with the curved mask shape.

figure A-3 Create a circular shape to the left of the movie area.

3. In the Properties panel for the document, change the color of the Stage to black.
4. Rename Layer 1, **spotlight**.
5. Select the Text tool in the Tools panel and type the word SPOTLIGHT across the center of the Stage. Make the text fairly large (about 90 pts), bold, and a light color.
6. Make a new layer above the **spotlight** layer and call it **mask**.
7. On the **mask** layer create a filled circle shape (no stroke, any fill color) and place it off Stage and to the left of the movie. See Figure A-3.

ABOUT THE AUTHOR

Annesa Hartman holds a Masters in Teaching with Internet Technologies, focusing her attention on instructional design for online technologies, and Web and graphic design concepts and programs. Currently, she is an Instructional Designer for Landmark College's Institute for Research and Training in Putney, Vermont, where she designs and develops online courses for educators. For over 14 years she also has taught computer graphic courses and is a freelance graphic designer with clients from around the world. She is the author of *Exploring Adobe Photoshop CS4*, *Exploring Adobe Illustrator CS4*, and *Producing Interactive Television*. When she is not pushing pixels, she is performing community theater and teaching yoga classes.

ACKNOWLEDGMENTS

I've been itching to write this book for sometime and I thank Cengage Delmar Learning for giving me the opportunity to bring it to life. First, I acknowledge with great gratitude my fellow colleagues at Landmark College—Linda Hecker, Ellen Engstrom, Alicia Brandon, Jim Baucom, Julie Strothman, and Steve Fadden, and Landmark students/alumni—Katie Culpepper, Mike Tranchina, and Ryan Ward. Next, a big thanks to the talented artists highlighted in the Explorer Pages—Ellis Neder, James Couture, and Justin Lerner, and my Flash students from Modesto Junior College—Edvin Eshagh, Ashley Gonsales, and Joan Powell Kennedy. Also, much appreciation to Veda Crewe Joseph, The Roxbury Latin School, Joshua Hirsch, and photographer aficionado, Dan Marx. Finally, thank you to my dear boyfriend, Dave Marx, for providing encouragement and support during my most stressful, book-writing moments. Ah, that's better!

Cengage Delmar Learning and I would also like to thank Toni Toland for ensuring the technical accuracy of this text.

QUESTIONS AND FEEDBACK

Cengage Delmar Learning and the author welcome your questions and feedback. If you have suggestions you think others would benefit from, please let us know and we will try to include them in the next edition.

To send us your questions and/or feedback, you can contact the publisher at:

Cengage Delmar Learning
Executive Woods
5 Maxwell Drive
Clifton Park, NY 12065
Attn: Media Arts & Design Team
800-998-7498

Or Annesa Hartman at:

Landmark College
Instructional and Graphic Designer
P.O. Box 820
River Road South
Putney, VT 05346
ahartman@landmark.edu

| a discovery tour |

1

A DISCOVERY TOUR

charting your course

No time, but the present—in this chapter, we begin with a hands-on exploration of Adobe Flash. You may start the lesson right away, or read through it carefully. Whatever method the intention is to give you a spark—or "flash"—of inspiration to delve further into all that Flash offers.

goals

In this chapter you will:

- **Discover the purpose of Flash, who uses it and why**
- **Explore some of Flash's tools and features**
- **Create an animated business card**
- **Get excited about Flash**

THE FLASH PHENOMENON

Since its inception in 1996, Adobe Flash (previously called Macromedia Flash) has made a huge impact in the digital content creation industry—strutting its stuff in animation and games, television and Web advertisements, and Internet and mobile device applications. As a content authoring program, it offers a multi-faceted set of tools and features for online designers and developers, animators, illustrators, programmers, educators, and off-the-shelf enthusiasts. You can assemble, create, animate, and interact with content, such as images, text, audio, and video (all of which you will get to explore in this book) and output the content into a highly compressed form for viewing via the Flash Player in online environments (more on that later).

Lesson: An Animated Business Card

In this lesson, you get to explore a bit of the Flash phenomenon. Using a document containing a virtual version of a business card you will navigate the interface, translate and animate an object, add a button, and publish the movie for online delivery.

Exploring a Document

1. Open Flash.
   (A trial version is available for download at *http://www.adobe.com/products/flash.*)

2. A welcome screen opens. Choose the Open option (see Figure 1–1), and open the file **chap1L1.fla** in the **Exploring Flash CS4/chap01_lessons** folder.

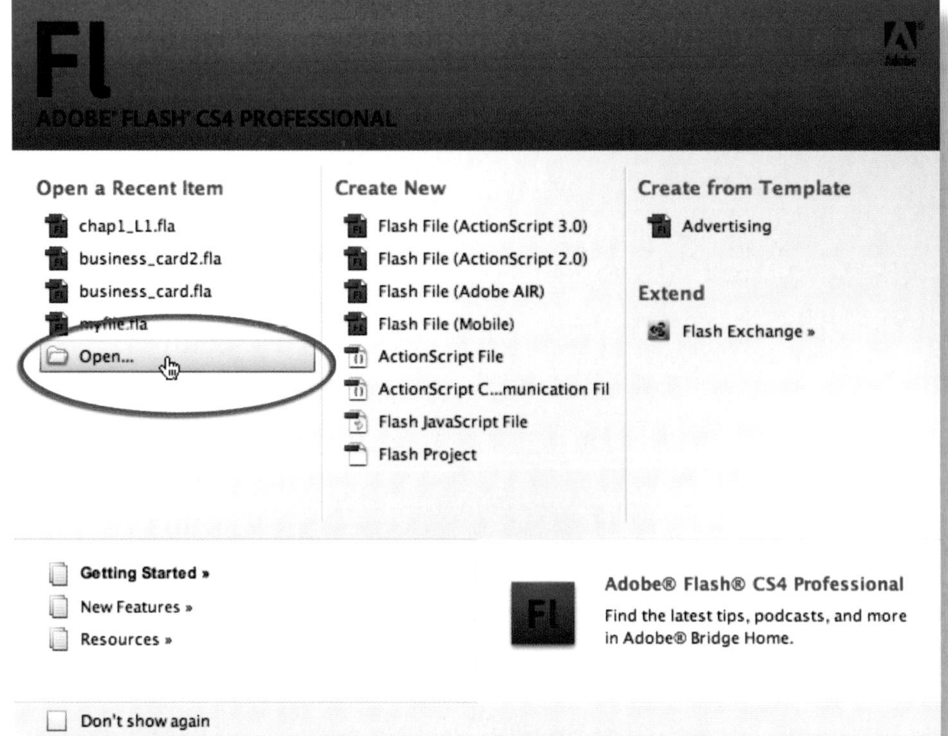

figure 1–1

The Flash Welcome screen.

Note: As mentioned in File Setup in the preface, before starting the lessons, create a folder on your computer. Name it **My_Lessons** (or whatever name you prefer). From the CD, drag a copy of the lesson files to your folder. As you work on the lessons, open the lessons, assets and sample files from this location. You can save your work in the same place.

3. In the upper right corner of the interface click on the Default button and choose the "Classic" workspace from the submenu. See Figure 1–2.
4. From the menu bar at the top of the Flash program, choose View > Magnification > Fit in Window for a zoomed in view of the movie area you will be working on. See Figure 1–3. This is a sample design of a business card that you will use to explore some features in Flash and add interactivity. This business card is not designed for print, but rather delivery as an email attachment, a Web advertisement, or in some other digital form.

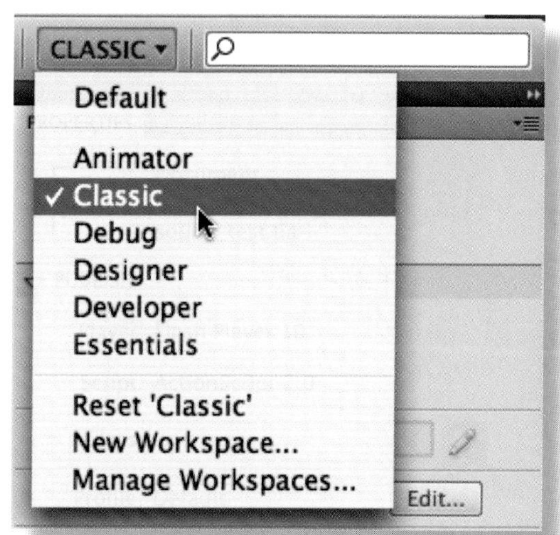

figure 1–2

Choose the Classic workspace.

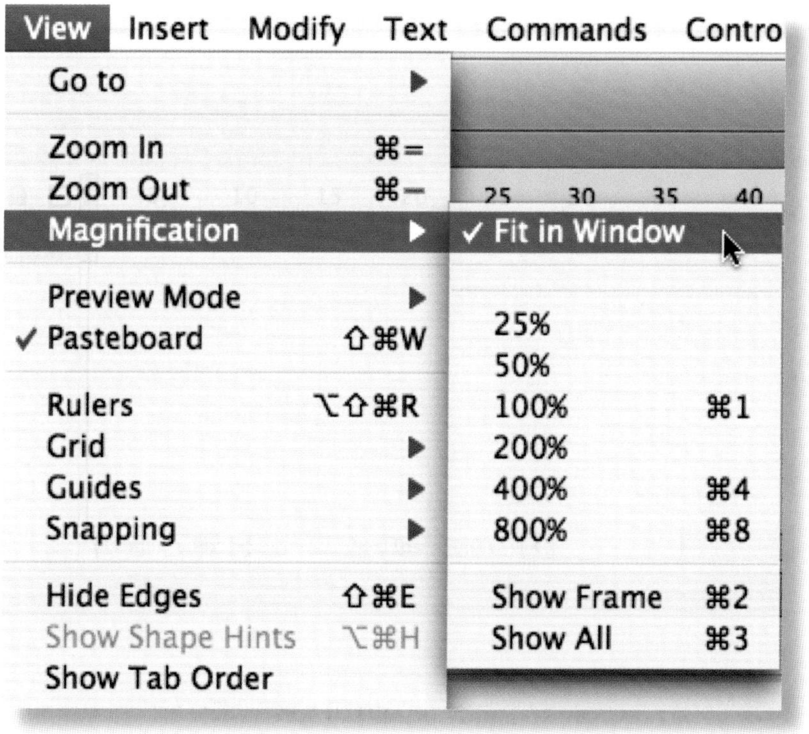

figure 1–3

Set magnification from the Menu bar.

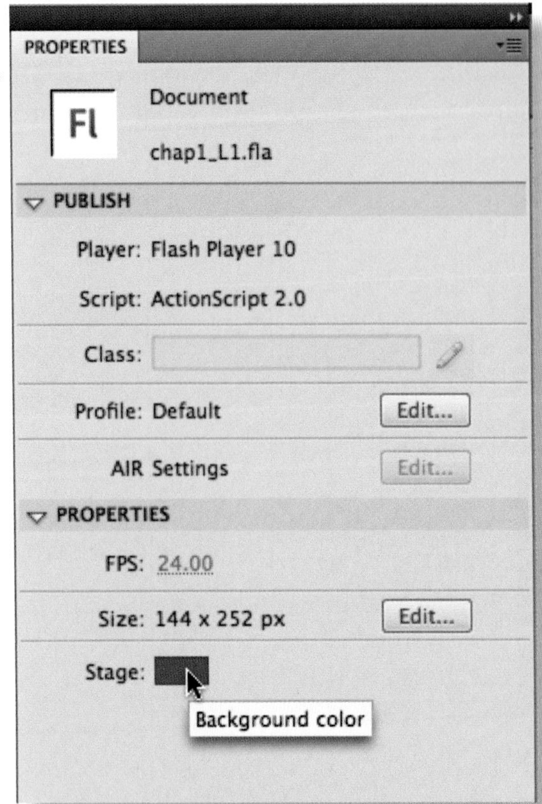

Adjust document properties in the Properties panel.

5. First view the document's properties located in the Properties panel on the right. Panels in Flash show valuable information about whatever element is currently selected on the Stage, which at this moment is the whole document itself. Note that in the Document's Properties you can view the name of the document, its Publish options, and adjust its size, color, and the frame rate of any animation applied. See Figure 1–4.

6. Click on the Veda Crewe Joseph image at the top of the business card, and notice that the information on the Properties panel changes—the settings now include options for the selected bitmap, **logo.jpg**. See Figure 1–5.

7. Now click on the text in the layout and note that the Properties panel offers options for adjusting text (Position and Size, Character, and Paragraph). You will use the Properties panel a lot in this program.

figure 1–5

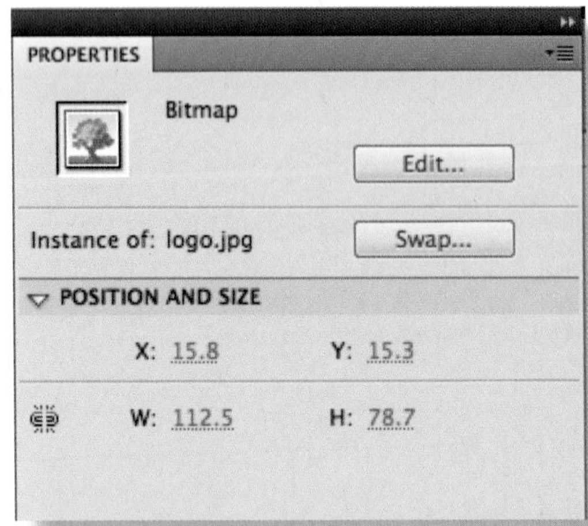

Properties for a bitmap image titled **logo.jpg**.

8. Now, check out the top of the interface—the Timeline. To see the Timeline clearly and all the layers of information that are contained on the Stage, click and drag down on the horizontal bar at the bottom part of the Timeline panel. See Figure 1–6. The Timeline panel is where you organize your objects on various layers, and animate them if you so choose. Right now, there is no animation in the scene—all the objects on each of the layers are positioned on frame

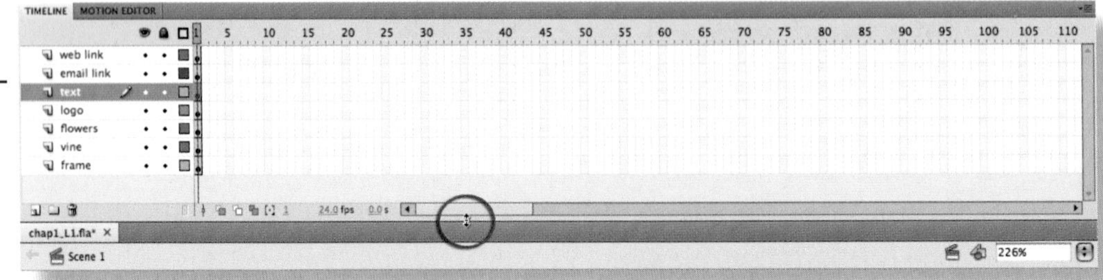

Resize the Timeline panel.

one (indicated by the single black dots in each layer called keyframes). See Figure 1–7.

9. Click on the **vine** layer to select it (it turns gray) and notice that the object on that layer is highlighted (selected) on the Stage.

10. Be sure the Selection tool is highlighted in the Tools panel on the left. Refer to Figure 1–11. Now, click and drag directly on the vine image on the Stage. You can move it around wherever you like.

11. Choose Edit > Undo from the main menu to bring it back to its original position. Be sure it's still selected (A blue box is still visible around the object.).

12. To the left of the interface is the Tools panel—there is a ton of fun things in this panel, but let's take one tool at a time. Click on the Free Transform tool. See Figure 1–8. You can scale, rotate, and move an object with this tool.

13. Click and drag on one of the black square handles on the Transform bounding box around the vine to change the scale of the vine image. See Figure 1–9.

14. Choose Command (⌘)-Z (Mac) or Ctrl-Z (Windows) on your keyboard to undo.

15. Click just outside of one of the black square handles until you see a circular icon. Click and drag to rotate the object. See Figure 1–10.

16. Command (⌘)-Z (Mac) or Ctrl-Z (Windows) to undo.

17. Choose File > Save, title your file **chap1L1_yourname.fla** and save it in your lessons folder.

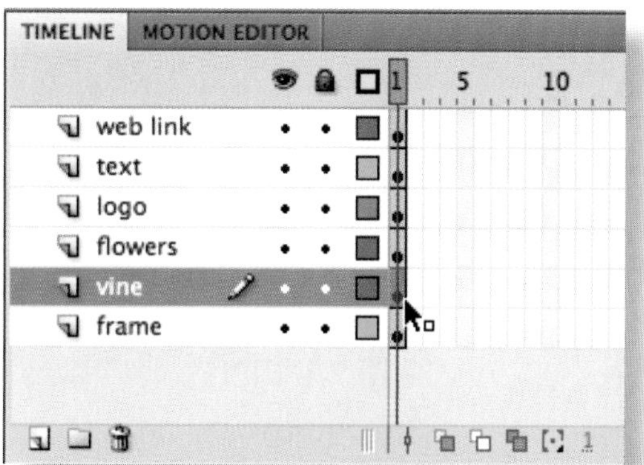

figure 1–7

Select the **vine** layer.

figure 1–8

Select the Free Transform tool from the Tools panel.

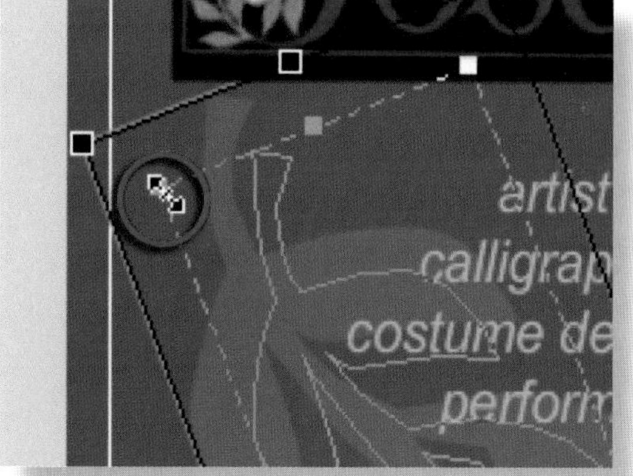

figure 1–9

Scale the vine graphic.

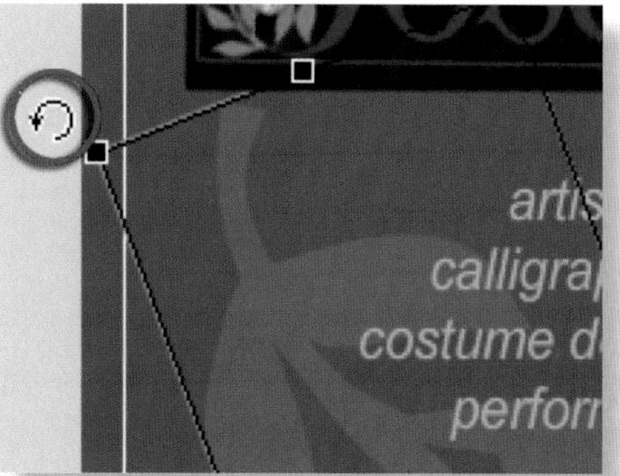

figure 1–10

Rotate the vine graphic.

figure 1–11

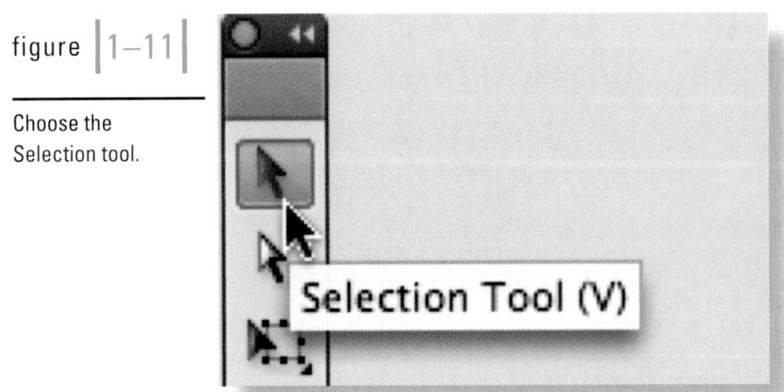

Choose the Selection tool.

Animating an Object

1. In the center of the card is a flower. Select the Selection tool in the Tools panel. See Figure 1–11. Click on the flower and choose Delete on the keyboard. Notice that in the **flowers** layer (up in the Timeline panel) there is now an empty circle in the first frame, which indicates there is nothing on that layer. See Figure 1–12.

figure 1–12

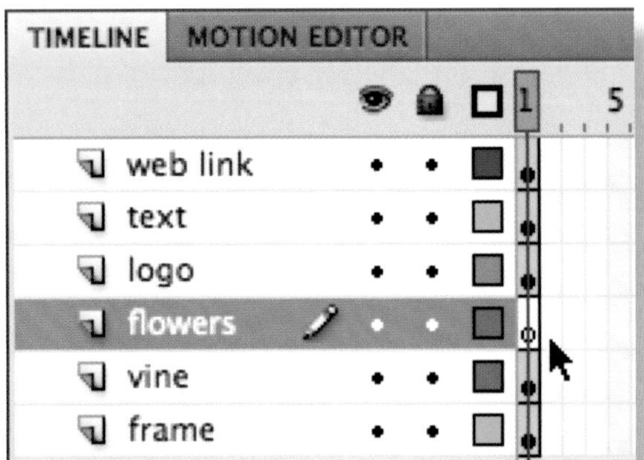

Delete the object on the flowers layer.

figure 1–13

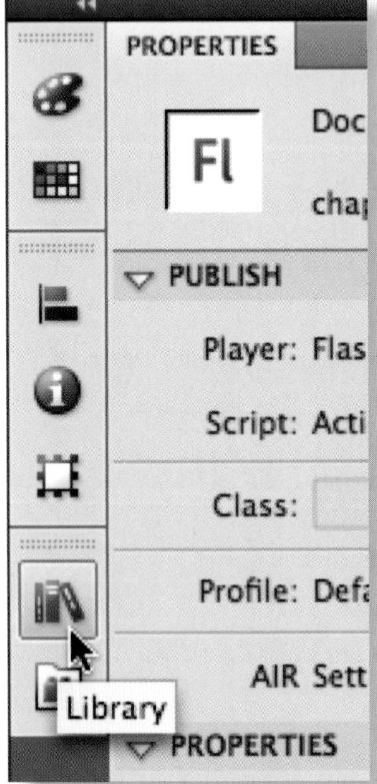

Expand the Layers panel.

2. Let's add a new flower from the Library. From the panel on the right choose the Library icon. See Figure 1–13 (You can also choose Window > Library).

3. In the Library are three items—**flower**, **logo.jpg**, and **vine**. The flower and vine were drawn as vector objects in Flash and saved as reusable objects called symbols. The **logo.jpg** is a bitmap image made elsewhere and imported into the program. These items are saved in a Library so you can use them in your scene whenever you would like.

> **Note:** What's a vector? What's a bitmap? And, uh, symbols? In short, vectors and bitmaps are ways in which digital images are constructed. And, symbols are special objects that you can convert these images into to use in animation and ActionScripting within Flash. All of these things are covered in upcoming chapters.

4. Click on the icon next to the flower name in the Library. See Figure 1–14. Drag a copy of the **flower** into the center of the card. Note on the **flowers** layer there is now a black dot on frame one indicating an object is on the Stage.

figure 1–14

Select the flower symbol.

Note: **As you learned, the flower is a symbol. As a symbol, you may drag from the Library as many flowers as you would like into the scene, and the interesting thing is that Flash will only calculate the size of only one of the flowers and a little more. Let's say, for example, the flower is 1 kilobyte in size. If you placed 10 instances of the flower from the Library to the Stage instead of the overall file size increasing by 10 kilobytes, it would only increase by a little more than 1 kilobyte. That's just one way Flash can make such small movie files.**

5. Click on the flower on the Stage and be sure the Free Transform tool is selected in the Tools panel (refer to Figure 1–8).
6. Click and drag on one corner of the transform bounding box around the flower and decrease the flower size by approximately 50%. See Figure 1–15.
7. On the **web link** layer on the timeline click and drag down to select frame 30 on all the layers (they should turn blue). (Be sure to click and drag as one action, rather than click and then click and drag—that will get a different effect than what we want right now. Choose Edit > Undo if necessary.) See Figure 1–16. You can also hold down your shift key and select each frame vertically down.

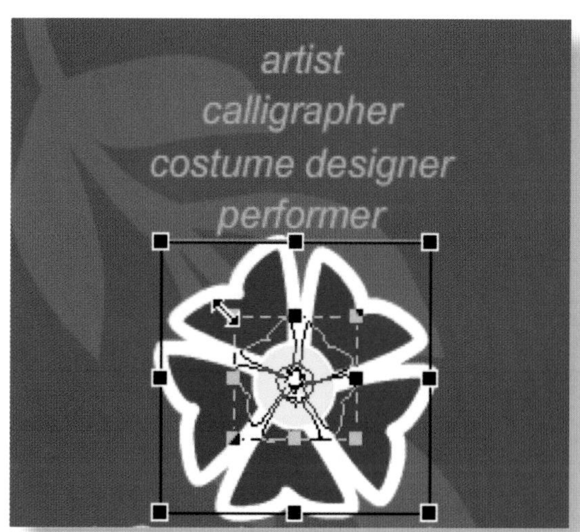

figure 1–15

Scale down the flower graphic.

Select frame 30 of all the layers.

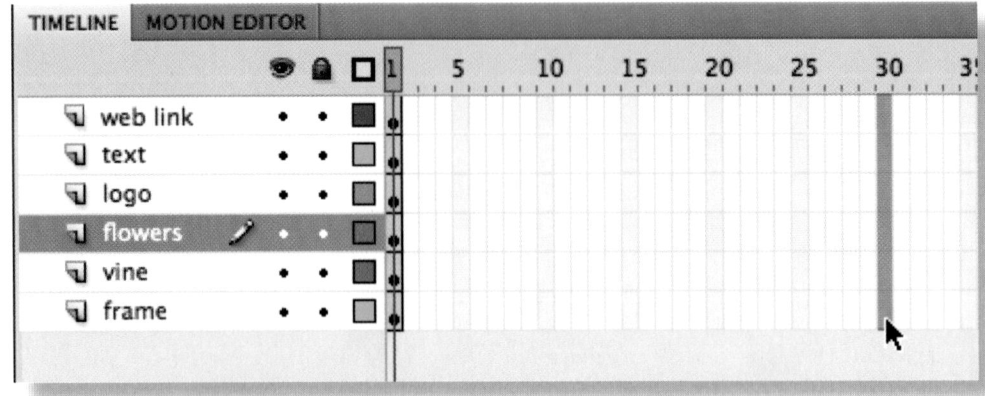

8. Once all frames are selected, click and hold (Mac) or right-click (Windows) on any of the selected frames and choose Insert Frame from the frame option's drop down menu. See Figure 1–17. Also you can choose Insert > Timeline > Frame from the menu bar or press F5 on your keyboard. Blank keyframes will be added from frames 1 through 30 on all the layers. This is so that you will be able to see all the items on the card over 30 frames (a little over 1 second of time considering the default frame rate is set at 24 frames per second).

Insert a Frame.

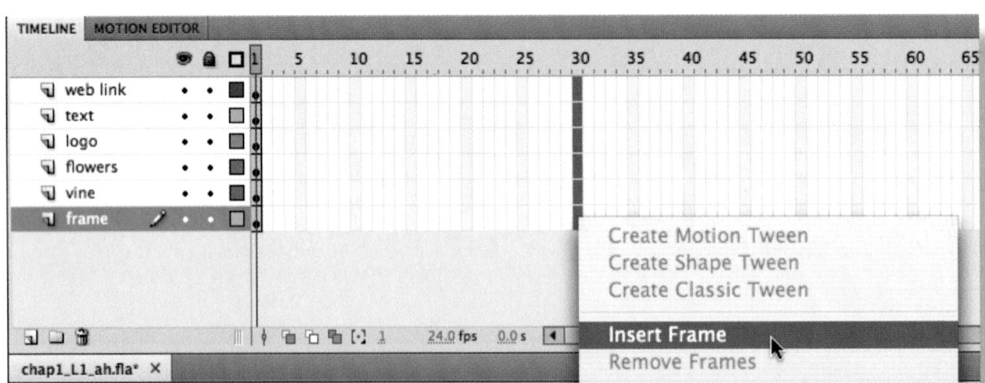

9. Now to rotate the flower. Click, then click and hold (Mac) or right-click (Windows) anywhere between frames 1 to 30 of the **flowers** layer to bring up the frame options menu—choose Create Motion Tween. See Figure 1 to 30. A blue bar extends between frames 1–30.

figure 1–18

Create a Motion Tween.

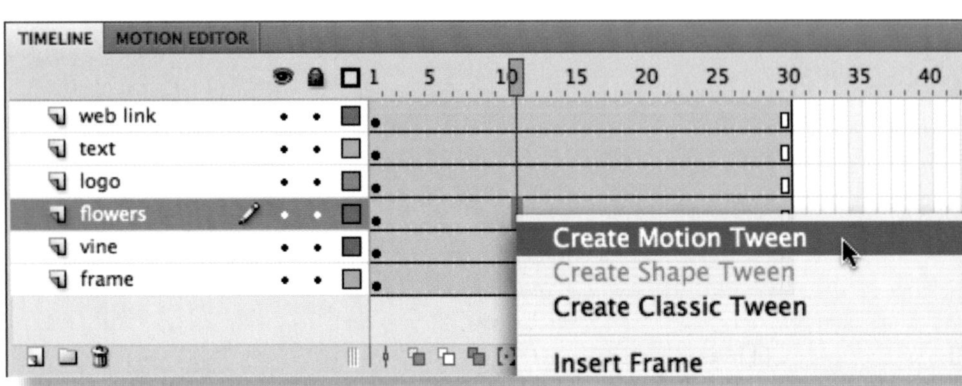

10. In the Properties panel on the right, position your cursor right below the word "time(s)" under Rotation—a two directional arrow will appear. Click and drag to the right or left (scrub, is the technical term!) to increase or decrease the amount of rotations the flower will complete over 30 frames. Settle on rotate 1 time(s). See Figure 1–19.

11. Hit Enter (Return) on the keyboard to play the animation. Amazing—Flash is calculating the rotation of the flower between frames 1 and 30—this is an animation technique called "tweening."

12. Save your file.

13. Choose Control > Test Movie from the menu bar to view a version of the movie in the SWF format (pronounced "swiff"). SWF is the compressed format of your movie used for delivery to the online environment. Note the flower object keeps rotating by default—it can be stopped, but that's for later learning. Close the output window.

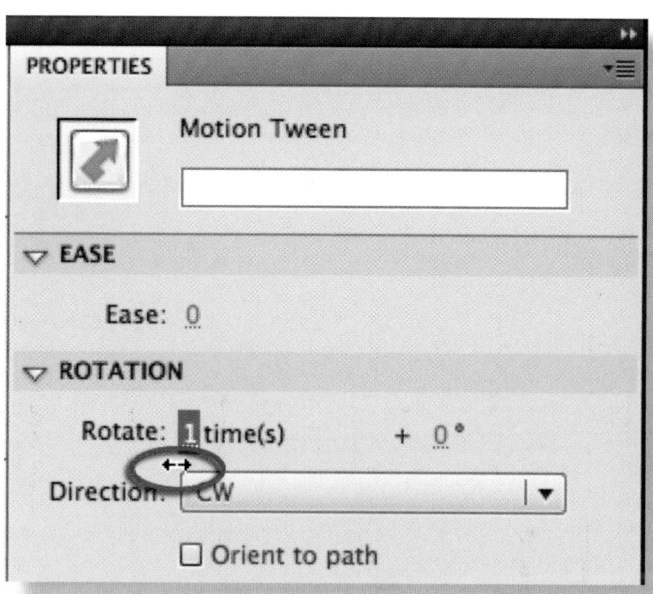

figure 1–19

Set rotation to once around.

Adding an Action

1. Select the Selection tool in the Tools panel. See Figure 1–20.

2. Click on the Web address text at the bottom of the card to select it. See Figure 1–21.

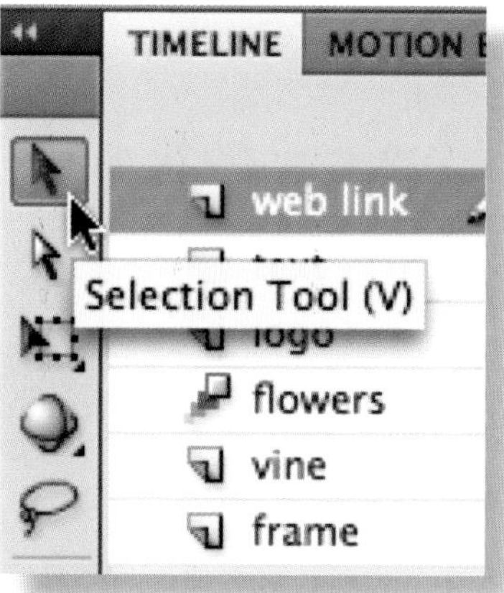

figure 1–20

Choose the Selection tool.

figure 1–21

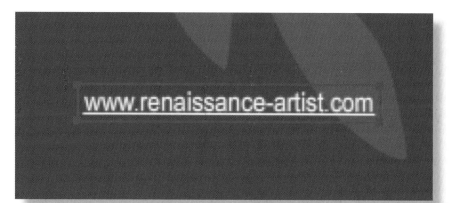

Select the Web link text.

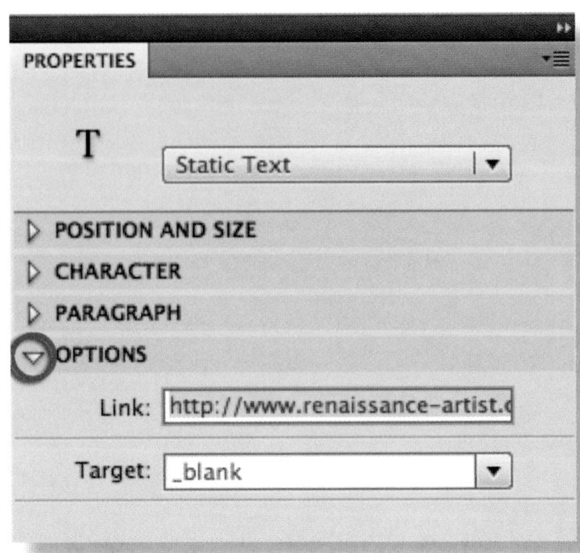

figure 1–22

In the Options menu in the Properties panel enter the URL (Web address).

3. In the Properties panel for the text (on the right side of the screen), click on the down facing arrow next to the Options menu to expand it.
4. In the Link field, exactly type the following in the URL field: **http://www.renaissance-artist.com**. Also, choose under Target: **_blank** and click OK. See Figure 1–22.
5. Choose Control > Text Movie to publish the movie as a SWF.
6. Roll the cursor over the Web link and note that a little hand icon appears—identifying this as a link (See Figure 1–23). Click on the link to open Veda's Web site. Excellent!
7. Ah, there is so much more you can do with this movie! However, that's for later discovery. Save your file (File > Save from the top menu bar), you're ready to move on to the next chapter.

figure 1–23

View the final movie as a SWF file. When you hover over a button object a hand appears.

SUMMARY

In this chapter, you have discovered that with Flash you can:

- Assemble and layout content, such as bitmap and vector images (and later include sound and video).
- Organize content on to layers.
- Import images and create new images that can be saved as symbols into a Library.
- Animate content.
- Add actions (interactivity) to content.
- Publish movies (SWFs) into a compressed format for online delivery or elsewhere.

Even if it's just a glimpse of what Flash is capable of, hopefully this chapter has encouraged you to, as Latin poet, Virgil once said, "go forth ... and win great victories."

in review

1. Name three features of Flash.
2. What are Panels in Flash?
3. What tool do you use to transform (move, scale, and rotate) an object?
4. What does the timeline panel do?
5. What is a black dot on the timeline called?
6. What are three ways to place a frame on the timeline?
7. What is tweening?
8. Where are symbols saved in Flash?
9. What is a SWF (swiff)?
10. What does the Link option do?

exploring on your own

1. Read about the history of Flash—it's been an amazing journey!

   - From *flashmagazine.com, The Flash History: http://www.flashmagazine.com/news/detail/the_flash_history/*

   - AppleInsider presents, *Flash Wars: Adobe in the History and Future of Flash: www.appleinsider.com/article.php?id=4026*

   - Flash Player Penetration statistics—the popularity of Flash has been tracked and compared to other Internet-based plug-ins: *http://www.adobe.com/products/player_census/flashplayer/*

2. Visit some Flash-based Web sites. Go to Adobe's Showcase Web site: *http://www.adobe.com/cfusion/showcase/index.cfm*. In the Browse By Product area, choose Flash to bring up all sites in the showcase that contain Flash.

3. How do you know a site contains Flash-based content? Try this: open one of my favorite sites: *http://www.miniusa.com/*. Note as the site opens a loading screen comes up. See Figure 1–24. A loading screen is what you view as a Flash movie loads in the background—this is a first indication that the site is using Flash technology. Once the page is loaded Ctrl-click (Mac) or

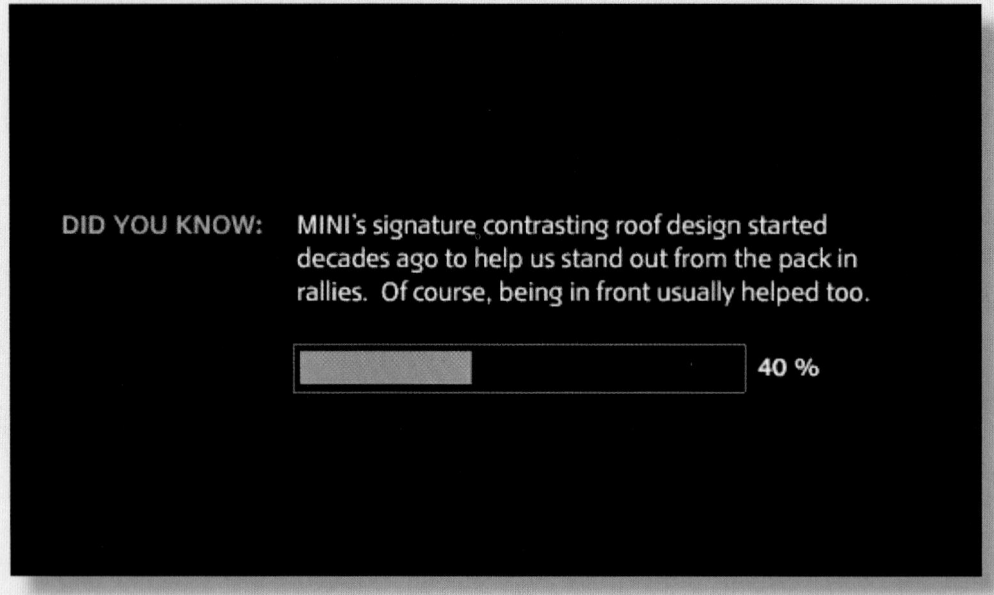

figure | 1–24 |

The loading screen of a Flash-based Web site.

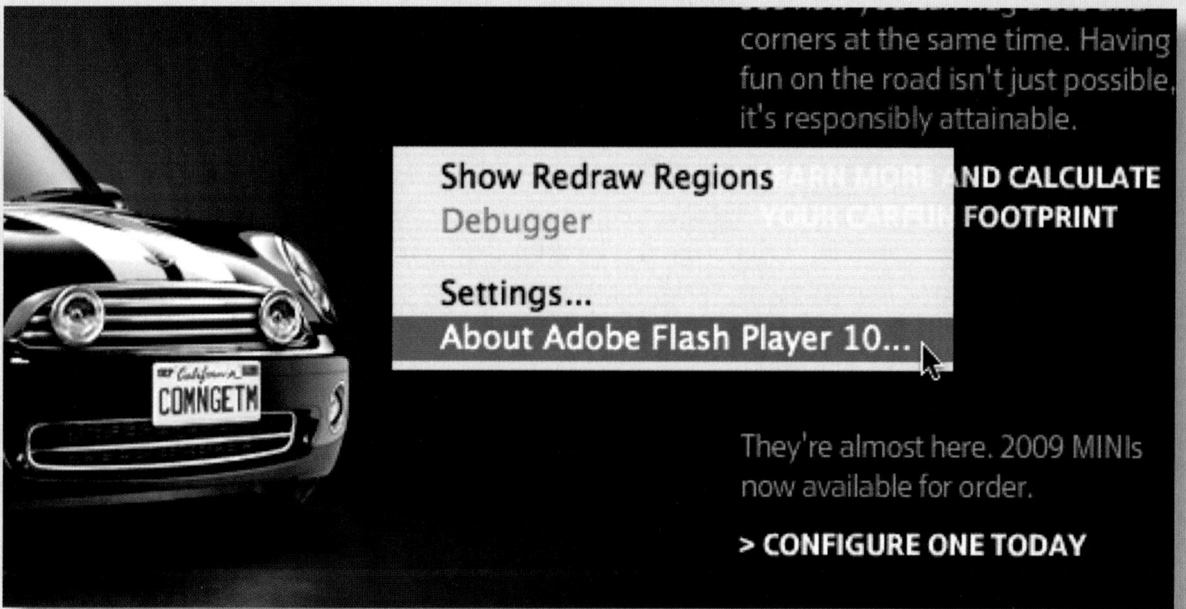

figure 1–25

Ctrl-click (Mac) or Right-click (Windows) over an area in a Web site to see if it's being viewed through the Flash Player.

Right-click (Windows) over the page and an option to learn more about the Flash Player will appear, an indication that what you are clicking on is being viewed through the Flash Player, the plug-in required to view Flash content. See Figure 1–25.

| getting around |

2

charting your course

There are many parts to Flash—lots of tools and features to distract you, confuse you, overwhelm you. This chapter presents a tour of the main parts of the interface along with an overview of bitmaps and vectors—two ways in which digital images are created and used extensively in Flash. Don't skip this chapter!

goals

In this chapter you will:

- **Explore fundamental sections of the Flash interface**
- **Develop a basic understanding of the two types of digital images: bitmap (raster) and vector**

GETTING AROUND

There are many routes you can take to get the same results in Flash. Some routes are more roundabout than others. Practice and familiarity with the Flash landscape, keyboard shortcuts, and customized workspaces will eventually get you where you want to go faster. For now, however, I will guide you through what will be the most well-traveled routes in the program—the sections of the program you will use the most in your initial stages of learning. The rest will come as we wander through the program in subsequent chapters.

Lesson: Interface Highlights

In this lesson, you identify the main interface elements of Flash.

1. Open Flash. In the Welcome window under Create New, choose Flash File (ActionScript 2.0). See Figure 2–1. A new, untitled document appears.

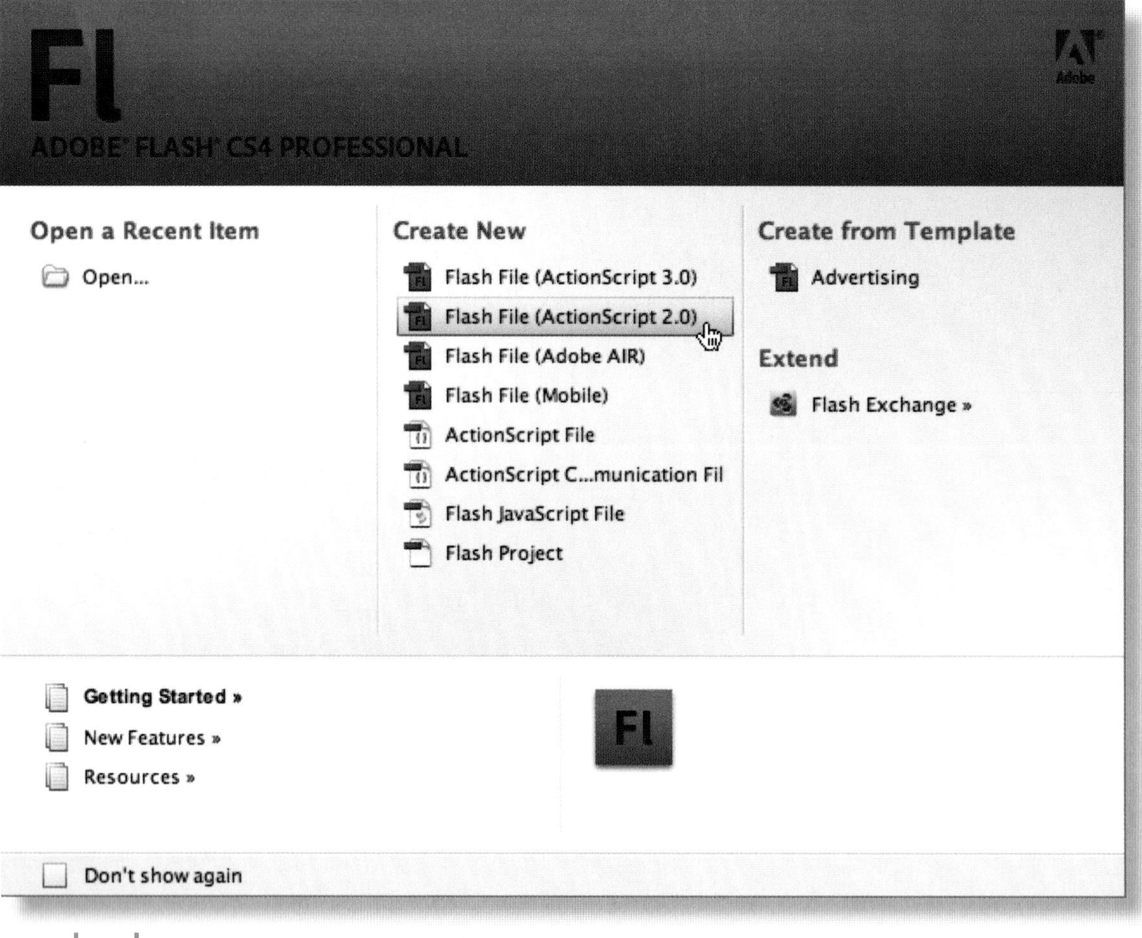

figure |2–1|

Select Flash File (ActionScript 2.0) for a new file.

Note: **Why ActionScript 2.0 and not 3.0? In this instance choosing the Flash File (ActionScript 2.0) vs. (ActionScript 3.0) will not make much difference since we will not be getting into ActionScript in this lesson. Nevertheless, see explanation of ActionScript 2.0 and 3.0 in the Preface, Background of This Text section.**

2. In the upper right corner of the interface, click on the Default button and choose the "Classic" workspace from the submenu. Refer to Figure 1–2 in Chapter 1.

3. Choose File > Save from the menu bar at the top, title the document **myfile.fla** and save in your lessons folder.

4. The Flash interface may look different depending on whether you are a Macintosh or a Windows user. The main elements, however, are the same. Compare your Flash interface with Figure 2–2 (Mac) and Figure 2–3 (Windows), and note where the various parts of the program are located.

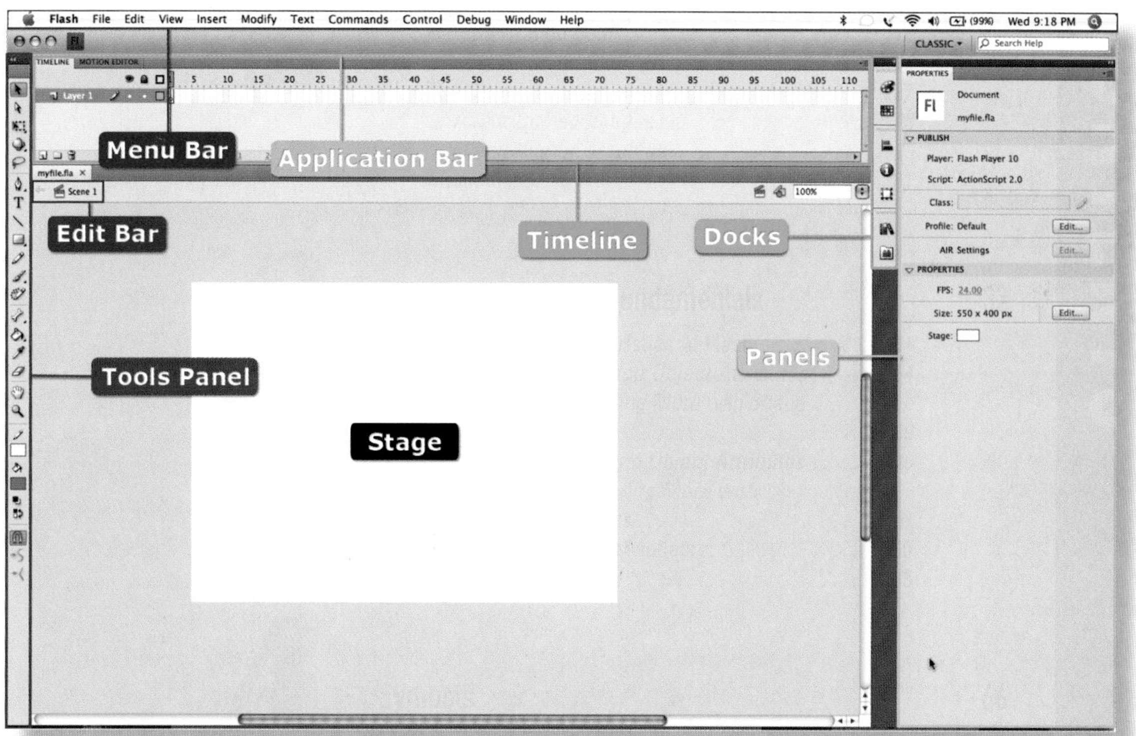

figure |2–2|

The Flash interface (Macintosh).

- *Document/Stage Area:* This blank, white area in the center of the interface is where you do all of your work. The gray area around the document area is what you might call "off stage"—items can be placed in this area to use later in a scene or be animated on to it.

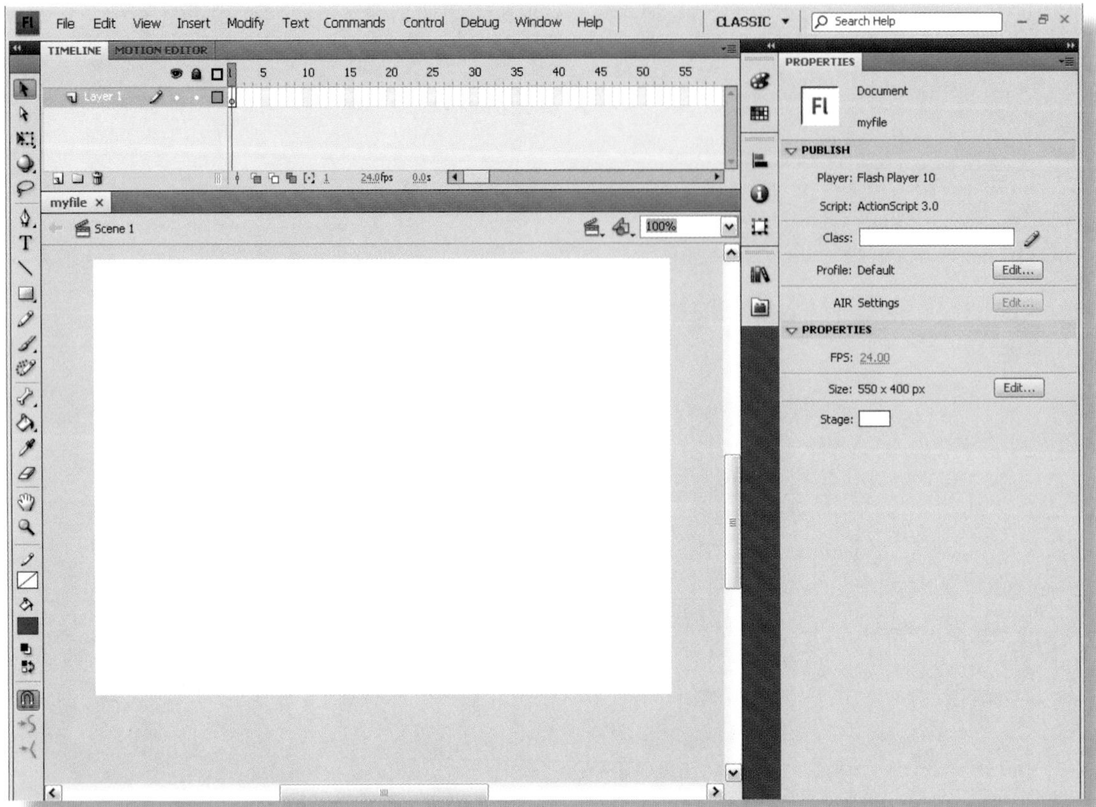

figure 2–3

The Flash interface (Windows).

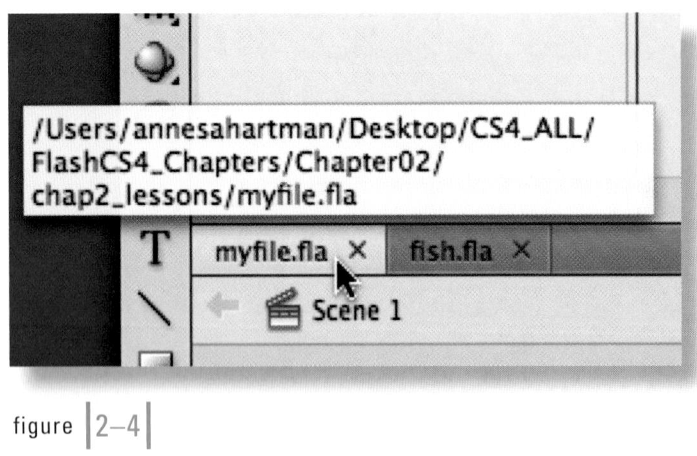

figure 2–4

File information is made available when you hover over a document title tab.

Items in the gray area are not published in the final Flash movie. At the top of the document area is a document title tab, which shows the documents name and provides a close (X) button. If you hover over the close button a note comes up indicating where the file is saved. See Figure 2–4. You can open numerous files in Flash and move between them. To view a document, click on the document tab at the top of the document area to bring the document forward in the window. To close a document, click the X icon on its tab. Below the document tab is the Edit bar that indicates where you are working

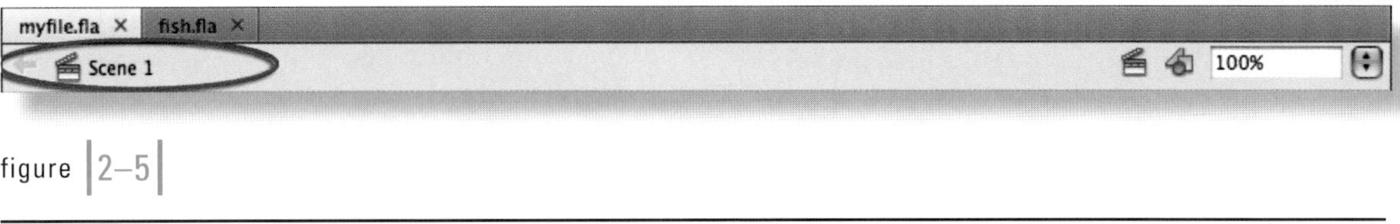

figure 2–5

The Flash Edit bar.

within a document (the default is set to Scene 1, but you can have many scenes, and editing options within each scene). The Edit bar also gives options to switch between scenes, edit symbols, and set magnification. See Figure 2–5.

- *Menu Bar:* Along the very top of the interface is the menu bar, which contains all of the commands to perform certain tasks: Flash, File, Edit, View, Insert, Modify, Text, Commands, Control, Debug, Window, Help. The commands are categorized so you can find them easily (so do not bother memorizing them all!). For example, if you want to open a panel, click the Window menu and a list of options will pop up. If you want to test your movie and control its playback, go to the Control menu. You get the idea.
- *Application Bar:* A new feature in all Adobe Creative Suite applications is the Application bar. The bar extends along the top of the program below the menu bar on the Macintosh interface and as part of the menu bar on the Windows interface. It contains universal commands found across the Creative Suite programs, such as the application's icon, workspace options, and a search feature. See Figure 2–6. Workspaces are pre-defined panel sets for particular tasks in Flash. If you click the button on the far right of the Application bar (it is set to Classic as we did in step 2 above, but the default is actually called "Default") a drop-down list will appear with a list of preset workspaces. See Figure 2–7. If you use Flash more for design you might choose the Designer workspace, for ActionScripting and development you might choose the Developer workspace. I use the Classic view as the starting point for all the lessons in this book. I prefer it because it puts the Tools panel on the left side of the screen and the Timeline panel at the top, which is how Flash is set up in previous versions. You might eventually prefer to use one of the other workspaces or create your own workspace, but for consistency with the lessons throughout this book stick with the Classic workspace.

figure 2–6

Application bars for Macintosh and Windows.

figure 2–7

Workspace options.

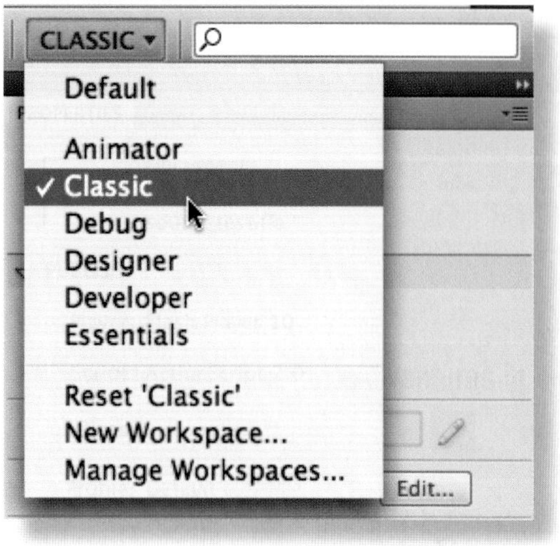

- *Tools Panel/Toolbox:* Located to the left of the document area in the Classic workspace view is the Tools panel or Toolbox. This is where you choose the tools you need to select, edit, modify, and create your Flash masterpieces (see Figure 2–8 for tool names and shortcut keys). Tool icons with a black arrow in the corner contain hidden, related tools. With your cursor, click and hold down on that tool's icon to reveal the other tool choices (see Figure 2–9). You will be using the Tools panel a lot, so always keep it handy. If you close it by mistake you can reopen it by choosing

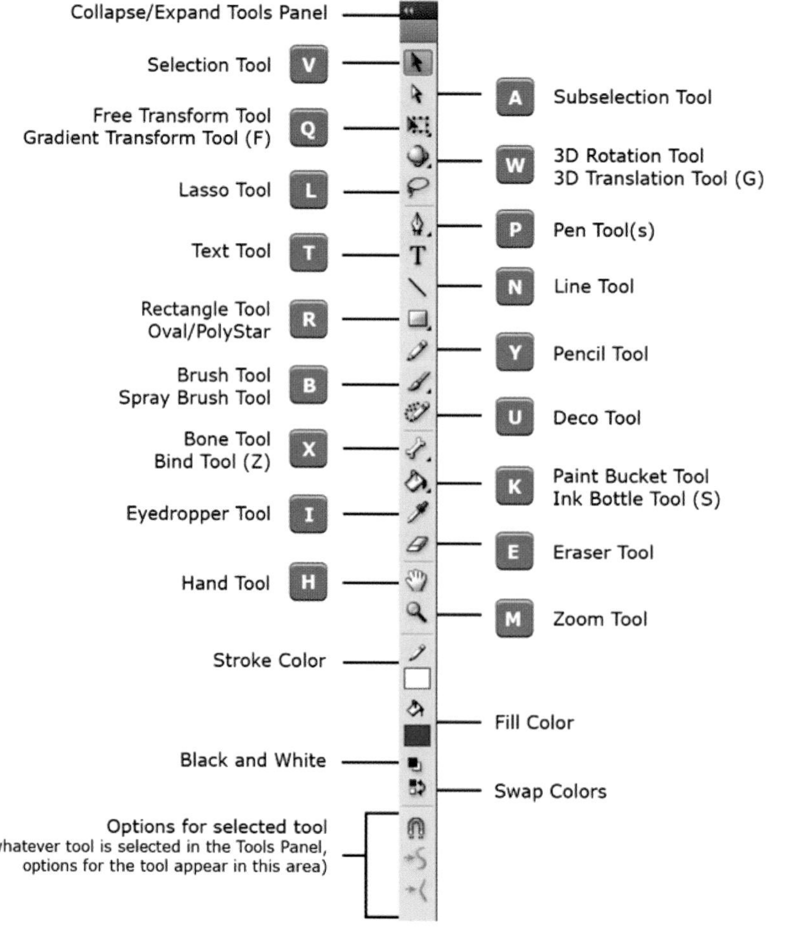

figure 2–8

The Flash Tools panel.

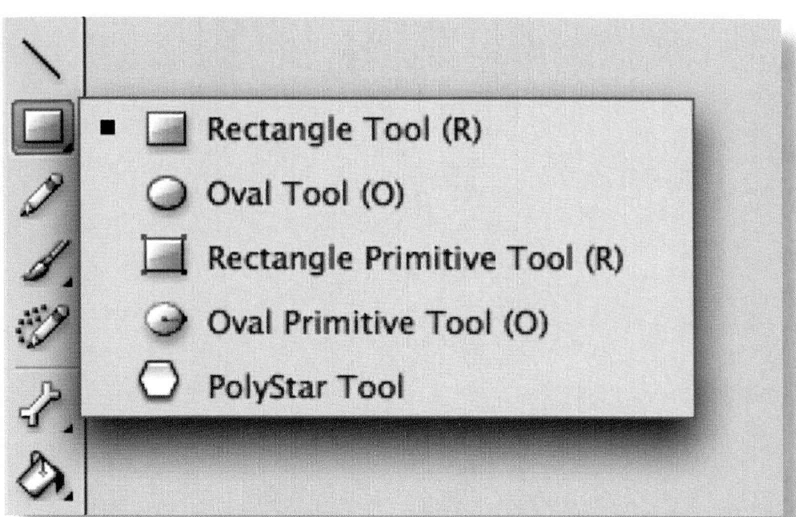

figure 2–9

Click and hold on a tool in the Tools panel to reveal more tools.

Window > Tools from the menu bar. You will learn about most of the tools in the next chapters, but if you are the curious type and cannot wait, choose Help > Flash Help on the menu bar and search for Tools or type "Tools" in the search field on the Application bar.

- *Panels:* Panels, usually located to the right of the work area, help you modify and monitor elements you are using in the program. By default, panels are tabbed together in groups—for instance the Color panel and Swatches panel are in one group. See Figure 2–10. However, you can separate them. Simply click on their title tabs and drag them to another area of the workspace. See Figure 2–11. Of course, you can dock any panel back into a group by dragging its title bar over the desired panel group—the panel is ready to be docked when a blue highlight appears around the docking area. See Figure 2–12. There's more on Docks in the next section. If you don't see a particular panel, choose Window from the menu bar and select the panel name. Panel names with checks by them are already open. To close a panel, go to Window on the menu bar and select the checked panel name to toggle it off—close it from view.

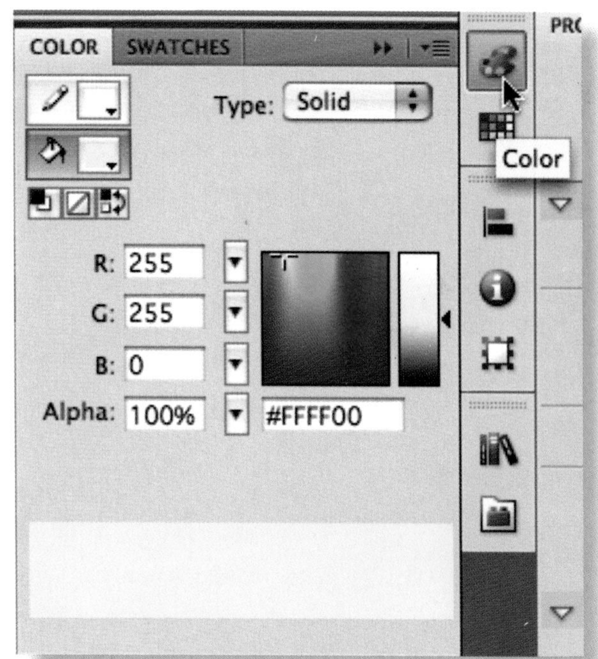

figure 2–10

Panels come tabbed together in groups.

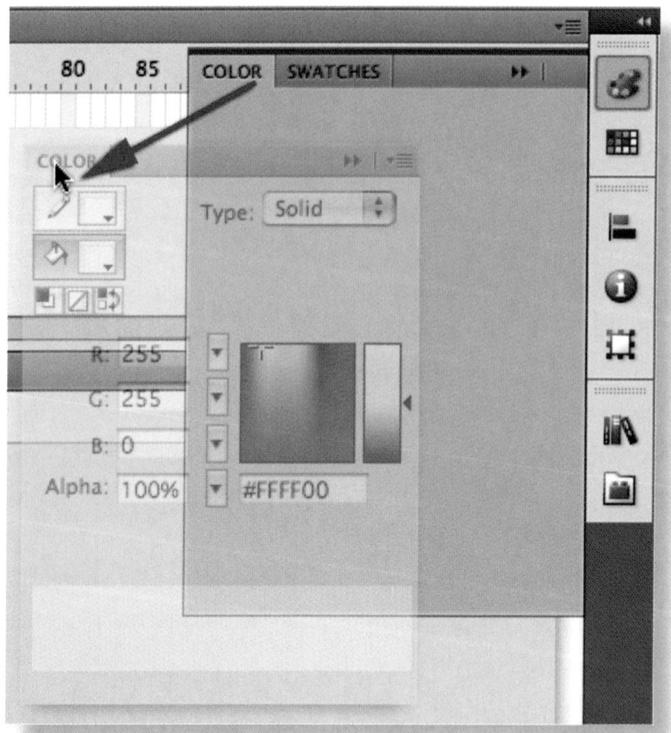

figure 2–11

Drag on the title bar to undock the Color panel.

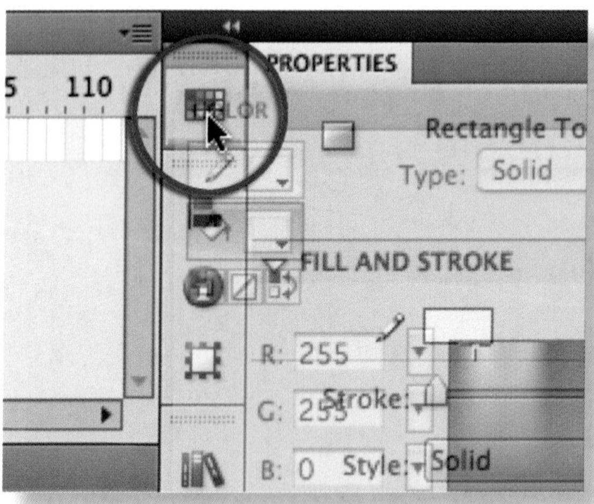

figure 2–12

Look for the blue highlight when redocking a panel.

One of the most useful panels in Flash is the Properties panel (sometimes referred to as the Properties Inspector). In the Default, Classic, and Essential workspaces it is the expanded panel on the right. The Properties panel provides options for whatever is selected on the Stage (Document area). If text is selected, for example, the Properties panel provides options for setting the font type, size, color, and more! See Figure 2–13. Or, another example, if a sound object is selected then the Properties will provide options for editing its audio track.

- *Docks:* Flash CS4 offers a handy way to organize your favorite panels called docks. Docks are located on the right and/or left sides of the screen and can hold a single panel or groups of panels. To familiarize yourself with using the docks, try the following:

1. Be sure the Classic workspace is selected in the Application bar (upper right corner of the screen).

figure 2–13

Change the color of text and other features in the Properties panel.

2. Expand the Color panel: click the Color panel icon. See Figure 2–14.

3. Click on the title bar of the Color panel and drag it to another area of the screen to undock it from its group. See Figure 2–15.

4. Collapse the panel by clicking on its title bar. Expand it, by clicking on the title bar again. See Figure 2–16.

figure 2–14

Expand the Color panel.

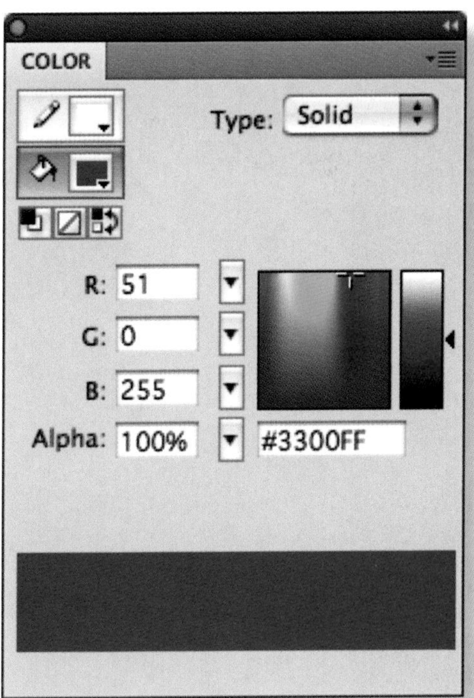

figure 2–15

The Color panel undocked.

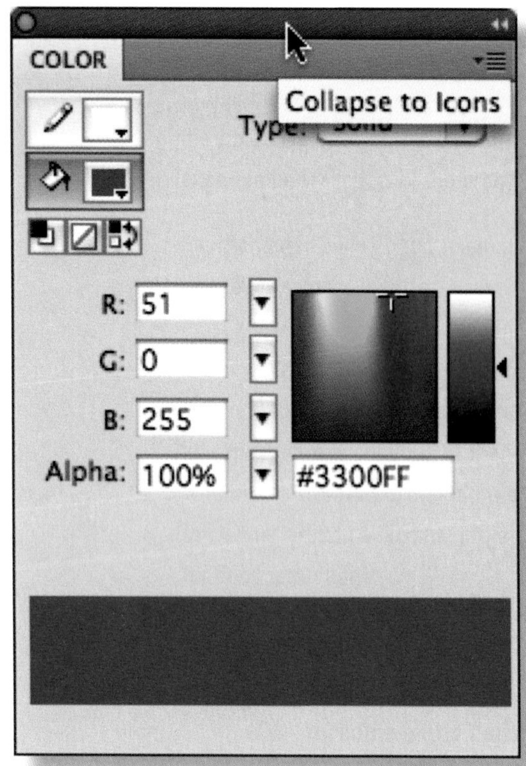

figure 2–16

Click a title bar to collapse or expand a panel.

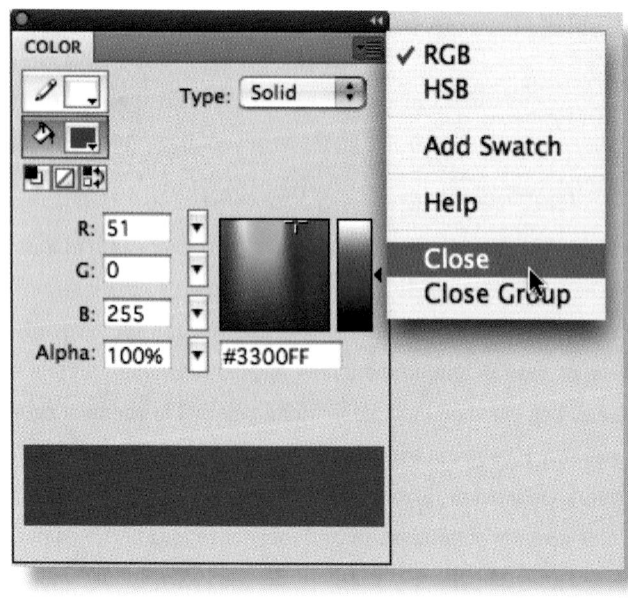

figure 2–17

Close a panel from its submenu.

5. Close the panel, by clicking on the submenu to the top right of the panel and choosing Close from the drop down (see Figure 2–17), or Ctrl-click (Mac) or right-click (Windows) over the title bar and choose Close.
6. Choose Window > Color to reopen the Color panel.
7. Re-dock the panel, by clicking in the title bar of the panel and dragging it over the docked panels already on the right side of the screen until you see a blue outlined dock shadow appear. Refer to Figure 2–12.

- *Timeline:* In the Classic view above the document area is the Timeline panel. A lot of things happen in this panel—it's where you organize all your stage elements on layers and animate them if you so choose. See Figure 2–18. You will get lots of practice using the timeline.
- *Context Menus:* Context menus appear when you Control (Ctrl)-click (Mac) or right-click your mouse (Windows) in the document area. They are drop-down menus that give you quick access to various features of any tool you are currently using. See Figure 2–19.

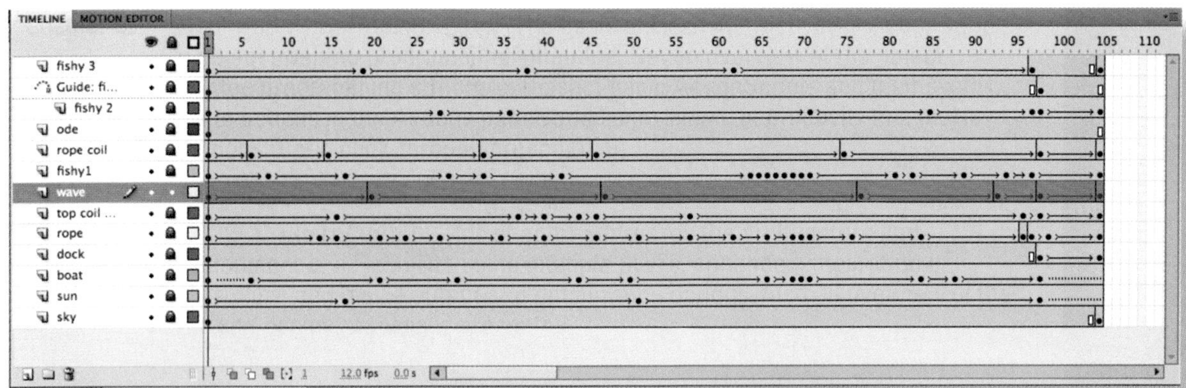

figure 2–18

Example of animated objects on the Flash Timeline.

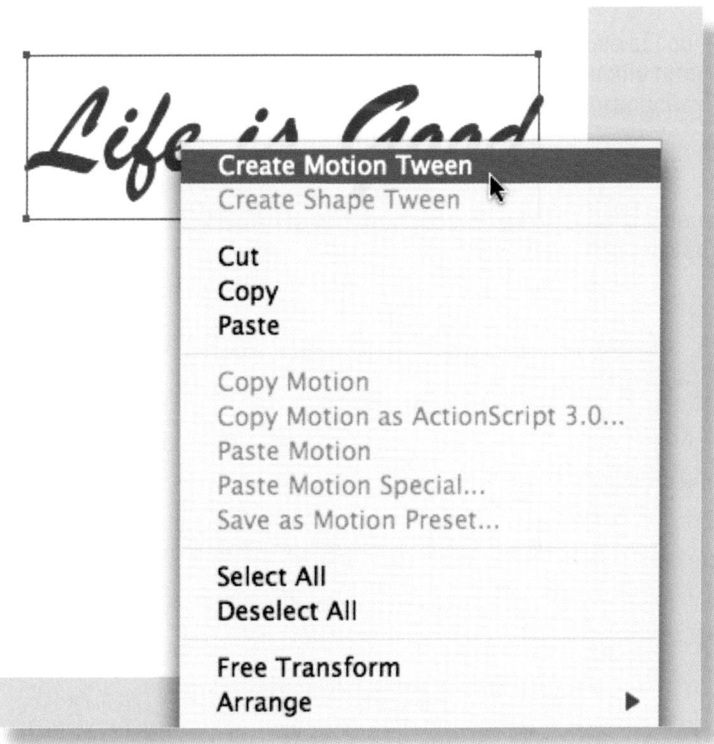

figure 2–19

Control-click (Mac) or right-click (Windows) over an object to open its context menu.

THE CHARACTERISTICS OF BITMAPS AND VECTORS

There are two types of digital graphics: bitmap (or raster) and vector. Having a clear picture of the differences between bitmaps and vectors enables you to more effectively create, format, and edit digital artwork. This is important in Flash and in every other computer graphics program you might encounter. Some programs, such as Adobe Photoshop, are designed to color correct and manipulate bitmapped images, like photographs. Some are well equipped for drawing

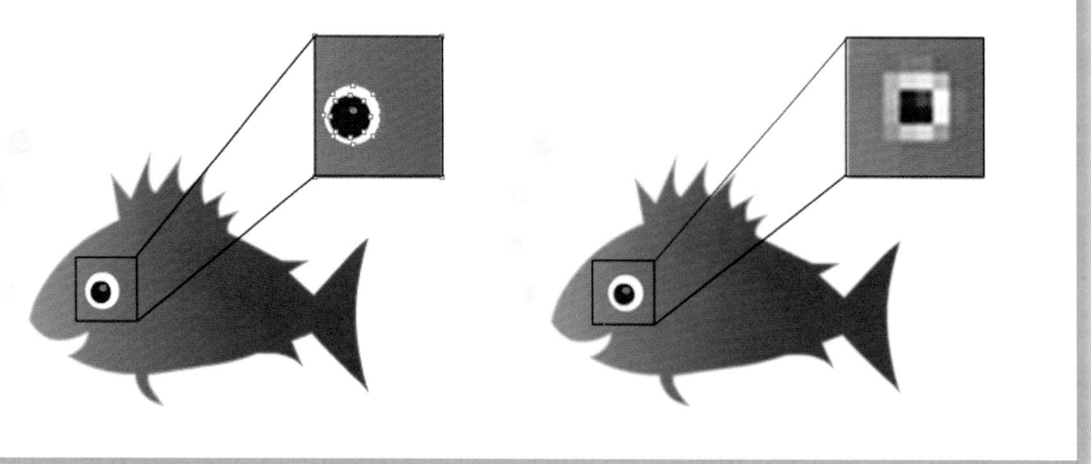

figure |2–20|

A graphic in the vector and bitmap formats.

and manipulating vector images, such as Adobe Illustrator. Flash has limited tools for users to create vector-based illustrations and edit bitmaps, but it's a whiz at assembling, animating, and compressing them for online delivery. Let's look further into the characteristics of each type of graphic. See Figure 2–20.

About Bitmap Images

When describing bitmap images (also called raster images), I like to think of beautiful mosaics composed of individual tiles. Each tile has its own color and location, and when combined with other tiles it produces a complete image, pattern, or design. To equate this with computer graphics, each complete image, pattern, design, or grid is what would be defined as a bitmap, and each tile (individual piece of the bitmap) is a pixel, a square element containing specific information (bits), such as color and location data. Figure 2–21 demonstrates this makeup.

A bitmap image contains a fixed number of pixels (information), measured by pixels per inch (ppi). This measurement is called the image's *resolution*. The quality and size (both dimensionally and in file weight) of a bitmap image is dependent on its resolution. An image with a high resolution contains more pixels per square inch than an image of the same dimensions with a low resolution. If an image is destined for print the resolution would be anywhere from 150 ppi to much higher to accommodate the needs of the output device, a printer. An image to be viewed via a screen, such as in a Web browser, 72 ppi (Mac) and 96 ppi (Windows) is the standard resolution. Setting the proper resolution of an image is key to reproducing it at the desired quality. Our concern in Flash is not about working with high resolution images, but rather working with low resolution images (72–96 ppi), since most content in Flash is developed for the online/screen environments. A goal in Flash is to import bitmap images that are already cropped and compressed for the most optimal performance in the program.

figure 2–21

A close-up view of bitmapped pixels. Hummingbird photo compliments of Dan Marx.

Remember these things about bitmap images:

- They are unique because they are comprised of a grid of pixels, and because of this their visual quality, file size, and intended use are dependent on resolution.
- They are most common for continuous tone images, such as photographs; they are really good at representing subtle gradations of color and shading.
- You can import, transform, and animate images in Flash, which you'll get plenty of chances to try out in upcoming chapters.

About Vector Graphics

As you have discovered, when dealing with bitmap images, an image's resolution and pixel dimensions are interdependent. Adjusting the amount of pixels in a bitmap image affects its resolution, not to mention its visual quality, and vice versa. There is no way around it, unless you are working in vectors. Vectors are another way of constructing digital images. The flower you animated in Chapter 1 was a vector image. Vector graphics are comprised of points and lines (paths) that describe an object's outline or shape. Instead of being comprised of a grid of square pixels a vector image is drawn based on mathematical calculations of X and Y coordinates. Refer to Figure 2–20 again and Figure 2–22. This means vectors are resolution independent: they can be scaled large (billboard size) or small (postage stamp size) and printed to any output device without loss of detail or clarity. Vectors are great for creating bold and illustrative graphics and free-form drawings that can be easily scaled while retaining crisp lines and solid colors.

Vectors play an important role in Flash. Most images you see on the Web are comprised of bitmaps. With one exception, Web browsers only support bitmap-based images in three formats—JPEG, GIF, or PNG (see Exploring on Your Own section for more details on these

figure 2–22

A vector graphic shown in three different views within Flash.

formats). The exception is the Scalable Vector Graphics (SVG) format, an XML specification that can describe two-dimensional vector graphics, both static and animated.

While the SVG format has been in development for some time, it is not as commonly used, however as another vector supported format—SWF—Flash's output format (see note below). Content published as a SWF can be viewed within any browser through the Flash Player plug-in.

Why is it so important to be able to use vector technologies on the Web? Images comprised of vectors are usually smaller in file size and can be scaled without loss of visual quality, which are both vital characteristics when downloading content via an Internet connection and viewing the content on different sized screens with varying resolutions. Also, because of vectors and Flash's ability to compress content so efficiently into the SWF format, we have the ability to view more complex animations (which occurs from the movement of hundreds of single images, usually drawn via vectors). Flash has been a boon for animators who previously could not show off their work via the Internet because their files were incompatible or unwieldy to download.

Remember these things about vector graphics:

- They are unique because they are comprised of lines and points that are drawn mathematically, which makes them resolution independent and thus scalable without loss of visual quality.
- They are most commonly used in free-form drawing and the creation of bold and illustrative types of graphics with crisp lines and solid colors.
- Flash's drawing tools only create graphics using vector technologies, which you can easily transform and animate in Flash and will get plenty of practice in the upcoming chapters.

Note: The question is often asked—what does SWF (pronounced "swiff") stand for? You will find a fine debate on this issue if you search the Web. Some say it stands for Shockwave File (a file format derived from Macromedia's Director program). Some say it stands for Small Web File. I go for "Small Web File" since I heard it as such from a Macromedia developer many years ago when I was designing Flash curriculum for the company.

SUMMARY

This chapter presented an overview of the main interface elements of Flash and characteristics of the two digital image types—vectors and bitmaps. With this fundamental information you are set to get hands-on with Flash.

in review

1. What is another name for the Document Area in Flash?
2. Describe Workspaces in Flash.
3. What's so useful about the Properties panel?
4. How do you get to context menus in Flash?
5. Describe two differences between bitmap and vector graphics.
6. What graphic formats are viewable in a browser?
7. What type of graphics is created with the drawing tools in Flash?
8. What is a SWF?

exploring on your own

1. Review the options available in the Flash Preferences. In Flash, choose Flash > Preferences (Mac) or Edit > Preferences (Window) and explore the options in each category.
2. Research on the Web the characteristics of image formats, such as GIF, JPEG, PNG, TIFF, and EPS. Visit, for example: Wikipedia—Image File Formats at *http://en.wikipedia.org/wiki/Graphics_file_format*, or one of my favorite Web design and developer resources, Web Monkey—Web Graphics for Beginners at *http://www.webmonkey.com/tutorial/Web_Graphics_for_Beginners*.

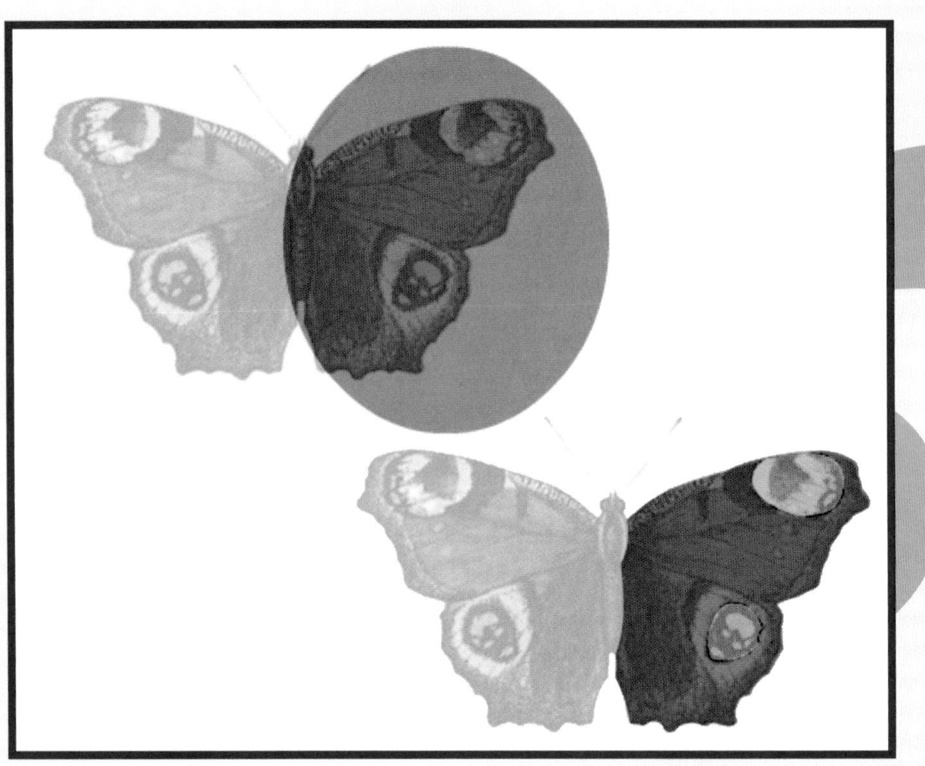

| object and drawing fundamentals |

charting your course

I mentioned not to skip the last chapter and it goes for this one too. Understanding the structure of objects and the use of the drawing tools in Flash—what you cover in this chapter—might seem tedious at first, but will prove to be the basis for more exciting things to come.

goals

In this chapter you will:

- **Identify the characteristics of shape and grouped graphics (symbols are covered in Chapter 4)**
- **Create and modify drawn objects as shapes and groups**
- **Select and adjust colors, make new ones and save them**
- **Apply gradients and alpha effects to objects**
- **Import a bitmap object and turn it into vectors**
- **Play with various drawing and text tools**
- **Identify the differences between the Merge Drawing and Object Drawing models**

THE OBJECT CHARACTERISTICS OF FLASH

Flash is not as intuitive to use as one might hope. It has a way with dealing with objects (images, text, audio, or video) that can get quite confusing if some basics aren't covered first. (In fact, ActionScripting in Flash is referred to as object-oriented programming, a method whose title hints to the idea that orienting objects correctly in the program is kind of important.) From my experience of teaching hundreds of students about Flash, the most important concept to grasp before any other in this program is how objects in Flash are identified, created, and used as shapes, groups, and especially symbols. An object can be saved as a shape, a group, or a symbol. You can switch an object between these states to perform commands on the object that can only be done when it's in that particular state (if I just lost you here, don't worry, it will become clearer as you work through the lessons). Let's start with some simple lessons on identifying and exploring the attributes of shape and group objects in Flash's default Merge Drawing model. (See section later in this chapter on Flash's two drawing models—Merge Drawing and Object Drawing.) Then in Chapter 4, you study the third and most important object type in Flash—symbols.

Lesson 1: The Shape Object Attributes

When you first create a vector object on the Flash stage the graphic is saved as a shape. A shape object has the following attributes, which you will identify in this lesson:

- A shape object has a dotted pattern when selected;
- Two sections can be selected on a shape object—a fill and a stroke (outline);
- A shape object can be modified, such as changing its fill and stroke colors and overall shape;
- A shape object can intersect another shape of a different color;
- A shape object can unify (merge) with another shape graphic of the same color.

Attribute #1

1. Open the Flash program. Choose Open from the Welcome window or File > Open from the menu bar and browse for the **chap3L1.fla** in the **chap03_lessons** folder.

2. Be sure the Classic workspace is selected.

3. Choose View > Magnification > Fit in Window. This document is a template to assist you in identifying the parts of shape objects.

4. Select the Zoom tool in the Tools panel. See Figure 3–1.

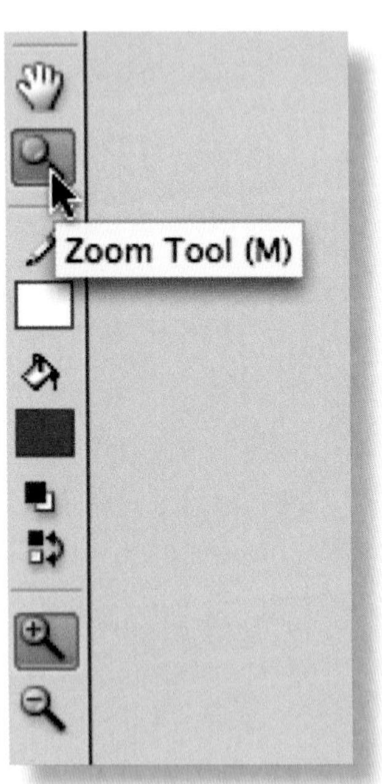

figure 3–1

Select the Zoom tool.

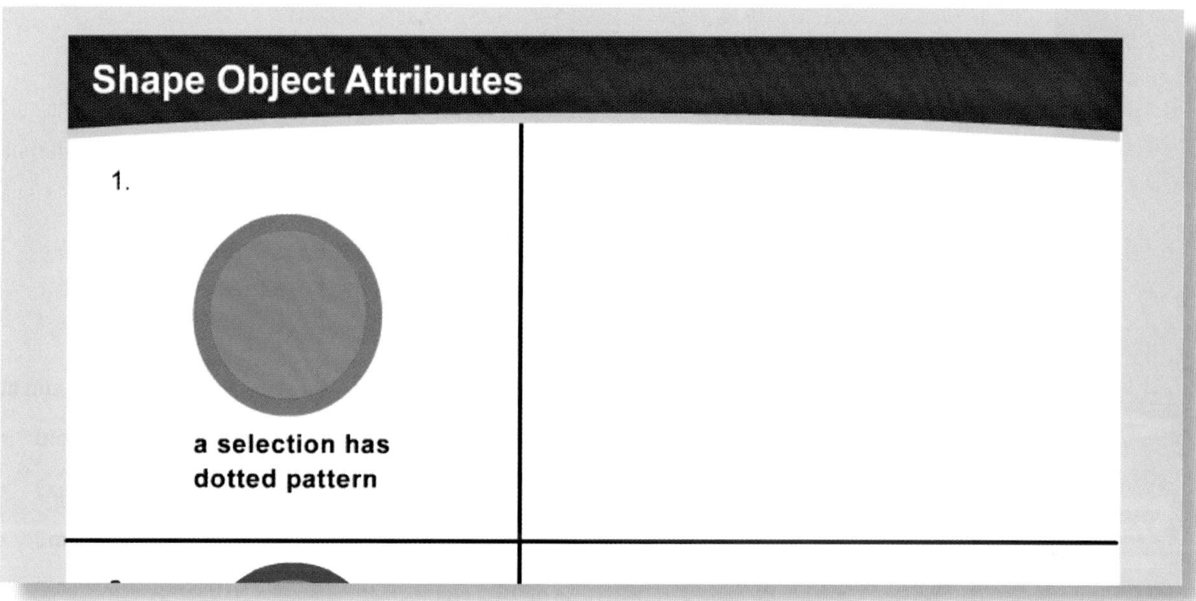

figure 3–2

The attribute #1 area of the document.

5. Click in the middle of the top area of the document to magnify it. This is the attribute #1 area. Attribute #1 shows that a shape graphic has a dotted pattern when selected. See Figure 3–2.

6. Choose the Selection tool in the Tools panel. See Figure 3–3.

7. Click on the center (fill) of the circle (colored blue)—notice the dotted pattern when you select it. This indicates a shape object.

8. Click on the stroke (outline) of the circle (colored orange)—also a dotted pattern.

9. Double-click on the center of the circle to select both the stroke and the fill.

10. Click on the white area outside the circle to deselect it.

11. Select the Oval tool in the Tools panel (be careful to choose the Oval tool and not the Oval Primitive tool). See Figure 3–4.

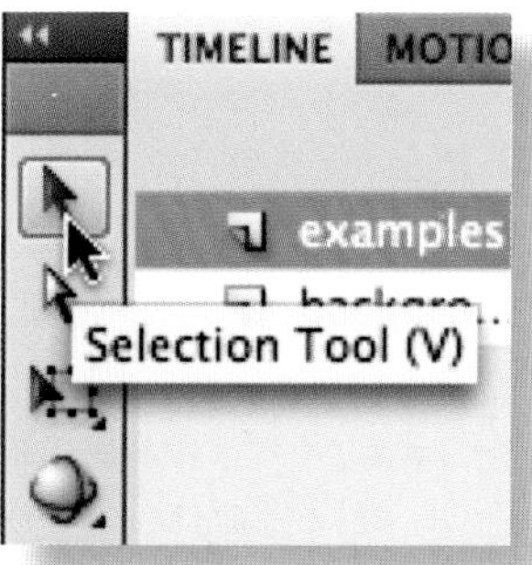

figure 3–3

Select the Selection tool.

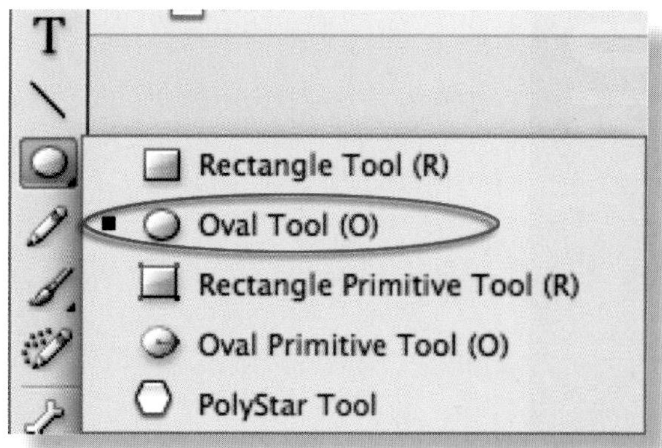

figure 3–4

Select the Oval tool.

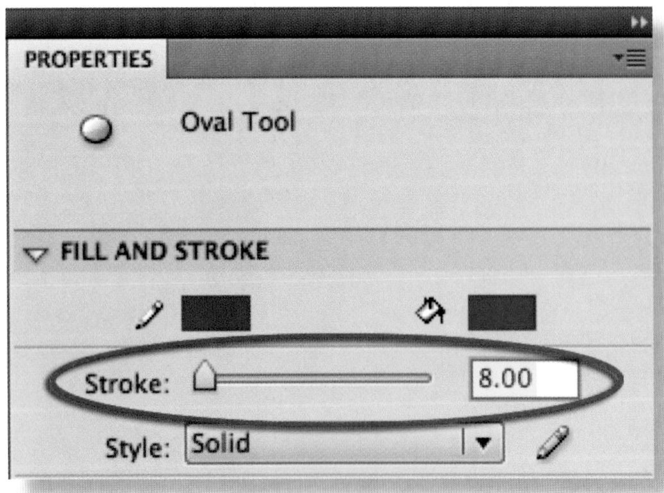

figure 3–5

Set options for the stroke width in the Properties panel.

12. In the Properties panel (or the Tools panel), click on the Stroke color box and choose a new color. Click on the Fill color box and choose a new color. For Stroke width choose 8. See Figure 3–5.

13. Click and drag on the blank area to the right of attribute #1 to draw the shape.

> **Note: To constrain the shape to a perfect circle, hold down the Shift key as you draw the shape.**

14. With the Selection tool, click on the center of the object you created—it has a dotted pattern.

15. Now, select the stroke (outline) of the oval you created—also a dotted pattern.

16. Double-click on the center of the oval to select both the stroke and the fill.

17. Click and drag the object around in the white area—both parts of the object move simultaneously.

Attribute #2

1. Move the document to see the attribute #2 area—either use the Zoom tool or try the Hand tool (right above the Zoom tool) in the Tools panel. Refer to Figure 3–1.

2. Attribute #2 is the ability to modify an object's stroke and fill color. Create an oval shape to the right of the second attribute.

3. Select the fill of the object. In the Property panel change the Fill color (the second color box with a paint bucket icon next to it). Note that the color is updated in the selected area. See Figure 3–6.

4. Now select the stroke area of the oval. In the Properties panel, change the Stroke color (the first color box with a pencil icon next to it).

Attribute #3

1. Attribute #3 is the ability to alter the shape of an object. Select the Rectangle tool from the Tools panel (same place as the Oval tool). Be sure to select the Rectangle tool and not the Rectangle Primitive tool. Create a rectangle shape on the right side.

2. Be sure the object is deselected—you should not see the dotted pattern. If necessary, choose Edit > Deselect All.

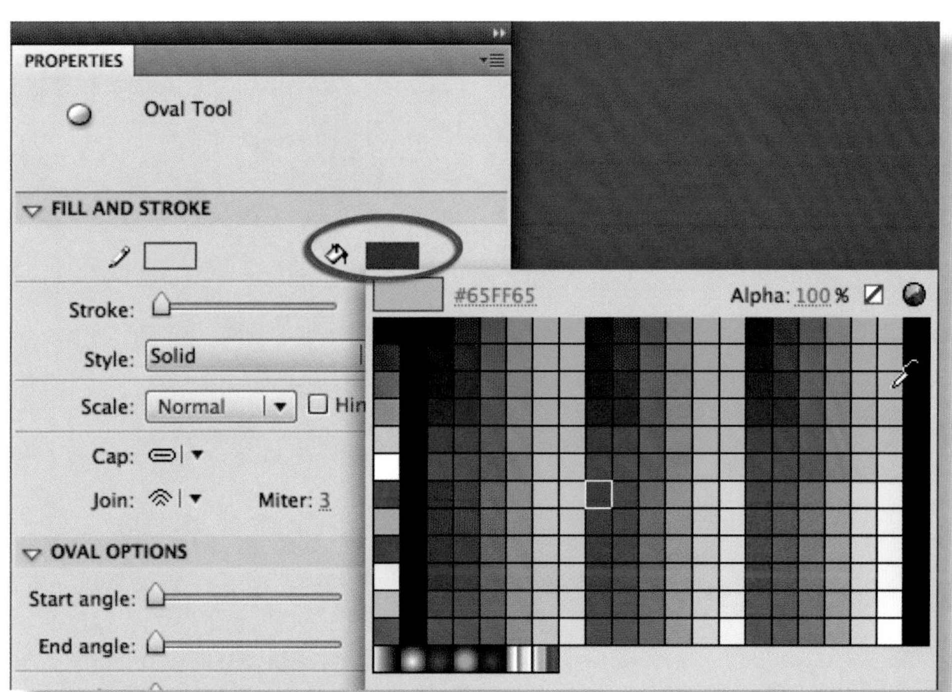

figure 3–6

Choose a fill color for the object.

3. Choose the Selection tool. Hover the Selection tool close to a corner of the rectangle (you might need to zoom in). This is tricky; you'll notice the icon next to the Selection tool changes to a corner shape. See Figure 3–7. Once you see this icon, click on the object's corner and drag. The corner shape will change. See Figure 3–8.

figure 3–7 and figure 3–8

Click and drag on a corner edge of the object to change its shape.

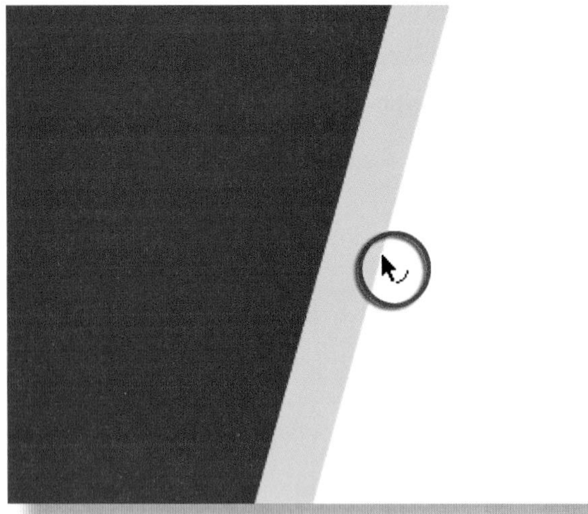

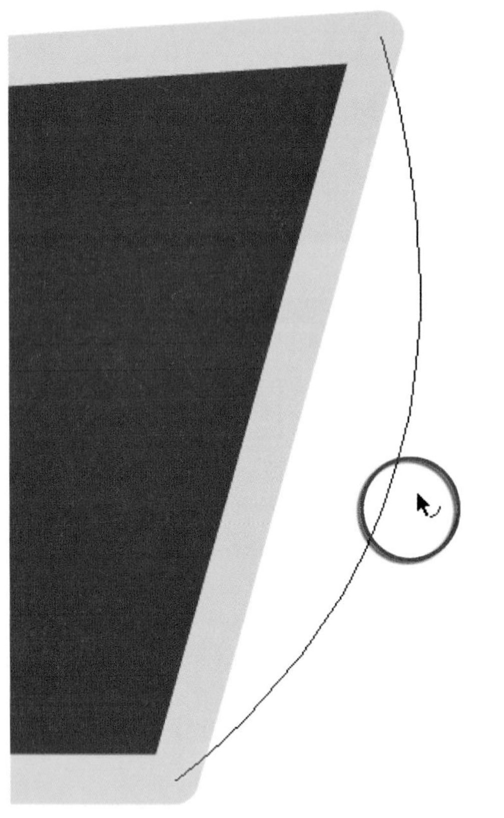

figure 3–9 and figure 3–10

Click and drag on a straight edge of the object to change its shape.

4. Hover the Selection tool over a straight edge of the rectangle. The icon next to the Selection tool changes to a curved shape. See Figure 3–9. Once you see this icon, click on the object's edge and drag out to create a curved shape. See Figure 3–10.

> **Note: Pushing and pulling the lines in the shape can only be done when the object is *deselected*. If you accidentally select the object, click on the white area outside the object to deselect and try altering the lines again.**

Attribute #4

1. Attribute #4 shows how you can intersect two shapes of different colors. Choose the Selection tool, then click on the green circle in the front of the blue circle in the left column. Move the green circle to the right a little bit. A cutout (intersection) of the circle shape is created in the blue circle behind it. See Figure 3–11.

2. On the right side, create two new shapes (use the Rectangle, Oval or PolyStar tool, but not the Primitive Rectangle or Oval). Make each a different color and make sure they are overlapping. Click and drag one shape away from another to view the intersection.

> **Note: Explore what happens if you make the shapes with or without strokes. To turn off the stroke color of a shape, select a shape tool (Oval, Rectangle, or PolyStar—but not the Rectangle Primitive or Oval Primitive) and in the Properties panel, choose the "none" option for the stroke color (a white box with a red slash through it). See Figure 3–12.**

> **Note: You may wonder why you would break up vector objects like this, but when you start drawing a lot this feature comes in handy. For instance, you may want to create a wall with a window shape punched out of it. If you want to protect objects from one another you must convert them to a different state—next lesson! Or put them on layers—another lesson later on.**

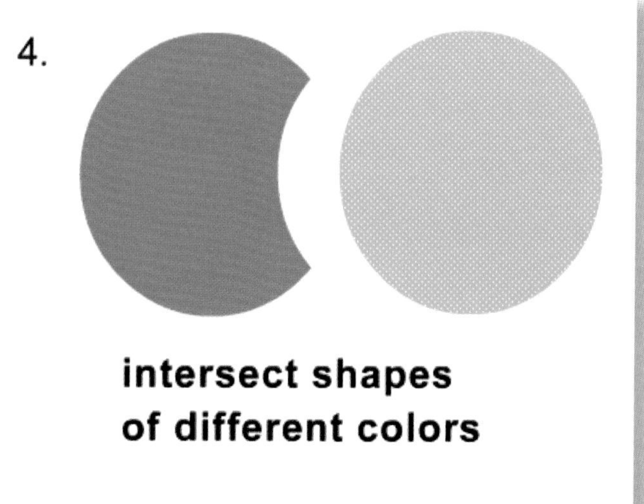

figure 3–11

Overlapping shapes of different colors creates an intersection.

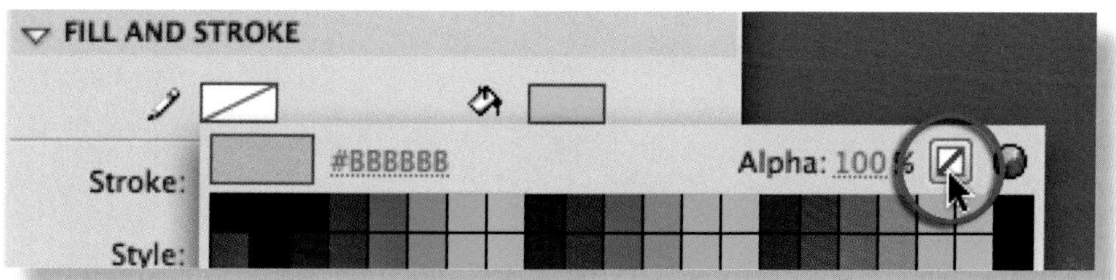

figure 3–12

Choose "none" for the stroke color.

Attribute #5

1. Attribute#5, shows how you can unify two shapes of the same color. Select the Oval tool in the Tools panel and choose the "none" stroke option in either the Tools panel or Properties panel. See Figure 3–12 again.
2. Select a Fill color. Refer to Figure 3–6.
3. Draw an oval on the right side area.
4. Create another oval of the same color overlapping the first oval shape.
5. Select the shapes and move them—they have been united into a single shape.
6. Choose File > Save and save this exercise in your lessons folder. You've learned the main attributes of shape objects. Review these attributes as listed at the beginning of this tutorial.

Lesson 2: Discovering More with Shape Objects

As you learned in the last lesson, objects as shapes have specific attributes. You further explore these attributes—editing the stroke and fill, union and intersect, and line alteration—while you discover more with shape objects.

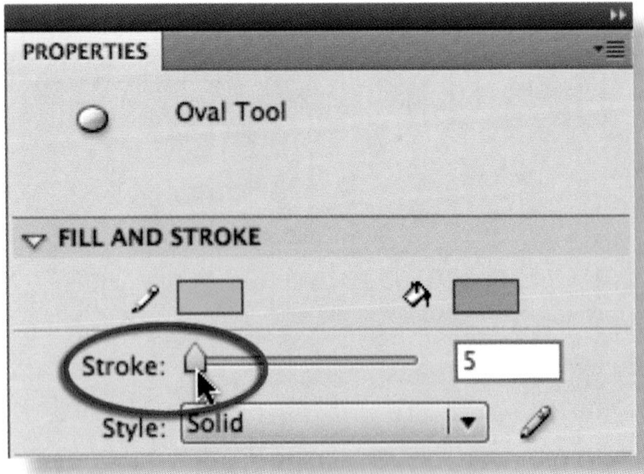

figure 3–13

Set the stroke width in the Properties panel.

The Stroke and the Fill

1. Choose File > New > Flash File (ActionScript 2.0) to open a new file in Flash.
2. Be sure the Classic workspace is selected.
3. Select the Oval tool (not the Primitive Oval) in the Tools panel. Choose a color for the Fill and Stroke.
4. In the Properties panel, set the Stroke width to 5. See Figure 3–13.
5. Click and drag on the Stage to create a circular shape.

> **Note: Like all vector objects in Flash this object is comprised of two parts—a stroke (outline) and a fill. Strokes and fills can be removed, added, or modified.**

6. Select the Selection tool (black arrow) from the Tools panel. Click in the center (the fill) of the circle and move it—notice you've left behind the stroke.
7. Choose Edit > Undo to undo your last command.

> **Note: By default you have up to 100 Document and Object Undos. To set undo amounts go to Flash > Preferences (Mac) or Edit > Preferences (Windows). The more undos set the more memory intensive Flash will be. I suggest leaving it at the 100 undos and save your file often.**

8. Now, double-click on the center of the object with the Selection tool—it should select both the stroke and the fill. Move the complete object around.
9. Hit Delete on your keyboard to delete the circle.
10. Select the Oval tool again. Define a new stroke and fill color in the Properties panel.
11. Click and drag to draw the shape on the Stage.
12. Let's modify the stroke of this object. Double-click on the stroke (outside edge) of the object to select the whole stroke (and nothing but the stroke!). In the Properties panel adjust the strokes width and color—note how changes are automatically updated on the selected stroke.
13. Choose the Style drop down and select Hatched. You won't see the hatched style until you deselect the object. Click elsewhere on the stage to deselect the stroke and admire the hatching effect. See Figure 3–14.

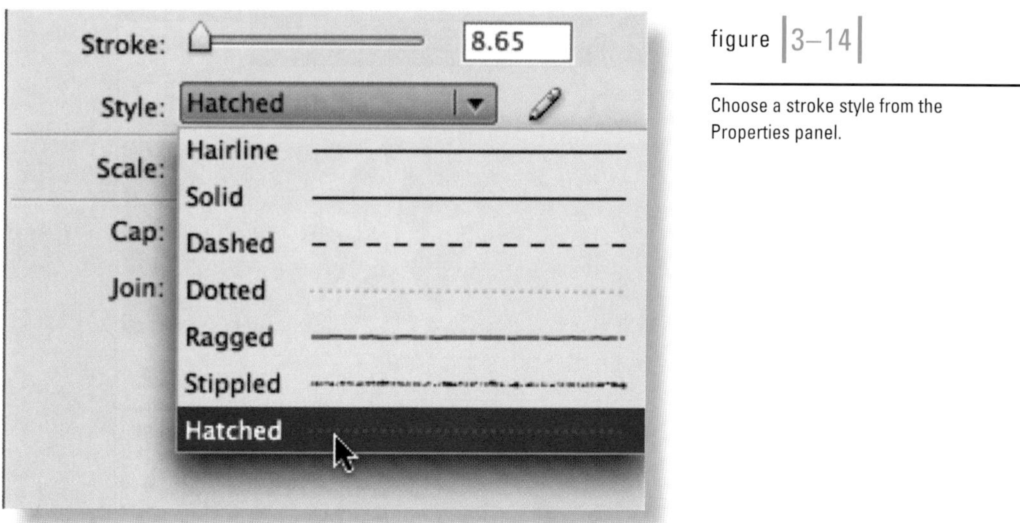

figure 3–14

Choose a stroke style from the Properties panel.

14. Select the stroke again and adjust the style options by clicking on the Edit Stroke Style icon to the right of the Style drop down menu. See Figure 3–15.

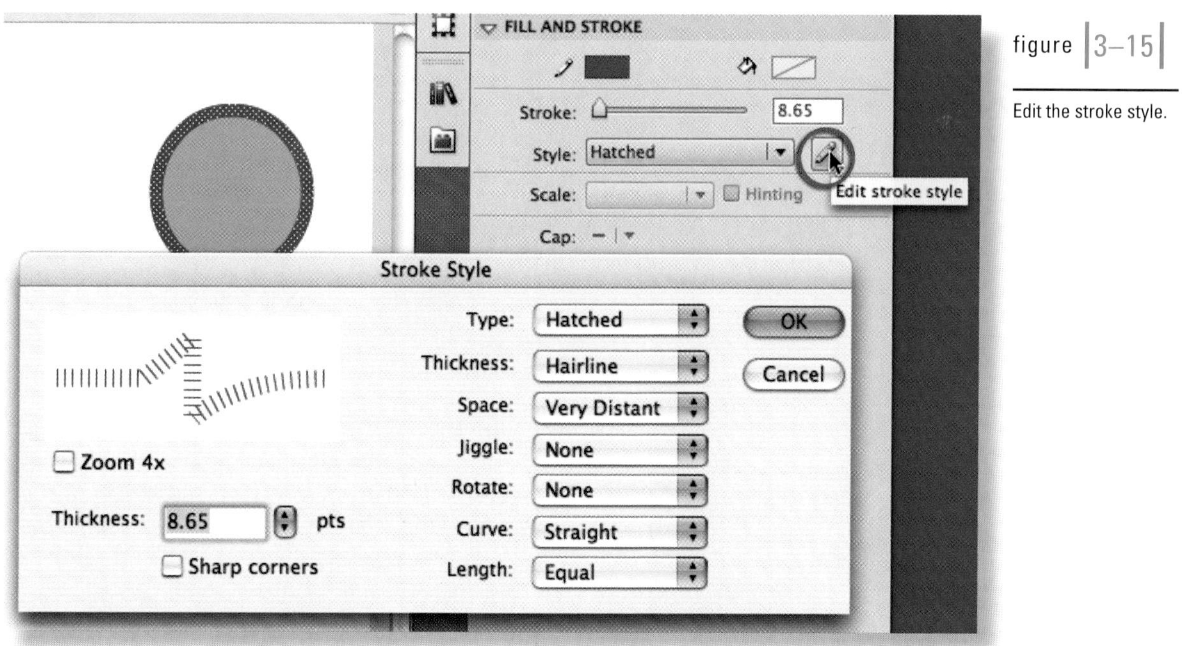

figure 3–15

Edit the stroke style.

15. Select the fill of your object.

16. In the Properties panel adjust the fill color and note it updates automatically on the selected fill.

17. Delete all the objects on the Stage.

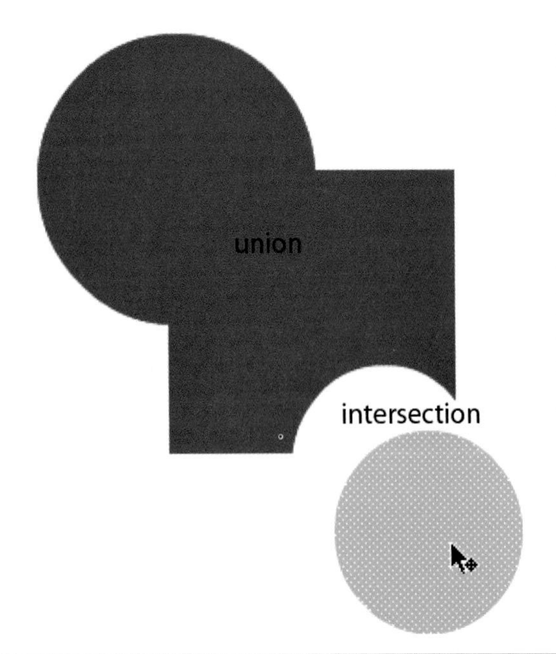

figure |3–16|

Overlapping shapes of the same color merge together; different colors intersect.

Intersect and Union

1. Select the Oval tool and for the stroke color choose the "none" option.
2. Choose a fill color to your liking.
3. Hold down the Shift key as you draw the oval on the stage—it makes a perfect circle (Shift proportionally constrains an object as you draw it).
4. Select the Rectangle tool and choose none for the stroke color and the same fill color as the circle.
5. Draw the rectangle overlapping the circle.
6. Select the rectangle and move it—what happens? The circle object has blended or merged with the rectangle. Shape objects of the same color and overlapping are combined. See Figure 3–16.
7. In contrast, objects of different color intersect. Try it. Select the Oval tool again and change the fill color.
8. Draw a circular shape over the unified shape.
9. Move the new colored circle—it cuts away the object underneath, or intersects it. See Figure 3–16 again.

figure |3–17|

Note the two crossed arrows icon of the Selection tool—this icon indicates that the object can now be clicked and moved.

Pushing and Pulling Shapes

1. Delete all objects on your Stage. Draw a rectangle (not a primitive rectangle) on the Stage.
2. Select the Selection tool and hover (but don't click!) it over the rectangle and notice the icon that comes up—it should be two arrows crossed—this is the icon indicating that you are about ready to click and move the rectangle. See Figure 3–17.
3. Now, position the Selection tool so that it is right over an edge of the rectangle—the crossed arrows should change to an arch shape—click and move the edge of the rectangle.

See Figure 3–18. By selecting an edge of a shape and pushing and pulling that edge you can change the shape of your object.

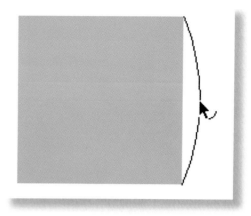

figure 3–18

Note the curved shaped icon of the Selection tool—this icon indicates that the edge of the object can be altered.

> **Note:** If you are having trouble selecting the edge of the object, it's possible the object is already selected. Click on an area of the Stage away from your object, or choose Edit > Deselect All and try again.

4. To create corner shapes, rather than curved shapes, select a corner of the rectangle—you should see a right angle icon, and pull. See Figure 3–19.
5. Create an Oval shape and push and pull its edges.
6. Add extra areas to push and pull by moving your cursor to the edge of a shape and holding down the Alt/Option key as you push and pull.

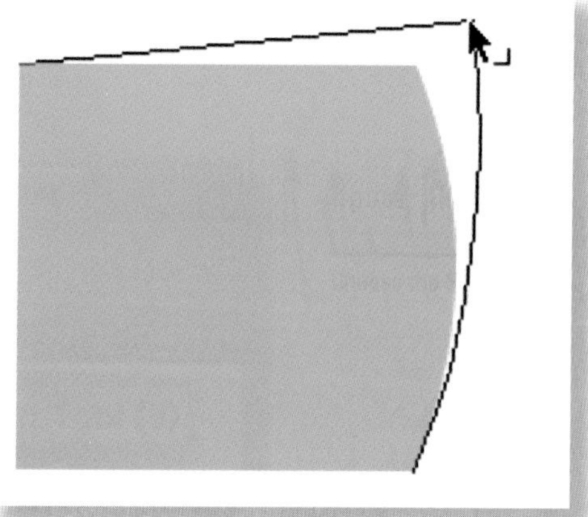

figure 3–19

Note the corner shaped icon of the Selection tool—this icon indicates that the corner of the object can be altered.

> **Note:** You can also manipulate the shape of an object by selecting the Subselection tool (the white arrow) in the Tools panel (see Figure 3–20). With the Subselection tool carefully click on the edge of an object. Points appear around the object. Click on a point and move it to alter a path. See Figure 3–21. Direction handles might appear with points on each end. Click on the end points of these handles to adjust curved paths (also called Bezier curves). To make new paths (or strokes as they are called in Flash) using Bezier curves select the Pen tool in the Tools panel and click or click and drag on the Stage to make straight or curved paths (strokes). See Figure 3–22. It's a nice option to make and edit points and paths on an object using this method, but we will not spend much time with it in Flash. A product where this method of drawing is more commonly performed is Adobe Illustrator. See my other book *Exploring Adobe Illustrator CS4*.

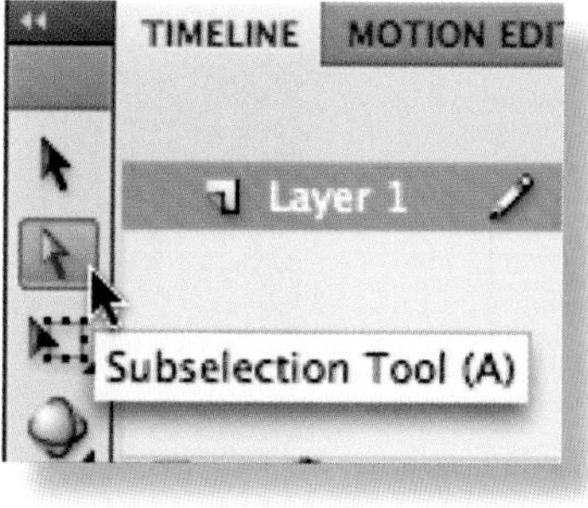

figure 3–20

Select the Subselection tool from the Tools panel.

Modifying Color, Transparency, and Creating Gradients

1. Delete all objects on the Stage. Create a shape (Oval, Rectangle, or PolyStar) on the Stage. Double-click it to select both stroke and fill.

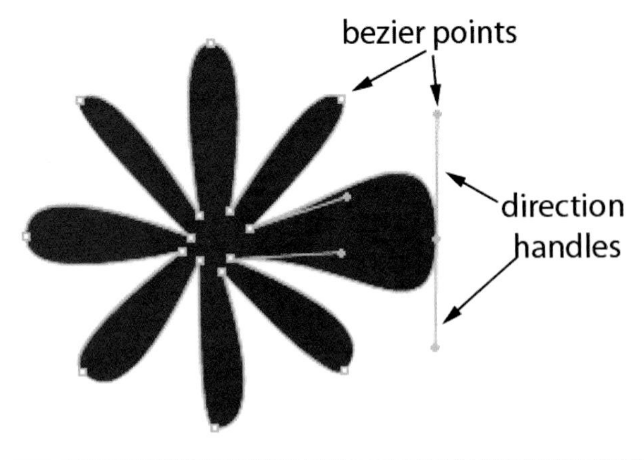

figure 3–21

Parts of the Bezier curve.

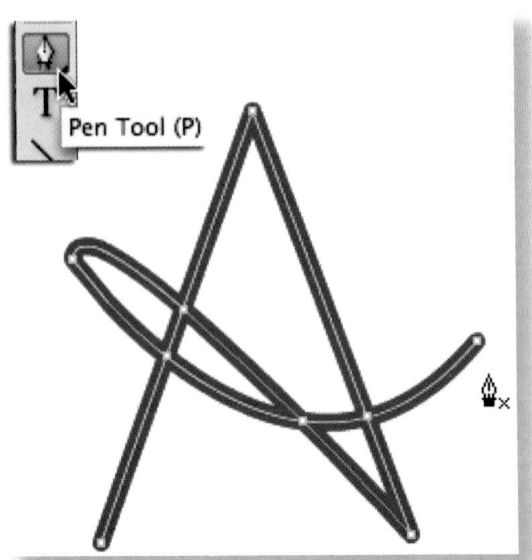

figure 3–22

Play with the Pen tool.

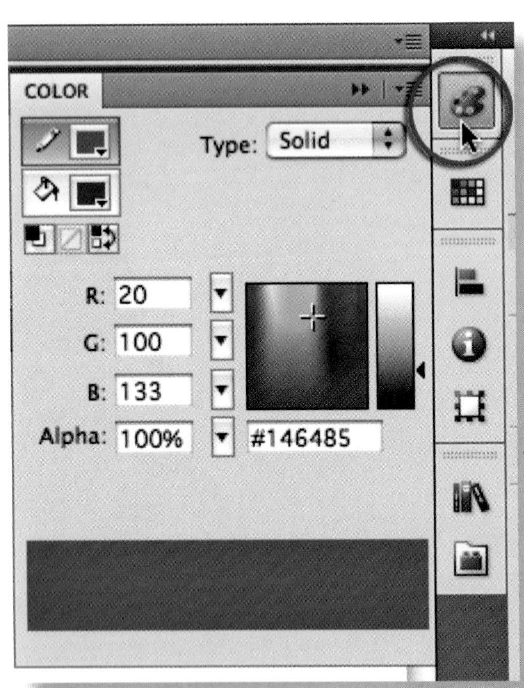

figure 3–23

Expand the Color panel.

2. Expand the Color panel from the docked panels on the right. See Figure 3–23.

3. Choose the Fill Color option in the Color panel. See Figure 3–24.

4. Click and drag your cursor over the color palette/mixer area (the rainbow colored box) in the Color panel to mix a new color. See Figure 3–25. The fill of the selected object on the Stage updates automatically.

figure 3–24

Click to fill color area in the Color panel.

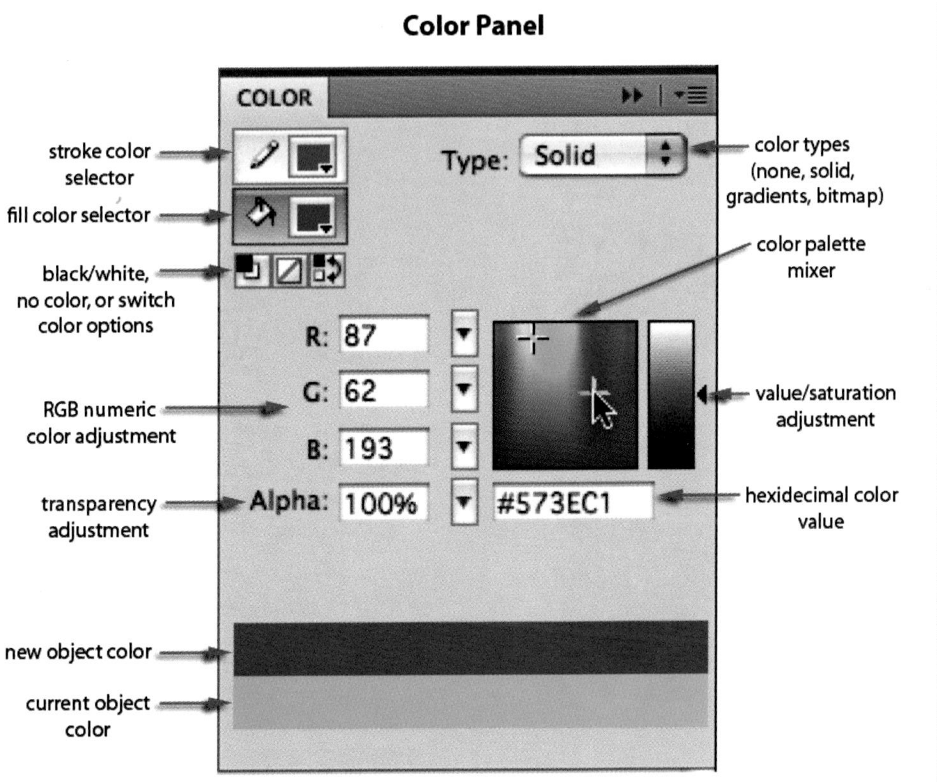

figure 3–25

The many parts of the Color panel. Create a new color by clicking and moving the cursor in the color palette mixer.

5. Adjust the saturation and value of the color by moving the slider along the vertical color ramp to the right of the color mixer area. Refer to Figure 3–25 again.

6. Save your color—open the options submenu in the upper right corner of the Color panel and choose Add Swatch. See Figure 3–26.

7. Expand the Swatches panel in the docked panels on the right to see your saved swatch. See Figure 3–27.

8. Be sure your shape and the Fill color box in the Color panel are selected. Create another color in the color mixer area.

9. Move the Alpha adjustment slider to 50% transparency (note: 100% is completely opaque, 0% is completely transparent). Refer to Figure 3–25 again.

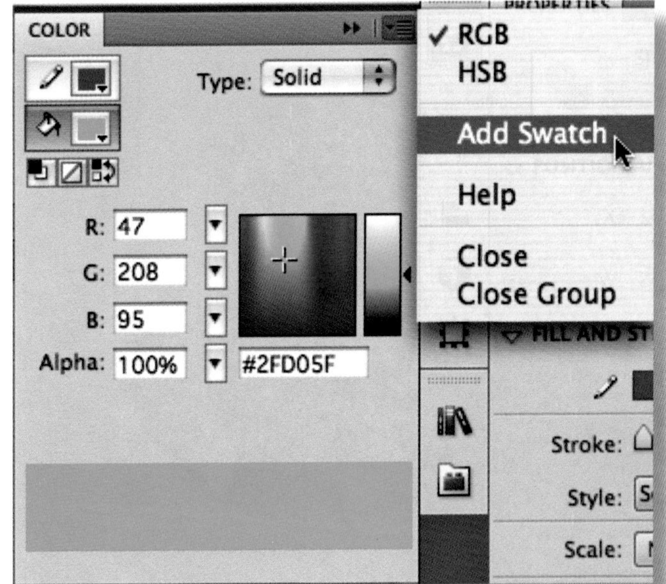

figure 3–26

From the Color panel's submenu choose Add Swatch.

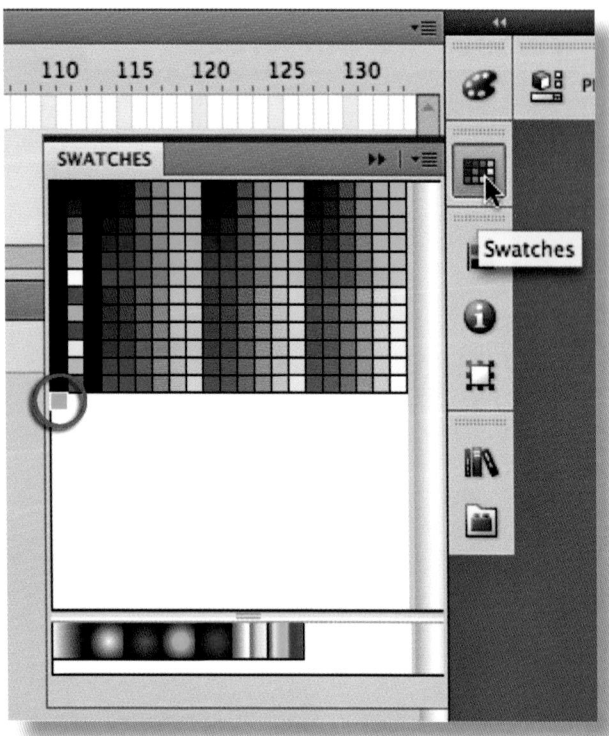

figure 3–27

Expand the Swatches panel and view a saved color swatch.

10. To see the alpha effect deselect the object and choose View > Grid > Show Grid. You should see the grid lines through the object. See Figure 3–28. You'll learn in a later chapter that you can animate the alpha of an object, which is a very useful special effect.

11. Now, let's create a gradient (see note below). Select the fill of your object and expand the Color panel, if not already open. In the Type drop down menu instead of Solid choose Linear. See Figure 3–29.

Note: A gradient is a smooth blend of colors. There are two types of gradients in Flash—Linear and Radial. See Figure 3–30. You will find, as you practice with gradients in the lessons of this book, that you can choose any combination of colors for your gradients, and transform, add levels of transparency, and animate them.

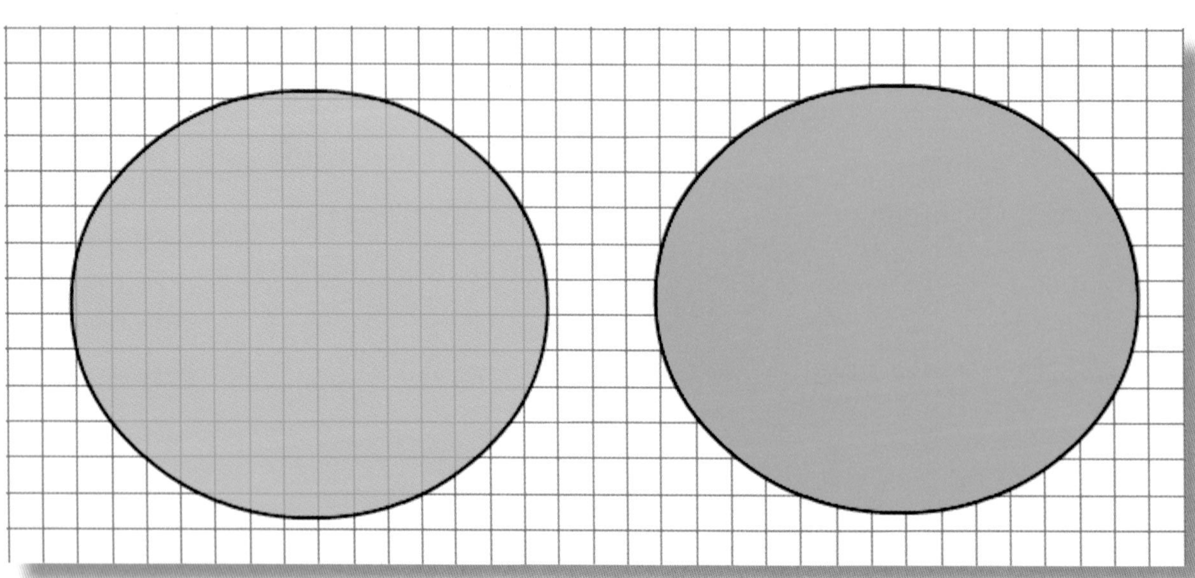

figure 3–28

Choose View > Grid > Show Grid to see the transparency setting you have created.

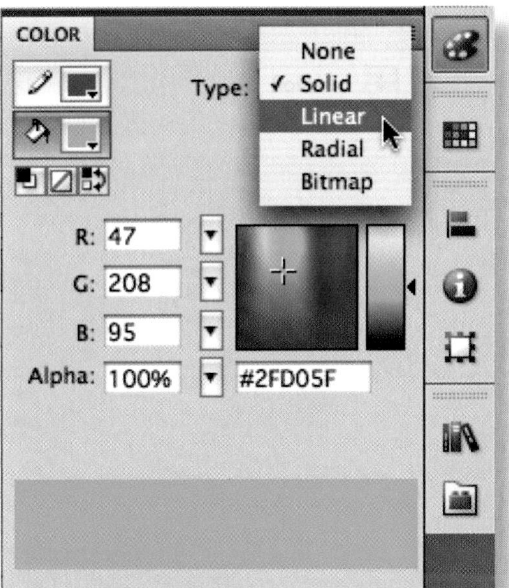

figure 3–29

Choose the Linear gradient color type from the Color panel.

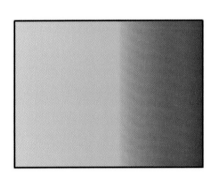

figure 3–30

On the left an example of a linear gradient. On the right, a radial gradient.

12. The default gradient options come up in the Color panel.

13. Select the left color stop on the gradient ramp (the triangle on the top of the color stop turns black when selected). See Figure 3–31.

14. Mix a color for the left color stop in the color mixer area. Adjust the value and saturation slider if necessary.

15. Select the right color stop. Select a color in the color mixer area.

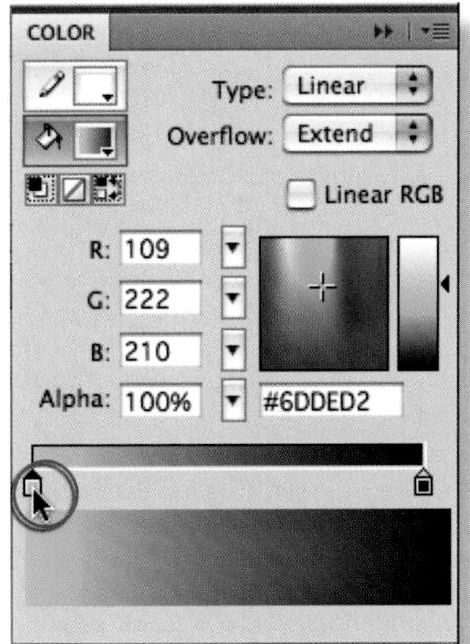

figure 3–31

Select the left color stop.

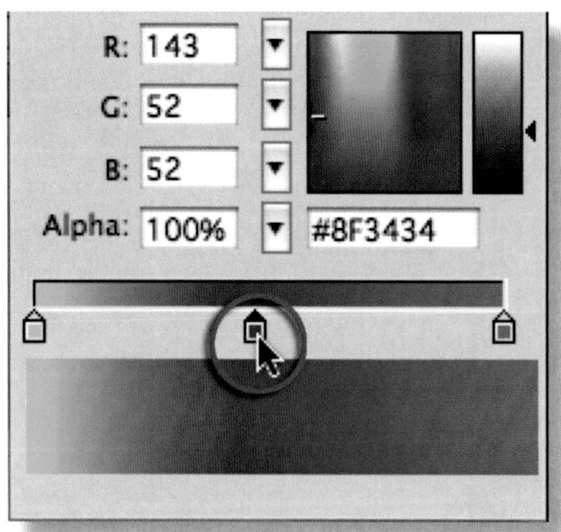

figure 3–32

Add a color stop to the color ramp.

16. Edit the gradient by sliding the left or right color stop along the gradient ramp.

17. Add a new color to the gradient. Click below the color ramp to add a color stop. Make a new color. See Figure 3–32.

18. Delete a color stop—click on the stop you just created and drag it down and away from the Color panel.

19. For fun: make a Radial gradient—choose the Gradient from the Type drop down menu in the Color panel.

> **Note:** Learning how to create gradient colors can be a bit tricky at first. I recommend doing a search for "About Creating Gradients" in the Flash Help files (Help > Flash Help from the Menu bar) to learn more.

Lesson 3: The Group Object Attributes

One way to protect shapes from each other so they don't intersect or merge with one another on the same layer is to group them. To group an object, or objects, you select the object(s) and choose Modify > Group from the Menu bar. Grouping is similar to grouping in other programs, such as Adobe Photoshop. Grouped objects in Flash have the following attributes:

- A selected grouped object has a bounding box.
- Grouped objects can be arranged front and back of one another on the same layer.
- Imported GIFs, JPEGs, and PNGs act like grouped objects.
- Text is grouped.
- Groups of objects can be nested within other groups.

Attribute #1

1. Open the Flash program. Choose Open from the Welcome window or File > Open from the menu bar and browse for the **chap3L3.fla** in the **chap03_lessons** folder.

2. Be sure the Classic workspace is selected.

3. Choose View > Magnification > Fit in Window. This document is a template to assist you in identifying the parts of grouped objects.

4. Select the Zoom tool in the Tools panel.

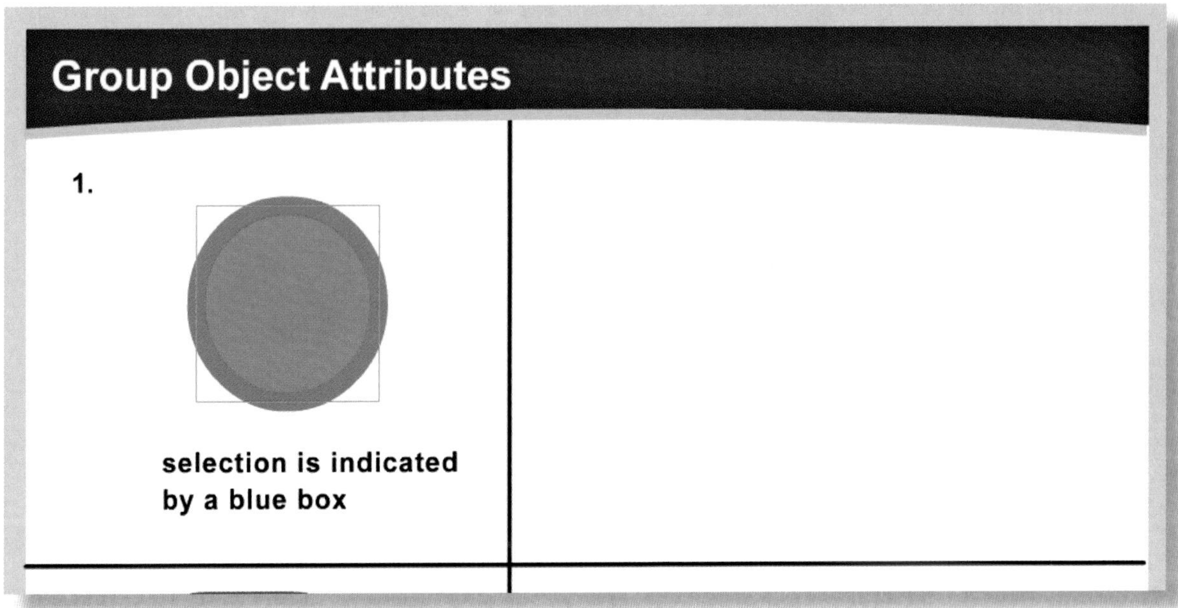

figure 3–33

The attribute #1 area of the document.

5. Click in the middle of the top area of the document to magnify it. This is the attribute #1 area. See Figure 3–33.

6. Attribute #1 is that a grouped graphic has a blue bounding box when selected. With the Selection tool select the circle—notice the bounding box; this tells you this is a grouped object.

7. Select the Oval tool in the Tools panel. Select a color for its stroke and fill. Draw the shape in the blank area to the right of attribute #1.

8. With the Selection tool (first tool in the Tools panel), double-click on the oval to select its stroke and fill and choose Modify > Group. Yes, you can group an individual object!

9. The shape object has been converted to a group—it has a bounding box around it.

Attribute #2

1. Adjust the window view to see the attribute #2 area of the document.

2. Attribute #2 shows how grouped objects can be arranged in front and in back of one another on the same layer.

3. Select the little, blue circle in the attribute #2 area.

4. From the menu bar, choose Modify > Arrange > Bring to Front.

5. Select the maroon rounded rectangle and choose Modify > Arrange > Send to Back.

Note: On the Timeline, notice that these grouped objects are on the same layer called **examples**. Grouped objects on the same layer can be arranged forward and back from each other using the Modify command.

6. To the right of attribute #2 create three objects (make sure they don't touch one another), and then Modify > Group each object group separately. Practice arranging these three objects in front of and in back of each other.

Note: Something to ponder… what happens if you arrange a shape object with a grouped object on the same layer? Are you able to arrange the object front or back with the grouped objects, or does it remain at the bottom of the stack?

Attribute #3

1. Attribute #3 shows that objects imported in the Web image formats GIF, JPEG, and PNG act like grouped objects. The butterfly graphic is an imported GIF. Select the butterfly—it has a bounding box around it. Bitmap objects imported into Flash have a bounding box around them; they also can be arranged in front or in back of other bitmap or grouped objects.

Note: For more information on Web image formats, see the Exploring on Your Own section at the end of Chapter 2.

2. From the Menu bar, choose File > Import to Stage. In the **chap03_lessons/assets** folder open the **kota.jpg**.
3. Move the imported photo to the right side of the attribute #3 area.

Attribute #4

1. Attribute #4 indicates that text created in Flash is grouped by default. Select the word TEXT to see it has a bounding area.
2. Select the Text tool in the Tools panel. See Figure 3–34.
3. Click once in the blank area to the right of attribute #4 and type your name.
4. Click and drag over the text to select it. Adjust its font, color, and size in the Properties panel to the right.
5. Choose the Selection tool in the Tools panel. Click on the text and position it elsewhere within the attribute #4 area.
6. To modify the text properties again, reselect the Text tool and click and drag over the text to select it. Make new adjustments (color, size, font) from the Properties panel.

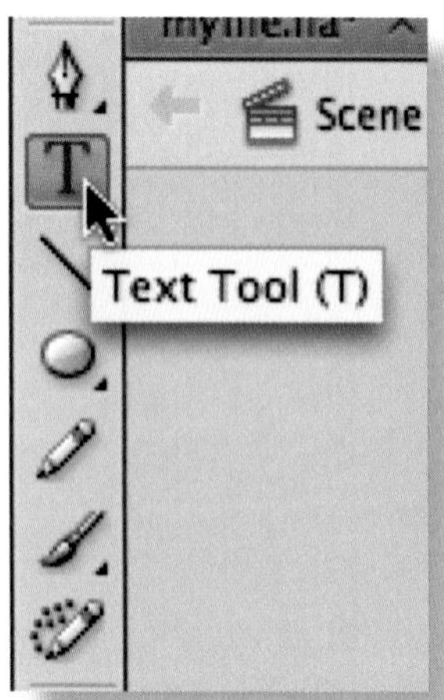

figure 3–34

Select the Text tool.

7. To break the text apart into individually grouped letters, select the text and choose Modify > Break Apart. This would be a good thing to do if you want to edit or animate each letter individually—more on that in a later chapter.

Attribute #5

1. Attribute #5 represents a grouped object with other groups nested inside of it. By nesting groups you can more easily organize and modify individual areas of a drawing.

2. With the Selection tool, move the Flag graphic to the right side area and note that all the pieces of the flag stay together.

3. Now, double-click on the Flag graphic. By double-clicking you are literally going inside the group. This workspace is called *editing mode*. Notice two very important things about editing mode:
   a. The rest of the objects on the Stage are faded;
   b. In the upper left corner of the Stage there is an icon and the word "Group" indicating where you are. See Figure 3–35.

   Later, when you learn about symbols, you will be moving in and out of *editing mode* quite a bit.

figure 3–35

The editing mode for the grouped object.

4. Click on the anchor in the center of the flag—it is its own group. Move it somewhere else on the Stage.

5. Exit the editing mode—go back to Scene 1—by clicking on the Scene 1 icon in the upper left corner of the stage. Refer to Figure 3–35 again.

6. With the Selection tool, move the flag again on the Stage—notice the anchor, although positioned elsewhere, is still part of the group.

7. For fun: can you get back into the group editing mode and place the anchor object back into the center of the flag?

> **Note: If the concept of nested objects is making your head spin—it's expected. You will experience this concept much more in this program. The key for now is to know where you are in the program at all times—are you in a Scene or within the editing mode?**

8. Save your file in your lessons folder.

Lesson 4: Discovering More with Grouped Objects

As you learned in lesson 3, grouped objects have specific attributes. You will further explore these attributes in this lesson, and also learn about the use of layers, importing images, and the trace bitmap feature.

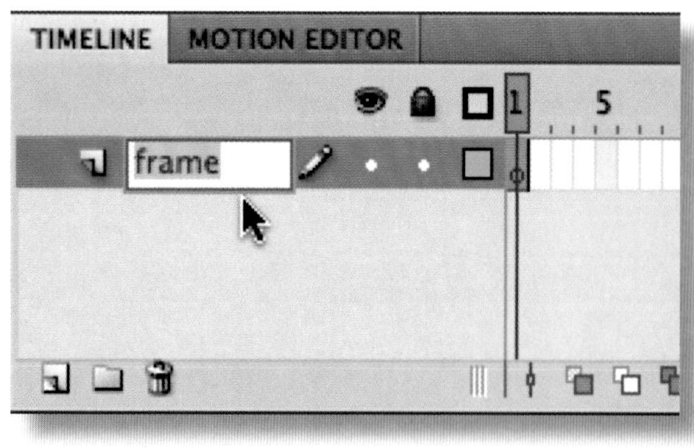

figure 3–36

Rename the layer.

Grouping and Modifying an Object

1. Open a new Flash movie—choose File > New > Flash File (ActionScript 2.0).

2. Choose File > Save, title your file **chap3L4.fla**, and save it in your lessons folder.

3. Be sure the Classic workspace is selected.

4. On the Timeline, double-click on the word **Layer 1**. Type in **frame** for the layer name. See Figure 3–36.

5. In the Tools panel, choose the Rectangle tool. Select a stroke and fill color for the rectangle.

6. Click and drag on the Stage, creating the rectangle shape, and without letting go of the mouse click the page down arrow key on your keyboard to create a rounded edge rectangle (click the page up arrow key to make a beveled rectangle). See Figure 3–37.

figure 3–37

Use the page up or page down arrow keys on your keyboard to create rounded or beveled corners on a rectangle shape.

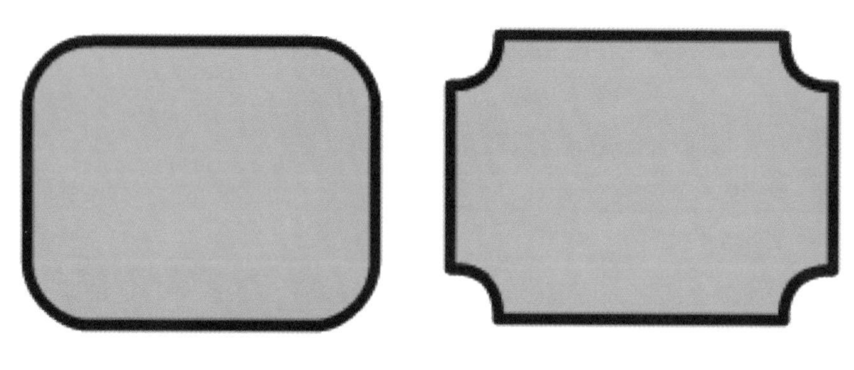

7. Select the rectangle and choose Modify > Group. A blue bounding box appears around the rectangle indicating that it is now grouped.

8. In the Properties panel, click on the width (W) field and enter in 250. For height (H) enter 270.

> **Note:** If you can't seem to enter a width and height individually the "lock width and height values" icon (an image that looks like a link to the left of the width (W) parameter) might be clicked on. Click it again to unlock the relationship.

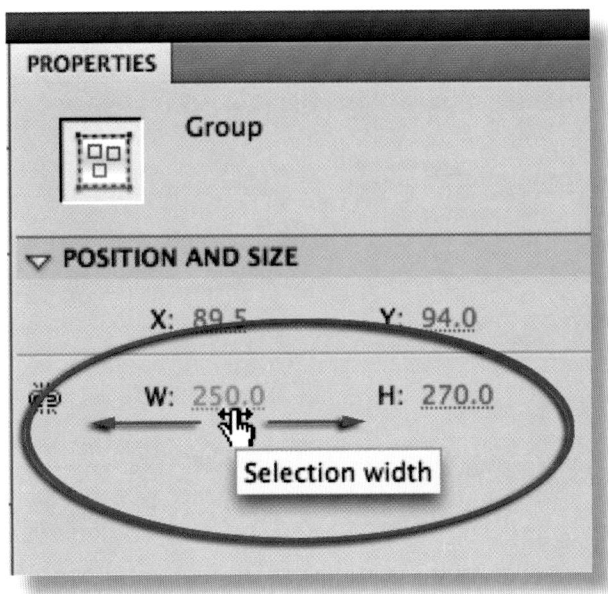

figure 3–38

Click and drag (scrub) right or left to decrease/increase the width value.

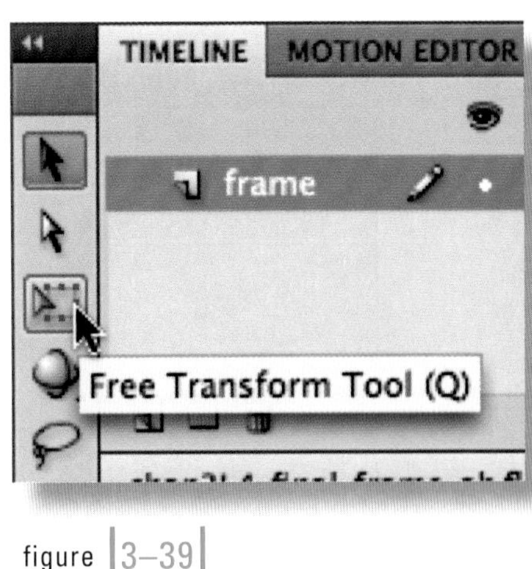

figure 3–39

Select the Free Transform tool.

Note: You can also set the width and height using the "scrubbing" method—hover your cursor right below the W field (selection width) until you see an icon of a hand over a double-sided arrow. Click and drag right or left to decrease/increase the value. See Figure 3–38.

9. Holding down the Option/Alt key click and drag the rectangle on the Stage to the right to create a duplicate or select Edit > Duplicate.
10. Select the Free Transform tool in the Tools panel. See Figure 3–39.
11. A bounding box appears around the selected rectangle. Click and drag on a corner of the bounding box and scale the duplicate rectangle to fit like a picture inside the larger rectangle. See Figure 3–40.

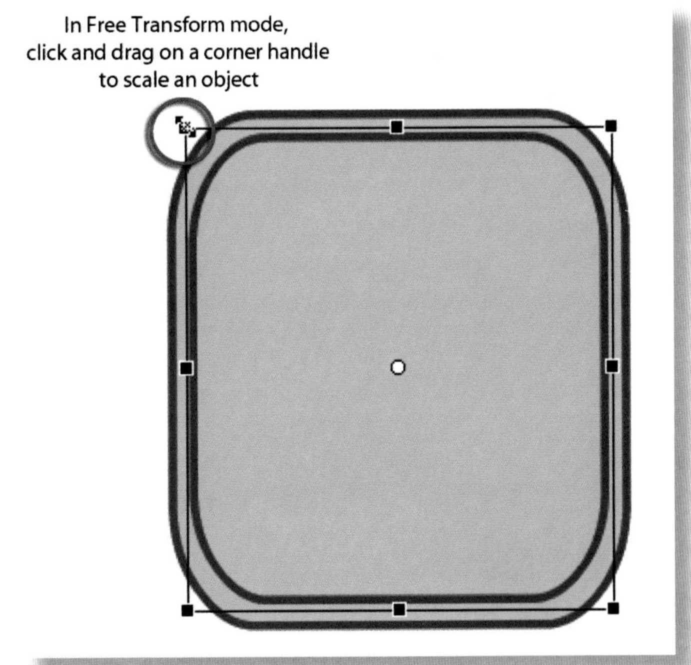

In Free Transform mode,
click and drag on a corner handle
to scale an object

figure 3–40

Adjust the frame with the Free Transform tool.

Note: To constrain the scaling hold down the Shift key on your keyboard as you click and drag a corner.

12. Let's modify the color of the smaller, inside rectangle. To do this the grouped object must be switched to a shape. (Remember an attribute of a shape object is the ability to modify a graphics fill or stroke color.) Double-click on the small rectangle to enter editing mode. This shifts the object to a shape, while preserving the integrity of the group. You know you are in editing mode by looking at the indicator in the upper left corner of the Flash interface. See Figure 3–41.

figure 3–41

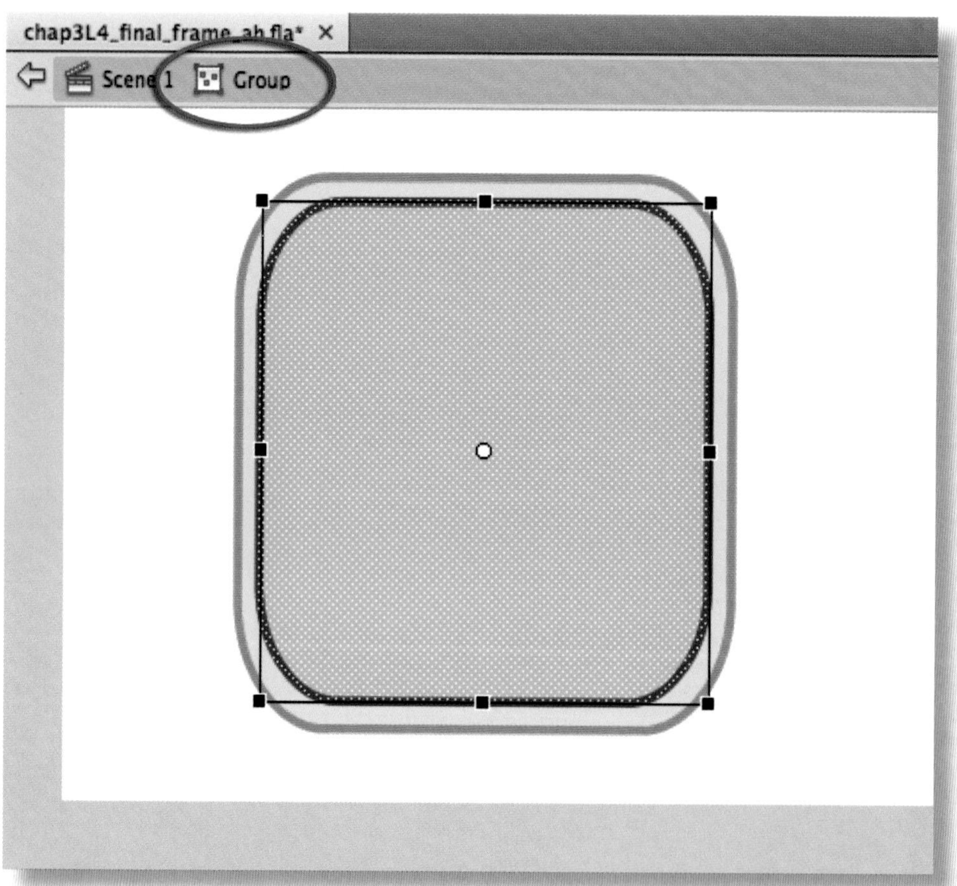

Double-click the object to enter editing mode.

13. Select a new color for the fill of the small rectangle. Remember, you have to select it before you can modify it.

14. Exit out of editing mode by clicking on the Scene 1 icon in the upper left corner of the Flash interface. Refer to Figure 3–41 again.

15. Choose File > Save and save your file in your lesson folder.

Importing a JPEG Image

1. Choose File > Import > Import to Stage and navigate to the **chap03_lessons/assets folder**. Select the **clouds.jpg** and click Import. A cloud image will appear on the document.

2. Select the **cloud.jpg** and hit Delete on the keyboard.

3. Expand the Library panel from the docked panels to the right or choose Window > Library. Notice the cloud JPEG has been saved in the Library. See Figure 3–42.

figure 3–42

The cloud image has been saved in the Library.

> **Note:** A Library in Flash is where all your objects, such as images, sounds, and symbols, can be stored until you are ready to place them on the Stage. All imported bitmaps (GIFs, JPEGs, and PNGs) are saved in the Library, making them always available even if you delete them from the Stage. You will use the **cloud.jpg** later in the lesson.

4. Save your file.

Using a Bitmap Fill

1. Double-click on the smaller, inside rectangle to enter its editing mode.

2. Select the fill of the small rectangle.

3. Expand the Color panel from the docked panels on the right. Select Bitmap from the Fill type list. See Figure 3–43. The cloud bitmap fills the selected fill of the small rectangle. See Figure 3–44.

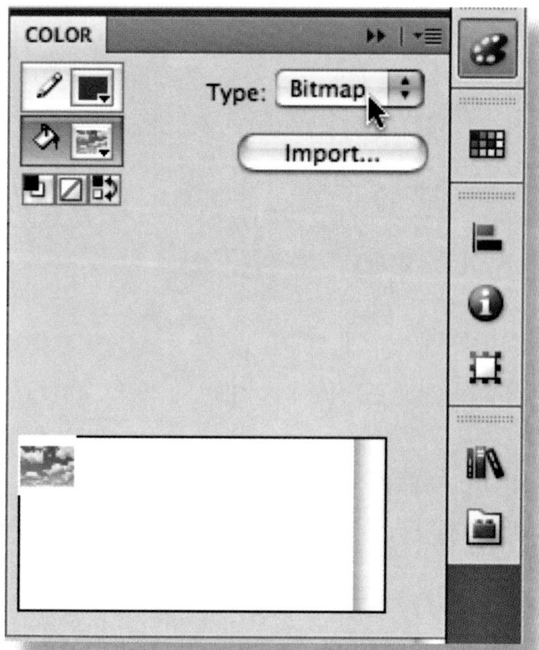

figure 3–43

Choose the Bitmap type in the Color panel.

figure 3–44

The cloud bitmap fills the selected object.

figure 3–45

Select the Gradient Transform tool.

4. Select the Gradient Transform tool in the Tools panel (click and hold on the Free Transform tool to show the Gradient Transform tool). See Figure 3–45.

5. Click once over the selected cloud fill to activate the Gradient Transform bounding box. Explore each of the handles on the bounding area to scale, skew, or rotate the bitmap. Fit it to your liking. See Figure 3–46.

> **Note:** Gradient Transform is designed to scale and rotate a bitmapped fill or gradient color within a shape. This feature allows for a variety of effects with bitmaps, such as masking and tiling an image.

6. Go back to the main scene of the movie by clicking on the Scene 1 icon in the upper left corner of the Flash interface.

7. Save your movie.

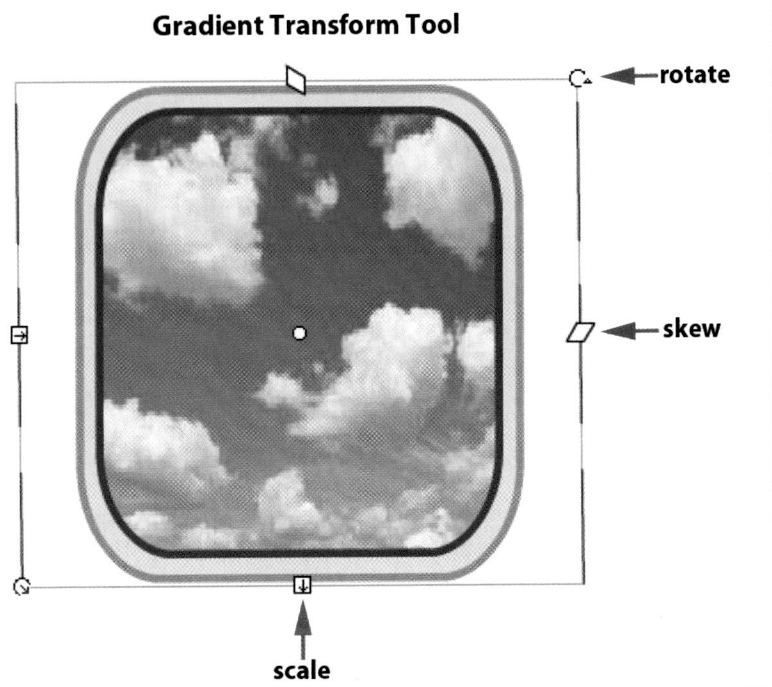

figure 3–46

Transform handle options for the Gradient Transform tool.

Using the Trace Bitmap Feature

1. Create a new layer—choose the New Layer button at the bottom left of the Timeline. See Figure 3–47.

2. Double-click on the new Layer name and rename it **dog**. See Figure 3–48. Be sure the layer is selected (highlighted in blue).

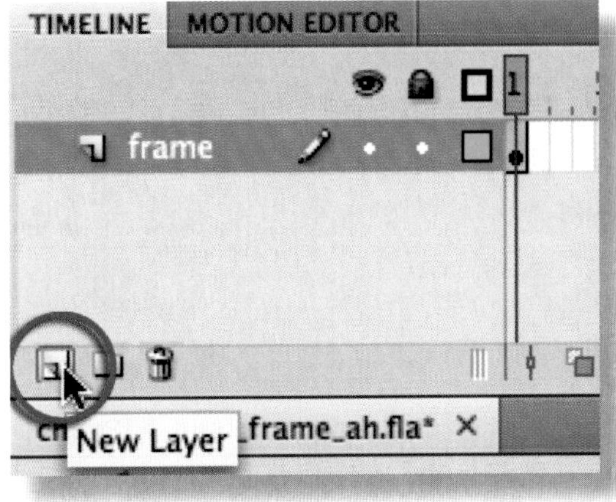

figure 3–47

Create a new layer.

figure 3–48

Name the layer.

Enter settings for Trace Bitmap.

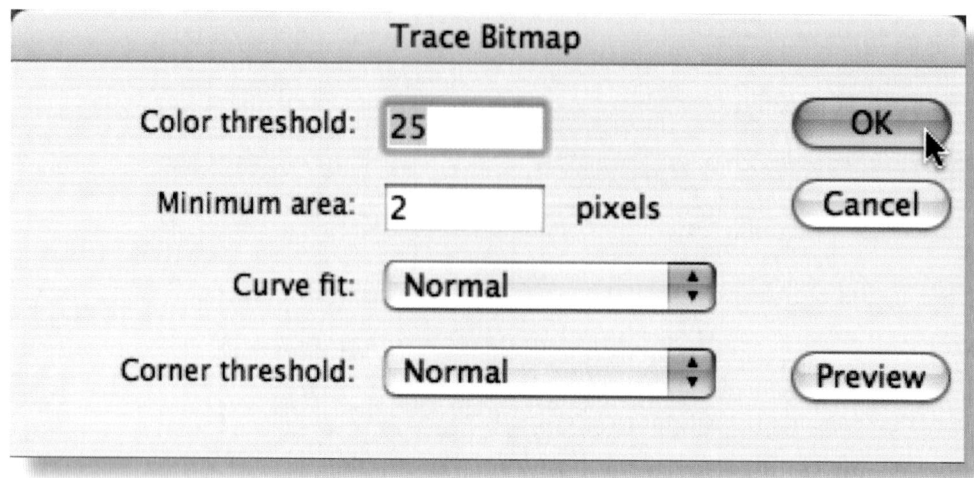

3. Choose File > Import > Import to Stage and open the **dog.jpg** in the **chap03_lessons/assets** folder.

4. Be sure the dog image is selected. Choose Modify > Bitmap > Trace Bitmap and add the following settings in the options box:
   - Color Threshold = 25
   - Minimum Area = 2
   - Curve Fit = Normal
   - Corner Threshold = Normal

   See Figure 3–49. Click OK.

> **Note:** The Trace Bitmap feature converts a bitmap graphic to vector form. The settings for Trace Bitmap will vary depending on the color complexity of the bitmap object and how accurate you would like the desired trace. In general, the Trace Bitmap settings determine the trace accuracy, based on color sampling, of the bitmap to vector conversion. The lower the sampling numbers the more accurate the trace.

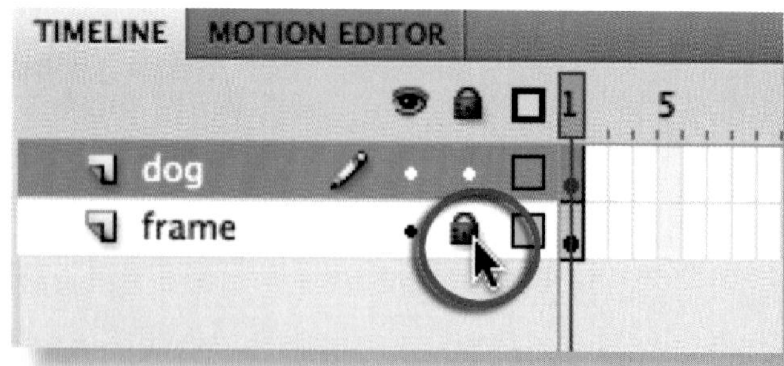

figure 3–50

Lock a layer.

5. Choose Edit > Deselect All to prepare you for the next step.

6. Lock the **frame** layer by choosing the lock option on the **frame** layer on the Timeline. See Figure 3–50.

7. With a vector version of the dog image you can select and remove individual areas of color on the image. Zoom in close to the **image**.

8. Select the Eraser tool in the Tools panel. See Figure 3–51. Click and drag over areas of the dog that you would like to remove (the background). See Figure 3–52.

> **Note:** Options for adjusting the erase size are located at the lower portion of the Tools panel when the Eraser tool is selected. See Figure 3–53.

> **Note:** You can also select, edit, and delete areas of the image by drawing around the area with the Lasso tool. See Figure 3–54. Note the options for the Lasso tool in the lower part of the Tools panel.

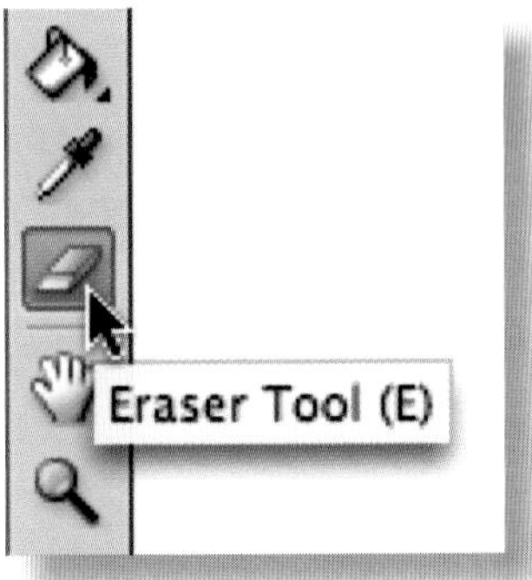

figure 3–51

Select the Eraser tool.

figure 3–52

Erase away areas of the image.

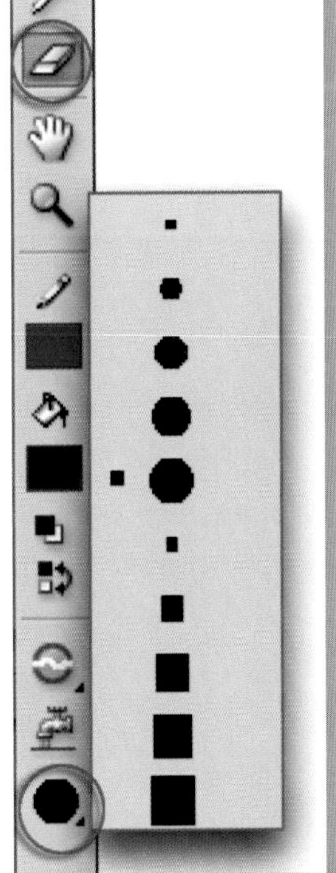

figure 3–53

Adjust Eraser settings from the Tools panel.

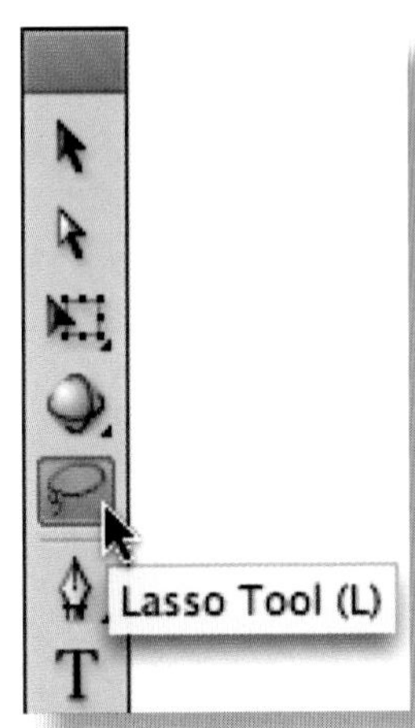

figure 3–54

Select the Lasso tool.

9. With the Selection tool marquee around the image to select all its parts (or choose Edit > Select All). Choose Modify > Group to convert the object to a Group.

10. Position and/or scale the dog image to fit in the frame.

Adding Text

1. One last thing, create a new Layer by selecting the New Layer icon at the bottom of the Timeline. Refer to Figure 3–47 again.
2. A new layer is created above the **dog** layer. Double-click on the Layer name and rename it **text**.
3. Select the Text tool in the Tools panel.
4. Click and drag within the top part of the frame to create a text block—type in the name of your dog.
5. From the Properties panel select a color, font, and font size for your text. Remember the text must be selected to make the character changes; click and drag over the text line to select the text.
6. Now, with the Selection tool, select the text box (automatically a Grouped object!) and position it to your liking.
7. Wow! You're done—save your file!

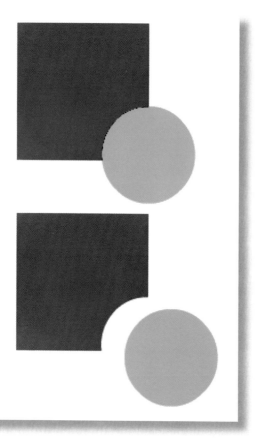

figure 3–55

The Merge Drawing model.

ABOUT FLASH DRAWING MODELS

Now that you have some idea of what it's like to move, draw, and edit objects in Flash, there is something else you should know. Flash provides two drawing models for drawing shapes. In the last lessons you worked with objects in Flash's default Merge Drawing model. The Merge Drawing model automatically merges shapes that you draw when you overlap them. As you discovered, if you select a shape that is merged with another, and move it, the shape below it is permanently altered. See Figure 3–55.

The Object Drawing model draws shapes as separate objects that do not automatically merge together when overlaid. This overlaps shapes without altering their appearance if you move them apart, or rearrange their appearance. See Figure 3–56. Flash creates each shape as a separate object that you can individually manipulate in the drawing object mode. When you select a shape created using the Object Drawing model, Flash surrounds the shape with a rectangular bounding box. Only certain drawing tools support the using of the Object Drawing model—Pen, Line, Rectangle, Oval or PolyStar, Pencil, or Brush. Admittedly working in

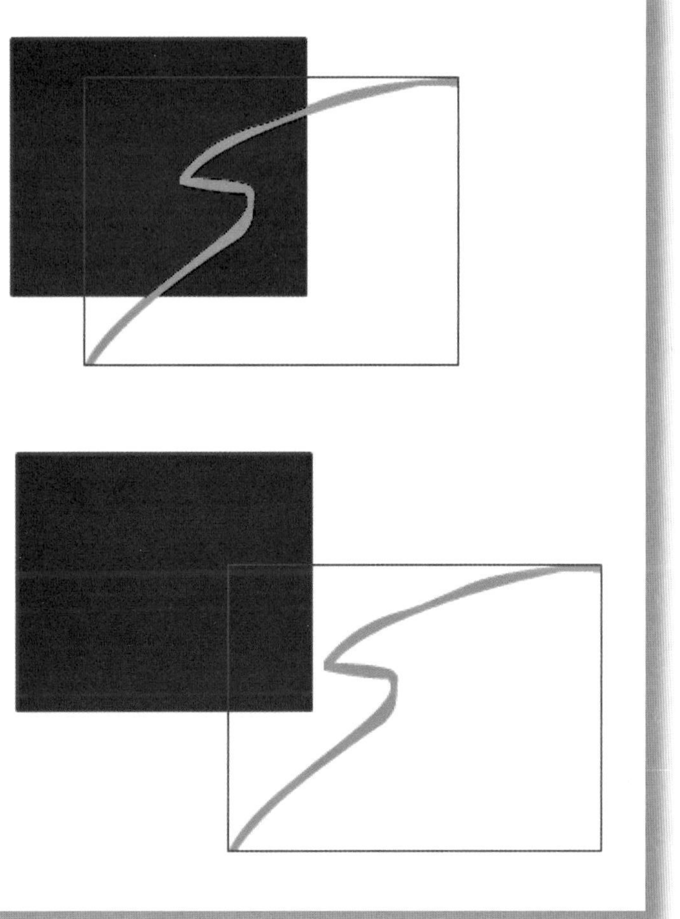

figure 3–56

The Object Drawing model.

the Object Drawing model is similar to working with grouped objects, but with the ability to alter the fill and stroke color of the object without having to go into editing mode.

Try this:

1. Select a drawing tool in the Tools panel that supports the object drawing model—Pen, Line, Rectangle, Oval or PolyStar, Pencil, or Brush.
2. In the lower part of the Tools panel choose the Object Drawing mode. See Figure 3–57.
3. Draw an object on the Stage. Draw another of the same object overlapping the first object. Move one object away from another.

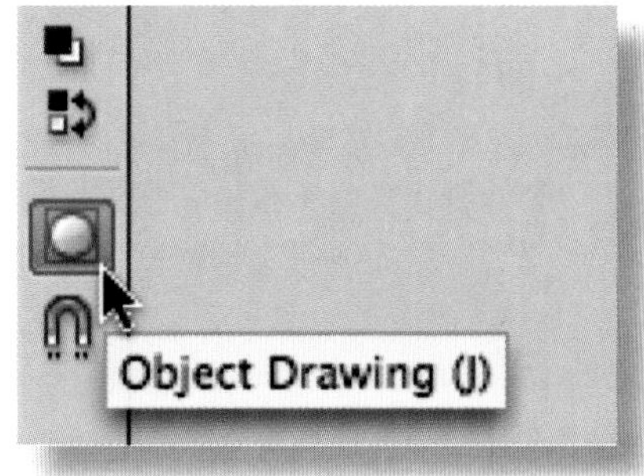

figure 3–57

Select the Object Drawing mode in the Tools panel.

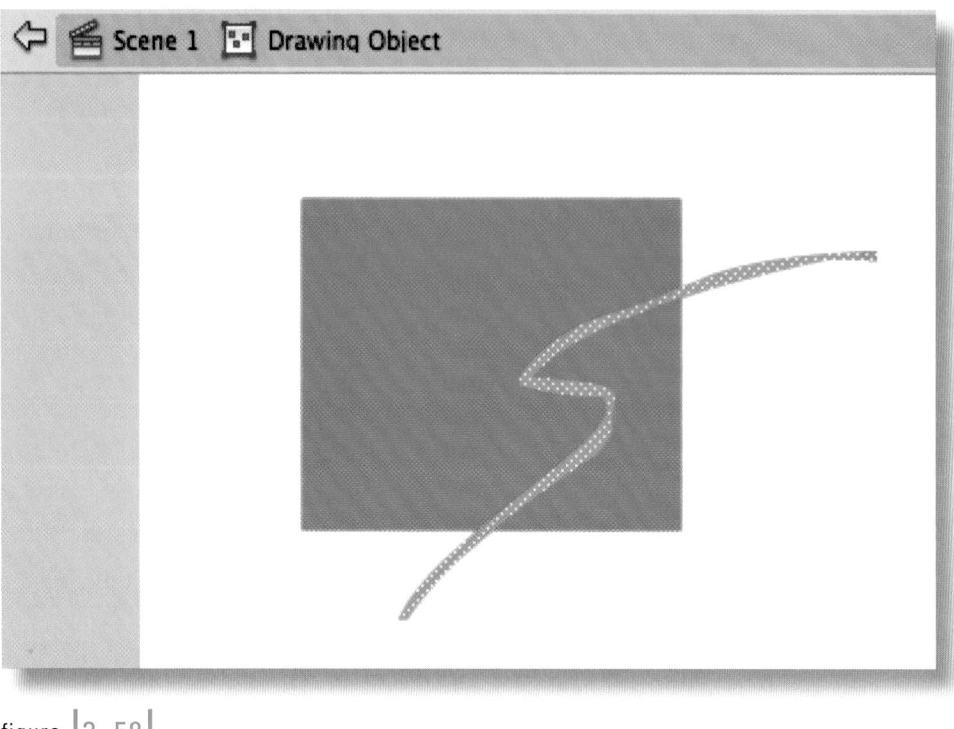

figure 3–58

Double-click to enter the editing mode of the drawing object.

4. Select an object and in the Fill box change its color—it updates automatically.
5. Double-click on one of the objects to enter the drawing object mode (see Figure 3–58). This reduces the object to a shape.
6. To exit out of the Drawing Object mode, click on the Scene 1 icon (refer to Figure 3–58 again).

Another quick note here—just to muddy the waters a bit more—as you worked through the lessons in this chapter I kept reminding you not to use the Rectangle or Oval Primitive tools grouped in the same area as the Rectangle and Oval tools in the Tools panel. The Primitive tools work similarly to objects created in the Object Drawing model except angle and radius options are made available in the Properties panel. Check it out and see what I mean—draw a Rectangle Primitive on the Stage, note, and play with the Rectangle Options available in the Properties panel.

SUMMARY

This chapter provided a substantial and critical overview of shape and group object attributes. In addition, it introduced you to various drawing tools and techniques in the program, and identified the differences between the Merge Drawing and Object Drawing models.

in review

1. Why is it important to understand the fundamentals of object characteristics in Flash?
2. What are at least three attributes of shape objects?
3. What are at least three attributes of grouped objects?
4. What are the names of the two parts that make up a vector object in Flash?
5. To select both parts of a vector object in Flash, what must you do?
6. How do you know you are in editing mode of an object in Flash?
7. How do you get out of editing mode?
8. Why is the Library panel useful?
9. Name three areas in Flash where you can modify the color of an object.
10. What does Trace Bitmap do?

exploring on your own

1. Explore the Pencil, Brush, and Deco Drawing tools. For example, select the Pencil tool in the Tools panel. See Figure 3–59. Draw a circular shape and note what happens to the shape—does it try to smooth itself out? Adjust the pencil settings that appear at the bottom of the Tools panel when the Pencil tool is selected. See Figure 3–60. What happens if you choose the Ink option, then draw a circle? The Smooth option? The Straighten option? Next, play with the Brush tool (right below the Pencil tool in the Tools panel) and adjust its options.

figure | 3–59 |

Play with the Pencil tool.

Also, explore the Deco tool (below the Brush tool in the Tools panel) and adjust its properties in the Properties panel.

2. Play with the Paint Bucket tool. See Figure 3–61. The Paint Bucket tool allows you to fill a shape with color. Use the Pencil tool to draw a circular shape. Select the Paint Bucket tool, choose a Fill color, and click inside the circular shape to fill it. If the shape doesn't fill, it might not be completely closed or has gaps in the outline of the shape you can't necessarily see. Adjust the gap options for the Paint Bucket tool from the settings that appear at the bottom of the Tools panel when the Paint Bucket is selected. See Figure 3–62.

3. Practice pushing and pulling the edges of a shape object. Using the **bfly_part1.fla** found in the **chap03_lessons/samples** folder, push and pull along the edges of the transparent oval shape to match the butterfly's wing underneath. See Figure 3–63. To refresh your memory on the push/pull technique, review the section Pushing and Pulling Shapes in Lesson 2: Discovering More with Shape Objects. See a completed example in **chap03_lessons/samples/bfly_part1_final.fla**. You will have opportunity to play more with this butterfly in the Exploring on Your Own sections of later chapters.

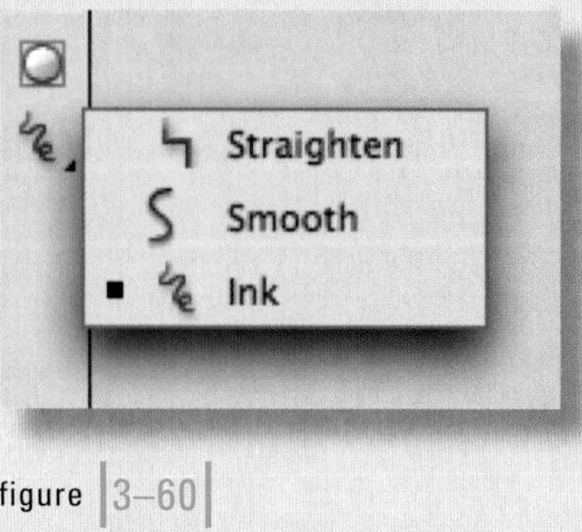

figure 3–60

Adjust the Pencil tools options from the Tools panel.

figure 3–61

Play with the Paint Bucket tool.

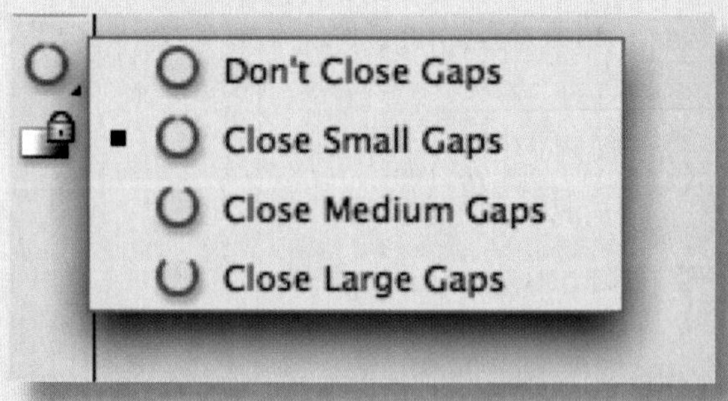

figure 3–62

Adjust the gap detection levels of the Paint Bucket tool from the Tools panel.

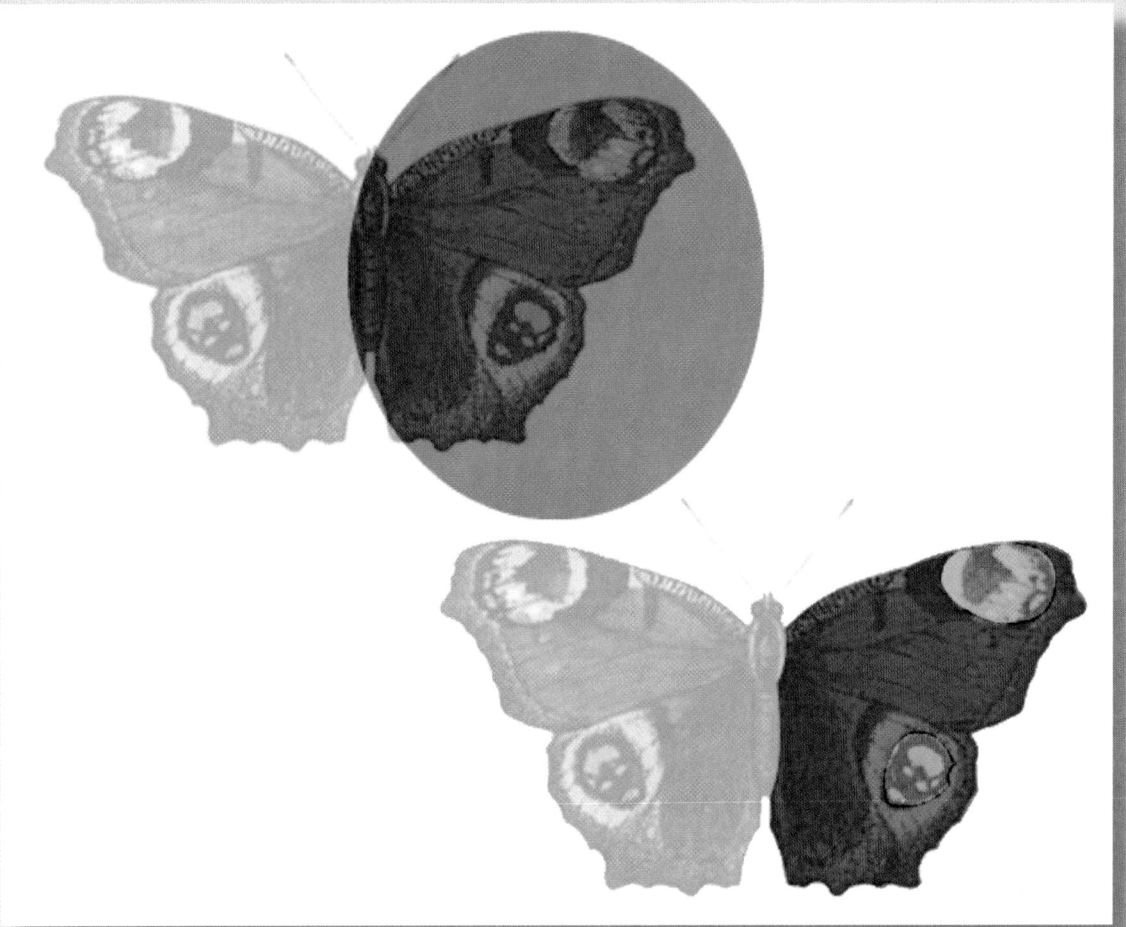

figure 3–63

Use the shape editing options learned in this chapter to create a butterfly wing.

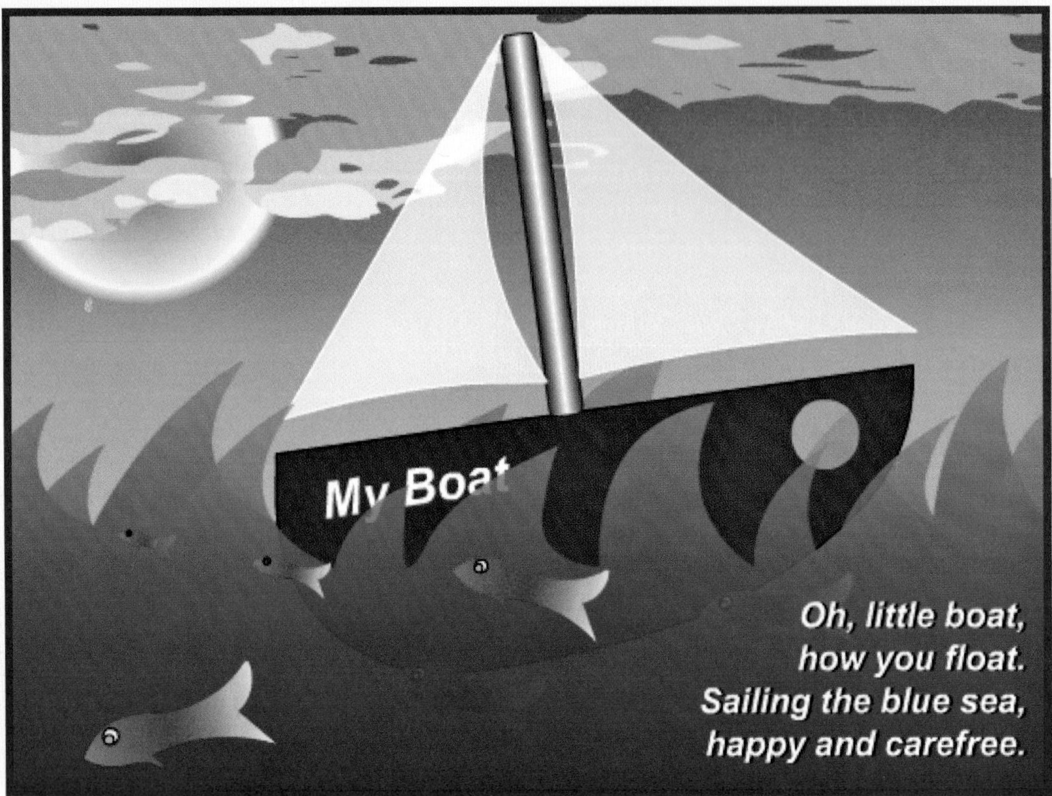
My Boat
Oh, little boat,
how you float.
Sailing the blue sea,
happy and carefree.

| symbols |

4

charting your course

In the last chapter, we covered the attributes of shape and group objects in Flash and played with them further using the drawing tools. This chapter is dedicated to the third and most versatile object type—symbols. Symbols are the heart of Flash objects.

goals

In this chapter you will:

- **Identify the characteristics of symbols.**
- **Play with symbols.**
- **Modify instances of symbols.**
- **Create a sailboat scene combining all that you have learned in the first four chapters of this book.**

SYMBOLS

Symbols are reusable objects that are stored in the Flash Library. They are an important aspect to making fast downloadable Flash files. Symbols have all the same attributes as shape and group drawing objects, and more. You ask, "so why did we spend so much time with shapes and groups when symbols have it all?" Well, to prepare you for symbols, of course! Symbols have special attributes that are used when creating sophisticated animations and interactive effects. I recommend all your objects be saved as symbols.

Lesson 1: The Symbol Object Attributes

This lesson offers a quick overview of the important attributes of symbols, including:

- Symbols have three behaviors—movie clip, button, and graphic.
- Selected symbols have a registration mark that you can use to set the origin of an object.
- Symbols have a name and are saved in the Library.
- Symbols can be reused, adding very minimal file size. Symbols on the Stage are called "instances."
- Like group objects, you double-click on a symbol to edit it.
- Symbol instances can be modified in size, shape, and name and be called by actions (interactive code).
- Symbols have their own set of layers and timelines.

Attribute #1

1. Open the Flash program. Choose Open from the Welcome window or File > Open from the menu bar and browse for the **chap4L1.fla** in the **chap04_lessons** folder.

2. Be sure the Classic workspace is selected.

3. Choose View > Magnification > Fit in Window. On the left is a list of attributes for symbol objects, on the right is a practice area where you learn these attributes.

4. Select the circle in the attribute #1 area. See Figure 4–1. Notice it contains a white registration mark (white dot with an X) in the center of the graphic. This mark indicates that the object is saved as a symbol. It can be moved to indicate a new origin, or pivoting point, for the symbol object; this is a useful feature when you start animating (next chapter!). See Figure 4–2 for a review of what shape, group, and symbol objects look like when selected.

5. On the right side area of attribute #1 create an oval shape with a stroke and fill color. Select the shape by double-clicking on it with the Selection tool.

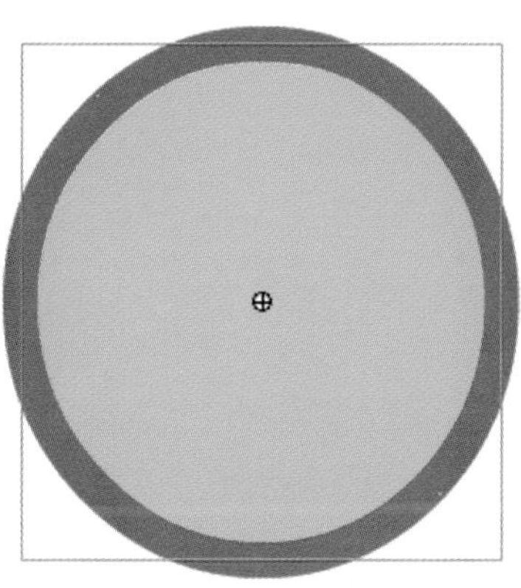

figure 4–1

The first attribute area of the lesson.

figure 4–2

What shape, group, and symbols look like when selected.

6. Choose Modify > Convert to Symbol (F8). See Figure 4–3. In the Symbol dialog box, name the symbol **my_object**, select the Movie Clip behavior from the Type pop up menu, and choose the center dot on the Registration point grid. See Figure 4–4.

> **Note:** More about symbol types will be covered later, but, for now, always save your graphics as a movie clip.

figure 4–3

Convert to Symbol command (F8).

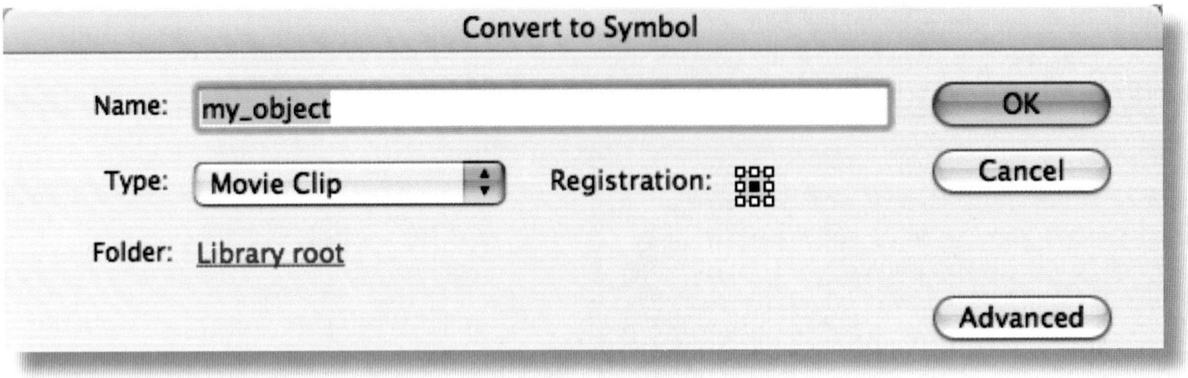

figure 4–4

Name your symbol in the Convert to Symbol dialog box.

figure 4–5

View symbols in the Library panel.

7. Choose OK to close the Symbol dialog box. Notice your object is now a symbol—with a white mark in the center.

8. Expand the Library panel or choose Window > Library. See Figure 4–5. Notice your **my_object** symbol is now in the Library, along with some other symbols. When you select the item in the Library, a thumbnail of the item will show up in the Library panel's window. Refer to Figure 4–5 again.

Attribute #2

1. Attribute #2 shows how you can create *instances* of symbols. An *instance* is a symbol on the Stage.

2. Open the Library panel again, if not already open. In the Library panel, click on the icon of the **my_object** movie clip symbol you just made and drag an instance of it to the Stage. Place it in the blank area to the right of attribute #2. See Figure 4–6.

3. Drag out two more instances—you now have three instances (virtual copies) of the symbol.

> **Note:** All three instances are using much less memory than if the objects were created using a duplication method, like Copy, then Paste or Edit > Duplicate. This is good, because the smaller the file size of your movie the faster and more efficient it will download from the Internet. You might ask, however… "when would you use more than one copy of a symbol in your movie?" Well, let's say you have 25 buttons on your site. Create one graphic as a button symbol and use 25 instances of it on your site—this saves some memory!

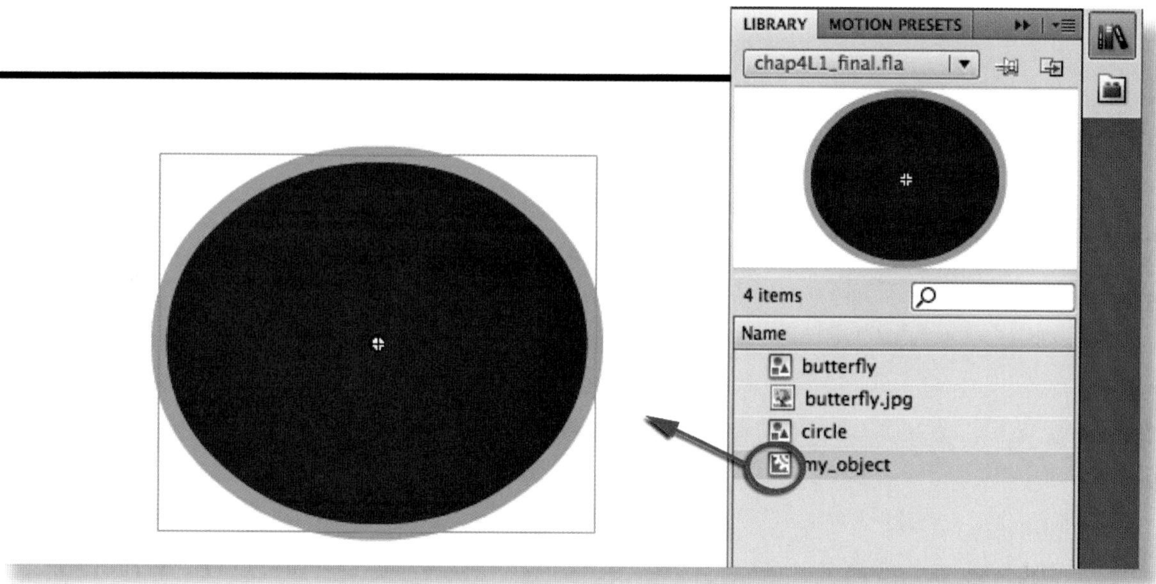

figure 4–6

Drag a symbol from the Library to the Stage to create an instance.

Attribute #3

1. Let's edit a symbol. Double-click on the circle in the attribute #3 area to get to editing mode of the graphic. Notice in editing mode that all areas of the Stage fade and that the symbol is titled **circle**. In editing mode, the circle is modified to a shape object. See Figure 4–7.

2. Click on the Scene 1 icon or the arrow in the upper left corner of the interface to practice exiting out of editing mode. See Figure 4–8.

3. From the Library drag two more instances of your **my_object** movie clip to the right of attribute #3.

4. Double-click on one of the instances (it doesn't matter which one). This puts you in the Edit > Symbol mode for the **my_object** movie clip symbol. Notice in the upper left corner of the Flash interface that you are no

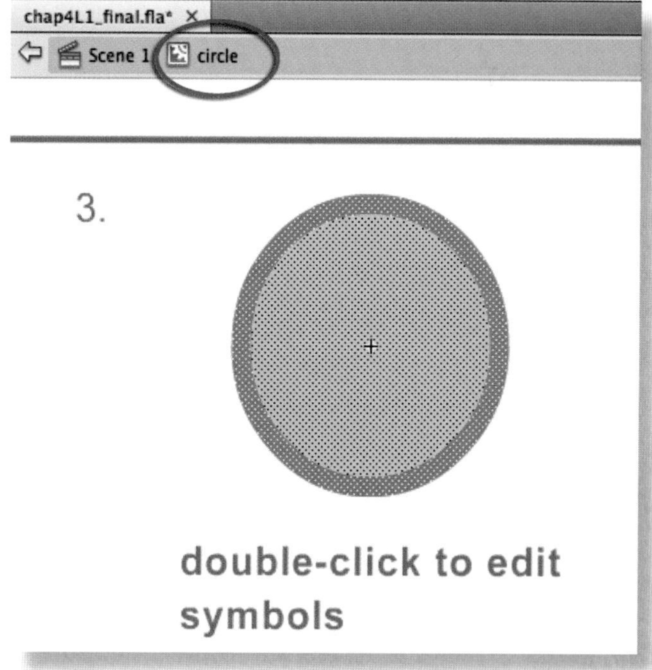

figure 4–7

Inside the editing mode of the **circle** symbol.

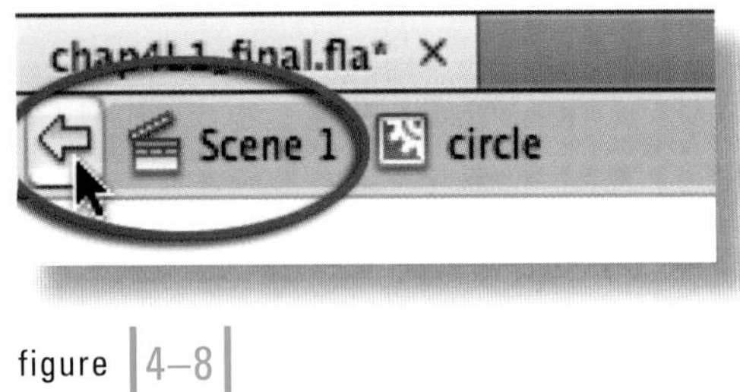

figure 4–8

Exit out of the editing mode by clicking Scene 1 in the Edit bar.

longer on Scene 1, but inside the **my_object** symbol, in editing mode.

> **Note:** This editing mode is just like editing mode for grouped objects, except now your object has a name, **my_object**. Also, note in the editing mode that the object has its own timeline with Layer 1 as the default. See Figure 4–9.

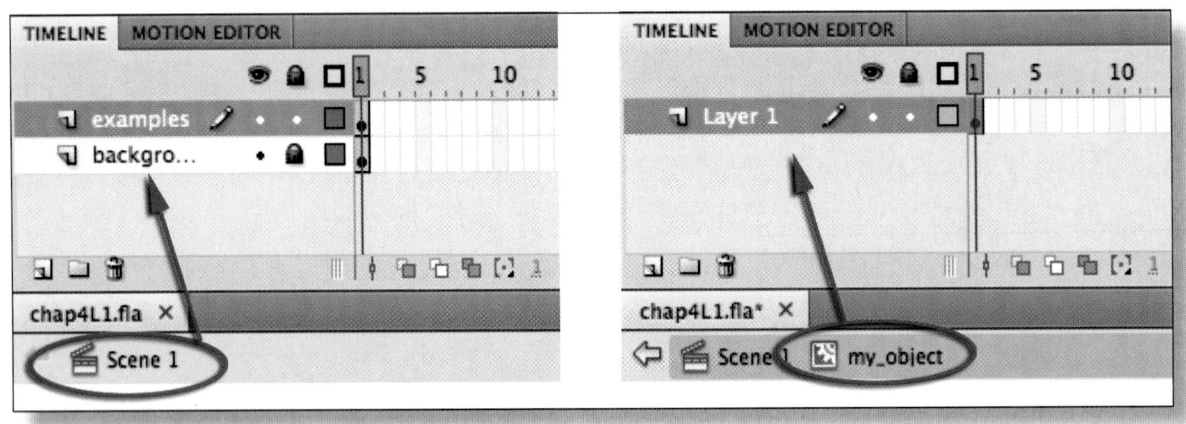

figure 4–9

Same as in Scene 1, there is a timeline in the editing mode of the movie clip called **my_object**.

figure 4–10

The Free Transform tool.

5. When in editing mode, the object is modified to its shape state. Change the color of the symbol.
6. Go back to Scene 1 by clicking on the Scene 1 icon or arrow in the upper left corner of the interface. What has happened? All the instances of the symbol that you had on the Stage have been updated to reflect the new color.
7. Double-click again on the object you changed the color of to enter its editing mode. Select the Free Transform tool in the Tools panel. See Figure 4–10.
8. Reduce the size of the object by dragging inward a corner handle of the transform tool. See Figure 4–11.
9. Exit editing mode.

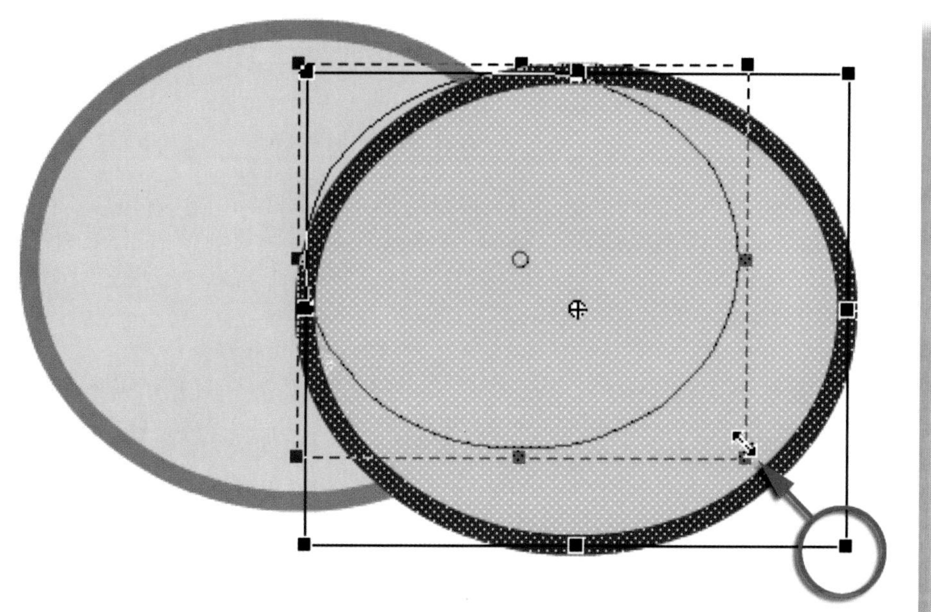

figure 4–11

Use the Free Transform tool to scale an object.

> **Note:** You learned in the last step that changes made to a symbol object affect its instances on the Stage. So, why is this so great? Consider again the 25 buttons example. Let's say, I place 25 instances of a blue button symbol on my Stage. I spent hours placing them properly in my scene. The creative director comes into my office and tells me that the client doesn't want blue buttons anymore, but orange buttons. How can I easily change the 25 button graphics from blue to orange? Edit the original symbol!

Attribute #4

1. Let's modify the symbol instances. Place two instances of the **my_object** symbol into the right side area of attribute #4.
2. Select one of the instances (don't double-click it, just click it once) and in the Properties panel, under Color Effect, choose the Tint style from the drop down menu. See Figure 4–12.
3. Move the Tint slider to change the tint of the instance. Play with the Red, Green, and Blue adjustments as well. The instance is still based on the original symbol, but modified in color.

figure 4–12

Change the color of an instance in the Color Effect area of the Properties panel.

> **Note: You can modify the color, size, and rotation of an instance. This is a good thing, if for example—going back to the 25-button scenario—you want all 25 buttons to be orange except for one. One of them you want to be purple and bigger in size. You can do this on a single instance of a symbol.**

4. Choose File > Save. You've learned the main attributes of symbol objects. Review these attributes in the bulleted list at the beginning of this lesson.

Lesson 2: Practicing Symbol Basics

Ultimately every graphic you create or import into Flash should become a symbol. It takes awhile to learn all the attributes of symbols and their behaviors. In this lesson, review the basics of symbol creation and then be prepared to practice with symbols in just about every other lesson from here on out.

Creating a Symbol Object

1. Create a new Flash file (File > New > Flash File (ActionScript 2.0)).
2. Be sure the Classic workspace is selected.
3. Draw a simple circle object on the Stage.
4. Choose Modify > Convert to Symbol (F8).
5. Call the symbol **my_object** and choose the movie clip behavior in the Type pop up menu. Select OK. Notice the object on the Stage now has a crosshair, and a white mark in the middle indicating that this is a symbol.
6. Expand the Library panel or choose Window > Library and note the **my_object** is saved in the Library.
7. In the Library window, click on the icon for **my_object** and drag two duplicates of the symbol onto the Stage. Remember a symbol when placed on the Stage is called an instance. An instance is, in essence, a "virtual copy" of the symbol in the Library—it references the attributes and file size of the symbol in the Library.

Editing a Symbol

1. Double-click on one of the instances on the Stage to enter editing mode.
2. Change the color of the symbol and notice what happens to the instances on the Stage—they are updated with the change. Any modifications made in editing mode will apply to all instances of that symbol within the movie. This is great when you start animating and need to make a change throughout a movie.
3. Try other modifications to the symbol in editing mode—change its color, or size, push and pull the edges, add another object, etc.
4. Exit editing mode.

Modifying an Instance

1. On the Stage, select one of the instances of the **my_object** symbol (don't double-click it, just click on it once).
2. In the Properties panel, under Color Effect choose Alpha and change the opacity (transparency) color of the instance from 100% to 50%. See Figure 4–13. An instance can be scaled, rotated, positioned, its color changed, and animated.

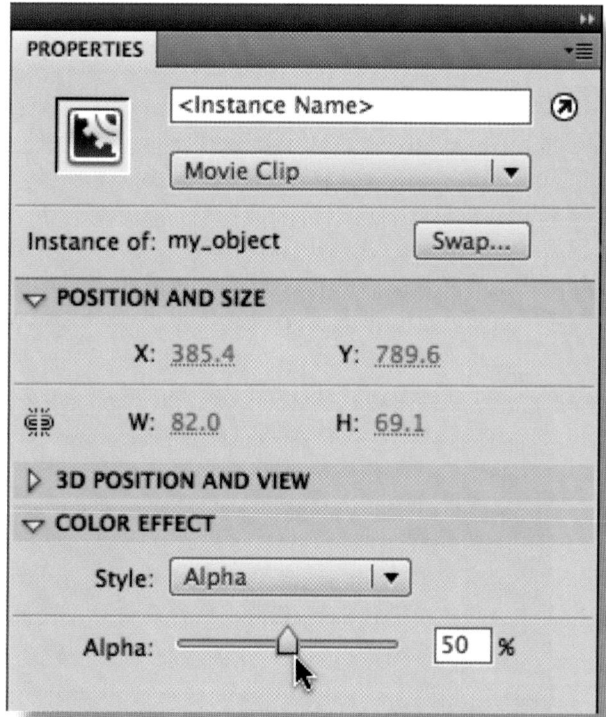

figure 4–13

An instance's alpha (transparency) can be adjusted in the Color Effect area.

3. Deselect the instance to see the transparent effect.
4. Double-click on the instance to enter editing mode.
5. Change the color of the symbol.
6. Exit out of the editing mode and note that all the instances on the Stage have changed color, but the transparency on the one instance is still applied. An instance of a symbol can be modified in addition to any modifications made directly to the symbol in the Library.
7. Explore other modifications on the instances—use the Free Transform tool to scale and rotate them, and change their color effects in the Properties panel. Then, add modifications to the objects' symbol by entering editing mode (double-click on an instance) and adjusting color, scale, rotation, or shape.
8. Exit out of editing mode and note the combination of effects. See Figure 4–14 as an example.
9. Save your file, if you'd like. You've completed this practice lesson.

figure | 4–14 |

Example modifications on instances of a symbol.

PROJECT: THE SAILBOAT, PART 1

The sailboat project is designed to review and solidify your understanding of objects in the shape, group, and symbol states, and to get you comfortable with moving around and organizing objects in the program. Once completed (see Figure 4–15), the scene will be used in the next chapter (The Sailboat, Part 2) to demonstrate and learn the animation features of Flash.

For reference, check out a demonstration version of this project in **chap04_lessons/ project_part1_final.fla**. Please note that the sailboat drawing in the demo is not intended to be copied. It's just an example. Create your own variation of a sailboat using the following steps as a guideline—don't worry about artistic ability, just have some fun with drawing shapes and choosing colors.

If you need to refresh your memory on how to do something, like how to make a gradient or rotate an object, you can always refer to previous lessons or the Help files within the Flash program (Help > Flash Help). I find the Help files very useful and refer to them often.

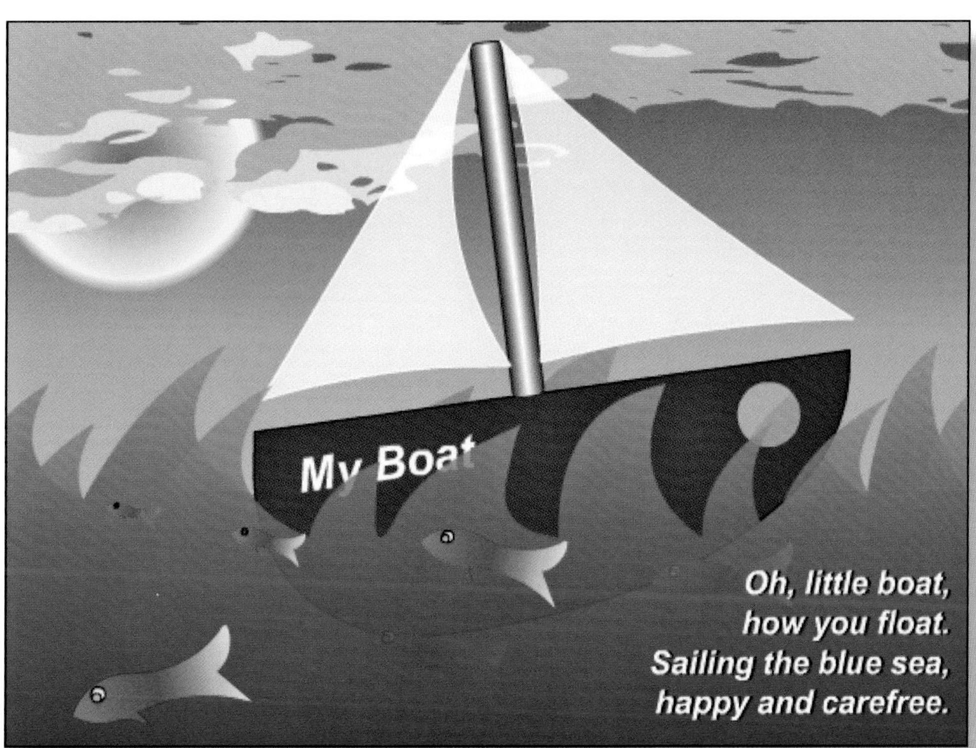

figure 4–15

An example of the completed sailboat project.

Building the Boat

1. Open Flash and create a new file: Flash File (ActionScript 2.0).
2. Choose File > Save and save the file in your lessons folder. Title it **my_boat.fla**. Click Save.
3. In the Properties panel under Properties, then Stage, choose a color for the background of your scene. See Figure 4–16.
4. Double-click on the Layer 1 title in the timeline and rename it **boat**. See Figure 4–17.
5. On the Stage draw a sailboat. Start with basic geometric shapes for the design. If you're not sure what a sailboat looks like, find a picture to reference. Keep it simple, though. Make the bottom part first (the hull), then group it (Modify > Group). Then make a mast (a pole to hold the sail). Group that as well. And, then make a sail

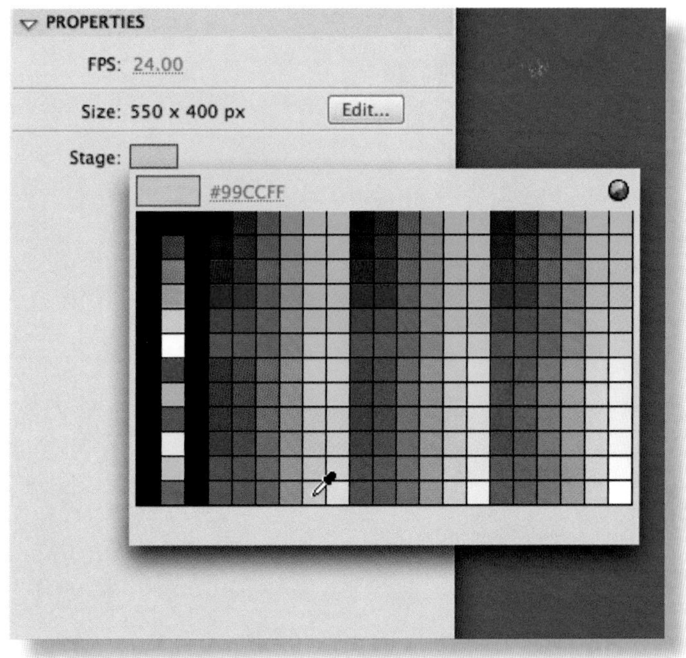

figure 4–16

Choose a new color for the Stage background.

figure 4–17

Rename your layer to describe what is on that layer.

and group it. The sail is the part that will be animated later—imagine it moving with the wind. See Figure 4–18 for an example of each part grouped.

6. If necessary, arrange each grouped part to complete the boat. For example, I selected my mast object and chose Modify > Arrange > Send to Back to move it behind the boat's hull.

7. Once completed, select all the parts of the boat and choose Modify > Convert to Symbol (F8). Title the symbol **boat** and

figure 4–18

Objects of the boat are individually grouped to protect the objects from each other.

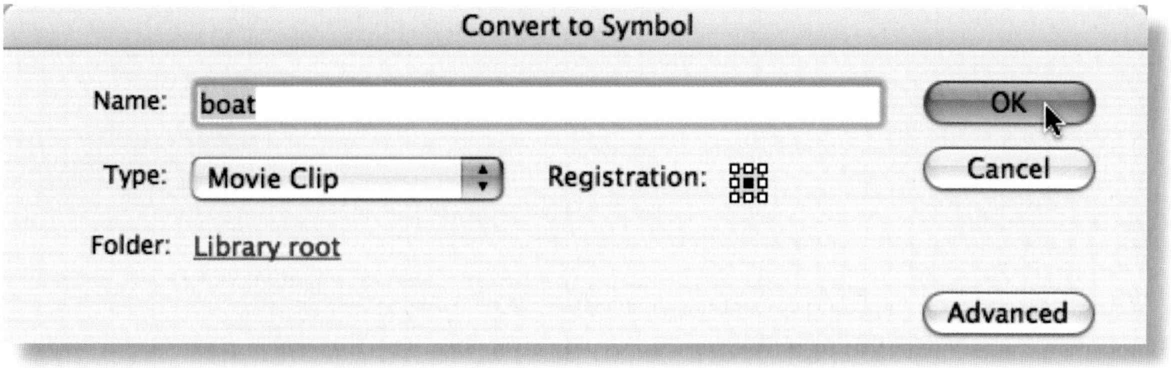

Convert to Symbol

Name: boat

Type: Movie Clip

Registration:

Folder: Library root

OK

Cancel

Advanced

figure 4–19

Name the symbol.

assign it the Movie Clip type. Leave the registration point in the center of the grid. See Figure 4–19. Click OK.

8. Double-click to enter editing mode for the **boat** symbol.

9. Select the Text tool and click on the boat's hull. Type in a name for your boat (for example, My Boat, Prince of the Sea, Floating Mistress, Minnow). See Figure 4–20.

10. Be sure the text is selected with the Text tool, and adjust the font, size, and color in the Properties panel. See Figure 4–21.

figure 4–20

Add some text to your boat.

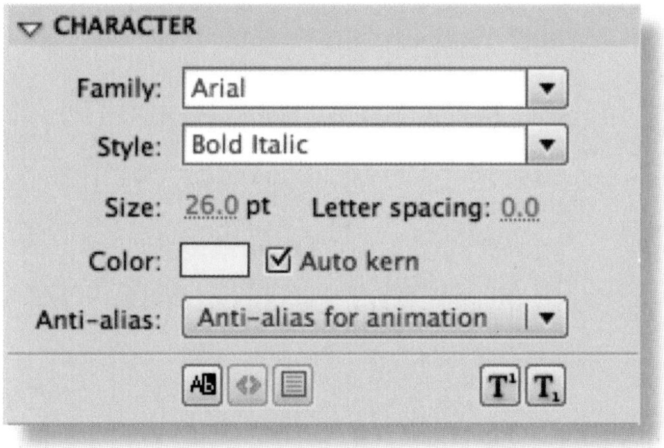

CHARACTER

Family: Arial

Style: Bold Italic

Size: 26.0 pt Letter spacing: 0.0

Color: Auto kern

Anti-alias: Anti-alias for animation

figure 4–21

Text options are available in the Character panel.

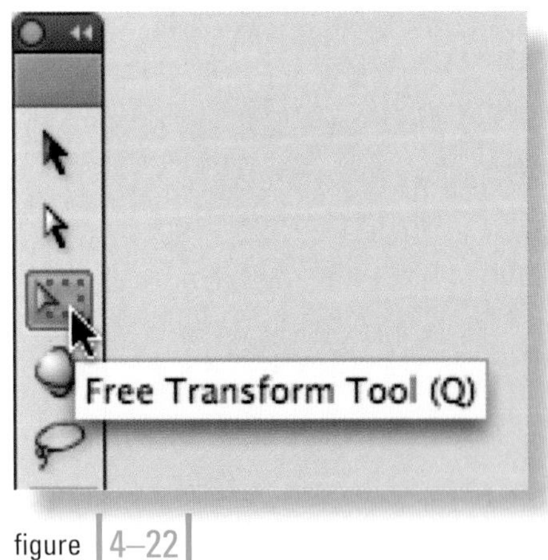

figure 4–22

Select the Free Transform tool.

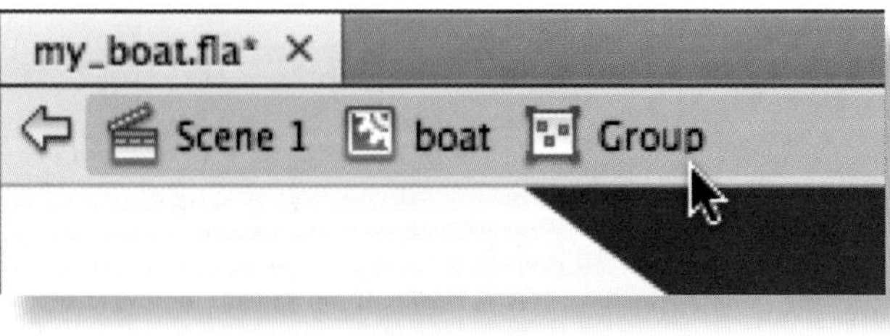

figure 4–23

The editing mode of a grouped object in the **boat** symbol.

11. Select the Free Transform tool from the Tools panel (see Figure 4–22) and rotate the text to the angle of your boat's hull.

12. Double-click on the boat's hull to go into the editing mode for the grouped object. See Figure 4–23. The object should be modified a shape.

13. Select the Oval tool in the Tools panel. Choose a fill color that is different from the color of the hull.

14. Draw a circular shape for the porthole somewhere on the hull of the boat. See Figure 4–24.

15. Select the fill of the circle. In the Properties panel, click on the fill color box to open the swatches panel. Hover your cursor under the Alpha percentage area—a two-sided arrow will appear (called a "scrubby"). Click and slide the scrubby to the left to lower the alpha percentage (making the color more transparent). I set mine to about 40%. See Figure 4–25.

figure 4–24

Create a circular shape on the boat to represent a porthole.

figure 4–25

Use the scrubby to change the alpha percentage of an object.

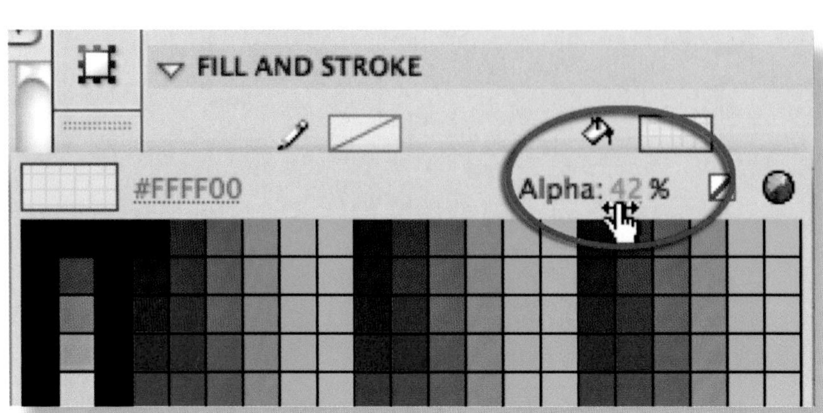

16. Click anywhere away from the selected object to deselect it. Choose View > Grid > Show Grid. Note that the grid appears within the porthole you created—it's see-through!

17. Choose View > Grid > Show Grid again to remove the grid.

18. Exit out of editing mode—click on the Scene 1 icon in the upper left corner of the interface. See Figure 4–26.

19. Save your file.

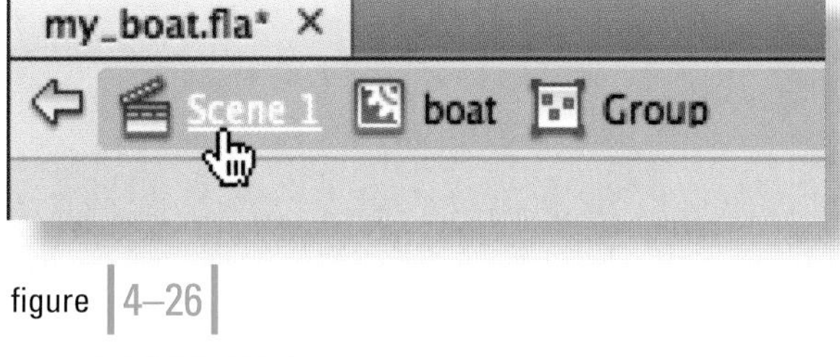

figure 4–26

Choose Scene 1 on the Edit bar to exit out of the editing mode.

Creating Waves

1. Choose View > Magnification > 100% so you can see the whole scene and some of the gray area around it.

2. Click on the New Layer icon in the lower left of the timeline. See Figure 4–27. Title the layer: **frontwave**. Be sure it is above the **boat** layer. Note: if the layer is not above the **boat** layer click and drag the layer above the **boat** layer.

3. Be sure the **frontwave** layer is selected. Draw a wave like shape. You can use any method you would like to draw the shape. I used the Pencil tool with the Smooth option selected in the Tools panel. See Figure 4–28. Be sure it's a closed shape that extends outside the movie area. See Figure 4–29. It doesn't have to be perfect—this lesson is just to practice with the tools, not to be the next Michelangelo.

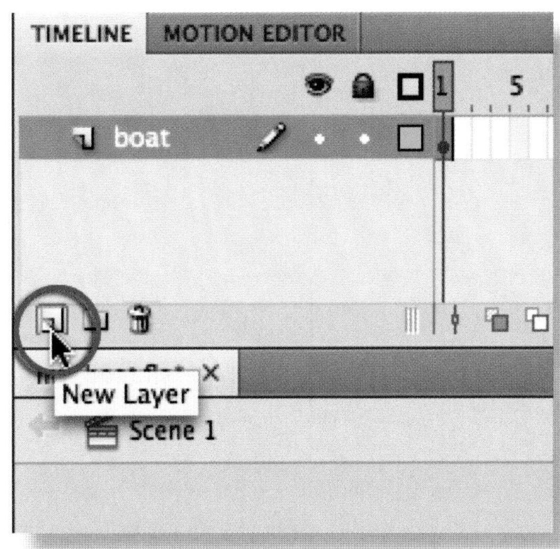

figure 4–27

Create a new layer.

figure 4–28

Choose the Smooth option for the Pencil tool.

figure 4–29

Make some waves using the Pencil or Pen tool.

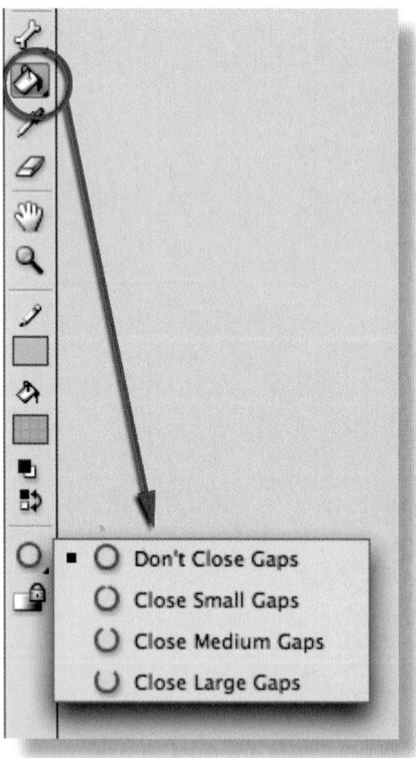

figure 4–30

Adjust the gap detection option for the Paint Bucket tool to properly fill an object with color.

4. Fill the wave with a color using the Paint Bucket tool in the Tools panel. See Figure 4–30.

> **Note: If the wave doesn't fill with color, it might be that the shape is not completely closed. Adjust the gap detection for the Paint Bucket tool found in the Paint Bucket tool options at the bottom of the Tools panel. Refer to Figure 4–30. The Gap Detection option detects any openings in the shape that you can't see.**

5. Select the fill of the wave. Expand the Color panel and change the fill to a linear gradient with a blue tint. For fun, see if you can make the lighter portion of the gradient slightly transparent (use the Alpha setting on one of the color stops of the gradient), so you can see the boat through the wave. See Figure 4–31.

6. Select the Gradient Transform tool in the Tools panel (hidden under the Free Transform tool in the toolbox). See Figure 4–32. Hover just outside the top right corner of the Gradient Transform bounding area around the object until you see the rotate icon, then click and drag to rotate it 90 degrees, so that the lighter portion of the gradient is on top. See Figure 4–33 for a reference on how to use the Gradient Transform tool.

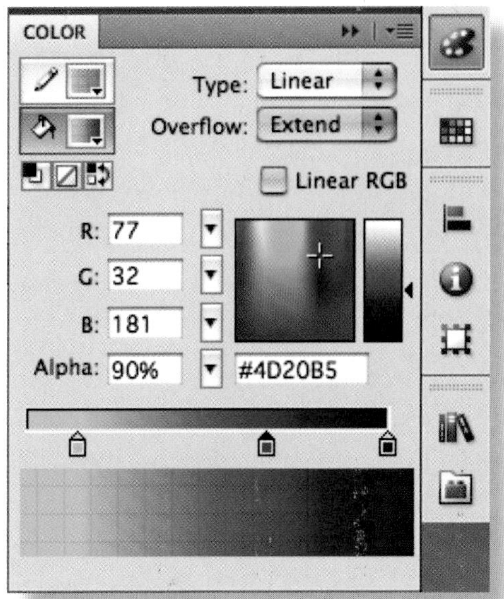

figure 4–31

The linear gradient options in the Color panel.

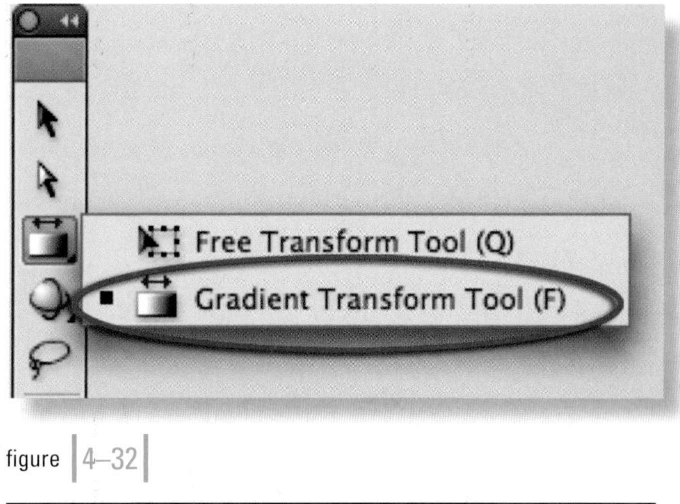

figure 4–32

Select the Gradient Transform tool.

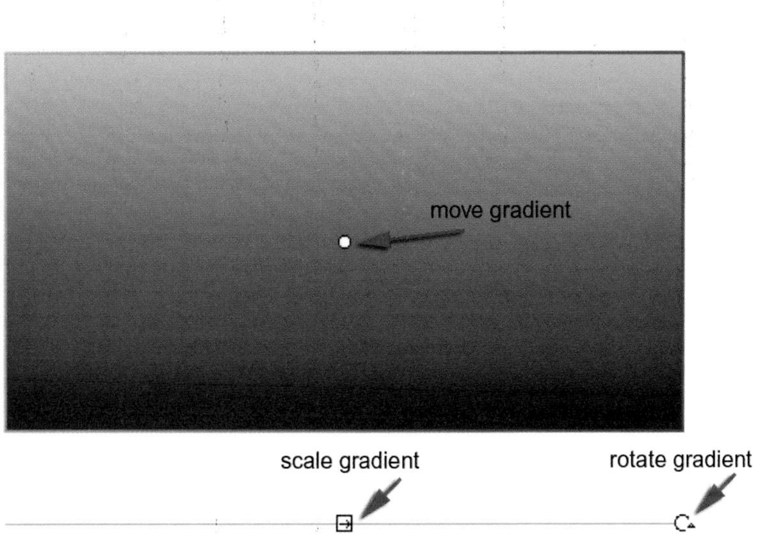

figure 4–33

Transform options of the Gradient Transform tool.

> **Note: If you don't see the Gradient Transform bounding area around your object, try zooming out on the scene.**

7. Select the wave and convert it to a symbol (F8). Call it **wave** and assign it the Movie Clip type.
8. Create a new layer and call it **backwave**. Drag it below the **boat** layer.
9. Select the **backwave** layer. Open the Library panel and drag an instance of the **wave** symbol on to the Stage. Position the wave so that it is offset from the **frontwave**. Refer to Figure 4–15 for an example of how the waves should be positioned.
10. For fun: create a new layer and call it **background**. Drag it below the other layers. Create a background sky by drawing a rectangle and filling it with a gradient. Adjust the gradient if necessary with the Gradient Transform tool. This new background will go over the colored background you chose at the beginning of this lesson.
11. Save your file in your lesson folder.

Creating a Sun and Clouds

1. Create another layer and call it **sun**—place it below the **boat** layer.
2. With the Oval tool create a circular sun object with a radial gradient fill.
3. Select the sun and choose Modify > Shape > Soften Fill Edges.

   In the dialog box enter the following properties:

   - Distance = 20
   - Number of steps = 10
   - Direction = Expand

> **Note: If you make a mistake or want to change the effect of the Soften Fill Edges, choose Edit > Undo and execute the effect again on the original shape.**

4. Convert the sun object to a movie clip symbol and call it **sun**.
5. Create another layer above the **sun** layer and call it **clouds**.
6. Choose File > Import > Import to Stage and browse for the **cloud.jpg** found in **chap04_lessons/assets**.
7. Choose Modify > Bitmap > Trace and choose the following settings:

   - Color Threshold = 75
   - Minimum Area = 8 pixels
   - Curve Fit = Normal
   - Corner Threshold = Normal

8. Select and delete the blue sky areas out of the vector graphic. Then select individual cloud areas, and group each one; use the lasso tool to select just the areas you want.

9. Convert each cloud to a movie clip symbol and name them in the convert to symbol dialog box.

10. Position the clouds in your Scene.

11. Save your File.

Gone Fishing

1. Deselect everything on your scene by choosing Edit > Deselect All or clicking on a blank area outside the movie area.

2. Choose Insert > New Symbol. Call your symbol **fish** and make it a movie clip.

figure 4–34

The editing mode for the **fish** symbol.

Click OK. You will enter editing mode for the **fish** symbol—a blank screen with a crosshair (plus sign) in the middle. Note in the upper left corner of the Stage that you are working within the **fish** symbol. See Figure 4–34.

3. In the center (right over the crosshair), draw a fish. Make it unique—with eyes, a mouth, and fins. See Figure 4–35 for examples of fish my students have created.

figure 4–35

Example fishes drawn by students.

4. Once completed, go back to Scene 1. You should see your boat again.
5. Create a new layer and call it **fish**. Place it above the **frontwave** layer. Open the Library panel and drag an instance of the fish symbol to the Stage.
6. Drag out a couple more fish and position them in your scene—scale, rotate them, and/or modify their instance color using the tint option in the Properties panel.
7. Save your file.

Ode to Your Boat

1. Create a final layer and call it **text**.
2. Select the Text tool and click on a blank area of your scene. Type in an ode to your boat—a small poem about your boat and it's sea-worthy adventures. Refer to Figure 4–15 again for an example.
3. Choose a font, font size, and color for the text. Save it as a symbol.
4. Save your file.
5. Choose Control > Test Movie to see your boat rendered as a SWF. See Figure 4–36. Once you've previewed your masterpiece, close the SWF window to get back to the main file. Congratulations! Your boat is done and ready to be animated in the next chapter.

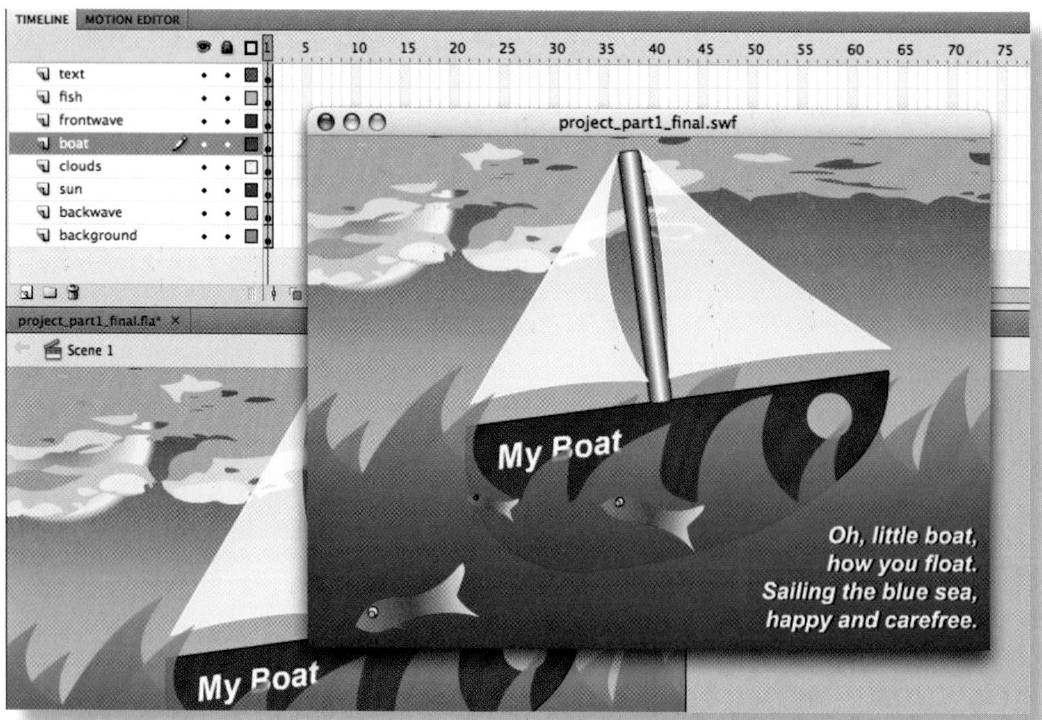

figure 4–36

View the final file in the SWF format.

SUMMARY

Identifying the attributes of symbols, and making and editing symbols and their instances should be a snap after this chapter. With this fundamental knowledge you can now begin to animate them and move on to a more advanced understanding of all that Flash has to offer.

in review

1. Name at least three attributes of symbols.
2. What is the shortcut key to convert an object to a symbol?
3. Where are your symbols saved?
4. What action do you perform to enter editing mode for a symbol?
5. Describe an instance and why it's useful.
6. What does the Gradient Transform tool do?
7. What is gap detection?
8. Describe how layers are useful.
9. What is the use of the crosshair/registration mark on a symbol?
10. What is the menu command to view a movie in the SWF format?

exploring on your own

1. Practice creating symbols and modifying instances on the butterfly document that was introduced in the Exploring on Your Own, Chapter 3. Open your version if you created one in Chapter 3, or open the sample version: **bfly_part1.fla** in the **chap04_lessons/samples** folder. Open the file, select the butterfly's wing, save it as symbol and create another instance of it to put onto the other side of the butterfly. Create the butterfly's body, group it, then save all the parts of the butterfly into a symbol that can be animated in the next chapter. See sample final version in **chap04_lessons/samples/bfly_part2_final.fla**.
2. In Flash, choose Help > Flash Help, do a search for "symbol" and read the documentation on symbols provided by Adobe.

| animation basics |

5

charting your course

OK, now we get into the fun part—the moving experience of animation! This chapter takes you on a whirlwind overview of tweening and frame-by-frame animation, the animation-specific features of Flash, and hands-on practice with various animation techniques. In conclusion, use the animation skills learned to animate the sailboat scene introduced in the last module.

goals

In this chapter you will:

- **Get an overview of Flash animation types—tweening and frame-by-frame**
- **Learn the parts of the Timeline, and identify animation types on the Timeline**
- **Get hands-on practice with tweening the motion, position, color, rotation, scale, and shape of objects**
- **Explore techniques for editing a tween's path**
- **Complete a frame-by-frame animation**
- **Discover the power of the movie clip Timeline**
- **Practice animation skills learned on the sailboat scene you created in the last chapter**

INTRODUCTION TO FLASH ANIMATION

If you have never animated anything before here's your chance. Flash is used to create small, animated enhancements that add extra sizzle to your site, or to create full scale, animated stories and sites.

Animation in Flash is 2D animation, objects are animated in two dimensions (*x* and *y*)—see exception note below. This is different from animation produced by 3D animation programs like Autodesk's Maya or 3ds Max where you can model and animate objects in three dimensions (*x*, *y*, and *z*). What might seem like 3D in Flash is actually fake. For example, a series of camera views of a 3D model can be imported from another source (like Swift3D or Plasma) and each position of it orbiting in space can be played back in Flash. Another option to simulate 3D movement is using ActionScript, which is essentially applying math to create the effect. Since this book is an introduction to Flash and caters to the more right-brained designer we will not get into that level of programming.

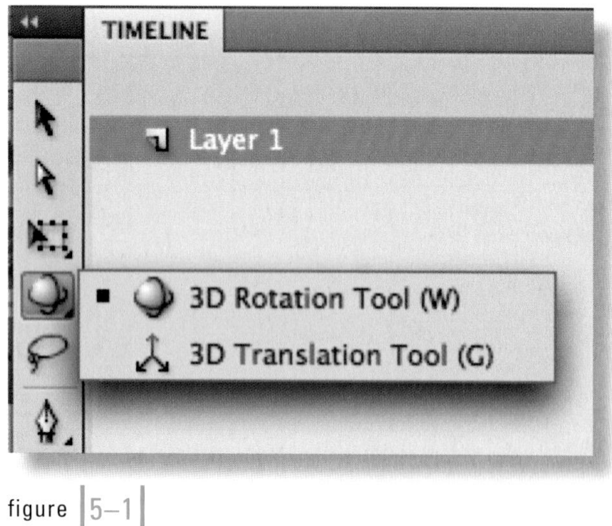

figure 5–1

The 3D transformation tools for 2D objects.

Note: In this version of Flash there are two new 3D tools, the 3D Rotation and 3D Translation tool (see Figure 5–1) that can be used to rotate or translate 2D movie clips along the *z*-axis, producing a simulated 3D perspective (see Figure 5–2). However, to use these 3D capabilities of Flash, the publish settings (File > Publish Settings) of your FLA file must be set to Flash Player 10 and ActionScript 3.0.

There are two types of animation created in Flash—tweening and frame-by-frame. Let's get the details on each of them.

Tweening Animation

Tweening is the most basic animation type and used to create most of the animated effects you see. Tweening is the process of recording two instances of a single object and having the computer calculate the images in the in-between frames. An instance can be altered in position, color, scale, rotation and, in the case of a shape tween, its shape. Usually simple objects are tweened in Flash, such as text, logos, buttons, and bitmaps.

Using tweens in Flash is an effective way to create movement and change over time while minimizing file size. View some SWF (Flash movies) of example tweens—**chap05_lessons/movies**. Descriptions of each movie are as follows:

- Simple motion tween example (**motion_tween.swf**): this is the simplest example of a tween—the moth moves in a straight path from one side of the scene to the other.

figure 5–2

Rotate a movie clip instance with the 3D Rotation tool.

figure 5–3

Animate the color of an object.

- Path motion tween example (**path_tween.swf**): the straight path produced by a simple motion tween is altered into a curved shape, producing more natural movement.
- Color motion tween example (**color_tween.swf**): the moth moves on a tweened path and changes color over time. See Figure 5–3.
- Shape tween example (**shape_tween.swf**): the moth shape "morphs" into a rectangle shape.

Previous users of Flash might be surprised to find that the way in which tweening is executed in Flash has changed significantly in version CS4. The now older method of tweening is still an option in the program—called "classic tweening" and classic tweens created in previous versions of Flash are supported. However, once you get the hang of the new tweening method, classic tweening is soon going to be history.

With the new motion tween model, tween paths can be edited directly on stage, tweens cannot be broken inadvertently, tween properties (rotation, color, etc.) are keyframed independently, and properties are auto keyframed. Motion can be easily altered in time and space by manipulating the points (that represent keyframes on the Timeline) directly on the path (see Figure 5–4), or using the Motion Editor (more on the Motion Editor in a later section). All these new features might not mean much to you if you have never used them before. But no worries ... you begin to use them in this chapter's lessons.

figure 5–4

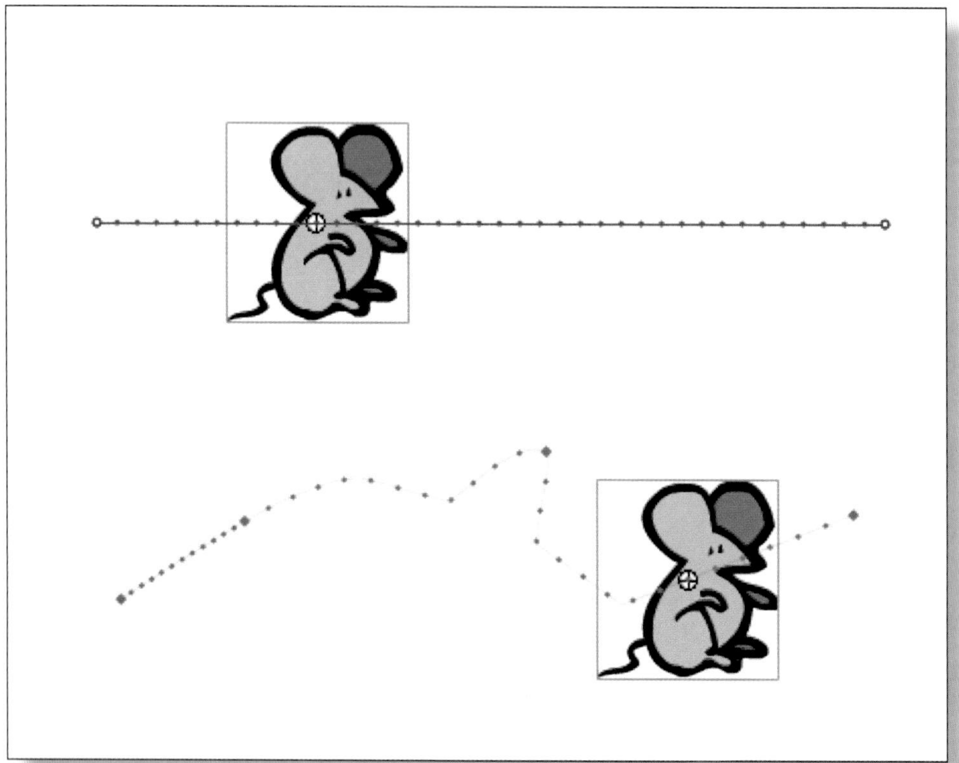

The tween path of an object.

Frame-by-Frame Animation

Frame-by-frame is a bit more complicated than tweening, and is used to create animations with complex movements, like a person walking and talking or a dog wagging its tail; any movements that alter shape in space and time. Unlike tweening, where the computer calculates "in-between" frames, an artist draws the contents of each frame of a frame-by-frame animation. Every picture is drawn to precision and played back, like a flipbook, fast enough that it simulates complex and articulate movement.

Cel animation, a classical animation used, for example, by Walt Disney to bring life to his characters such as Pinocchio, Mickey Mouse, and Bambi, uses the frame-by-frame method of animation. Individual illustrations are hand drawn, representing snapshots of the trajectory of an action, and then played back on film frame-by-frame. Cel animation was a breakthrough for traditional animation allowing some parts of each illustration to be repeated from frame to frame by using celluloid for the foreground and simply superimposing them over an opaque background, and thus saving labor. A full-length feature film produced using cel animation would often require a million or more drawings to complete. The process of frame-by-frame animation has been greatly expedited by computer technologies. Even so, any object that requires the changing of its shape over each frame of time, such as the swish of a fish tail or the growing of a nose, requires a skilled and patient artist to draw each individual picture of movement.

figure 5–5

Example frames of a frame-by-frame animation.

View some Flash movie examples of frame-by-frame animation—**chap05_lessons/movies**. Descriptions of each movie are as follows:

- Frame-by-Frame (**frame_by_frame.swf**)—the wings of the moth are changing shape at each keyframe (moment in time). Each shape must be individually manipulated to produce the effect. See Figure 5–5.
- Frame-by-Frame (**frame_by_frame_runner.swf**)—here's another example of a frame-by-frame drawn animation.
- Tweening and Frame-by-Frame Combo (**frame_by_frame_with_path.swf**)—the moth's body is tweening on a path and its wings are flapping frame-by-frame. Often motion tweened and frame-by-frame animation are used on the same object—this is where things get fun. You will create this same animation in an upcoming lesson.

I encourage you to look at Flash sites to get an idea of how animation is used—sometimes sites depend solely on animated content to make a point, while other sites use animation simply for eye-candy, and some sites could do just as well without it. See if you can distinguish which parts of the animation in the sites are created using the tweening method, the frame-by-frame method, or a combination of both.

Here are a few Flash sites with good animation examples (there are thousands more!):

- Dreamworks Animation: *http://www.dreamworksanimation.com/*
- Creative Commons: *http://mirrors.creativecommons.org/*
- Millan Flash eCards: *http://www.millan.net/anims/flash/flash.html*

The Flash Timeline

The Timeline is the heart of animation creation in Flash. It is not only the place where you organize your content into Layers, but also where you create, record, review, edit, and play back your animations. Learn the anatomy of the Timeline by reviewing the following list. For future reference, you can also review features of the Timeline in Flash's Help Files by choosing Help > Flash Help from the program's menu bar.

The Timeline organizes and controls a movie's content over time in frames and layers. Lengths of time are measured in frames (see note below). Layers organize objects (animated or still) within the animation. Only one object or symbol can be animated on a single layer.

Note: By default in Flash the frame rate for animations is set to 24 frames per second (fps). However, the final playback of a movie really depends on client-side factors, such as computer performance and Internet connection speed if the movie is downloaded from the Web.

The major components of the Timeline are layers, frames, and the playback head.

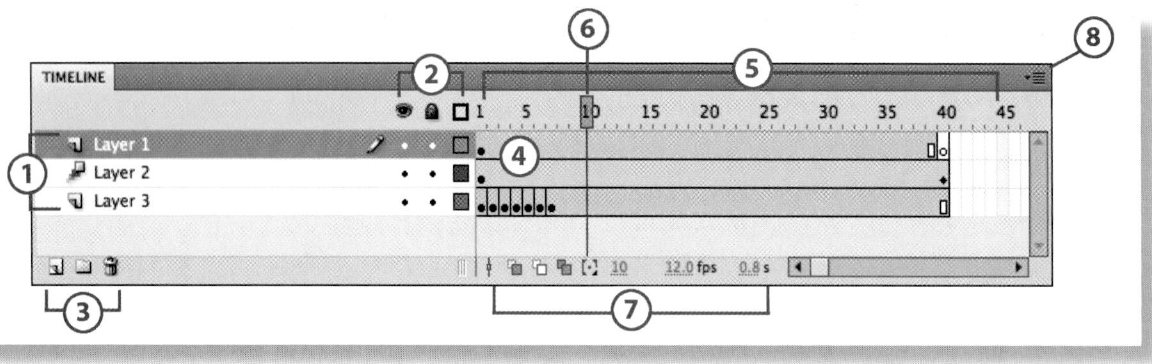

figure 5–6

The parts of the Timeline panel.

Refer to Figure 5–6 to identify each numbered item:

1. Layers in a document are listed in a column on the left side of the Timeline.
2. Hide, lock, or view as outlines objects on a layer. To do this, click a black dot of a specific layer that you see down the columns below the hide, lock, or outline icons at the top of the layer list.
3. Create a New Layer, a New Folder, or Delete a layer by choosing one of the icons in the lower left part of the panel.
4. Frames contained in each layer appear in a row to the right of the layer name. There are four types of frames: keyframe, property keyframe, blank frame, and frame.
   - **Keyframe**: A keyframe is indicated by a black dot on a frame. A keyframe records an object's point in time. To create a keyframe you choose Insert > Timeline > Keyframe (F6).
   - **Property Keyframe**: A property keyframe is indicated by a small, black diamond on a frame. A property keyframe defines the object's properties (rotation, scaling, etc.) that are associated with a motion tween.

- **Blank Keyframe**: A blank keyframe is indicated by an empty dot. A blank keyframe indicates that there are no objects on that frame at that point in time. To create a blank keyframe choose Insert > Timeline > Blank Keyframe (F7).
- **Frame**: A frame is colored gray on the Timeline. I call them "holding frames," as the frame holds, or freezes, an object's position on the Stage. The object is visible but not moving. To create a holding frame choose Insert > Timeline > Frame (F5).

5. The Timeline header at the top of the Timeline indicates frame numbers.
6. The playhead (colored red) indicates the current frame displayed on the Stage.
7. The Timeline status displayed at the bottom of the Timeline has buttons to turn on/off the onion skinning and editing multiple frames display. It also shows the selected frame number, the current frame rate, and the elapsed time to the current frame.

> **Note:** What's onion skinning? From the Flash help files, "Usually, one frame of the animation sequence at a time appears on the Stage. To help position and edit a frame-by-frame animation, onion skinning allows you view two or more frames on the Stage at once. When onion skinning is selected a frame under the playhead appears in full color, while surrounding frames are dimmed, making it appear as if each frame were drawn on a sheet of translucent onion-skin paper and the sheets were stacked on top of each other. Dimmed frames cannot be edited." You will experience onion skinning in later lessons.

8. Options for how to view items in the Timeline are found in the submenu in the upper right corner of the panel. See Figure 5–7.

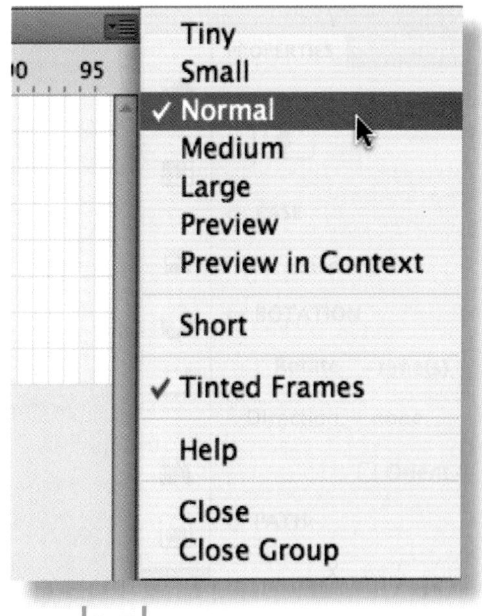

figure 5–7

Display options for the Timeline.

The Timeline indicates where there is animation in a movie, including tweened and frame-by-frame animation. You can insert, delete, select, and move frames in the Timeline. You can also drag frames to a new location on the same layer or to a different layer. You will experience how to do all these actions as you go through the upcoming tutorials. Flash indicates the type of a tween or frame-by-frame animation by visual cues in the Timeline. Refer to Figure 5–8 to identify each numbered item.

1. **Motion Tweens**: Motion tweens are highlighted on the Timeline in blue. The first frame will be a keyframe (black dot). Property keyframes (black diamonds) will also be visible along the span of the animation. Also notice the icon of a moving rectangle shape to the left of the layer name; another indication that there is a motion tween on the layer.

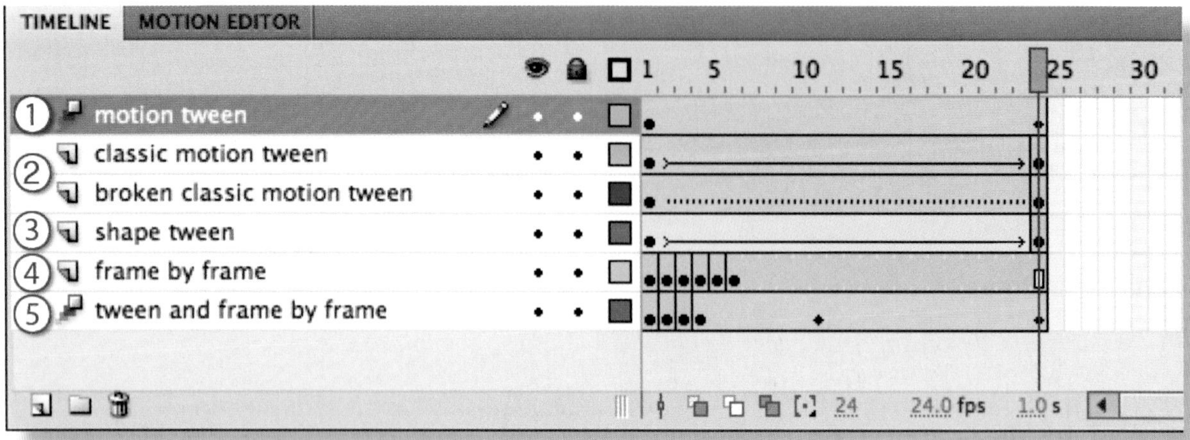

figure 5–8

Example visual of what various animations look like on the Timeline. Refer to text descriptions of each number.

2. **Classic Tweens**: Classic motion tweening is the method for creating tweens in previous versions of Flash. This method is still available to use in CS4 and is supported when opening older Flash files that contain motion tweens. Classic tweens are indicated in light blue with a keyframe (black dot) at the beginning and end of the time span. A black arrow extends across the span. A classic tween that is not working properly is indicated by dashed line. A broken tween can occur when the final keyframe is missing, or one of the objects on a keyframe is not part of the symbol.

3. **Shape Tweens**: Shape tweens are indicated in light green with a keyframe (black dot) at the beginning and end of the time span. A black arrow extends across the span.

4. **Frame-by-Frame**: Frame-by-frame animation is indicated by a series of keyframes.

5. **Tween and Frame-by-Frame**: Tween and frame-by-frame animation can be assigned to a single object. This is indicated by any combination of keyframes and motion tween spans (highlighted in blue).

The Motion Editor

The Motion Editor is a new feature in CS4. It provides a graph-like representation of tweened animation within a scene. See Figure 5–9. You can use the Motion Editor to edit the properties of a tween—keyframe positions, timing, and ease settings. To edit properties, select a span in the Timeline or a tweened object on the Stage and select the Motion Editor tab near the Timeline panel tab (or Window > Motion Editor). Admittedly the Motion Editor can be a confusing place to visit at first and this book doesn't go into great detail on this feature. To explore more, visit the Flash Help files (Help > Flash Help from the menu bar).

Lesson 1: A Basic Tween

In this lesson you learn how to create a basic tween and add some variations.

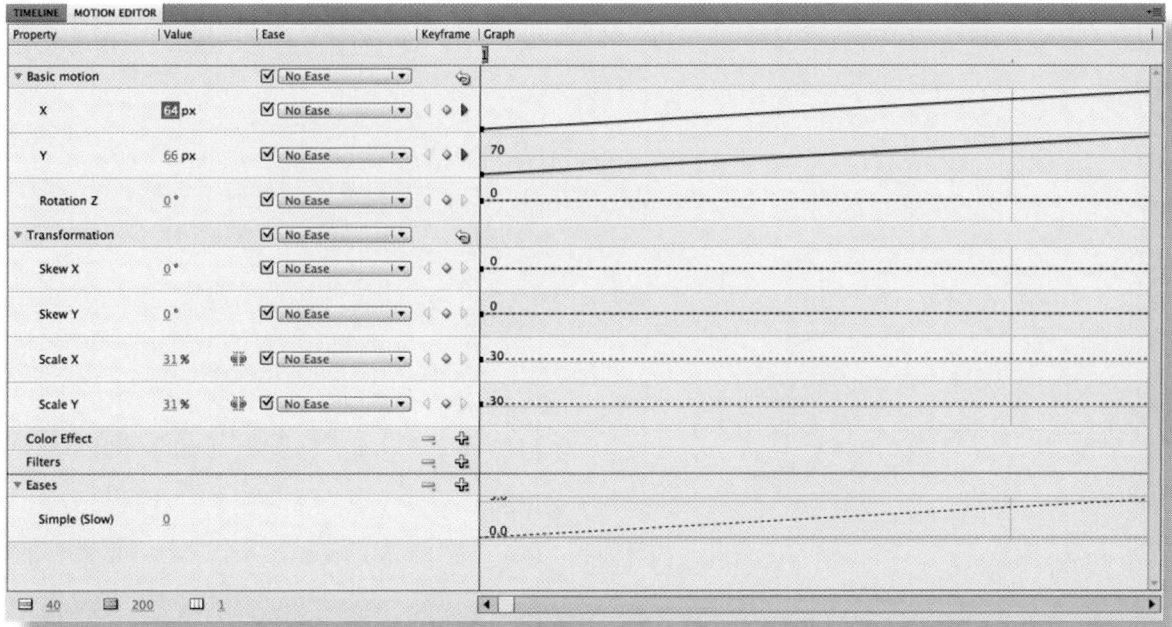

figure 5–9

The Motion Editor.

Setting up a Simple Tween

1. From the Flash program open the file **chap5L1.fla** in the **chap05_lessons** folder (File > Open). This file contains a butterfly graphic that has already been saved as a symbol. What indicators are there to tell you the butterfly is saved as a symbol?
2. Be sure your workspace is set to Classic.
3. Select frame 50 of both the **butterfly** and **background** layers by clicking and dragging through them in one movement. Ctrl-click (Mac) or right-click (Windows) over the selected frames and choose Insert Frame from the drop-down menu (F5) (see Figure 5–10).

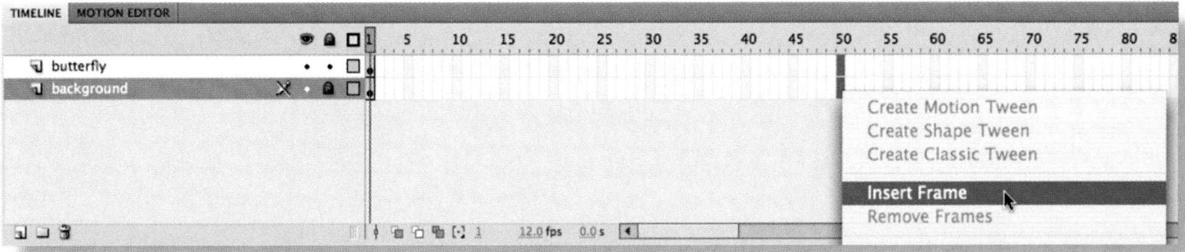

figure 5–10

Insert a frame on the Timeline.

4. Hit Enter (Return) on the keyboard and watch the playback head move through the 50 frames and loop back to 1.

> **Note:** What you have done in step 3 is create holding frames between 1 and 50 for all the layers on the Timeline (i.e., butterfly and background). This way you can see all the objects on all layers as you work on your animation.

5. Ctrl-click or click then hold (Mac) or right-click (Windows) anywhere between frame 1 and 50 on the **butterfly** layer, and choose Create Motion Tween from the drop-down menu. See Figure 5–11. A blue bar appears across the 50 frames of the **butterfly** layer.

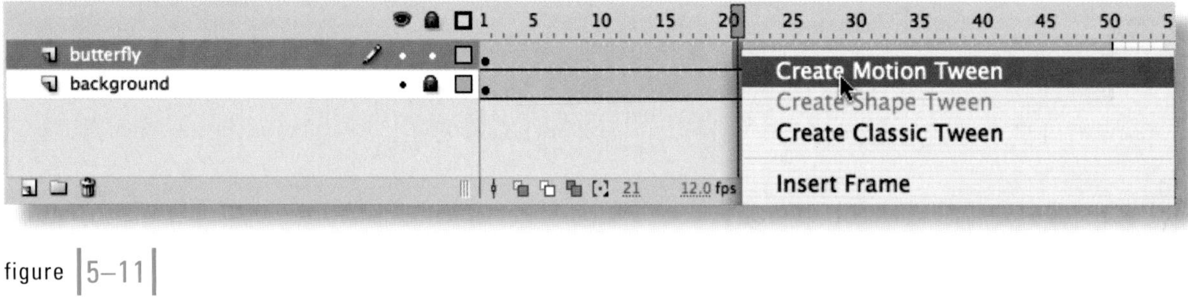

figure |5–11|

Create a motion tween.

6. Move the playback head to frame 50.
7. Then, move the butterfly off the Stage at the upper right corner. Notice a blue path is created. See Figure 5–12.

> **Note:** As you see in Figure 5–12, I positioned my butterfly off the Stage in the upper right corner, so when the animation is played back the butterfly will appear to be flying off the scene and out of view.

8. Hit Return (Enter) on the keyboard to play back the animation. The butterfly moves slowly and not really in the correct direction, but it moves!
9. Let's play a bit. Move the playback head to frame 1, and select the butterfly on the Stage.
10. Select the Free Transform tool in the Tools panel (see Figure 5–13) and rotate the butterfly so the front of the butterfly is heading forward on the path. See Figure 5–14.
11. Hit Return (Enter) to play back the animation. Ahh, better!

figure 5–12

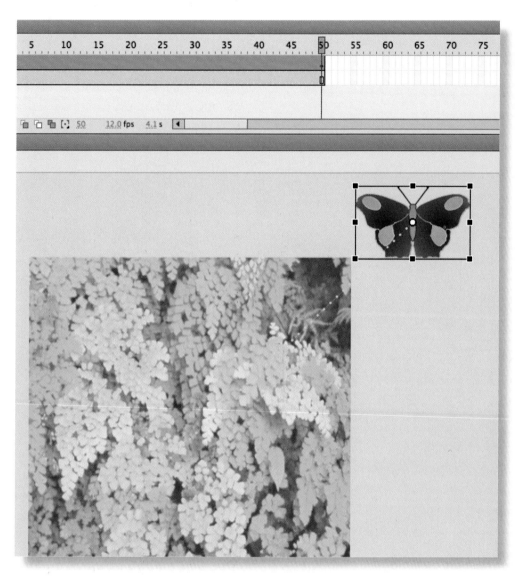

An editable path (light blue in this example) is created with a tweened animation.

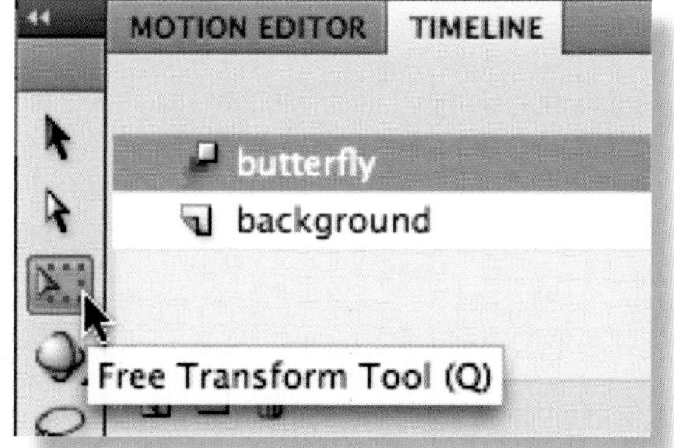

The Free Transform tool.

figure 5–14

Adjust the rotation of the animated object.

12. Let's get the butterfly to speed up over time. To do this, you need to reduce the amount of time the butterfly travels. Hover the cursor over the edge of frame 50 of the **butterfly** layer until you see a double-sided arrow icon. Click and drag the blue bar to frame 30. See Figure 5–15.

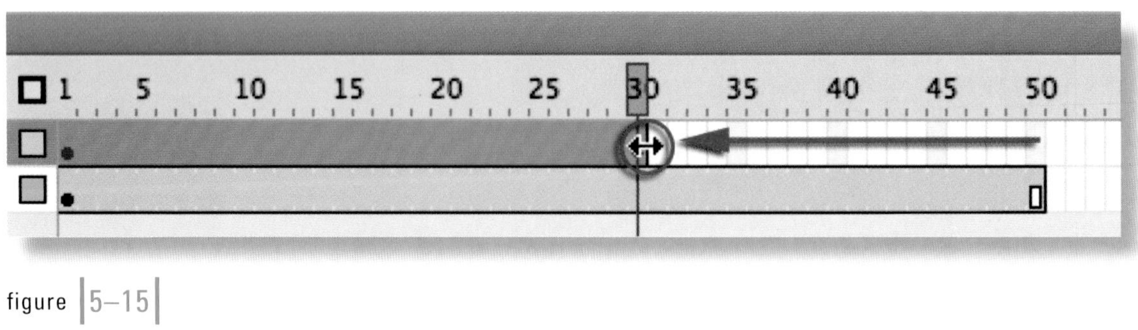

figure 5–15

Reduce the time on the Timeline.

13. Play the animation—the butterfly has a little more spunk!

> **Note:** Notice that the butterfly is now moving over 30 frames, yet the background remains visible for 50 frames. If you want to edit the **background** layer to end at frame 50 it's a different process than what we just did on the motion tween. To remove the holding frames on the **background** layer, click on frame 30 of the layer. Then hold down the Shift key and click on frame 50—all the frames between 30 and 50 are selected. Finally, Ctrl-click or click then hold (Mac) or right-click (Windows) over the selected span and choose Remove Frames from the submenu.

14. Save your butterfly in your lessons folder.

> **Note:** A word for Mac users—it is not uncommon to Ctrl-click (use the Ctrl key) in Flash. The Ctrl key allows you to access information available to Windows users using the right button of a two-button mouse. Ctrl-clicking to access additional menu items can be done in any program on a Mac, not just Flash. That being said, I get tired of the all the Ctrl-clicking to access this information, so I bought a two-button mouse for my Mac (any type of mouse will work!). Now, I just click on my right mouse button to access these menus—much easier!

Modifying the Path

1. Let's add some variation to the butterfly's flight. Select the **butterfly** layer. The butterfly and its path are selected on the Stage.
2. You will be altering the path, so you need to be able to see it clearly. One way is to change its color—double-click on the layer outline button (a colored box) in the **butterfly** layer. See Figure 5–16. The Layer Properties opens—choose a new outline color that you might be able to see better in the scene (I chose a dark red). See Figure 5–16 again.

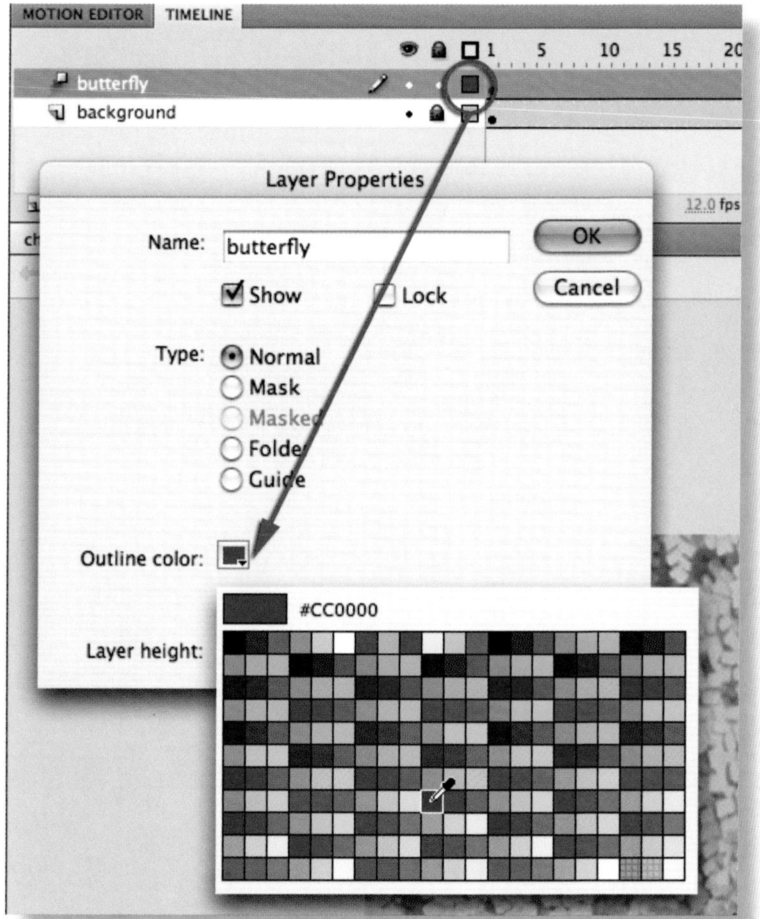

figure 5–16

Change the color of the layers outline view.

> **Note: Another option to improve the visibility of the path is to turn off the visibility of the background layer. See Figure 5–17.**

figure 5–17

Turn off the visibility of a layer.

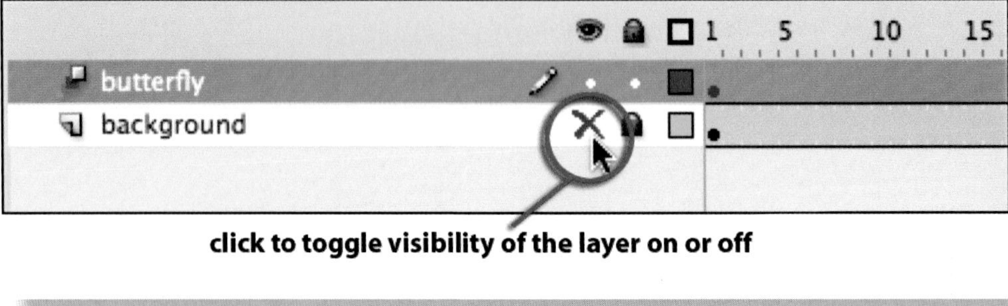

3. Hover over the motion path until you see a curved shape icon. Click and drag to the right and down on the path to create a curve to the path. See Figure 5–18. Caution: if you are unable to create the curve, be sure the path is not selected. Click elsewhere on the Stage to deselect it, then try again.

figure 5–18

Adjust the motion path.

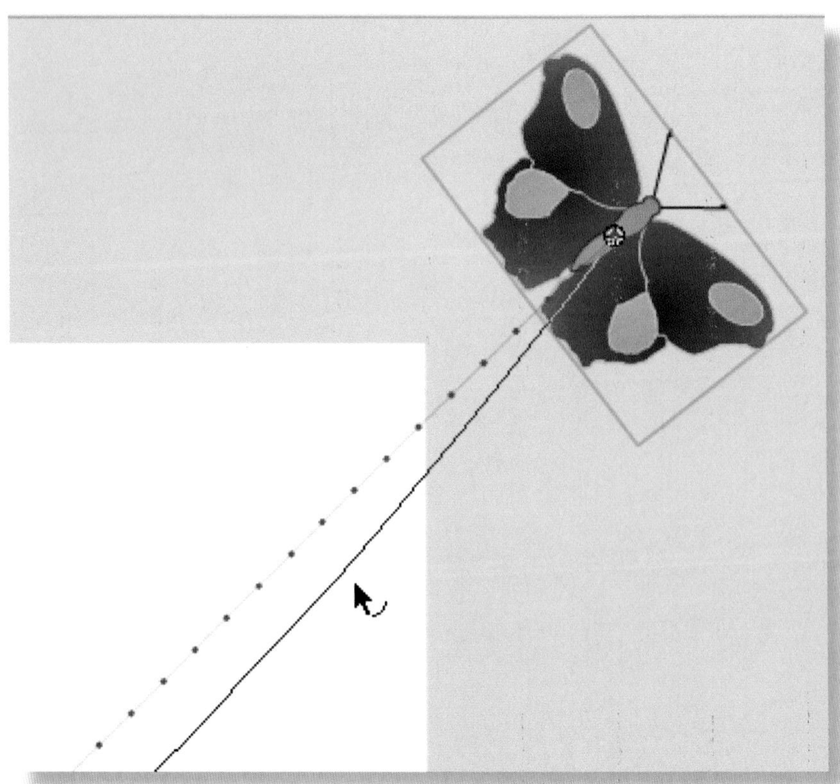

4. Play the animation—pretty cool, but the butterfly is not quite tangent to the path.

5. Now, click directly on the motion path to select it. In the Properties panel, choose the Orient to Path option. See Figure 5–19.

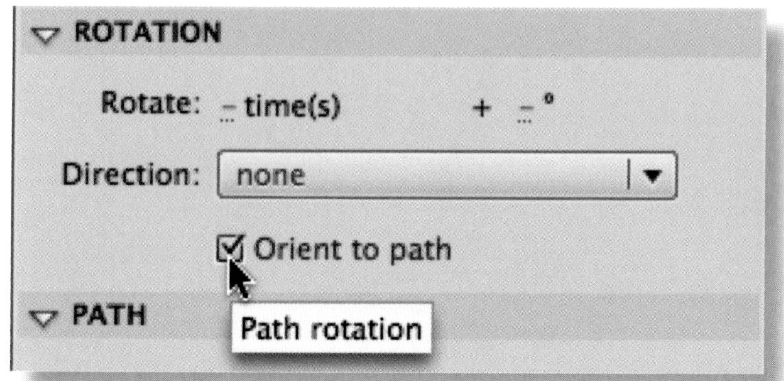

figure 5–19

Select the Orient to path option.

6. Choose Control > Test Movie to view the movie as a SWF file. Note that it keeps looping—that's the default action for Flash, which we will learn to control once you get into ActionScripting. Close the SWF file.

Adding Keyframes to the Motion Path

1. Let's alter the path of our butterfly. First, let's present an obstacle. Create a new layer, by clicking the New Layer icon at the bottom of the Timeline. See Figure 5–20.

2. Double-click the layer name and rename the layer **butterfly2**.

3. Drag an instance of the **bfly** symbol from the Library to the Stage. Be sure the **butterfly2** layer is selected and choose the Free Transform tool from the Tools panel (third tool down the list).

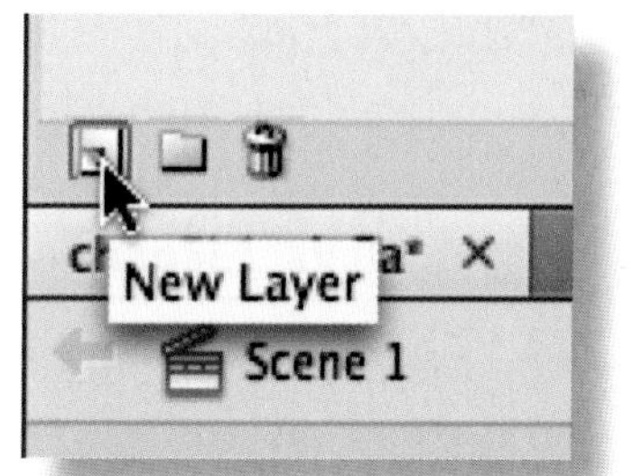

figure 5–20

Create a new layer.

4. Scale the butterfly smaller than the first butterfly and place it in the center of the Stage. See Figure 5–21.

5. Lock the **butterfly2** layer. See Figure 5–22.

6. Click on the **butterfly** layer—the one with the motion tween—to select it. Let's alter this butterfly's path so that it flutters around the smaller butterfly.

7. Move the butterfly's timeline to frame 1.

figure 5–21

Place another butterfly instance on to the center of the Stage.

figure 5–22

Lock the layer.

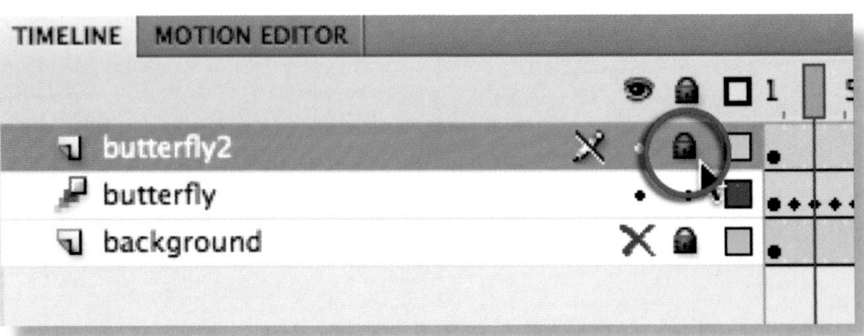

8. Choose the Selection tool. Click on the last point of the butterfly's motion path on the Stage, and drag the end of the path to curve around the small butterfly in the center. Refine the path around the smaller butterfly by clicking and dragging along the path. See steps in Figure 5–23.

> **Note:** A reminder: if you are having trouble clicking and dragging on sections of the path, the whole path might be selected. Deselect the path (click on a blank area somewhere on the Stage or choose Edit > Deselect All) and then try again.

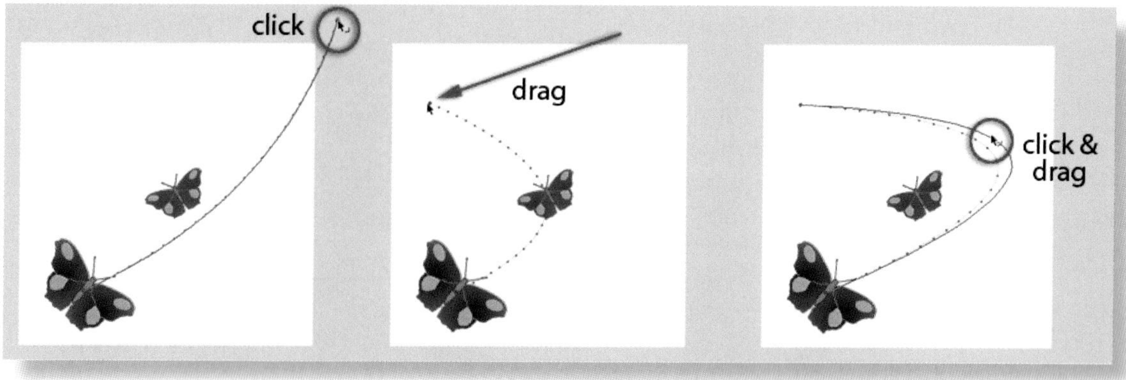

figure 5–23

Refine the motion path of the big butterfly around the smaller butterfly.

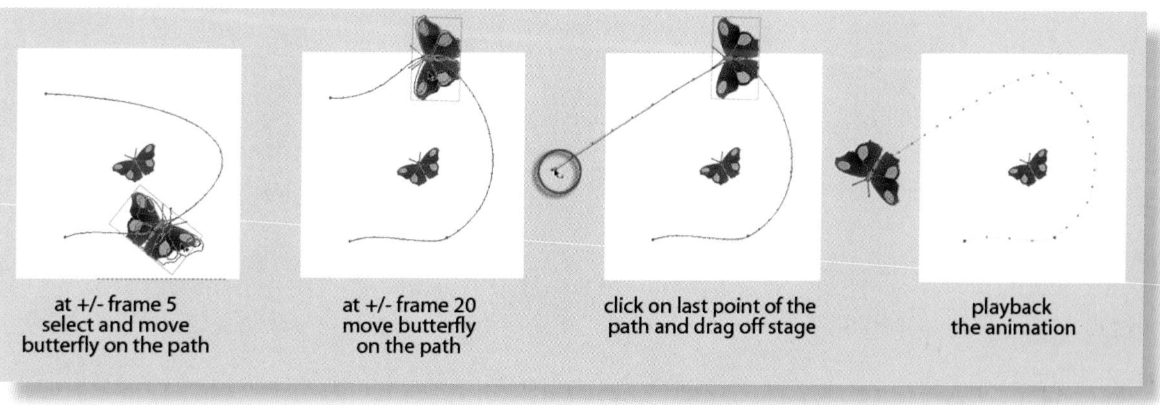

figure 5–24

Tweak the butterfly's orientation around the path.

9. More tweaking … move the playback head to frame 5. The butterfly should be approximately in the same spot as you see in the first image of Figure 5–24. Click and drag the butterfly down a bit to open the circular shape around the smaller butterfly.

10. Move the playback head to frame 20, click and move the butterfly up a bit to widen its path.

11. Click and drag the last point of the butterfly's path off stage to the left.

12. Play back the animation—the adjustments to the butterfly's path are automatically updated.

13. If you've hidden the **background** layer, turn it back on (click the red X next to its name in the Timeline).

14. Choose Control > Test Movie to view the animation as a SWF.

15. Close the SWF file. Save your FLA in your lessons folder.

More Variations to Explore

1. Let's modify the animation just a bit more—with the Selection tool, click directly on the path to select the whole path (the Properties panel will say Motion Tween at the top). Click and move the path and note that the path and the butterfly attached to the path are moving as a complete unit. Yes, you can place the complete motion elsewhere in the scene if you so choose. Give it a try and play back the animation.

> **Note:** To adjust the animation as a whole unit, be sure that you click and move the path, not the butterfly itself (that will result in recorded keyframes, like you explored in steps 9 and 10 above). You will know you have the path selected when it says Motion Tween in the Properties panel.

2. With the Free Transform tool you can also scale it and rotate the selected path, which will affect the timing and position of the path in the scene. Try this and play back the animation each time you make a transformation to see the effect. See Figure 5–25.

figure |5–25|

Use the Free Transform tool to alter the scale, position, or rotation of the motion tween.

3. For practice, animate the smaller butterfly fluttering throughout the scene (be sure to unlock its layer, and lock the **butterfly** layer so you don't mess that up by mistake!).

Lesson 2: Tweening Color and Rotation

This lesson covers some simple variations to motion tweening—changing the color and rotation of an object over time.

1. From the Flash program open the file **chap5L2.fla** in the **chap05_lessons** folder.
2. Be sure your workspace is set to Classic.
3. Notice the layer called **sun**—the first frame of the layer contains a blank keyframe (a circle with a clear dot).
4. Open the Library and drag an instance of the **sun** symbol to the Stage. The blank keyframe on the **sun** layer is now filled with a black dot (a keyframe) indicating that the layer is now filled with an object, the sun.
5. On frame 50, Ctrl-click or click then hold (Mac) or right-click (Windows) and choose Insert Frame (F5) from the drop-down menu.
6. Ctrl-click or click then hold (Mac) or right-click (Windows) anywhere between frames 1 and 50, and choose Motion Tween.
7. Move to frame 50 of the **sun** layer.
8. Ctrl-click or click then hold (Mac) or right-click (Windows) on frame 50 and choose Insert Keyframe > All. See Figure 5–26.

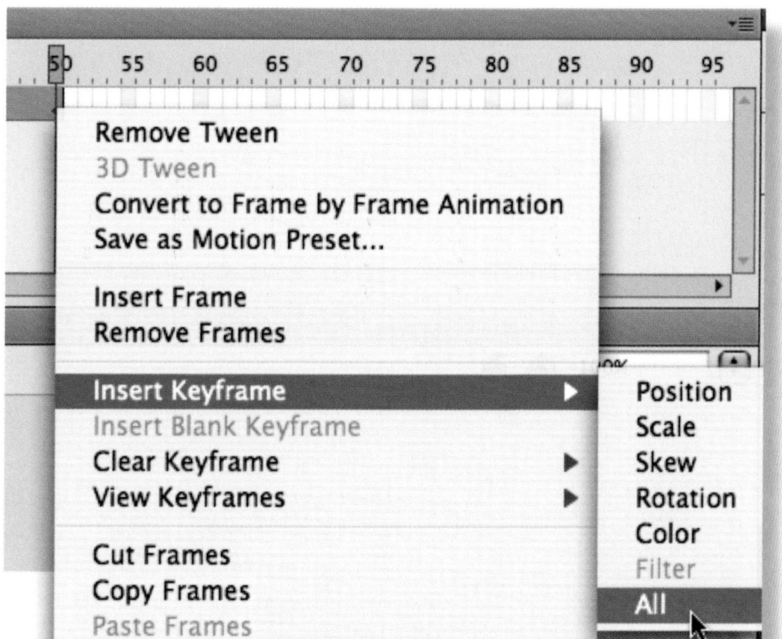

figure 5–26

Insert a keyframe with all available properties.

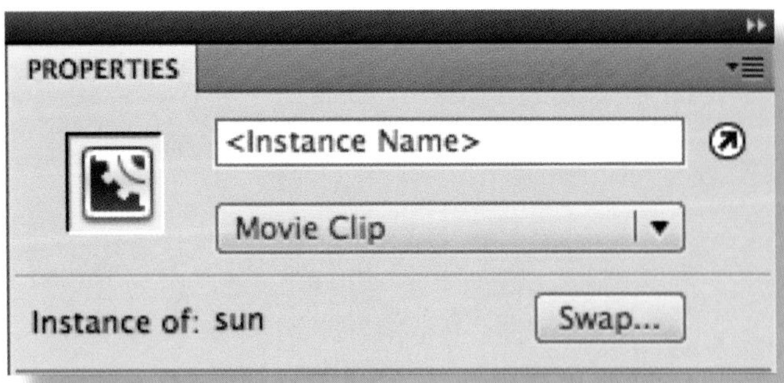

figure 5–27

Properties of the Movie Clip called **sun**.

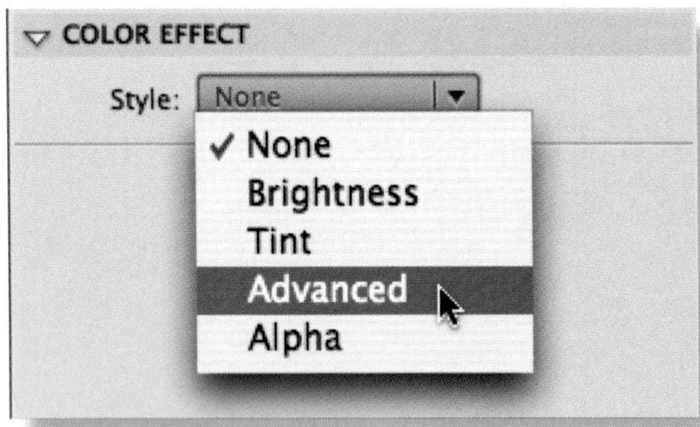

figure 5–28

Select the Advanced color style.

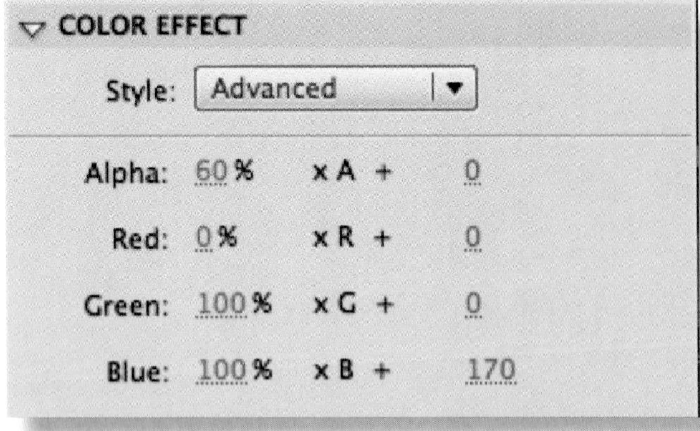

figure 5–29

For precise color adjustment, use the Advanced color effect option.

9. Now, select the instance of the sun on the Stage (be sure you select the object, the sun, not just the keyframe—the Properties panel will indicate it's a Movie Clip and display an instance name field). See Figure 5–27.
10. From the Properties panel under Color Effect, choose Style > Advanced. See Figure 5–28.
11. Change the color in the Advanced color box to the following (see Figure 5–29):
    - Alpha = 60%, offset keep at 0
    - Red = 0%, offset keep at 0
    - Green = 100%, offset keep at 0
    - Blue = 100%, offset to 170

    The result should be a slightly transparent, teal colored sun. If you don't like teal, feel free to adjust the advanced settings anyway you like. Explore what happens when you move various sliders in the Advanced box. If you don't like the result, use Edit > Undo.

> **Note:** The Advanced color option is a bit tricky, and more than we can get into right now. Consult the Flash Help files when you have the chance. Also check Help for information about the other Color Effect options—Brightness, Tint, and Alpha.

12. Play back the animation—the color shifts over time, including its transparency. Coolness!
13. Click anywhere between frames 1–50 on the sun's timeline. In the Properties panel, set the rotation to two time(s). See Figure 5–30.
14. Play back the animation again—the sun rotates and changes color!
15. Save your file in your lessons folder. For fun and practice, create a new layer, place another **sun** instance on the layer and animate its color, rotation, scale, and motion.

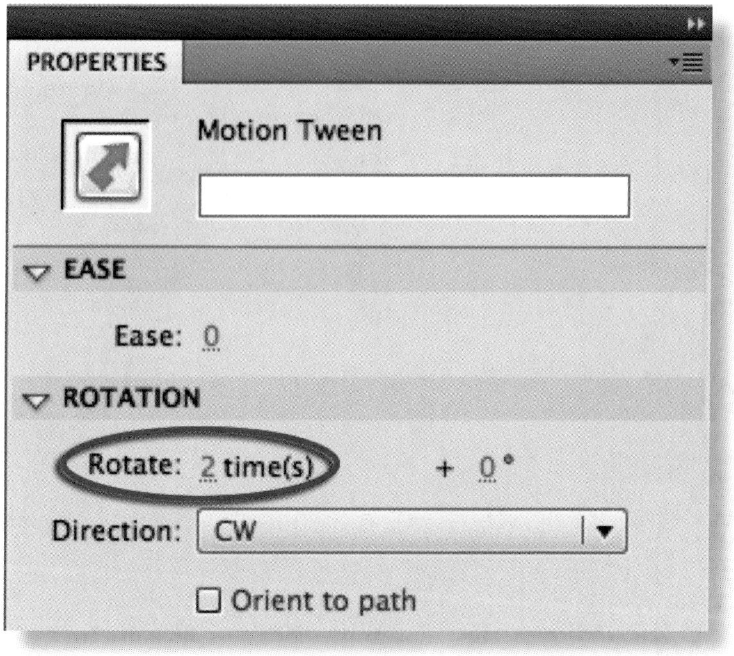

figure 5–30

Set rotation of an object in the Motion Tween properties.

Lesson 3: Shape Tween

So far, you have animated objects with motion tweens. When making motion tweens, the tweened object must be a symbol or it just won't work. If you forget to convert an object to a symbol before executing a motion tween a dialog box will come up asking what you would like to do. See Figure 5–31.

In contrast, shape tweens work on shape objects only. Shape tweens morph the edges of a vector object, so in order for Flash to read the edges or outline of the object, the object must be a shape. Try this simple tutorial to get an idea of how it works.

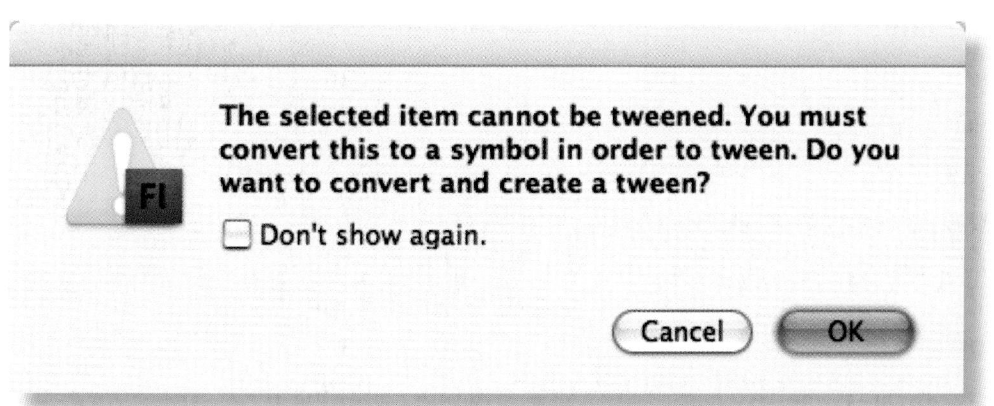
The selected item cannot be tweened. You must convert this to a symbol in order to tween. Do you want to convert and create a tween?
Fl
Don't show again.
Cancel
OK

figure 5–31

An object must be a symbol to be motion tweened. If it isn't a warning box will let you know.

1. In Flash, choose File > New, and choose the Flash File (ActionScript 2.0) option.
2. In the Properties panel, set the width and height of the Stage to 300 pixels. Change the background color to black.
3. Select the Oval tool in the Tools panel (click and hold on the Rectangle tool to reveal the Oval tool underneath).
4. Select any fill color and set the stroke to none. See Figure 5–32. Draw an Oval in the center of the Stage. If you hold down the Shift key while dragging, your shape will constrain to a perfectly round circle.

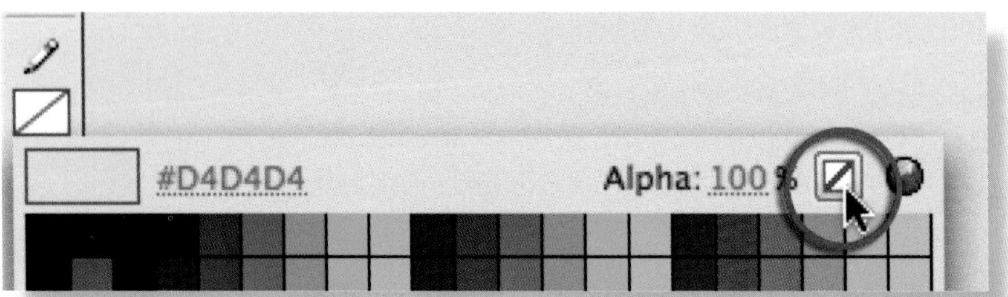

figure 5–32

Choose the none option for the Stroke color.

> **Note:** If you notice when you draw the object there is a blue bounding box around it, it's possible you are in Object Drawing mode for the shape (see Chapter 3 for a review of Object Drawing mode). You want to be in Merge Drawing mode for this lesson. Delete the object on the Stage. Select the Oval tool and in the lower part of the Tools panel be sure the Object Drawing mode is turned off. See Figure 5–33.

5. Ctrl-click or click then hold (Mac) or right-click (Windows) over frame 20 and choose Insert Blank Keyframe.
6. With frame 20 still selected, choose the Rectangle tool in the Tools panel. Select a fill color (make it different than the color of the Oval), and set the stroke to none. Draw a rectangle in the center of the Stage.
7. Ctrl-click or click then hold (Mac) or right-click (Windows) anywhere between frames 1 and 20 and choose Shape Tween from the drop-down menu. See Figure 5–34.

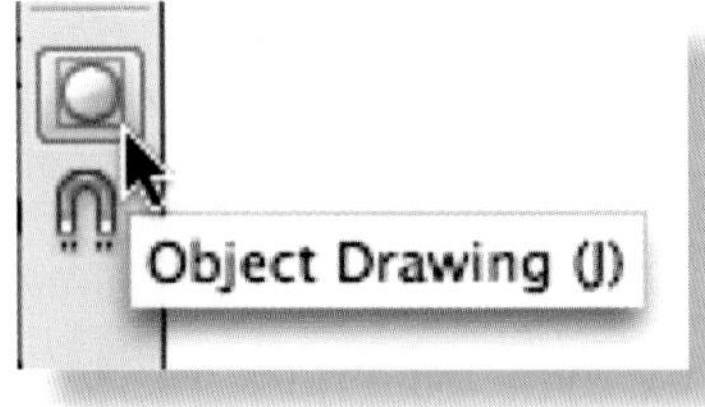

figure 5–33

Be sure the Object Drawing mode is turned off.

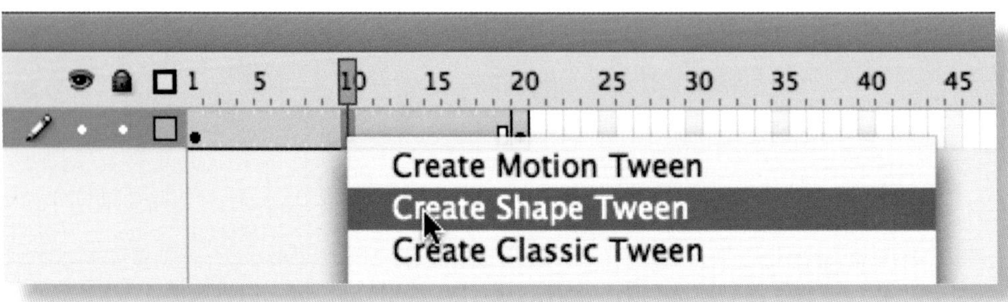

figure 5–34

Create Shape Tween is found as a submenu option from the Timeline.

8. Play back the animation. Whoa!

9. Extend the time it takes to morph by clicking once on frame 20, then click again on frame 20 and drag to frame 40.

10. Try variations on the shape—go to the first frame and push and pull the edges of the object to make a different shape. Also, change its fill color. See Figure 5–35. Play back the animation.

figure 5–35

Alter the shape.

11. Save your file.

Note: Shape animations in Flash work best with simple objects. To shape tween text and alter the way Flash determines the morph action, refer to the Exploring on Your Own section at the end of this chapter.

figure 5–36

Each moth drawing is saved as a symbol in the Library.

Lesson 4: Frame-by-Frame Basics

In this tutorial, the drawn positions of a flying moth have been created for you. All you need to do is add the frames!

Making the Moth Fly

1. Open the file **chap5L4.fla** in the **chap05_lessons** folder.
2. Be sure your workspace is set to Classic.
3. Rename Layer 1 to **moth animation**.
4. Open the Library. In the Library, click on each of the symbol icons of the moth positions (1, 2, 3, 4, and 5) to view the drawings that indicate the moth's wing pattern. See Figure 5–36.
5. Select frame 1 of the **moth animation** layer (the empty circle).
6. Click and drag from the Library the symbol "1," and place it in the center of the Stage.
7. Turn on the Onion Skin option in the lower portion of the Timeline panel. This feature will help you see where to place each drawing in the next steps. See Figure 5–37.

figure 5–37

Turn on the Onion Skin option for precise control when creating a frame-by-frame animation.

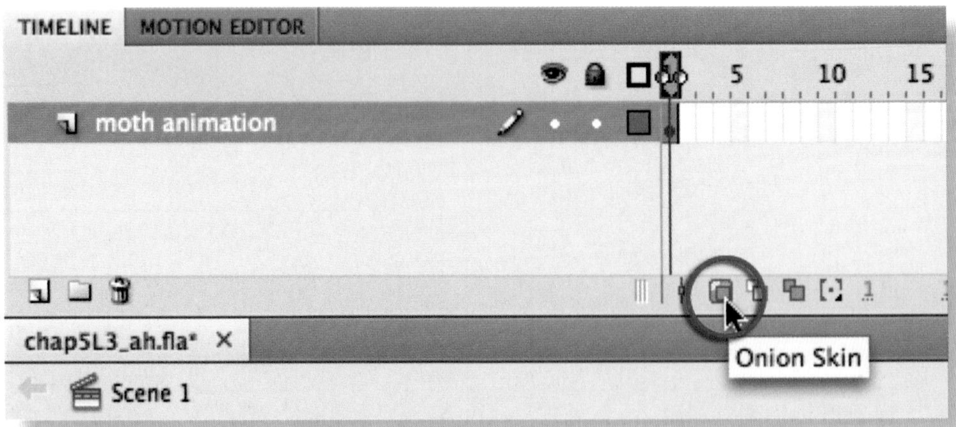

8. Insert a blank keyframe (F7) on frame 2 of the **moth animation** layer. Be sure it's a blank keyframe (an empty circle vs. a keyframe which is a filled black circle).
9. Click and drag from the Library the symbol "2," and place it in the center of the Stage over the first moth's outline.

10. Use your arrow keys to incrementally move the moth image on frame 2—position the moth directly over the faded version of the moth on the first frame. See Figure 5–38.

11. Insert a blank keyframe (F7) on frame 3 of the **moth** layer.

12. From the Library place symbol "3" into the scene, precisely over the other two moth objects.

13. Insert a blank keyframe (F7) on frame 4 of the **moth** layer.

14. From the Library, place symbol "4" into the scene. Once again, use the onion skinning effect to position it over the other moth objects.

15. Insert a blank keyframe on frame 5 of the **moth** layer.

16. You got it—from the Library place symbol "5" into the scene and position it over the other moth's image.

17. To see all the onion skins of the moth's frames adjust the amount of frames viewed in onion skin mode by clicking and dragging the markers near the playback head in the Timeline. See Figure 5–39. Note the onion skins of the five frames are visible in the scene. See Figure 5–40.

18. Play back the animation.

19. Now turn the Onion Skin option off—click on the Onion Skin icon at the bottom of the Timeline (refer to Figure 5–37).

20. Choose Control > Test Movie to view the movie as a SWF. The moth's wings are popping closed, and not very smoothly—let's fix this in the next section.

21. Save your scene in your lessons folder.

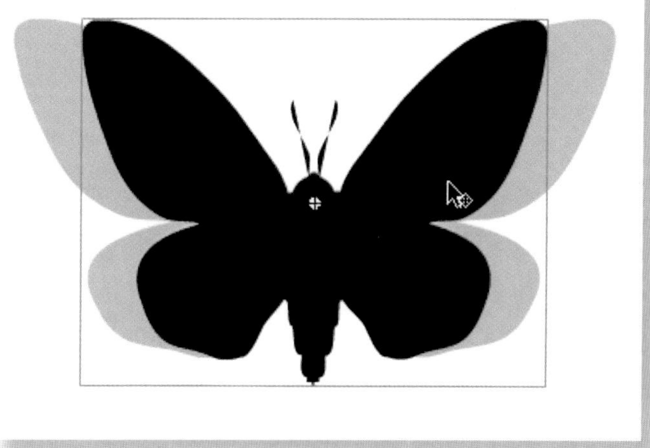

figure 5–38

Place the second moth drawing over the onion skinned version of the first moth drawing.

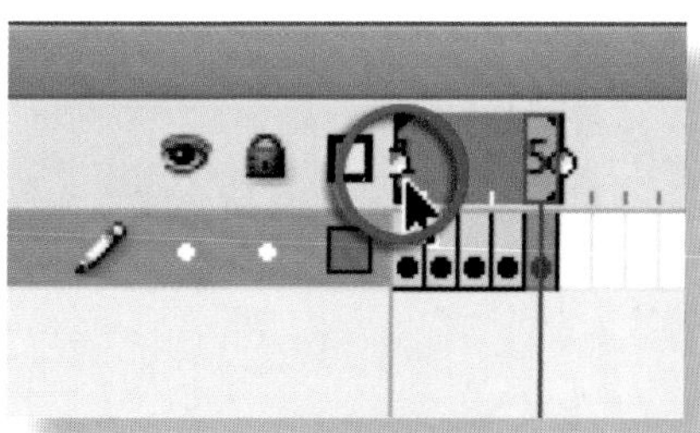

figure 5–39

Adjust the viewing range of the onion skin near the Timeline's playback marker.

figure 5–40

All frames are shown of the frame-by-frame animation.

Making an Animated Loop

1. Select all five frames. To do this, click on frame 1 of the **moth** layer, hold down your Shift key and click on frame 5. All the frames should turn blue, indicating they are selected.

2. Ctrl-click or click then hold (Mac) or right-click (Windows) over frame 5 and choose Copy > Frames. (Also, you can go to the Menu bar and choose Edit > Timeline > Copy Frames.) See Figure 5–41.

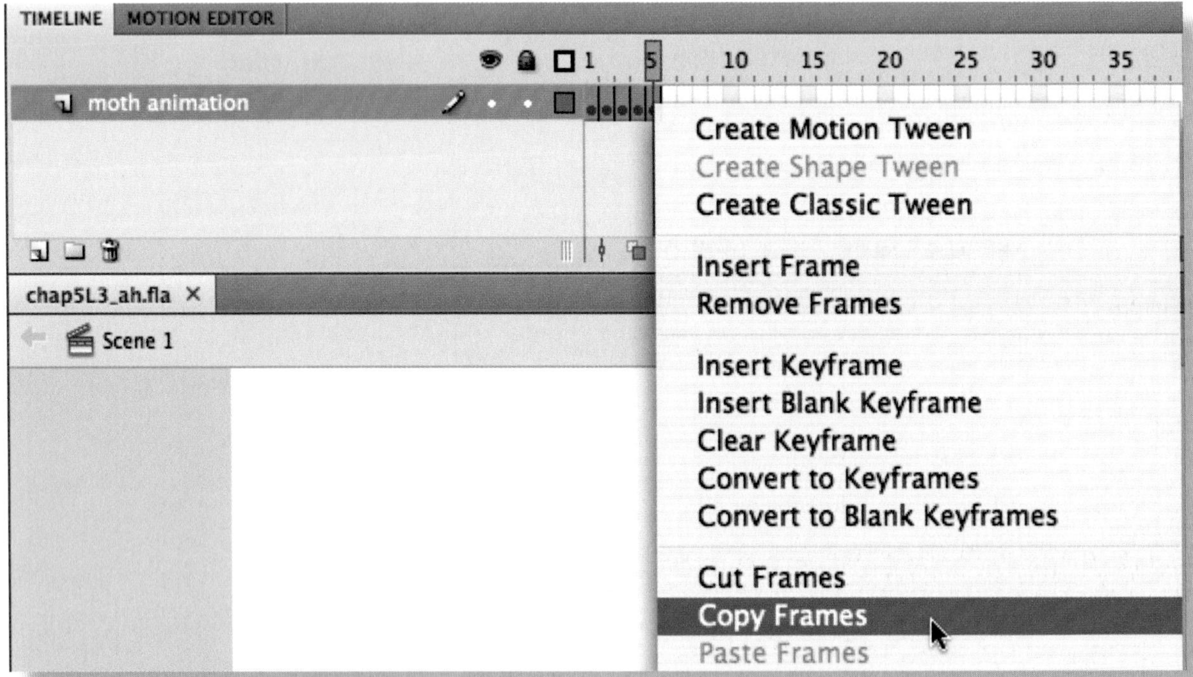

figure 5–41

Copy frames from the Timeline submenu.

3. Click on frame 6 of the layer. Then Ctrl-click or click then hold (Mac) or right-click (Windows) and choose Paste > Frames.

4. Here's a tricky part. If not already selected, Shift-select the frames you just pasted, frames 6, 7, 8, 9, and 10 (they should all be highlighted blue).

5. Ctrl-click or click then hold (Mac) or right-click (Windows) over frame 10 and choose Reverse Frames. See Figure 5–42.

6. Choose Control > Test Movie. Notice how the moth wings now open and close, creating a continuous motion. By default, all animations in the SWF format continue to loop.

7. Save your file. You've completed this lesson.

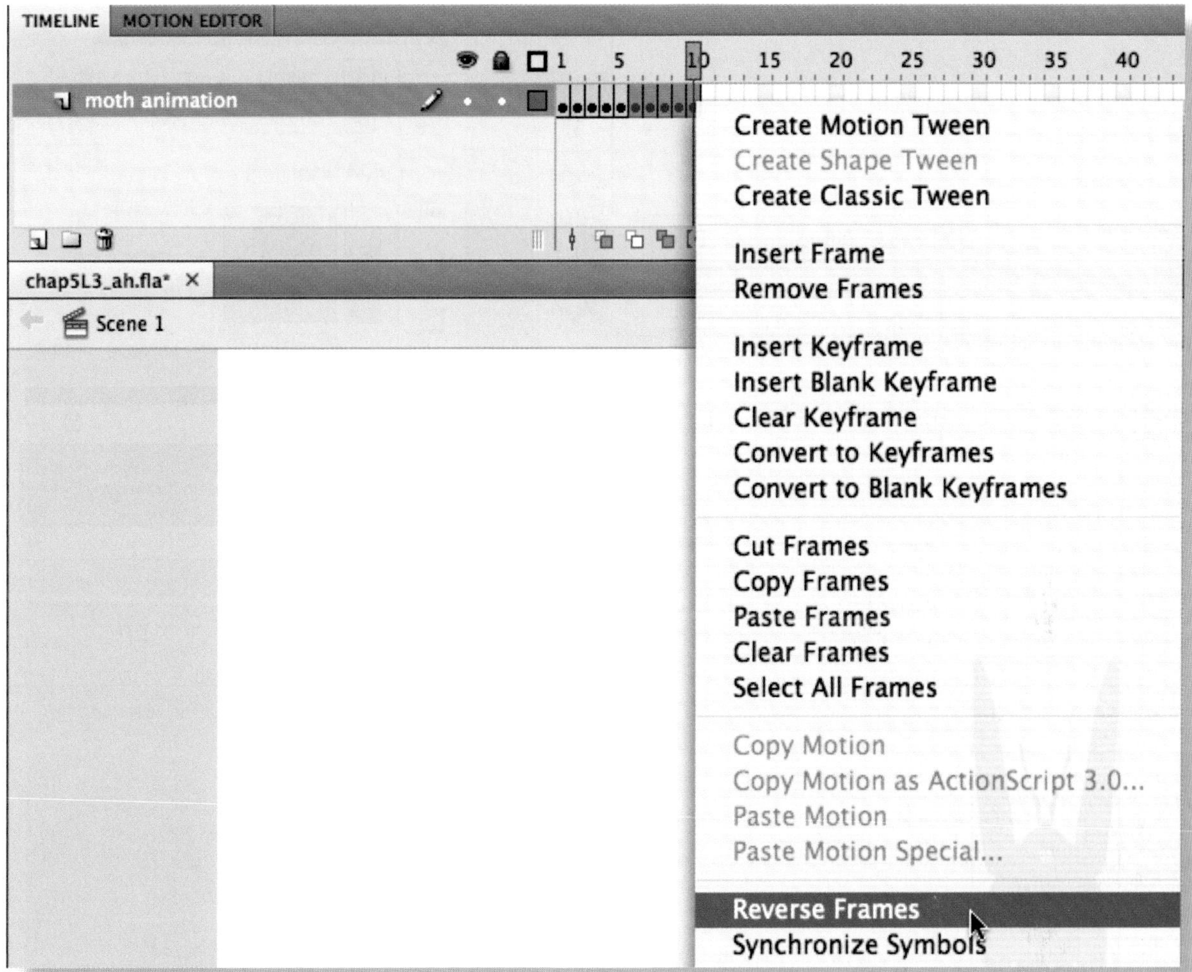

figure 5–42

Reverse selected frames.

THE MOVIE CLIP TIMELINE

When converting objects to symbols you have the option to choose three different types: Movie Clip, Button, and Graphic. See Figure 5–43. Each type has different attributes depending on how you want to use the symbol. In previous lessons, you have saved your objects as movie clip symbols. This is the most versatile symbol type and has many attributes that will be used when you delve into more advanced uses of symbols and ActionScripting. As you will discover, one of the most important things about a movie clip symbol is that it contains a Timeline that is independent from the main (or "root") Timeline.

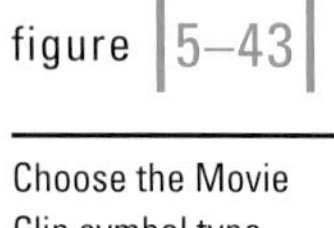

figure 5–43

Choose the Movie Clip symbol type.

Lesson 5: Animating on the Movie Clip Timeline

This lesson is particularly important. Here you will view an example then create an animation within a movie clip. This technique can add complexity to your animations, taking them to a whole new level.

Viewing an Example Movie Clip Animation

1. Launch Flash and choose File > Open. In the **chap05_lessons** folder open the file **chap5L5_example.fla**.
2. Hit Enter (Return) to play the animation—the moths move and change color on a path. This animation is created on the main, root Timeline.
3. Choose Control > Test Movie. Hmmm … the moths are still moving, but their wings are now flapping. Where is this wing animation coming from? Close the SWF.

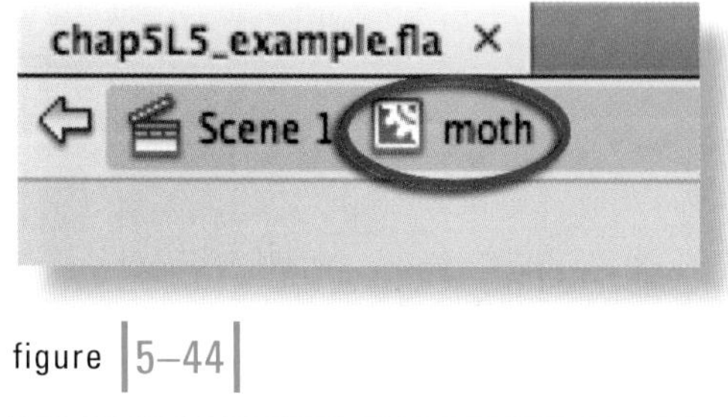

figure 5–44

The movie clip icon indicator for the moth in the upper left corner of the Stage.

4. Double-click on one of the moth instances to enter editing mode. This **moth** symbol is a Movie Clip type indicated by the blue movie clip icon in the upper left corner of the Flash Stage. See Figure 5–44.
5. Inside the moth movie clip notice the series of 10 keyframes. See Figure 5–45. The movie clip has its own Timeline—it works independently from the root (Scene 1) Timeline. Hit Enter to play the animation within the movie clip—ah, the wings move!
6. Exit editing mode (click on the Scene 1 icon in the upper left corner of the document, or the left-facing arrow).
7. View both animations again—the one within the movie clip and the one on Scene 1—by choosing Control > Test Movie. Notice also that the animation in both Timelines loops—this is the default setting for Flash animations.

figure 5–45

A series of keyframes are located within the moth's symbol.

Making Your Own Movie Clip Animation

1. Choose File > New, Flash File (ActionScript 2.0) to create a new file.

2. Choose Insert > New Symbol. Call it **morph** and save it as the Movie Clip type. Hit OK. See Figure 5–46. You will be sent to the editing mode of the **morph** movie clip. There's nothing on the Stage yet but a cross hair (plus sign) in the center.

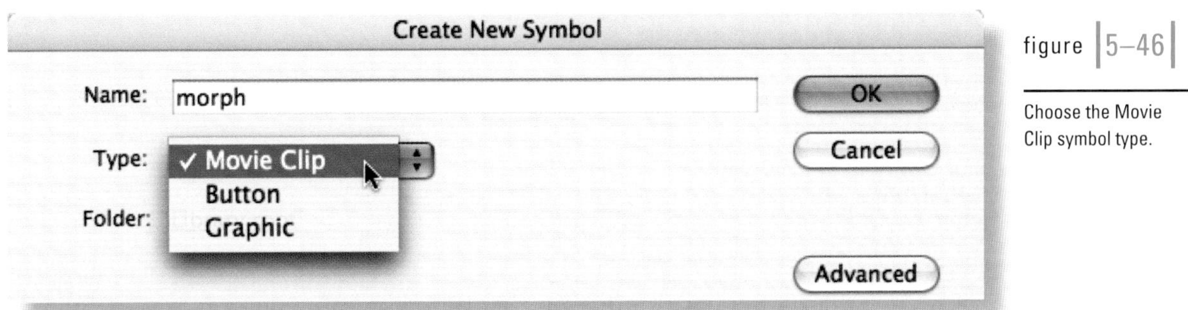

figure 5–46

Choose the Movie Clip symbol type.

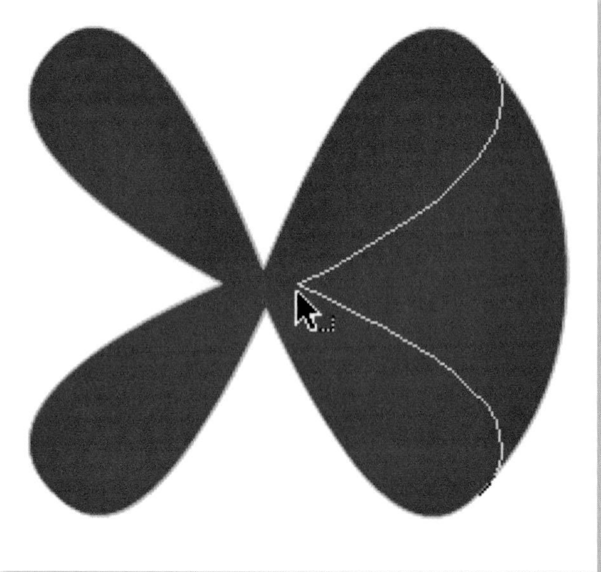

figure 5–47

Alter the shape.

3. Directly over the cross hair, create a colored circle. You can do this accurately by holding Alt/Option and drawing from the center.

4. Ctrl-click or click then hold (Mac) or right-click (Windows) over frame 15 and choose Insert KeyFrame (F6).

5. At this frame 15, change the color of the circle and modify it to make a clover shape. To do this, first deselect the shape. Then with the Selection tool, Alt/Option-click on the top edge of the circle and drag inward. Also, do this for the two sides and the bottom of the circle. See Figure 5–47.

6. Ctrl-click or click then hold (Mac) or right-click (Windows) anywhere between frames 1–15 and choose Create Shape Tween. Play back the animation.

7. Create a cycle for the morph. Ctrl-click or click then hold (Mac) or right-click (Windows) over the first frame and choose Copy Frames. Ctrl-click or click then hold (Mac) or right-click (Windows) over frame 30 and choose Paste Frames. Place a shape animation between frames 15 and 30.

8. Go back to Scene 1, the root Timeline.

9. Open the Library panel and drag an instance of the **morph** symbol to the center of the stage.

10. Create a motion tween with the **morph** symbol (refer to the first lesson in this chapter for a review on creating a simple motion tween).

11. Play back the movie by choosing Control > Test Movie. For reference: in my final version found in **chap05_lessons/chap5L5_final.fla** I added a scaling effect and rotation to the tween on the root Timeline. See if you can do the same!

PROJECT: THE SAILBOAT, PART 2

The Sailboat Project, Part 2 is the second part of the project started in Chapter 4. It's an opportunity to practice the animation skills you learned in this chapter on a scene you created. If you don't have access to the scene you drew in the last chapter, you can use the final example file found in **chap04_lessons/project_part1_final.fla** as your starting file.

The steps in this project are abbreviated with the assumption you have completed the first five chapters of this book before tackling this project. If you need to refresh your memory on how to do something, like how to make a motion or shape tween, refer to the previous lessons in this chapter or the Help files within the Flash program (Help > Flash Help).

An example of this completed project can be found in **chap05_lessons/project_part2_final.fla**. Examples created by my past students are available in the **chap05_lessons/movies/students**. See Figure 5–48 and Figure 5–49. Don't copy these example demos, but rather use them as guides, along with the steps below, as a basis for your own rendition of the scene.

figure | 5–48 |

A sailboat scene example from student Ashley Gonsales.

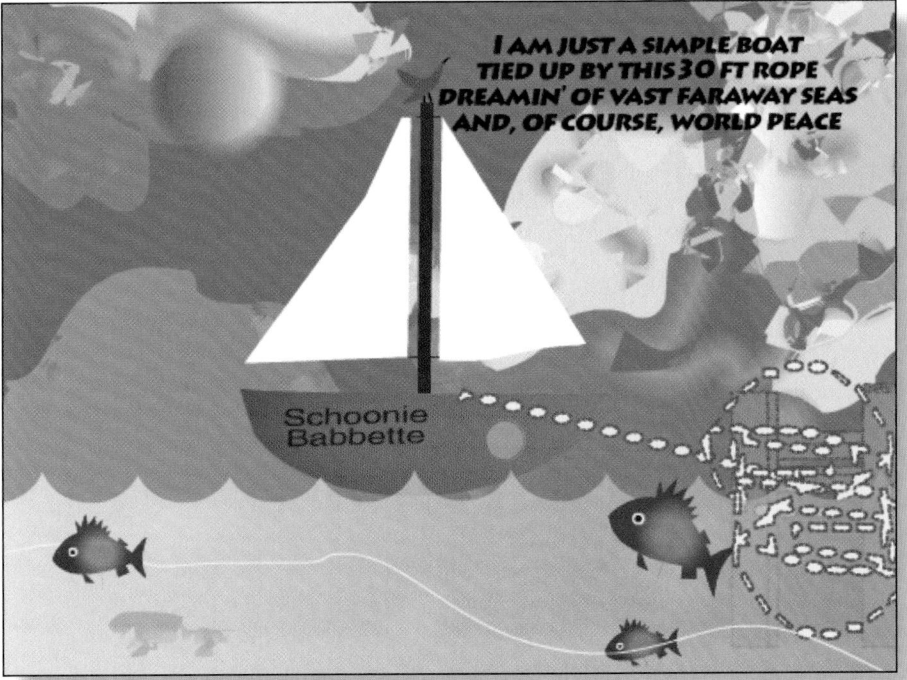

figure | 5–49 |

A sailboat scene example from student Joan Powell Kennedy.

Motion Tween the Boat and the Sun

1. Open the Sailboat Project, Part 1 that you created in Chapter 4. If you don't have a boat scene use the final version in **chap04_lessons/project_part1_final.fla**.

2. Expand the Timeline panel so that you can see all the layers in the movie—to do this click and drag down on the edge line between the Timeline and the movie area. See Figure 5–50.

figure 5–50

Expand the Timeline panel to see all the layers.

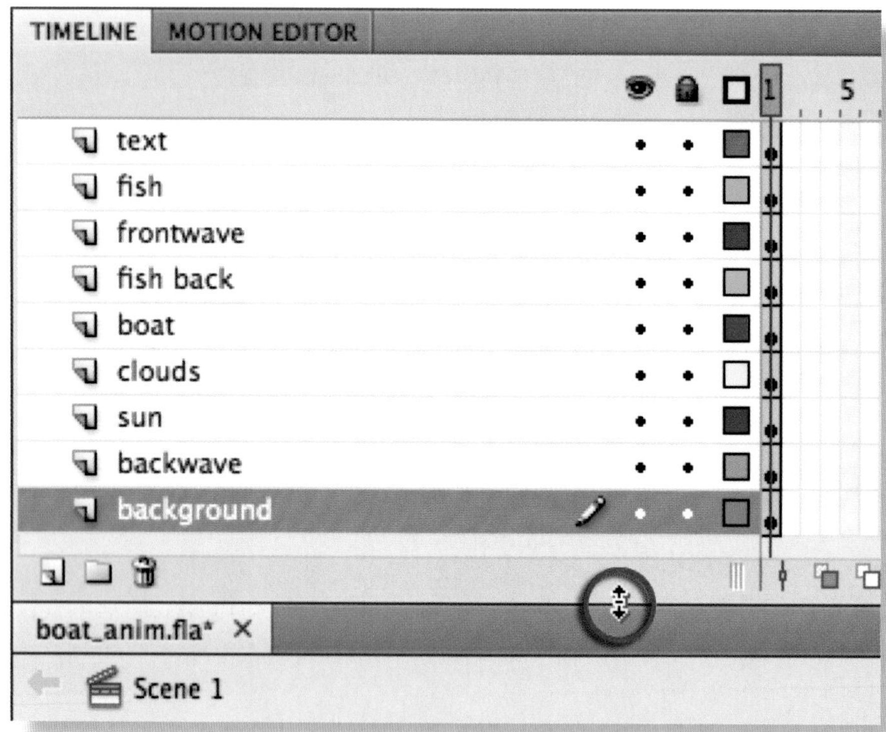

3. Add some holding frames to these layers by selecting all the frames at frame 100 of the Timeline. To do this at frame 100, click and drag down from the top frame to the bottom, then press F5 on the keyboard. See Figure 5–51. All frames between 1–100 will turn gray.

4. Using a motion tween, animate the sun rising and setting in your boat scene.

5. Change its color over time.

6. Next, using a motion tween, animate your boat entering into the scene and stopping in the middle of the scene.

7. On the Stage, make your boat rock slightly back and forth by adding keyframes within the tween and setting the rotation of the boat forward or back (Hint: use the Free Transform tool to set the rotations).

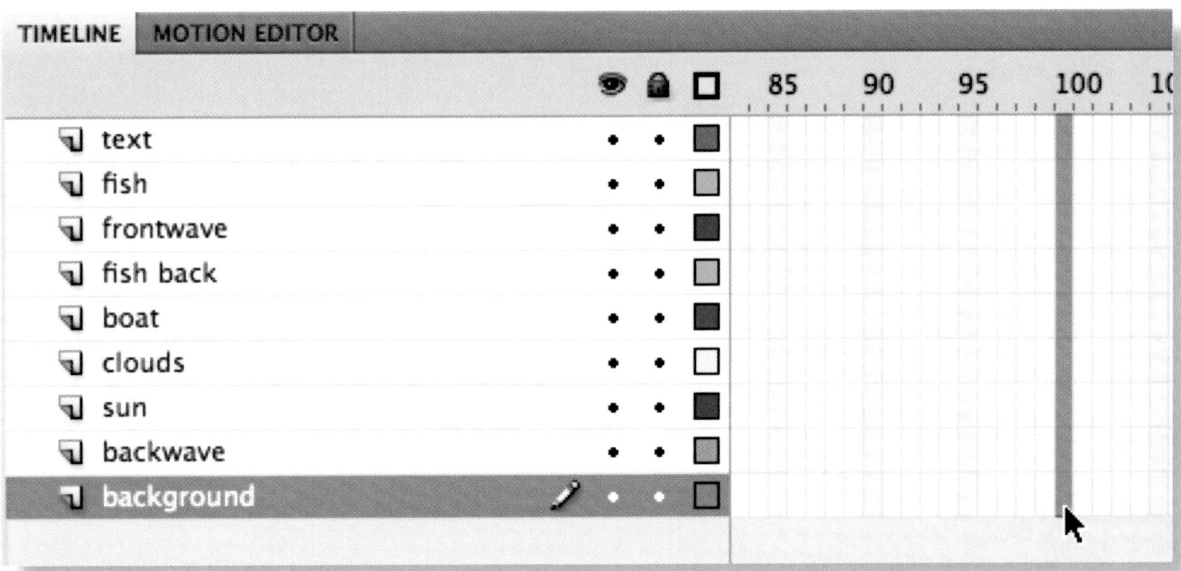

figure 5–51

Select the same frame number of all the layers.

8. Choose Control > Test Movie to publish and view the file as an SWF.

9. Save your file as **myboat_anim.fla** in your lessons folder.

> **Note:** It's possible you will want to adjust the timing of your boat's rocking action, which is a bit tricky. You need to be able to select and move a property keyframe. To do this . . .
>
> a. Be sure the layer that has the property keyframe you want to move is deselected.
>
> b. Command ⌘ (Mac) or Ctrl-click (Windows) on the property keyframe to select it. See Figure 5–52.
>
> c. Let go of the Command ⌘ or Ctrl key, then click and drag the selected frame, moving it right or left on the timeline to adjust its timing.
>
> To further refine a motion tween you can also explore the somewhat challenging Motion Editor panel. Visit the Flash Help files for more information.

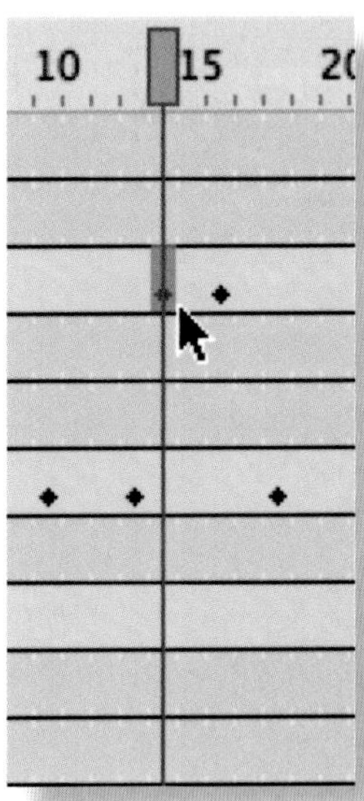

figure 5–52

Adjust a property keyframe.

Making a Fish Swim on a Path

1. In your **myboat_anim.fla** create a new layer and call it **fish swims**.
2. From the Library drag out an instance of the **fish**.
3. Using a motion tween, animate the fish jumping in and out of the water as it swims across the scene.
4. Try animating several fish swimming and jumping—make them different sizes and coming from different directions. Hint: to flip your fish so that it faces the opposite direction, choose Modify > Transform > Flip Horizontal. Also, remember: put each animating fish on its own layer!
5. Save your file.

More Variations to Explore

Using what was learned in the last lesson of this chapter—"Animating on the Movie Clip Timeline"—create an animation within the **boat** symbol (a flag waving or sail moving, for example) or within the **fish** symbol, such as fins undulating, bubbles floating, eyes blinking. Hint: be sure to put whatever you want to animate on its own layer, and if you create a shape animation be sure the object is a shape (if it's grouped you can reduce it to a shape by choosing Modify > Break Apart from the menu bar).

SUMMARY

A thorough overview of the important Flash Timeline was covered in this chapter, including how to organize and display objects on layers, create and edit frames, and alter the timing of animated objects. The animation methods of tweening (motion, scale, rotation, color, and shape), frame-by-frame, and animating within a movie clip symbol were also explained and practiced. The world of movement is now at your fingertips—play, play, play!

in review

1. Describe the difference between tweening and frame-by-frame animation.
2. Name the four types of frames that can be created on the Timeline.
3. Name at least three advantages of using layers in Flash.
4. What is the purpose of onion skinning?
5. What is the function of the Orient to Path option?
6. Describe shape tweening.
7. What is an advantage to animating within a movie clip?
8. What does Modify > Break Apart do?

exploring on your own

1. Study up on the history of animation: *http://en.wikipedia.org/wiki/Traditional_animation*
2. Create a shape animation using text. Try this:
   a. On a layer on the first frame create some text (use the Text tool in the Tools panel)—keep it simple, for example the word "cat," and use a large, bold font. Select the text and choose Modify > Break Apart to reduce it down to individual letters. Choose Modify > Break Apart again to reduce the letters into shapes.
   b. On the same layer insert a blank keyframe (F5) at frame 10 (for example). In that frame, create another line of text, i.e., the word "dog." Modify > Break Apart twice to reduce it into shapes.
   c. Create a shape tween between the frames by Ctrl-clicking or clicking then holding (Mac) or right-clicking (Windows) between the two keyframes and choosing Create Shape Tween from the drop-down menu.

d. Play back the animation. See an example version in **chap05_lessons/samples/text_shape_tween.fla**.

> **Note:** If the shape between the two objects is not morphing exactly the way you would like you can try adding shape hints. For more details on how to use the shape hints feature see the Flash Help files and do a search for "shape hints."

3. For more realistic, life-like motion explore the Ease option for motion tweens. Easing is an animation technique that subtly varies the pace (acceleration or deceleration) of an object. For example, in real life, when a car merges onto the highway the natural motion of the car is to speed up gradually as it travels along the ramp—you might want to create this same effect in Flash. Visit this great resource on easing in Flash-Timing: Easing In and Out from Cartoon Solutions—*http://www.cartoonsolutions.com/store/catalog/Timing-for-Animation-sp-7.html*, then try it on your own. Follow the steps below and create your own tweened object or use the sample file provided in **chap05_lessons/samples/easing.fla**.

   a. Create a simple object in Flash, and save it as a movie clip symbol.

   b. Motion tween the object over 25 frames across the Stage. For review of how to create a motion tween see Lesson 1: A Basic Tween, Setting up a Simple Tween, steps #1–8 in this chapter.

   c. Click on the motion tween (the blue bar) on the Timeline.

   d. In the Properties for the Motion Tween click and drag to the right (scrub!) on the Ease number field to about 80. See Figure 5–53. Hit Return/Enter on the keyboard to play back the animation. The object should subtly decelerate (slow down, ease out) over time.

   e. Now, reverse the ease, click and drag to the left of the Ease number field to about –80. Play back the animation. The object should subtly accelerate (speed up, ease in) over time.

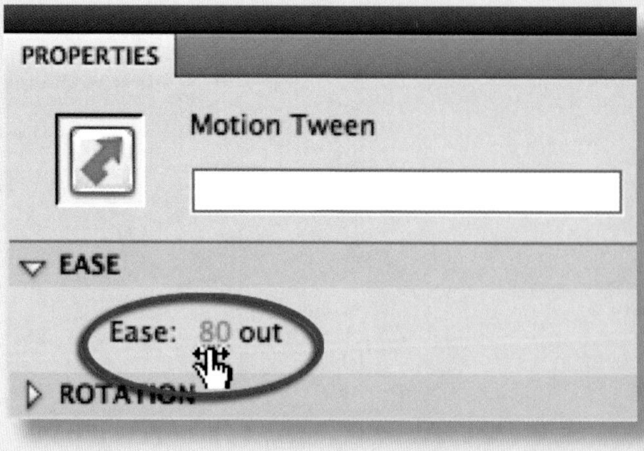

figure 5–53

Adjust the ease in or ease out of a tweened object.

4. There is an incredibly cool, new feature in CS4 called inverse kinematics (IK). Although IK is a complex feature that must be used in a file supporting ActionScript 3.0, it's worth mentioning. As described in the Flash help files, "Inverse kinematics (IK) is a method for animating an object or set of objects in relation to each other using an articulated structure of bones. Bones allow symbol instances and shape objects to move in complex and naturalistic ways with a minimum of design effort. For example, inverse kinematics lets you create character animation, such as arms, legs, and facial expressions much more easily." Try this:

   a. Create a new Flash file (ActionScript 3.0) in Flash.

   b. Use the Oval tool and create a simple arm shape with three parts—upper arm, lower arm, and a hand. See Figure 5–54.

figure |5–54|

An arm shape created using the Oval tool.

   c. Select the Bone tool in the Tools panel. See Figure 5–55.

figure |5–55|

Select the Bone tool in the toolbox.

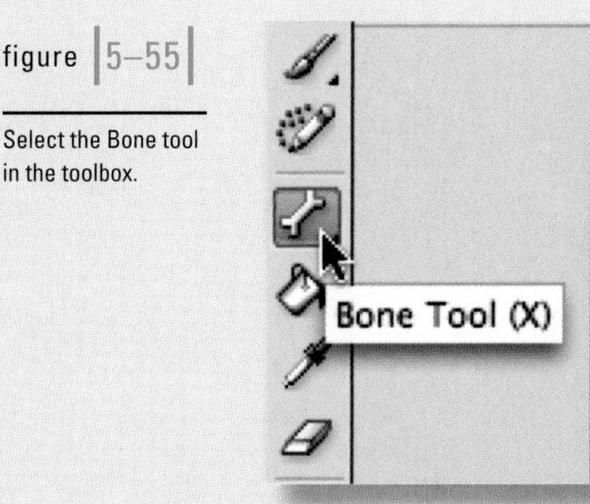

d. Click and drag the Bone tool from the top part of the arm down to the elbow—the top arm bone. Then, click and drag again on the end of the top arm bone to the wrist—the lower arm bone. Then click and drag on the end of the lower arm bone to create the hand. See Figure 5–56.

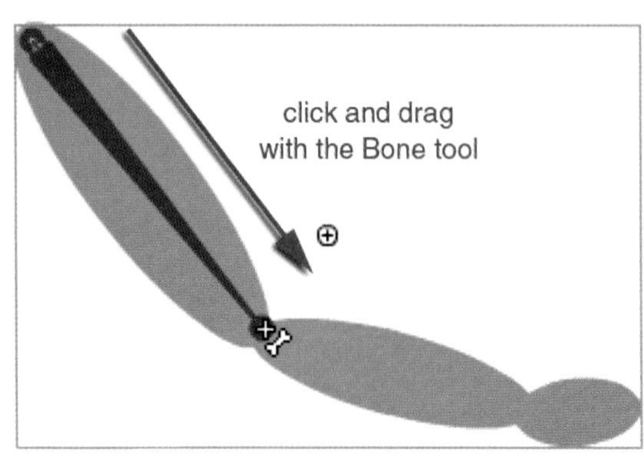

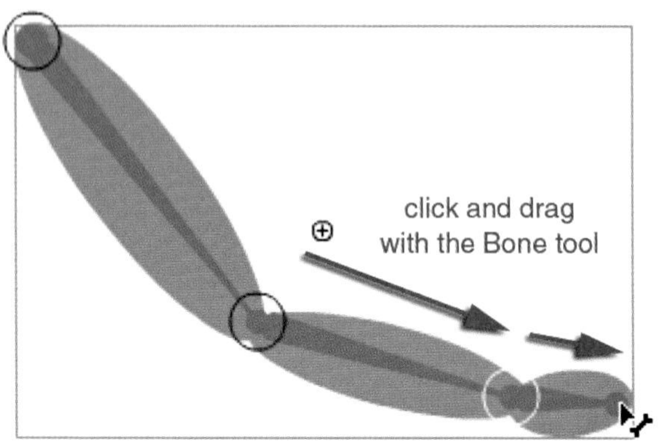

figure 5–56

Adding bones to the object.

e. Notice in the Timeline that an "Armature" layer is created.

f. Select the Selection tool, and click on the end node of the hand bone (the circle shape on the fingertips of the armature) and drag to articulate the full arm. See Figure 5–57.

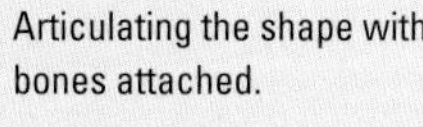
figure 5–57

Articulating the shape with bones attached.

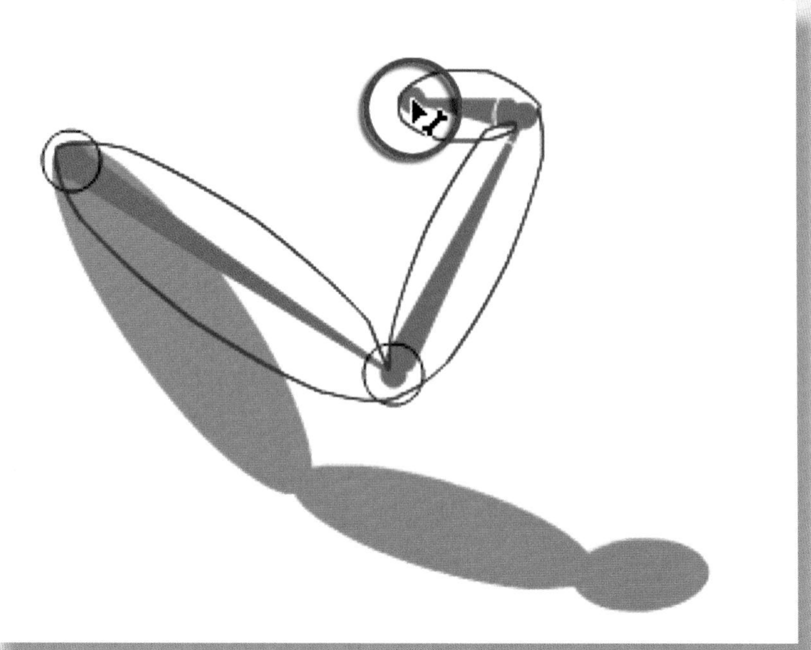

g. Animate the arm—set keyframes (poses) of the arm and hand waving. See Figure 5–58.

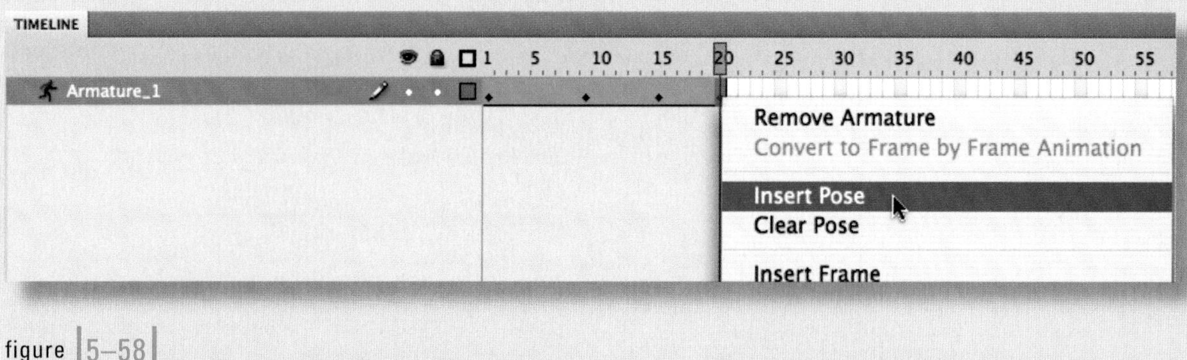

figure 5–58

Setting keyframes for the armature.

Study more about IK in the Flash help files > Timelines and Animation > Using inverse kinematics. Admittedly this feature is a boon for character animators!

ADVENTURES IN DESIGN

Masking

Masks are one of the most common effects used in computer graphics; to mask is to hide or reveal an object(s) or part of an object(s). In the instance of Flash any filled shape can be a mask. The filled area, when placed on a mask layer, represents a completely transparent window in which other shapes, graphics, etc., can be revealed behind it. Creating masks is easy, but how you use them is up to your imagination.

PROFESSIONAL PROJECT EXAMPLE

For the last few years, I have been asked by The Roxbury Latin School, an independent boys school in West Roxbury, Massachusetts, to create a Flash presentation for their annual online giving appeal. The presentations are always full of attractive photographs that I'm challenged to find the most appealing way to subtly transition one photo into another with text and music included. My favorite way to do this is to frame the photos within a mask shaped as the school's logo or design elements found on their Web site (*http://www.roxburylatin.org*). Figure A–1 is a screen shot of The Roxbury Latin School's presentation I designed in 2006, which shows an example of a photo framed by a mask in the shape of the school's shield. Photos are animated fading in and out within the mask shape.

Figure A–2 shows The Roxbury Latin School's presentation for 2007—another example of a mask, but one that swoops horizontally across the screen with photos that pass within the curved shape.

YOUR TURN

Now, it's your turn to make a mask and animate it.

Setting up the Mask

1. Open Flash and create a new Flash File (ActionScript 2.0).
2. Set the workspace to Classic.

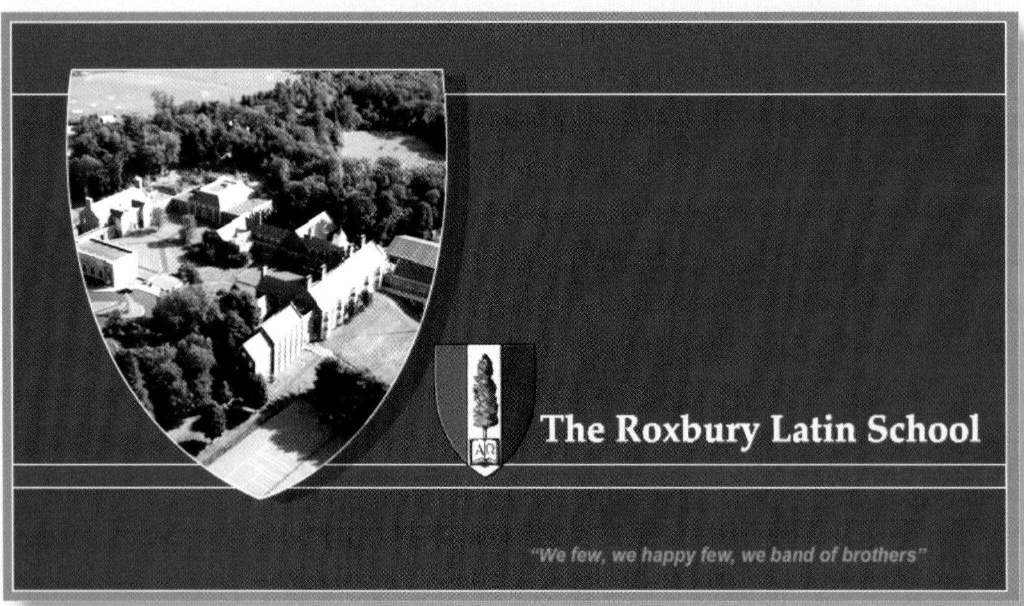

figure A–1 Example of a mask effect in a presentation for The Roxbury Latin School. The mask is in the shape of the school's logo.

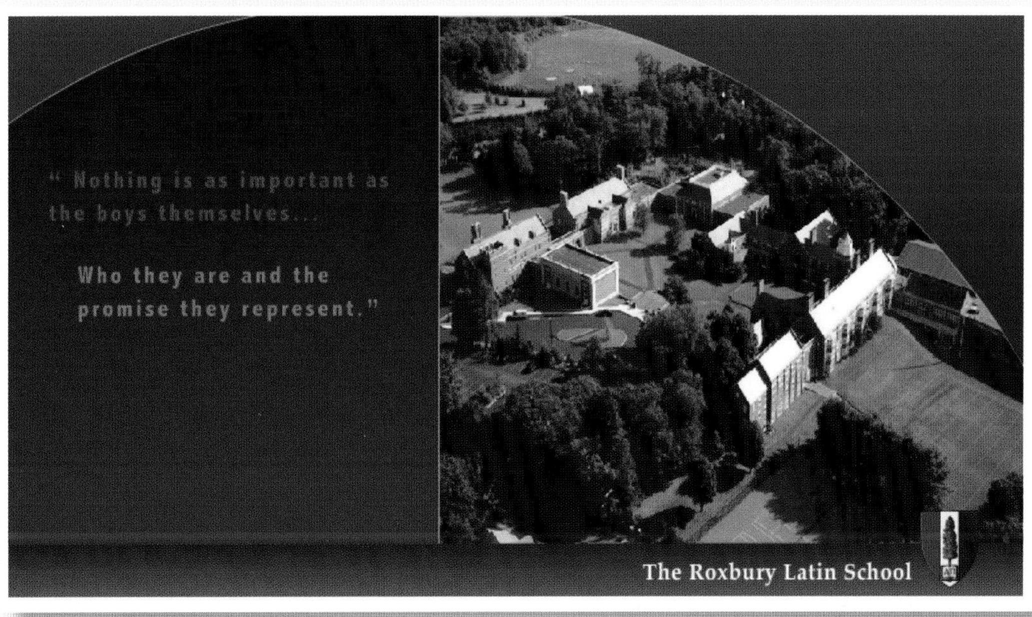

figure A–2 Another example of a mask effect in a presentation for The Roxbury Latin School. Photos are animated with the curved mask shape.

figure A–3 Create a circular shape to the left of the movie area.

3. In the Properties panel for the document, change the color of the Stage to black.
4. Rename Layer 1, **spotlight**.
5. Select the Text tool in the Tools panel and type the word SPOTLIGHT across the center of the Stage. Make the text fairly large (about 90 pts), bold, and a light color.
6. Make a new layer above the **spotlight** layer and call it **mask**.
7. On the **mask** layer create a filled circle shape (no stroke, any fill color) and place it off Stage and to the left of the movie. See Figure A–3.

ADVENTURES IN DESIGN

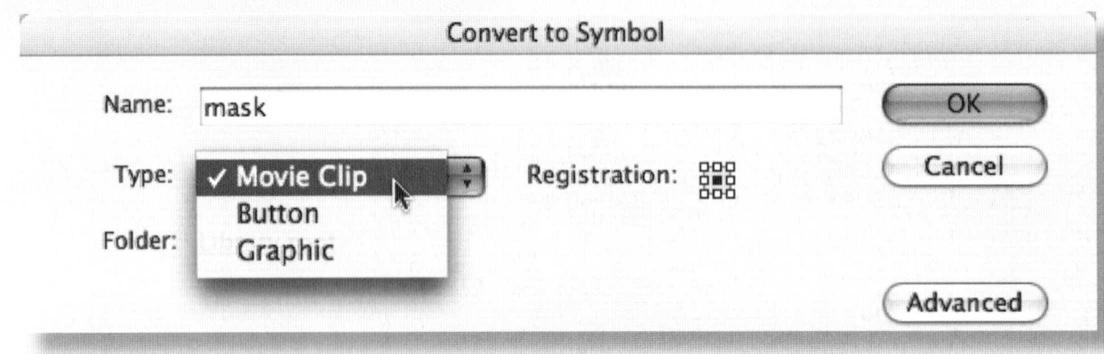

figure A–4 Save the shape as a Movie Clip symbol called **mask**.

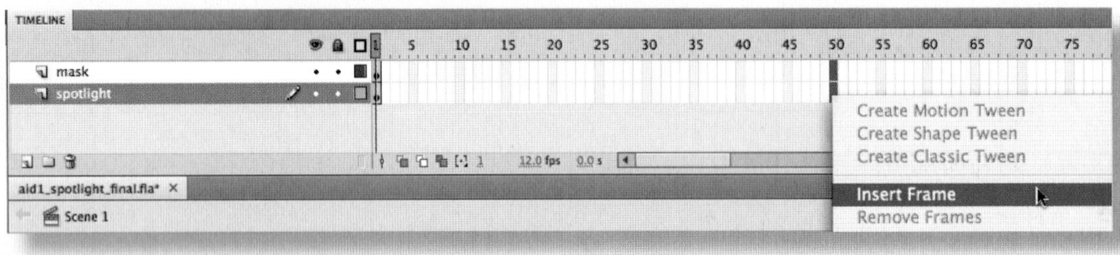

figure A–5 Insert holding frames from frames 1–50 of both layers.

8. Convert the circle shape to a symbol (F8), call it **mask** and save it as the Movie Clip type. See Figure A–4.

Animating and Applying the Mask

1. Create a frame at frame 50 of both the mask and spotlight layers—select frame 50 of both layers, then click and hold (Mac) or Ctrl-click (Windows) on one of the selected frames to reveal the submenu, and choose Insert Frame. See Figure A–5. All the frames from 1–50 of both layers will turn gray.
2. Create a motion tween on the **mask** layer—click anywhere between frames 1–50 of the mask layer, then click and hold to reveal the submenu. From the submenu, choose Motion Tween. The frames on the mask layer will turn blue.
3. Choose View > Magnification > 50%, so you can see the off Stage portion of the document.
4. Move the Timeline's playback head to frame 50.
5. Hold down the Shift key, then click and drag the circle mask shape to the opposite side of the Stage. A motion tween path will be created. See Figure A–6.
6. Hit Return (Enter) on the keyboard to test the animation of the circle moving across the Stage and over the word spotlight.
7. Ctrl-click (Mac) or right-click (Windows) on the tweening icon to the right of the mask layer's name

figure A–6 Create a motion tween of the mask object moving across the scene.

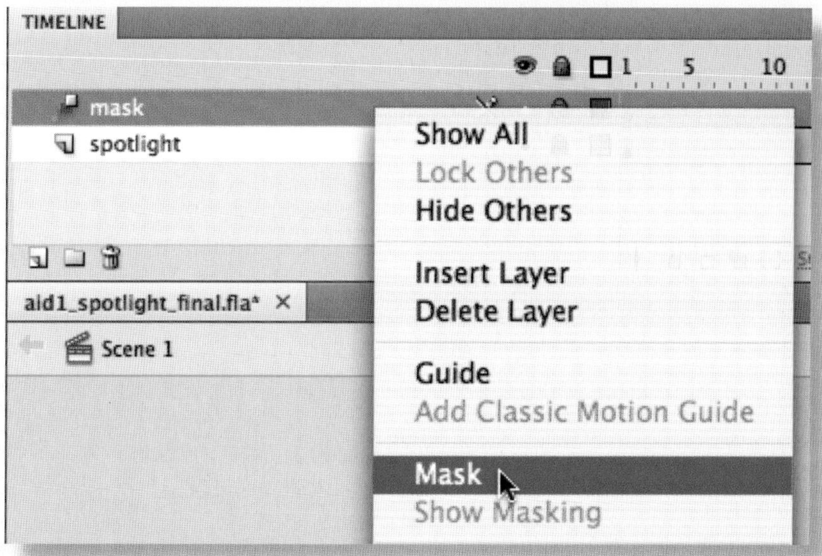

figure A–7 Turn on the mask effect.

and from the submenu choose Mask. See Figure A–7. Or, alternatively double-click on the tweening icon of the mask layer (to the left of the mask's name) to open the layer's properties and choose Mask.

8. Note the visual change in the layer icons—the spotlight layer is now indented under the mask layer and both layers are locked. The mask is turned on in this mode and since it's off Stage, you won't see your Spotlight text just yet. See Figure A–8.

ADVENTURES IN DESIGN

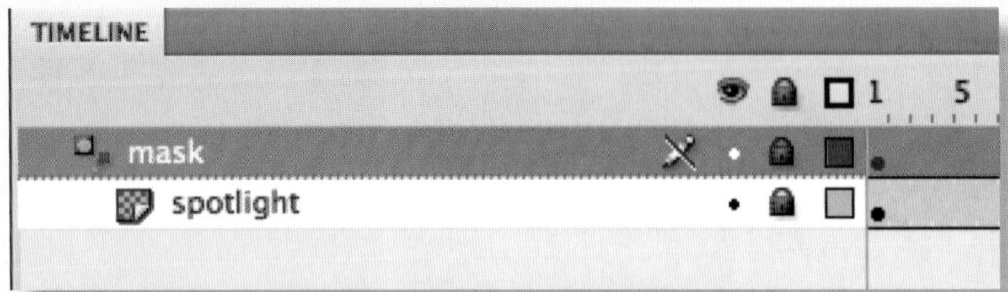

figure A–8 Note that the **spotlight** layer is now indented below the **mask** layer, indicating that it is the object to be masked. Both layers are also locked.

figure A–9 The mask effect working.

9. Play the animation—the circle on the mask layer is now a transparent window through which the word spotlight is revealed through as it animates across the Stage. See Figure A–9. Way cool, I think!

> **Note:** To edit the mask (make it bigger or smaller, for example) or the word spotlight (change its color, for example) you must unlock the layers. To apply the mask again, relock both layers.

10. Save your file.

Adding an Effect

1. Let's play with this mask a bit . . . click on the lock icon of the mask layer to unlock it.
2. Create a new layer above the **mask** layer and call it **light**.
3. Let's create a copy of the mask layer and its animation on to the **light** layer—to do this, click anywhere between frames 1–50 of the **mask** layer (the blue, tweened frames) to select it. Hold down Alt/Option on the keyboard and click and drag up to the **light** layer to place a copy of the **mask** layer animation to the **light** layer. See Figure A–10. This can be a bit tricky, so if you make a mistake copying choose Edit > Undo and try it again.
4. Remove the mask option from the light layer—Ctrl-click (Mac) or right-click (Windows) to the right of the **light** layer title and from the submenu choose Mask to toggle it off.

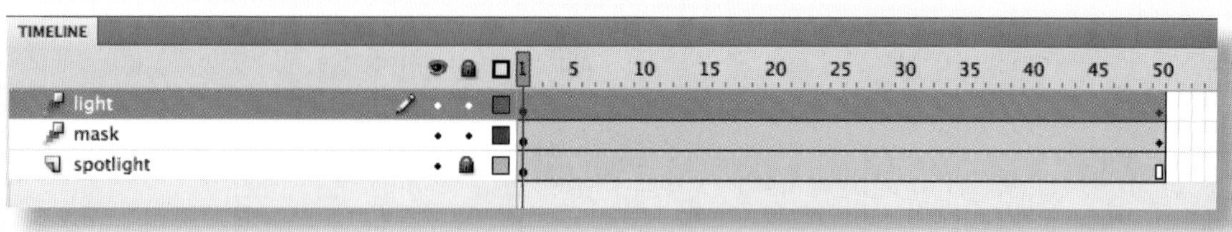

figure A–10 Create a copy of the mask animation to the **light** layer.

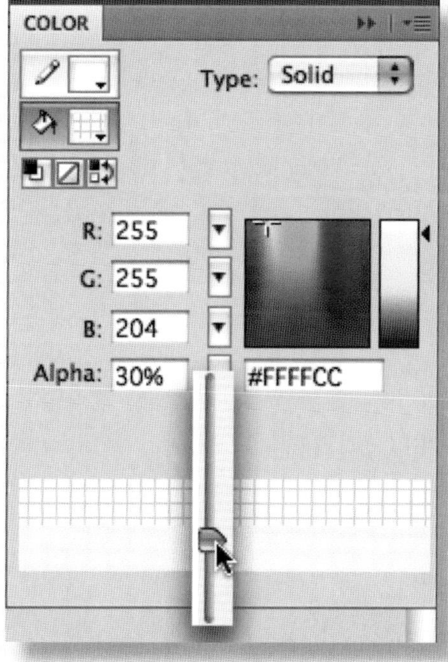

figure A–11 Change the color and add transparency to the mask movie clip.

figure A–12 Example of the final masking effect.

5. Lock the **mask** layer.
6. Double-click the circle shape on the Stage to enter its editing mode. Expand the Color panel (or choose Window > Color). Change the fill color of the shape to a light yellow and set the alpha to 30%. See Figure A–11.
7. Exit out of the symbol's editing mode (go back to Scene 1).
8. Be sure both the mask and spotlight layers are locked and that the **mask** layer is still set to mask the spotlight text (the **spotlight** layer is indented below it).
9. Play the animation. See Figure A–12. For an example see **aid_examples/spotlight/aid1_spotlight_final.fla** on the back of the book CD.
10. Save your file. That's it for this adventure!

FLASH EXPOSURE an overview of Flash
introduction
Adobe's Flash is the leading software for web-based animation,interactivity and design. With Flash you can create Web sites and presentations with vector and bitmap images, animation, sound, video and interactivity at a fraction of the file size of traditional HTML sites. This is due to the Flash vector-based format, creating compact movies that minimize network bandwidth requirements.
Each day on the World Wide Web, more and more sites are supporting the Flash format (SWF). More users are downloading the free Flash Player from Adobe to view these sites and experiencing a more exciting and interactive experience.
In this presentation, 4 distinct parts of the Flash program will be introduced:
drawing - animation - interactivity - output

6

| introduction to interactivity |

INTRODUCTION TO INTERACTIVITY

charting your course

Interactivity in Flash is created using ActionScript, a coding language based on Object Oriented Programming (OOP). This chapter offers a clear overview of the basic constructs of OOP and ActionScript, including the ActionScript panel, syntax, and simple interactive events. Also, you'll further explore interactivity and basic ActionScripting by constructing and outputting an animated movie and multi-scene presentation; all in all enlightening your continued comprehension of the power of Flash.

goals

In this chapter you will:

- **Master the fundamentals of Object Oriented Programming (OOP)**
- **Get familiar with ActionScript—its structure and syntax**
- **Create button and frame actions**
- **Add interactivity to an animated movie**
- **Construct a click-through Flash presentation using scenes**

AN OVERVIEW OF OBJECT ORIENTED PROGRAMMING

I confess I was hesitant, being a designer-type, to attempt to introduce the fundamentals of a programming (or scripting) language in this book. But it's an important concept to be aware of; a huge step toward comprehending all that Flash can offer. And, it really is not so scary.

Programming (or scripting) is the readable text, or code that is created by a programmer or developer. This code is a set of written instructions that is carried out by a computer or software application. There are many kinds of programming languages, and just like learning a foreign language, such as Russian, Spanish, or Japanese, it takes time to learn their syntax, grammar, and structure. In the next sections of this chapter, you will learn a bit of one programming language—ActionScript, the code that executes interactivity in Flash, such as the ability to click on a button and go to another page, control a sound, talk to a back-end database, or play a Flash video game.

Before we get into writing ActionScript, however, let's take a broader look at the organizational structure in which ActionScript derives from—Object Oriented Programming (OOP). OOP is said to be a more intuitive way to look at programming, because its structure can be associated with something we already understand—the function of real world objects that have characteristics and behaviors that we are familiar with. For example, consider the object of a cat; there are many kinds of cats, but in general they all have some basic characteristics and behaviors—they purr, have fur and whiskers, like to hunt, like to sleep, and have a wicked independent streak. In OOP when you group like-minded objects together, i.e., cats, they are called a "class." Each object derived from the class has similar characteristics and behaviors defined by the class. An individual object within a class—Simba, the lion cat, Garfield, the cartoon cat, Mina, my cat, for example, are in OOP terms "instances" of the class. Instances, you say? Haven't I heard this term before? Yes, when you learned about symbols in Chapter 4. The connection will make sense soon . . . hang with me. An instance object in OOP becomes the container in which events or actions are carried out upon it based on the predefined characteristics and behaviors of its class. These actions are in the form of messages and methods—scripts (instructions) that call out and do certain things to or with the object. These messages and methods are written in a certain code. For example, to my cat Mina, the message is from me in the code of English, "Get off the counter!" The method, the action, comes intuitively from the innate characteristics of the cat—it jumps off the counter and gives me a sour look, or the method could come from me—a push that causes the cat to jump off the counter and gives me a sour look and a hiss.

Before we get into a more abstract example of this OOP thing, study the diagram in Figure 6–1, which visually connects OOP terminology and structure with a real world example—cats!

OK, let's bring in another example of OOP structure as it relates to an object we are familiar with in Flash—an instance of a Movie Clip. A movie clip's characteristics and behaviors—its class—is predefined in the Flash authoring program. One characteristic we already know is that a movie clip can support nested timelines; we can have animations within animations (like

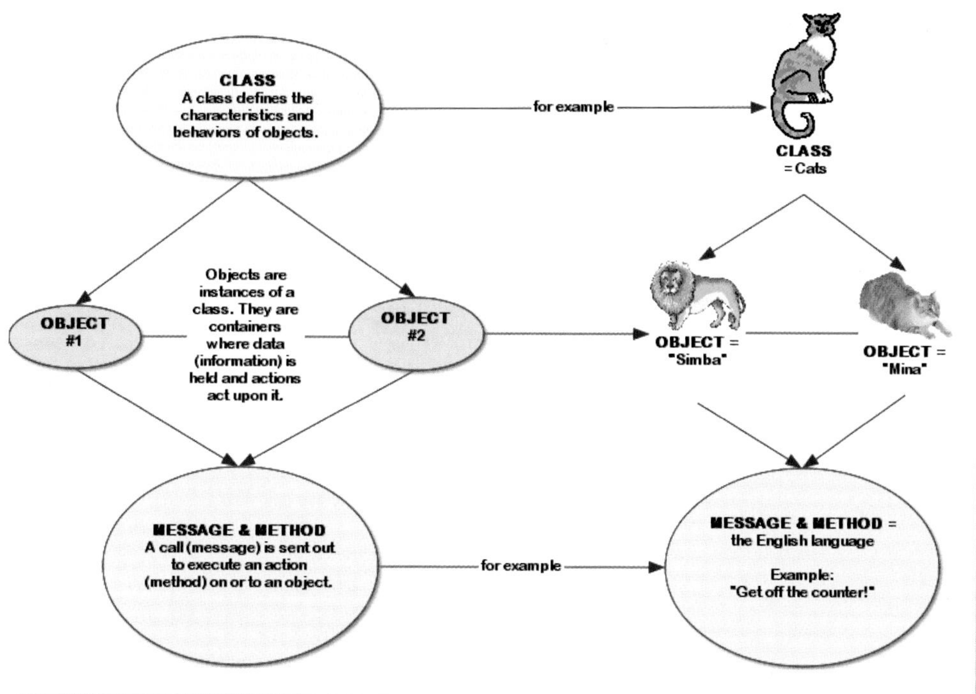

figure 6–1

A simplified explanation of Object Oriented Programming (OOP) represented by an example we know—Cats.

our moth flying and flapping its wings), and furthermore those animations can be controlled via ActionScript. Through ActionScript a movie clip can receive certain messages and execute certain methods. When you created tweens and altered colors of movie clips (their properties) in the last module you were actually creating ActionScripts—you just didn't know it because the language was being written behind the scenes. This is a fine way for doing some things in Flash, but not all the things possible. Eventually, you have to pull the curtain away and decipher the mystery.

View Figure 6–2 as a reference and note the connection of OOP terminology and structure with a familiar Flash-based object—an example movie clip called **myStar**. The class is **myStar** (a symbol). Object instances of **myStar** are named **myStar_shine** and **myStar_sparky**. **MyStar_shine** and **myStar_sparky** can have messages and methods applied to them via the language of ActionScript. We will do an example of this in the upcoming lesson.

Without the risk of getting further out of the realm of what we can cover in this book, there is one more point I want to make. Any interactivity in Flash is created through objects, but not necessarily objects that we can see. Remember an object is really just a container in which things can happen—the container is an instance of a class or sometimes referred to as a data type. Data types (classes) can be something visible like a movie clip, or something more abstract, like an Array, a String, or a Boolean. If you are feeling ambitious you can explore more about the data types supported by Flash in the Flash Help files. Choose Flash > Flash Help and search for "data types." In this book we stick with data types we can see—movie clips, buttons, and text fields.

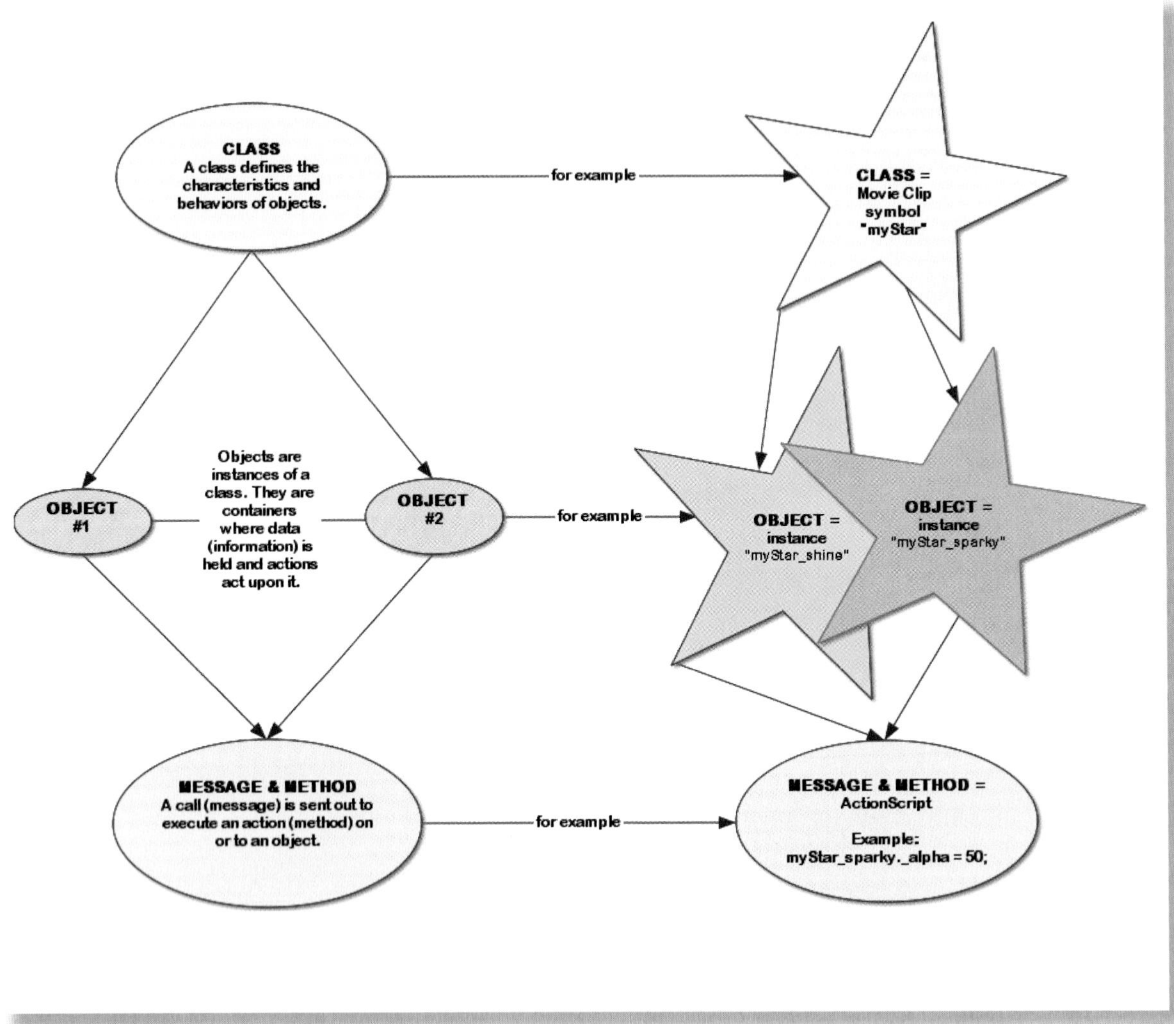

figure 6–2

Object Oriented Programming explained by an example in Flash—movie clips.

ACTIONSCRIPTING BASICS

As we learned in the last section, ActionScript is an Object Oriented Programming language used to run Flash-based applications. The basis of the language is ECMAScript, an international standard derived from JavaScript that is widely used on the Web. See ECMAScript's main Web site at http://www.ecmascript.org/ or Wikipedia at http://en.wikipedia.org/wiki/ECMAScript for more information. When you make action scripts you're "action scripting." For designers the thought of action scripting often evokes a queasy feeling, but hopefully those feelings will subside by the end of this chapter.

In the years since I have been using and teaching Flash, the ActionScripting language has become more sophisticated and more compatible with ECMAScripting standards. The result of this has made the language less intuitive for designers and more in line with what programmers want and need to make their coding more streamlined and flexible. That being said, however, if there is any program that provides a somewhat comfortable foray for designers to dabble in left-brain activity (i.e., coding), Flash is it.

ActionScript 2.0 versus ActionScript 3.0

ActionScript 2.0 and ActionScript 3.0 are the two current scripting languages supported by Adobe Flash CS4 and the latest version of the Flash Player (the engine that runs Flash movies within the Web environment, or as independent presentations). Each new version of ActionScript aims to be more compliant with ECMAScript. Here are a few features of ActionScript 3.0 that are making hard-core programmers much happier and willing to work in ActionScript:

- More compatible with ECMAScript, a common scripting language for Web applications.
- Faster computation and execution of code.
- More flexibility with class associations (how classes communicate and work together).
- The ability to hide or encapsulate information.

As you have already discovered when creating new files in Flash you have the option to set the file to be compatible with ActionScript 2.0 or ActionScript 3.0. I have made you save everything as ActionScript 2.0, because that's the form of ActionScript we are going to stick with throughout this book. As a novice to Flash, ActionScript 2.0 syntax and usage is easier to grasp until you get enough understanding under your belt to venture into ActionScript 3.0.

> **Note: If you are not sure if you will be using ActionScript 2.0 or ActionScript 3.0 in your movie, you can change the script version later in the movie making process. Choose File > Publish Settings and under the Flash tab adjust the script version option. See Figure 6–3. In the upcoming lesson, you will learn you can do this in the Actions panel as well.**

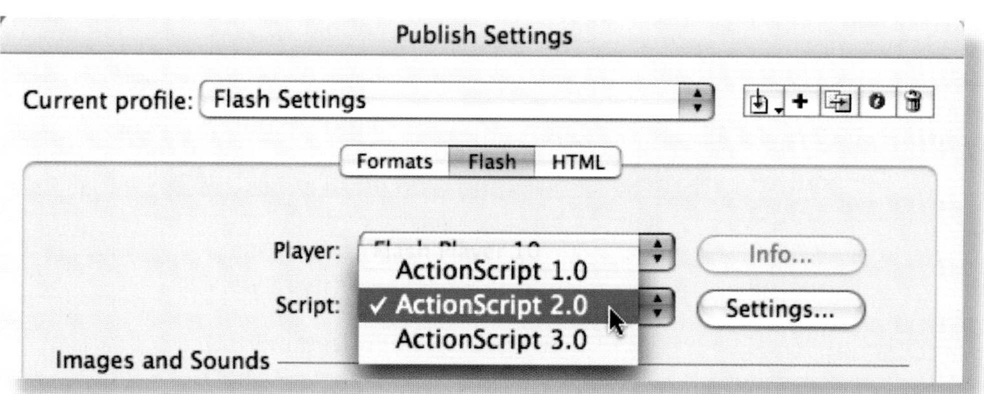

figure 6–3

Choose the ActionScript 2.0 option when working with ActionScript throughout this book.

About Behaviors and Components

Flash offers some automated ActionScripts in the form of Behaviors and Components (Window > Behaviors, and Window > Components). Behaviors are prewritten ActionScripts that you can add interactivity to an object, such as on a button to open a Web page link or mute an audio file. Behaviors are only compatible with 2.0 ActionScript. Components are scripted building blocks to streamline the functionality of an interactive application. From the help files, "components are designed to allow developers to reuse and share code, and to encapsulate complex functionality that designers can use and customize without using ActionScript." Behaviors and Components are designed for those who don't know how or don't want to write code, and this can be a positive thing! However, with just using Behaviors and Components you miss out on learning how to write your own code, and you're restricted to using only the automated scripts Flash provides for you. See Figure 6–4. As you work through some of the lessons in this book I will point out when using a Behavior or Component might be more efficient for you than hand-coding.

figure 6–4

Set a basic action for a movie clip in the Behaviors panel.

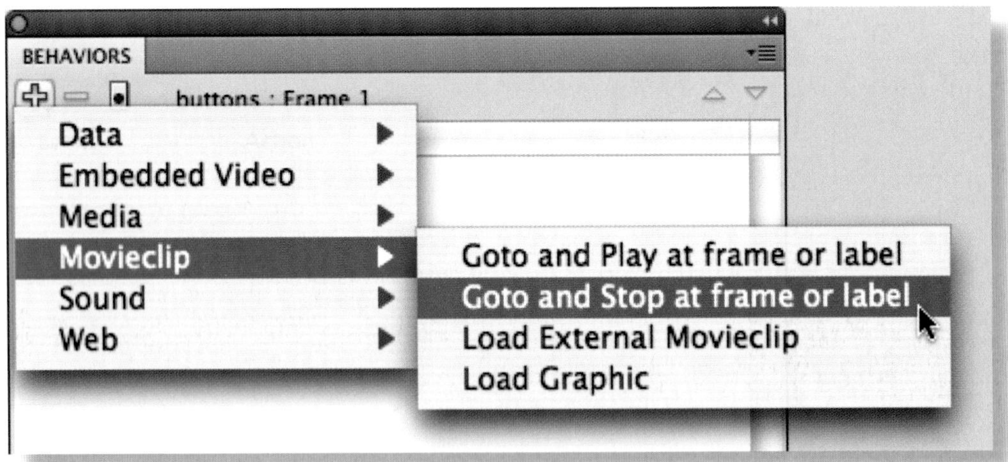

ActionScript Syntax

Chaos is not an option in ActionScripting. Every word and punctuation mark of a script must be written in proper order or it will not work. Figure 6–5 takes a closer look at the anatomy of an ActionScript, and its necessary syntax. Study it closely. See Figure 6–5.

See also the explanations of the syntax below:

- **Curly Brackets (Braces) {}:** Denotes logical blocks of code that function as a single unit.
- **Parenthesis ():** Encloses a property value, like the amount of alpha (transparency) on a movie clip, or the frame number or label of a Timeline event.
- **Semicolon ;:** Identifies where one method (action) begins and another ends.
- **Dot .:** Defines the target (path or location) of an object.

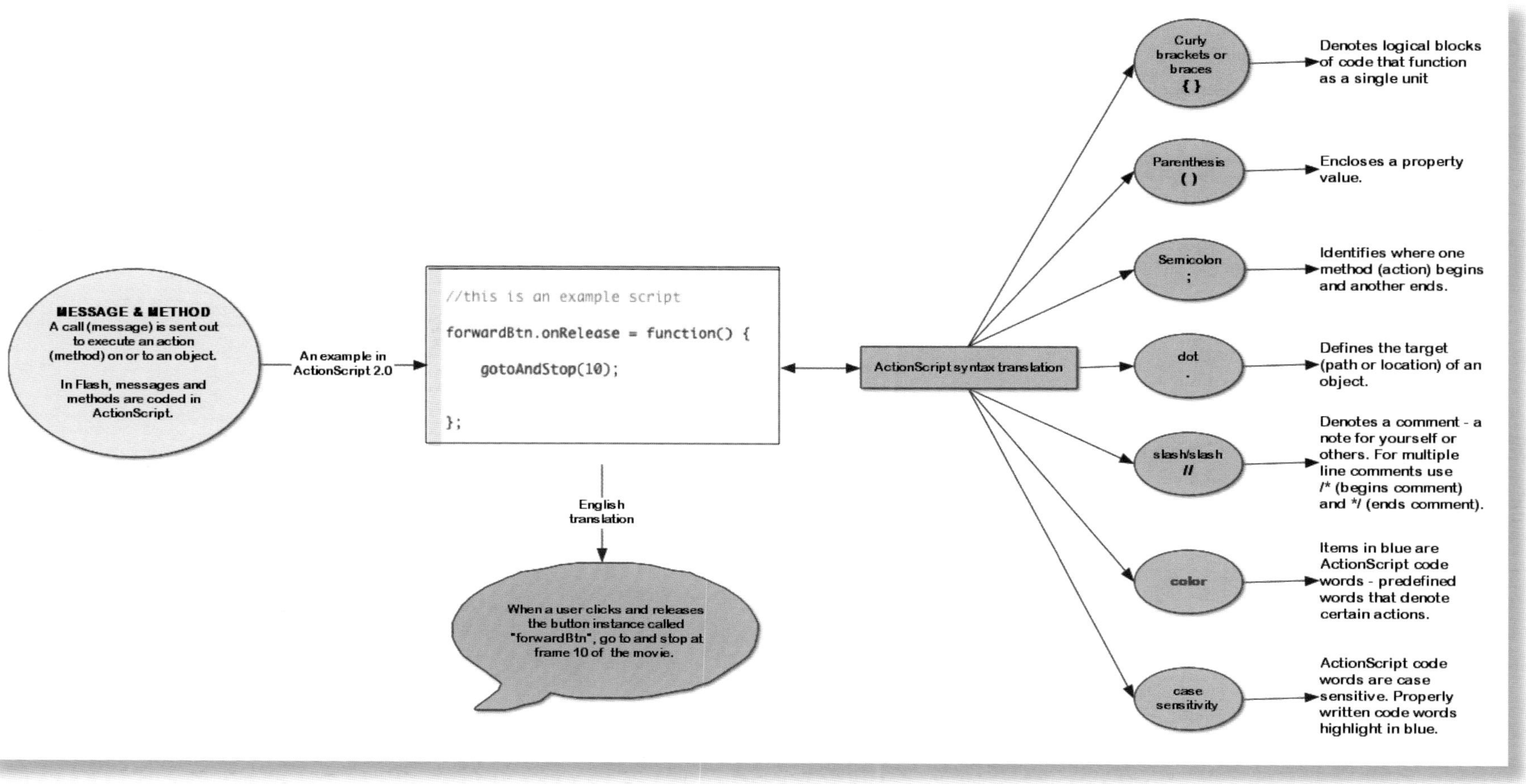

figure 6–5

The anatomy of an ActionScript.

- **Slash/Slash //:** Denotes a comment—a note for yourself or others within a script. For multiple line comments use /* (begins comment) and */ (ends comment).
- **Color:** Items in blue are reserved ActionScript code words—predefined words that denote certain actions.
- **Case Sensitivity:** ActionScript code words and instance names are case sensitive. Properly written code words highlight in blue.

Introduction to the Actions Panel

In Flash, actions are created in the Actions panel. To open the Actions panel choose Window > Actions (Alt/Option F9) in the Flash program. At first introduction the Actions panel can be an overwhelming experience; there is so much that you can do in this part of the program. There are many features, options, commands, and ActionScript components in this window—we only cover a few, which are highlighted in Figure 6–6 and the descriptions below.

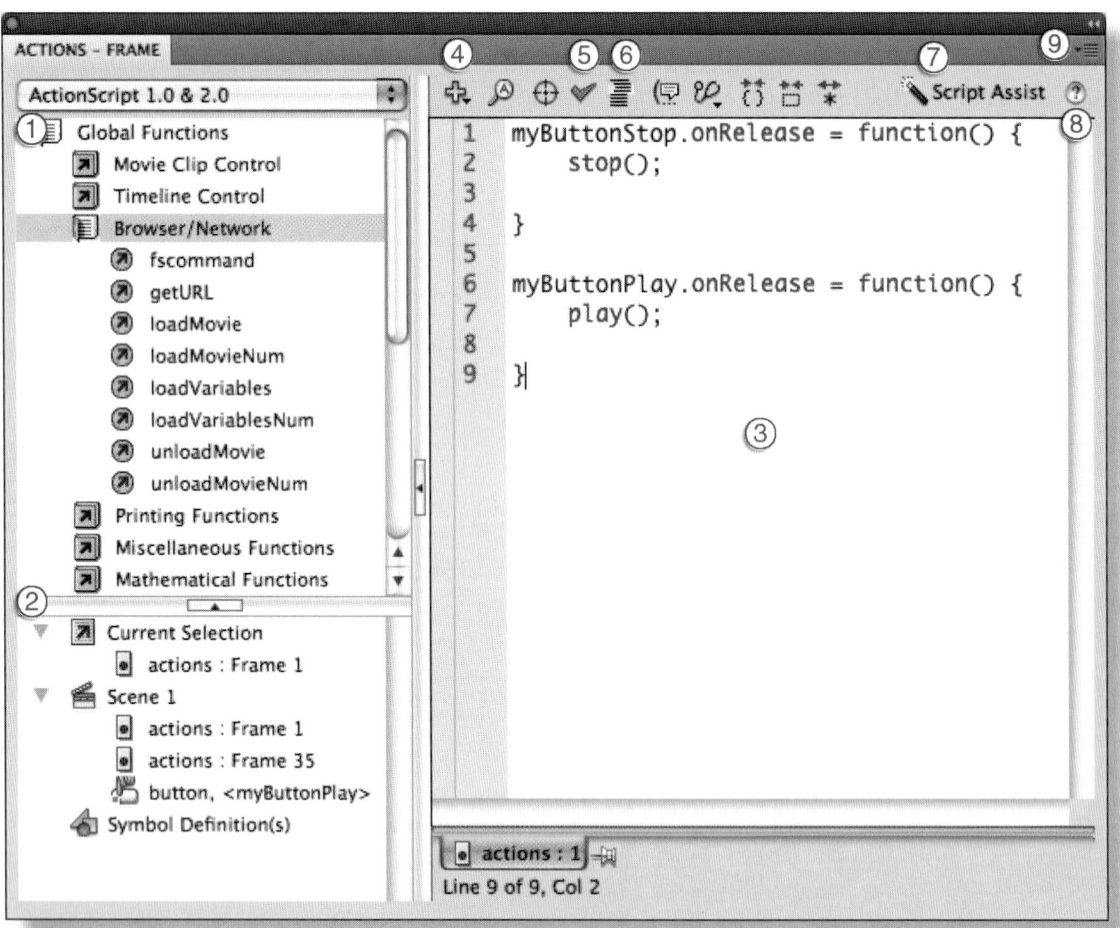

figure 6–6

Stop and play actions on a button in the Actions panel.

The Actions panel is divided into three windows:

1. The top, left window is the **Actions toolbox** and contains the keywords for constructing actions. They are in different categories depending on what they do. You click on the book icon of each category to open its submenus.

2. The bottom left window is the **Movie Explorer**, where you can see and select different scenes, frames, actions, and symbols in your particular movie.

3. On the right hand side of the window is the **script pane**, where actions are written. The blue tab located at the bottom of the pane indicates the item (frame, instance name, etc.) in which the action is being applied.

In the panel, there are a couple important commands to assist you in your learning of ActionScript:

4. **Add a new item to a script**—select from this drop down menu ActionScript items to add to your script (they are duplicates of what is also available in the Actions toolbox).

5. **Check syntax**—click this option to have Flash verify if you entered a script correctly or incorrectly. If there are errors in the message, they will be listed in the Compiler Errors panel. See Figure 6–7.

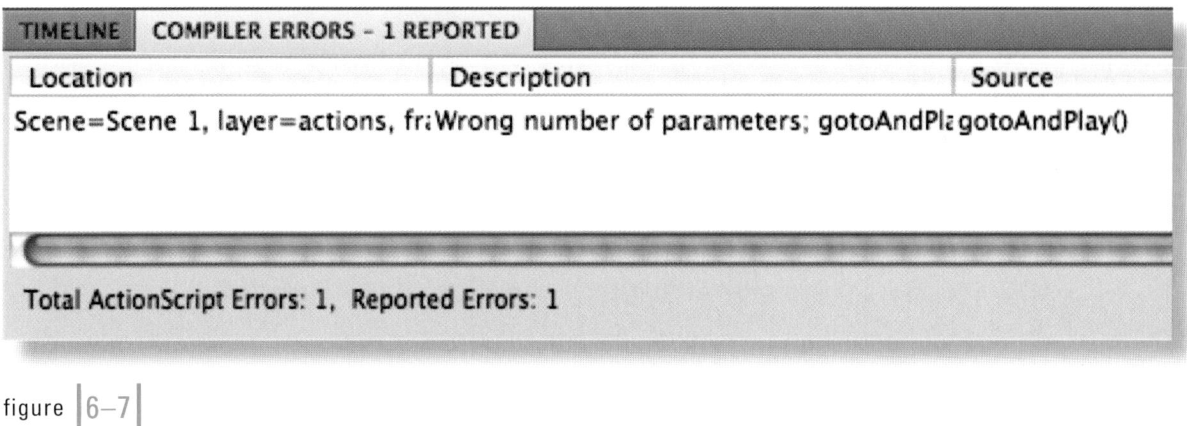

figure |6–7|

ActionScript error messages can be found in the Compiler Errors panel.

6. **Auto format**—formats your script in its proper line-by-line order, as long as your script has no errors.

7. **Script Assist**—provides options for ActionScript 2.0 users what needs to be included in a selected line of a script for it to work properly. See Figure 6–8.

8. **Help**—opens a browser and sends you to the help files specific to ActionScript—lots of good info here!

9. **Actions panel submenu**—choose from the submenu the same commands found along the top of the panel, as well as other options and preferences. For example, I set my script pane to list numbers along the side of the script,

figure 6–8

Use Script Assist to aid you in the coding of ActionScript 2.0.

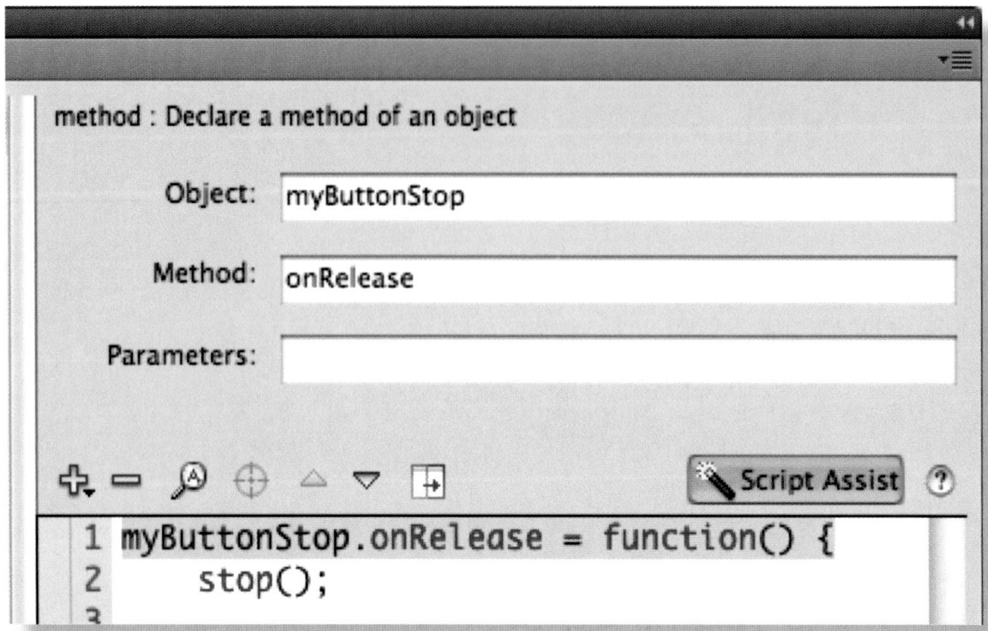

so I can easily identify areas within the script (especially if it gets really complex!). To do this, from the submenu choose the Line Numbers option (if there is a check by it already, then the option is already turned on).

You can enter actions in the Actions panel in several ways:

- Clicking on the folders and then commands in the Actions toolbox.
- Selecting commands under the "+" (Add a new item to a script) option.
- Typing the script directly in the pane (hand-coding).

> **Note:** If you curiously click through the Action panels toolbox you might find yourself overwhelmed by a bunch of unfamiliar terminology—operators, statements, arguments, directives, deprecated . . . Remember ActionScript is like a foreign language, and just as one has to study and practice to learn the words and grammatical structure of Spanish, French, Swahili, whatever . . . it is also so for ActionScript. This level of learning is beyond the scope of an introductory book. However, there are lots of resources available for further study—start with the Flash Help files.

Lesson 1: Stop and Play an Animated Movie

This lesson shows you how to control the looping of a movie and create two very useful actions—stop and play—on a movie clip instance.

Creating a Stop Action on a Frame

1. Open Flash. Choose File > Open and browse for **chap6L1.fla** in the **chap06_lessons** folder.
2. Be sure the Classic workspace is chosen.

3. Choose Control > Test Movie and play the animation. Notice the airplane keeps looping on its path over and over. By default Flash makes all animations loop in the SWF movie. You may not want this option, and prefer to have an animation stop after one pass across the screen. To do this, you must create a stop action.

4. Create a new layer, name it **actions** and place it at the top of the layers list. See Figure 6–9.

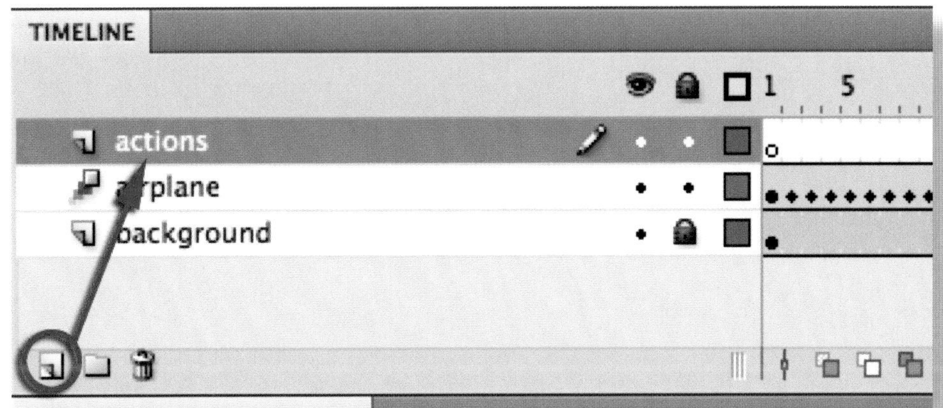

figure 6–9

Create an actions layer for all your actions.

> **Note:** Actions are often put on frames in the Timeline—think of frames as messengers, they hold messages, like "stop whatever is on the stage when a user clicks you" for objects on the Stage (such as a movie clip or button) until they are ready to be executed. It's best practice to make a separate layer for your actions. It's also a good idea to put the actions layer at the top of the layer list, so it, and all the actions that might be on its frames, can be found easily. You should also always lock your actions layer so you don't place content on the layer inadvertently.

5. Select frame 35 of the **actions** layer (the last frame of the airplane animation) and insert a keyframe (F6).

> **Note:** All frame actions must be placed on a keyframe, just like an action you record when doing an animation.

6. While keyframe 35 on the **actions** layer is highlighted, choose Window > Actions to open the Actions panel. If you need to expand the Actions panel pull on the lower right corner of the window to see all its parts—it's quite a big window!

7. Make sure the file is set to ActionScript 1.0 & 2.0. See Figure 6–10.

> **Note:** You might have noticed when selecting the ActionScript version the options to save your file to be compatible with Flash Lite ActionScript. Adobe's Flash Lite is a runtime engine for mobile and consumer electronic devices. Flash files can be created that are compatible with Flash Lite scripting language.

figure 6–10

Set the action version to ActionScript 1.0 & 2.0 in the Actions panel.

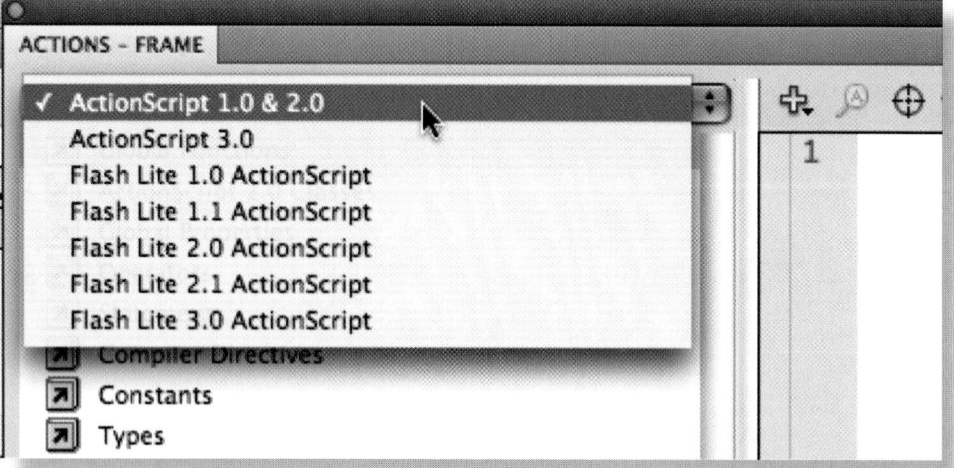

8. In the Actions toolbox click the Global Functions book icon, then the Timeline Control book icon to open them.

9. In the Timeline Control list double-click on the **stop** action to place it in the blank script pane. You can also click and drag the action to the script pane. See Figure 6–11.

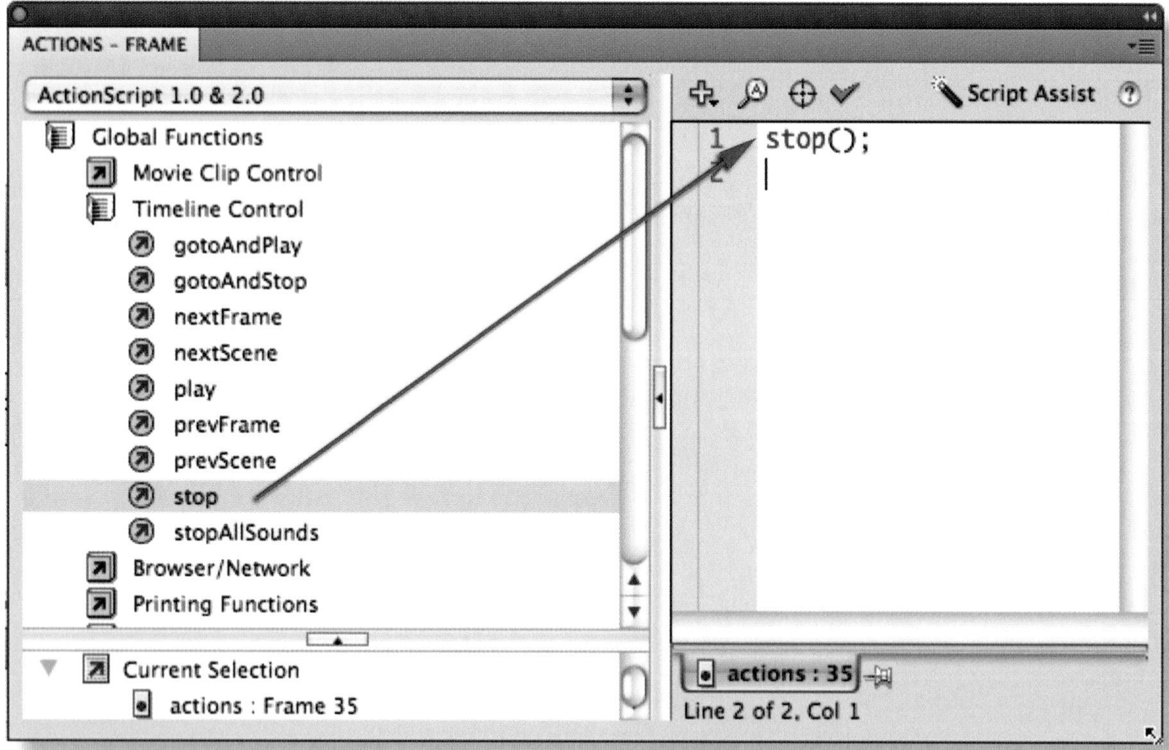

figure 6–11

Enter a stop action from the Actions toolbox into the script pane.

Note: You can also get to the stop action by choosing the Add (+) button at the top of the Actions panel. See Figure 6–12. To delete an action, select the part of the script you want to remove and press Delete on the keyboard.

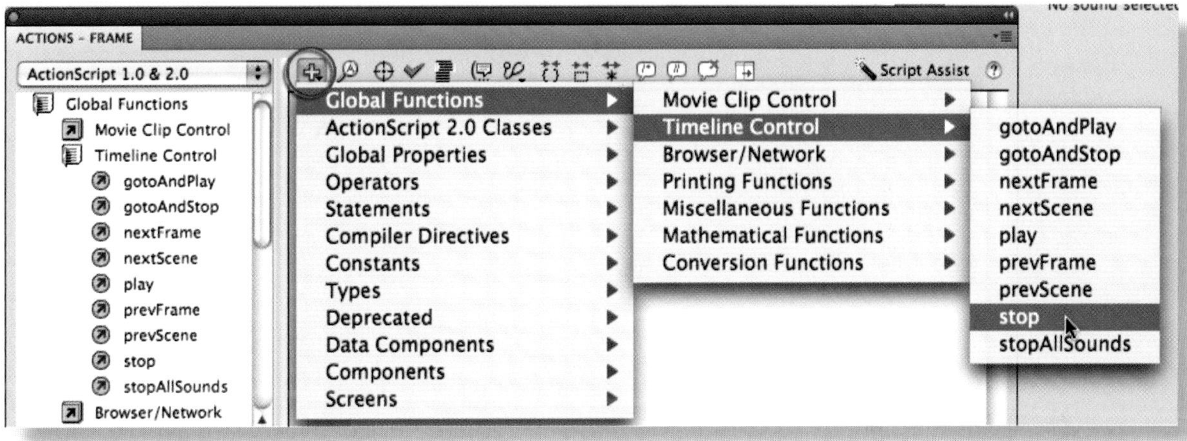

figure 6–12

Enter a stop action from the drop down menu under the "plus" icon.

10. Close the Actions panel. Note on frame 35 of the **actions** layer there is a little "a" in the selected keyframe; See Figure 6–13.

Note: If you don't see the little "a" in the frame, the action was not applied to the frame. Select the frame, open the Actions panel again and reset the stop script.

11. Choose Control > Test Movie. The airplane stops at frame 35. No more looping!

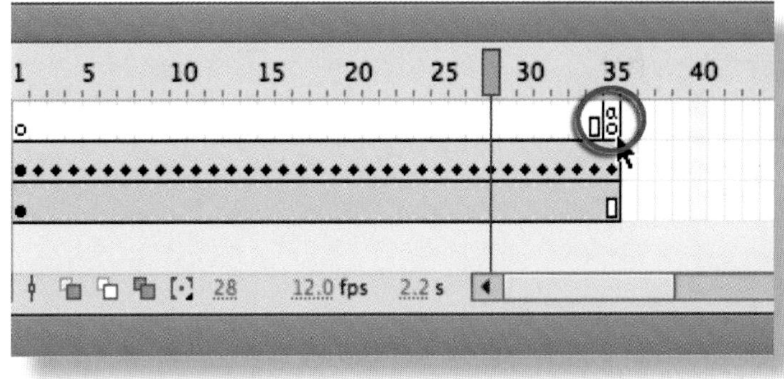

figure 6–13

An action defined on the Timeline.

Creating Stop and Play Buttons

1. Make a new layer and call it **buttons**. Place it below the **actions** layer.

2. Draw a red (with no stroke) dime sized circle shape in the lower right corner of the movie.

3. Select the button graphic and convert it to a symbol (F8). Name it **myButton** and choose the Button type. Set the registration point in the center. See Figure 6–14.

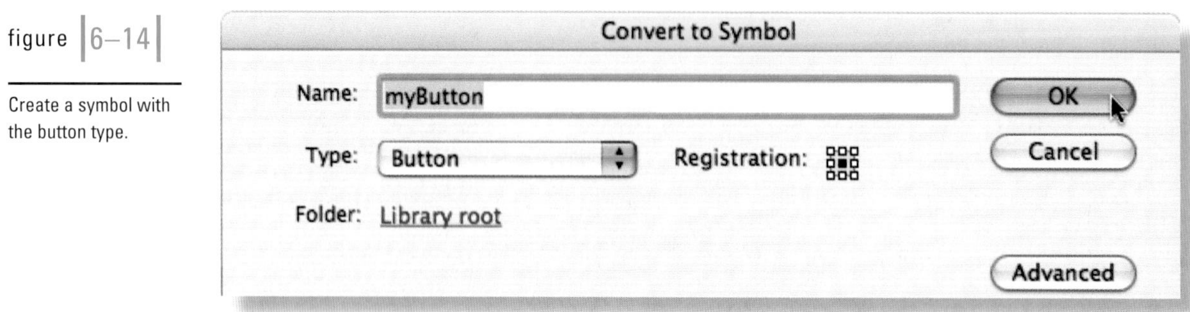

figure 6–14

Create a symbol with the button type.

4. Before moving on, let's examine the insides of this button. Double-click on the red button instance on the Stage to enter editing mode. In the Timeline you will notice right away what makes this a button—it has four preset frames—Up, Over, Down, and Hit. See Figure 6–15.

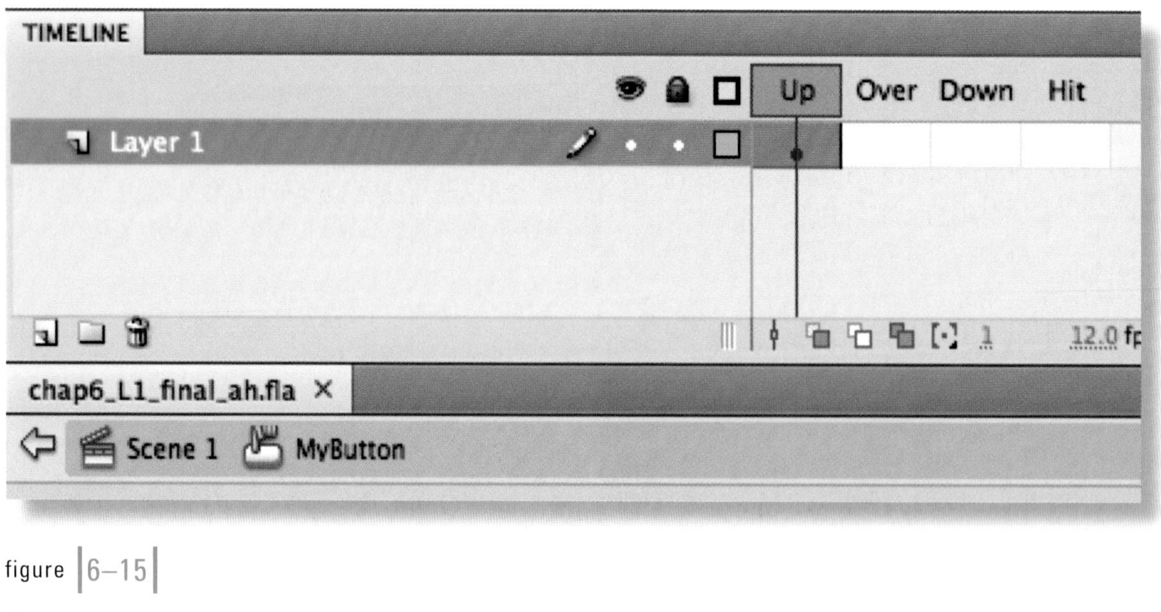

figure 6–15

The four states of a button—Up, Over, Down, and Hit.

5. Click on the Over keyframe and choose F6 on the keyboard to create a keyframe. Do the same for Down and Hit.

6. Click on the Over keyframe and change the color of the button selected on the Stage. Make it any color you want.

7. Click on the Down keyframe and change its color as well.

8. Choose Control > Test Movie. Rollover and click down on the button—it changes colors! You've just created a rollover button.

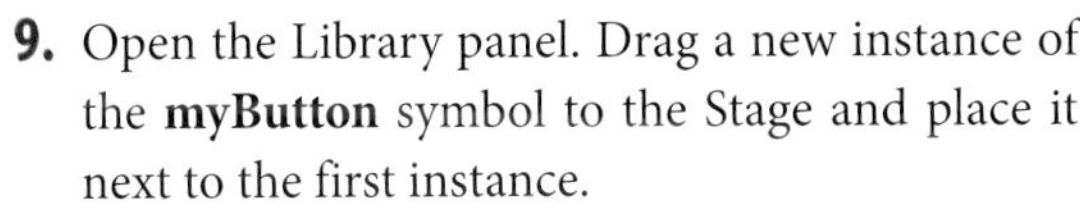

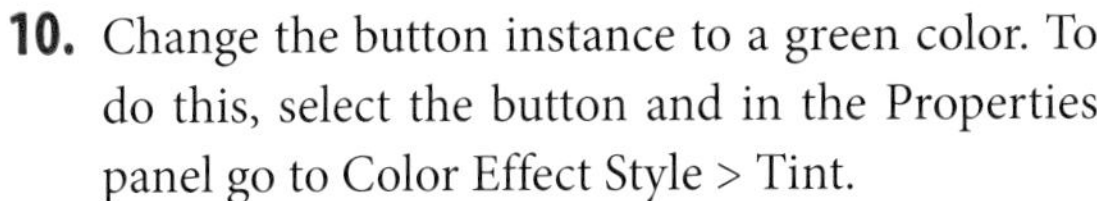

Note: **What about the Hit keyframe? The Hit state defines the area that responds to a user's mouse. This area is invisible in the SWF file. Any filled area of an object in the Hit area is the clickable area of the button. See Exploring on Your Own at the end of this chapter to learn more about and play with the Hit state.**

9. Open the Library panel. Drag a new instance of the **myButton** symbol to the Stage and place it next to the first instance.

10. Change the button instance to a green color. To do this, select the button and in the Properties panel go to Color Effect Style > Tint.

11. Create a new layer and call it **button_text**. Choose the Text tool in the Tools panel and over the red button type the word STOP. Over the green button type the word GO. Lock the layer. See Figure 6–16.

12. From the menu bar, choose Control > Enable Simple Buttons. With your cursor hover over the stop and go buttons. A little hand shows up indicating you've created a button symbol. See Figure 6–17.

13. Choose Control > Enable Simple Buttons again to toggle the command off.

Note: **This command must be off to do modifications to the button.**

14. Let's name the buttons so messages can be sent to them through ActionScript in the next section. Select the Stop button.

15. In the Properties panel, type in **myBtnStop** in the instance name field. See Figure 6–18.

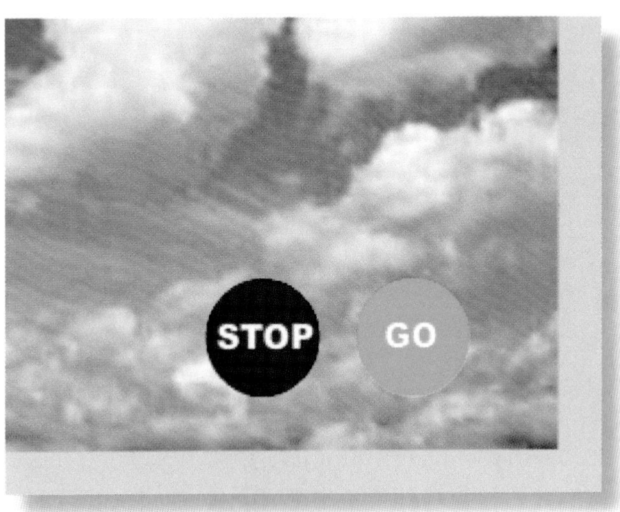

figure 6–16

Create text over each of the buttons.

figure 6–17

Enable the button—when rolled-over a hand icon appears indicating the button is activated.

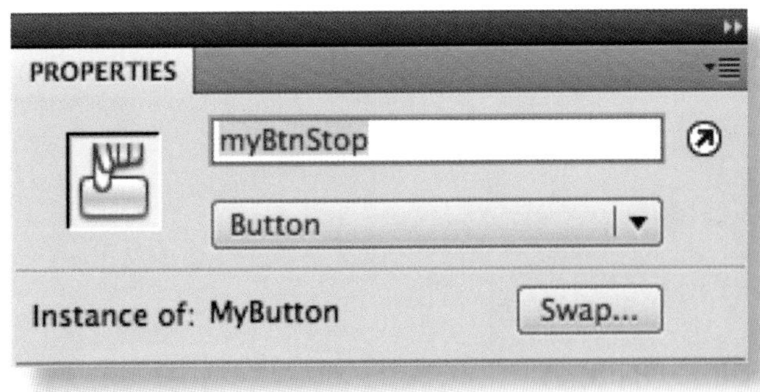

figure 6–18

Create a unique name for the button instance.

Note: You can name your instances whatever you want. Here, however, I have you name it **myBtnStop** for purposes of this lesson. The name should be short and descriptive with no spaces, no funky characters (like &%!?^, etc.), and the first letter in lowercase. Often the words "btn" or "mc" are indicated in the name identifying the class types, button or movie clip, respectively.

16. Select the Go button and in the Properties panel name it **myBtnPlay**.
17. Save your file in your lessons folder.

Adding Actions to the Buttons

1. Select the first frame of the **actions** layer. Choose Window > Actions to open the Actions panel.
2. In the Actions toolbox expand the ActionScript 2.0 Classes menu. From there, choose Movie > Button > Event Handlers, then double-click on the **onRelease** handler to place it in the script pane. See Figure 6–19.

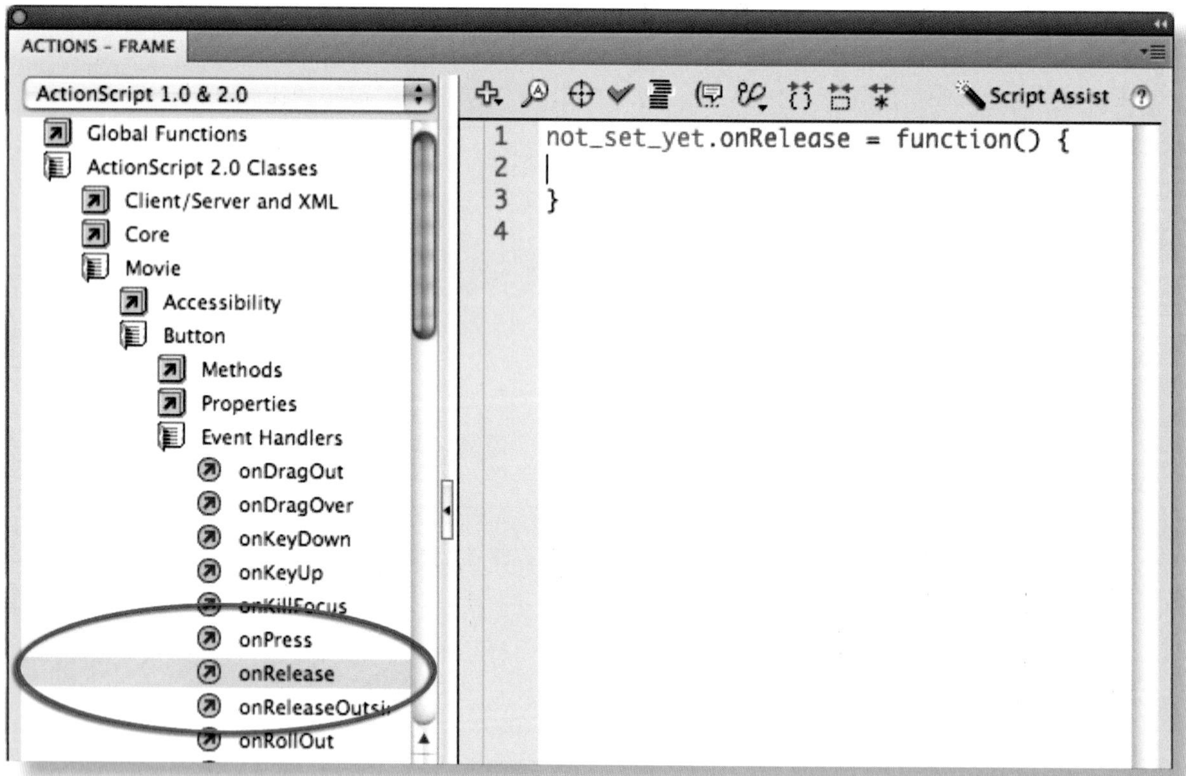

figure 6–19

Set the event handler for the script.

> **Note:** What's an event handler? An event handler is an instruction that you specify for a user-activated object (e.g., a button, the mouse, a key on the keyboard), that tells the object what to do when a specific event occurs. Buttons are activated by you and me (users) and can be done so whenever we choose. Although most button actions occur on the release of the button, other event handlers are available, for example, on press (onPress), on rollover (onRollover), and, if a short cut key is assigned, on the press of a key (onKeyDown), etc.

3. Select the red words **not_set_yet** and type in the name of the instance you want to call and execute this event—**myBtnStop** (remember you named this instance already in the previous section of this lesson). Be sure it's spelled exactly how you spelled it before or the action will not work. See Figure 6–20.

figure 6–20

Enter in the script the instance name of the object to be called by the script.

> **Note:** By the way, the words in blue are called keywords—they are predefined terms that are used by ActionScript.

4. The message is entered into the script, now let's add the action itself. Place your cursor after the first curly bracket. Scroll back up to the top of the Actions toolbox and choose Global Functions > Timeline Control and double-click on the word **stop**.

5. Choose the Auto Format option at the top of the Actions Panel to clean up the formatting of the script. See Figure 6–21.

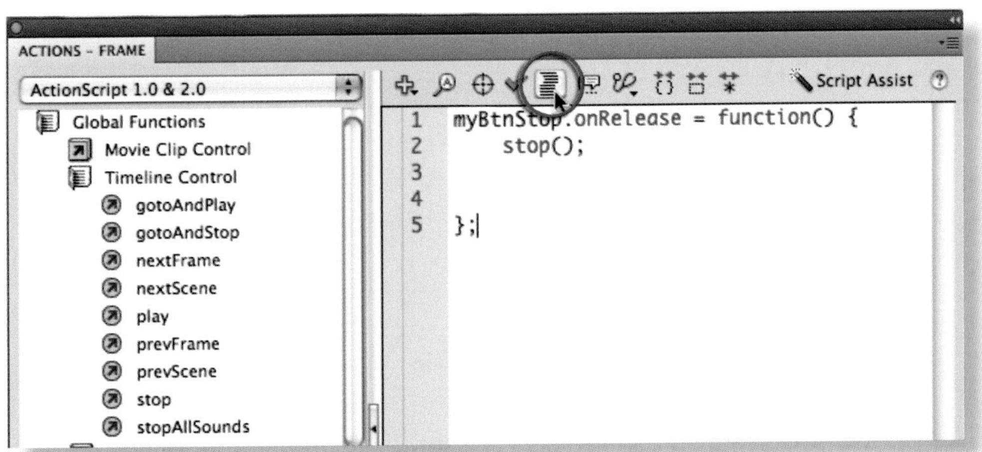

figure 6–21

Auto Format the script.

6. Check that your script looks like mine—refer to Figure 6–21 again. It should read exactly as follows:

```
myBtnStop.onRelease = function() {
        stop();
};
```

7. Let's add the action for the Go button now. Place your cursor after the semicolon at the end of the first action.

8. From the Actions toolbar, choose Classes > Movie > Button > Event Handlers, then double-click on the **onRelease** handler to place it into the script pane.

9. Select the red words **not_set_yet** and type in **myBtnPlay** (the name of the instance of your green Go button that you set in the previous section of this lesson).

10. Place the cursor after the first bracket of this action, and from the Actions toolbox choose Global Functions > Timeline Control and double-click on the word **play**.

```
myBtnStop.onRelease = function() {
    stop();


};
myBtnPlay.onRelease = function() {
    play();


};
```

figure 6–22

Check the script to be sure it is coded correctly.

11. Choose the Auto Format option at the top of the Actions panel (refer to Figure 6–21 again).

12. Your script should look like Figure 6–22 and as indicated below:

```
myBtnStop.onRelease = function() {
        stop();
};
myBtnPlay.onRelease = function() {
        play();
};
```

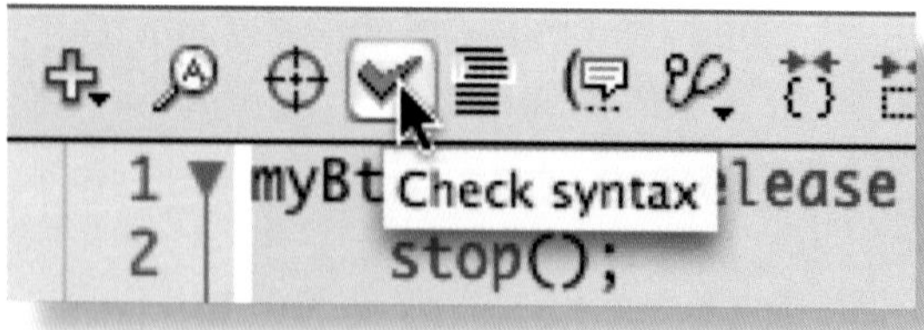

figure 6–23

Check the syntax of the script to verify that it has no errors.

13. Choose the Check Syntax option at the top of the Actions panel to have Flash verify that your script has no errors. See Figure 6–23. (If your script does have errors, read the messages in the Compiler Errors window to help you decipher what went wrong and/or carefully check the syntax of your code that all items are spelled and punctuated correctly as indicated in Figure 6–22.)

> **Note:** There are a couple of alternate ways you could have added the second action (for the Go button) in this ActionScript. You can copy the first action and paste it after the semicolon, then change the instance name and event. Or, you can place your cursor after the semicolon of the first script and hand-code (typed word for word) the new set of actions. Hand-coding will help you memorize a lot of the more common event handlers and behaviors.

14. Close the Actions panel and note that the action you just created should be indicated by a little "a" in the first frame of the **actions** layer.

> **Note:** If you don't see the little "a" it's likely the first frame of the **actions** layer was not selected (step #1) before entering the code and the code was inadvertently placed on an object. Open the Actions panel, click on the various objects on the Stage to see if the code has been assigned to an object. If so, select and delete the code, then follow the steps of this section again starting with step #1, selecting the first frame of the **actions** layer.

15. Choose Control > Test Movie and try out your Stop and Go buttons. Ah, interactivity!

> **Note:** Remember you still have the stop action at the end of the animation that you set in the first section of this lesson. If you'd like, you can remove this action to fully control the plane's movement using only the buttons. Select the last frame of the **actions** layer, go to Window > Actions, select the **stop ( );** action and press delete on the keyboard. The little "a" in the last frame should disappear. Play back the animation again and test your actions.

16. Save your file. Well done!

Lesson 2: Assembling a Presentation

Often Flash is used to create simple linear presentations or self-running movies by dividing sections of information into scenes. With ActionScript a user can click forward or back through each scene. It's similar to a PowerPoint presentation, but with options for more complex animations and interactivity within each scene. In this lesson, practice your newly found ActionScript skills by assembling a mock presentation. View the presentation beforehand and test out how it works, choose **chap06_lessons/demos/chap6L2_final.swf.**

> **Note:** Certain steps in this lesson have been abbreviated with the assumption that you have learned how to do those steps in previous lessons.

Setting up the First Scene

1. In Flash, choose File > Open. Open **chap06_lessons/chap6_L2.fla**.

2. The first scene of the presentation is created for you. Note the scene name has already been set—instead of Scene 1 (the default name), it's called **introduction**. See Figure 6–24. You will create other scenes and scene names in the next lesson section.

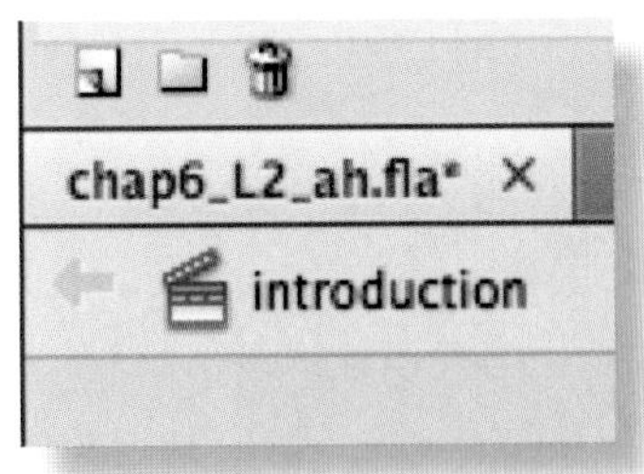

figure 6–24

The scene name.

3. Expand the Layers panel and click on each layer (or hide/unhide each) to identify and familiarize yourself with each item in the scene.

4. Select frame 25 of all the layers and click then hold or Ctrl-click (Mac), or right-click (Windows) and choose Insert Frames.

5. Create a tweened animation of the Flash Exposure title fading from completely transparent to completely opaque (adjust the Alpha from 0 to 100% over 25 frames).

6. Animate the tag line: **an overview of Flash** anyway you would like over 25 frames.

7. Create a new layer and title it **actions**. Place it at the top of the layers list.

8. Create a blank keyframe (F6) in the last frame (frame 25) of the **actions** layer.

9. Select the keyframe and choose Window > Actions.

10. In the Actions toolbox choose Global Functions > Timeline Control, and double-click on **stop** to enter it in the script pane. See Figure 6–25.

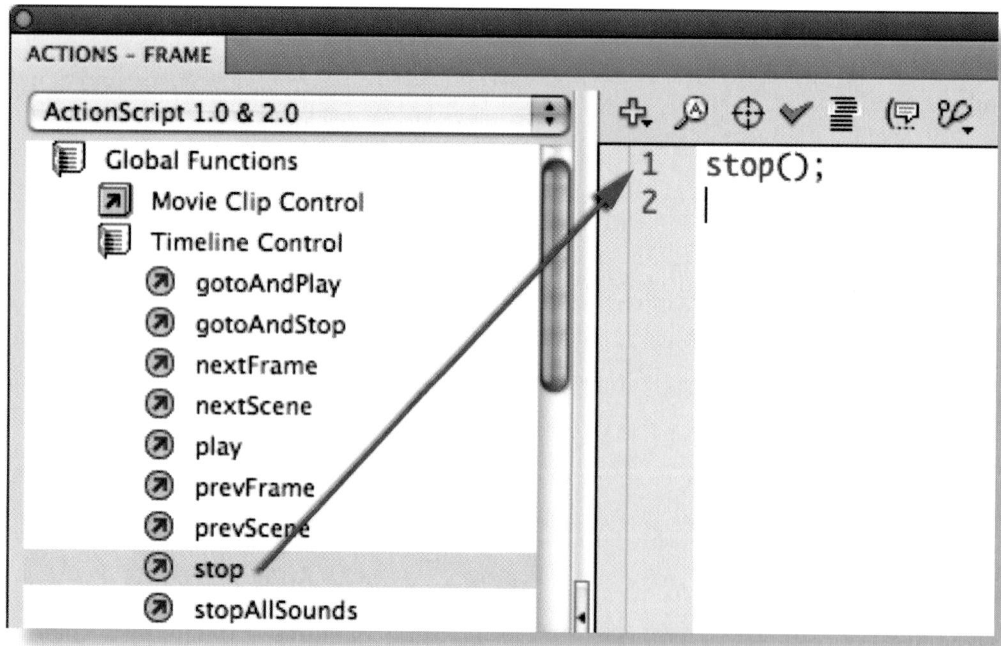

figure 6–25

Create a stop action.

11. Close the Actions panel. A little "a" should be visible on the last frame.

12. Create a new layer and name it **buttons**. Select the first frame of the **buttons** layer, and choose Window > Common Libraries > Buttons > playback flat. We'll use a predesigned button for use in this presentation. From the list, click and drag to the lower right corner of the scene the **flat grey forward** button. See Figure 6–26.

13. Close the Library. Select the button and in the Properties panel give the instance name—**forwardBtn**. See Figure 6–27.

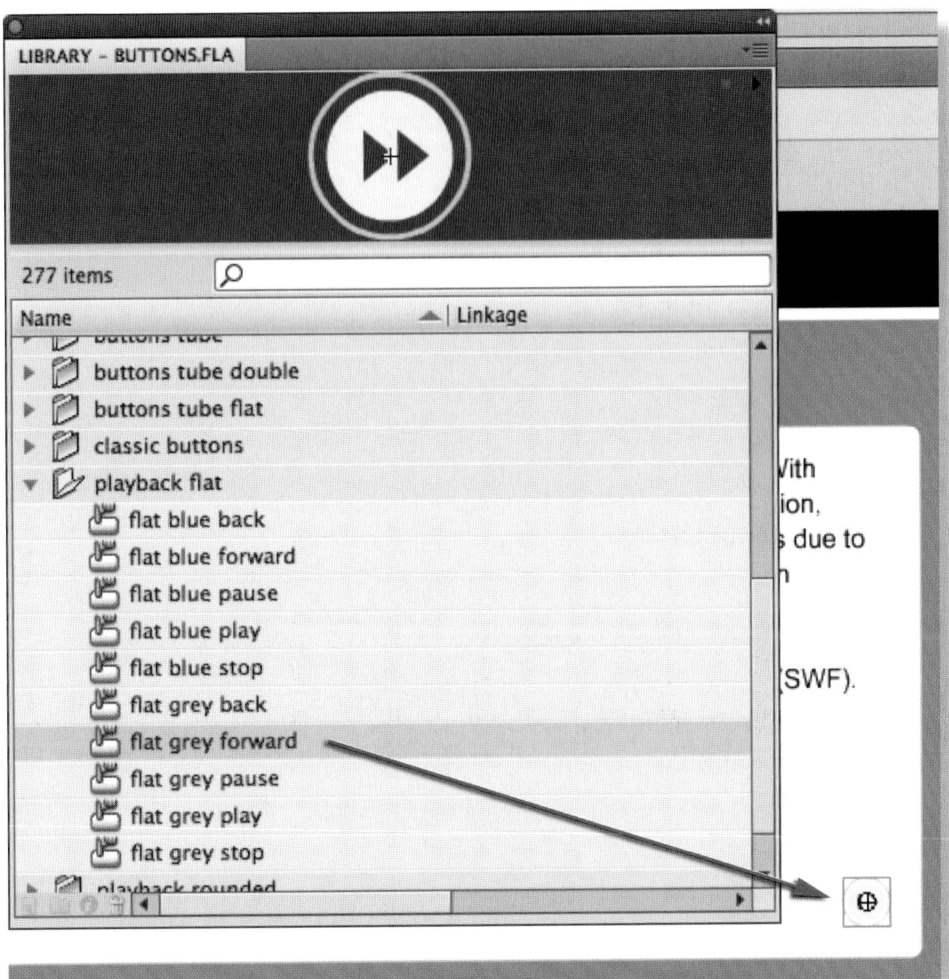

figure 6–26

Select a premade button from the Buttons Library.

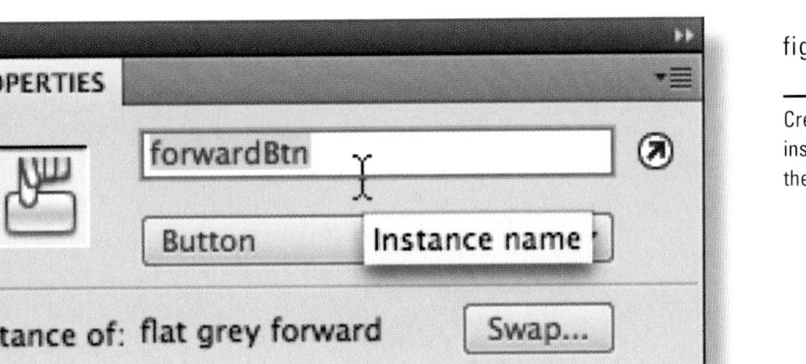

figure 6–27

Create a unique instance name for the button.

14. Select the first frame of the **actions** layer and choose Window > Actions.

15. From the Actions toolbar, choose ActionScript 2.0 Classes > Movie > Button > Event Handlers, then double-click on the **onRelease** handler to place it in the script pane.

16. Select the red words **not_set_yet** and type **forwardBtn**.

17. Place your cursor after the first bracket of this action, and from the Actions toolbox choose Global Functions > Timeline Control and double-click on the word **nextScene**.

18. Choose the Check Syntax option at the top of the Actions panel to have Flash verify that your script has no errors.

19. Choose the Auto Format option at the top of the Actions panel to align your script.

```
forwardBtn.onRelease = function() {
    nextScene();


};
```

figure 6–28

This action on the **actions** layer tells a button, when clicked, to go to the next scene of a movie.

20. Your script should look like Figure 6–28 and as indicated below:

```
forwardBtn.onRelease = function() {
        nextScene();
};
```

21. Close the Actions window. Your action is set to go to the next scene; however, we don't have the "next scene" set up yet so it has nowhere to go. Save your file and let's do that next.

Creating Multiple Scenes

1. Choose Window > Other Panels > Scene to open the Scene options box. Note in the Scene panel there is currently one scene indicated—**introduction**. See Figure 6–29.

2. Click on the Duplicate Scene button at the bottom of the Scene panel four times. Refer to Figure 6–29 again.

3. Double-click on the titles of each of the duplicate copies and rename them as follows (see Figure 6–30):
   - drawing
   - animation
   - interactivity
   - output

4. Click on each scene name in the Scene panel and note that the scene is selected in the movie area—the film-take clapper in the upper left corner of the document indicates the scene name. See Figure 6–31.

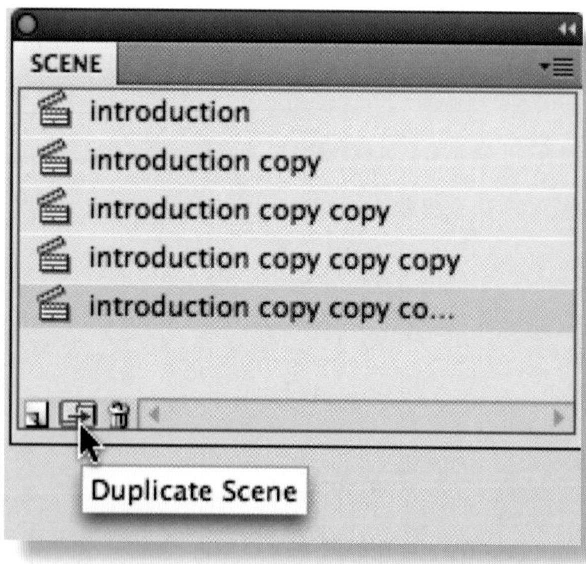

figure 6–29

Create four more scenes in the Scene panel.

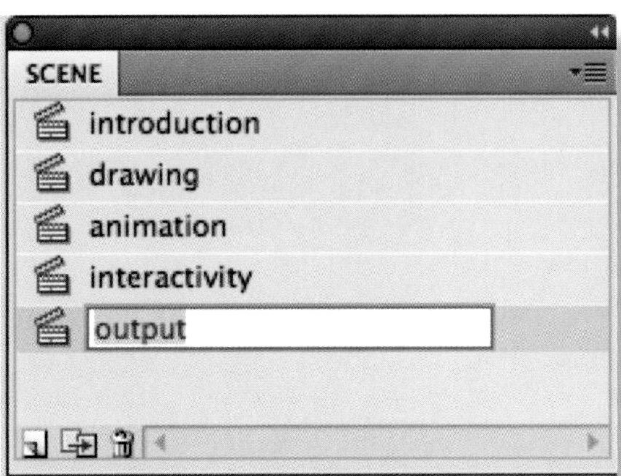

figure 6–30

Name each of the scenes.

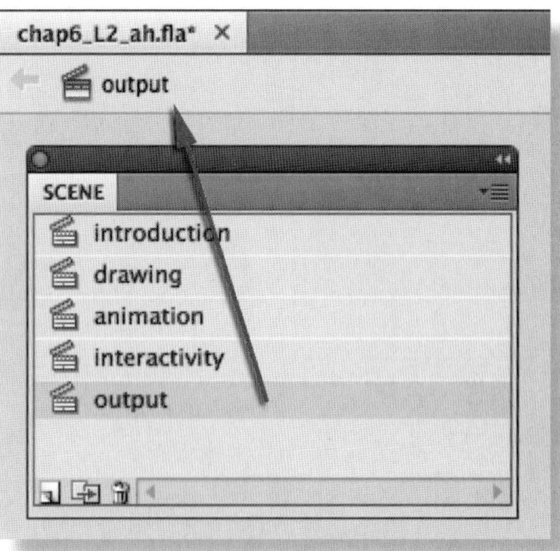

figure 6–31

Select each scene name in the Scene panel to view the scene on the Stage.

5. In the Scene panel, click the **drawing** scene title and be sure you have the **drawing** scene up in the movie window. Close the Scene panel. Note the drawing scene looks exactly like the **introduction** scene, because we just made a duplicate of it. Let's add elements to the drawing scene to differentiate it.

6. Expand the Library panel from the panels list or choose Window > Library.

7. Click on the **intro header** symbol in the Library—you won't see anything in the Library preview area because it's white text on a white background, but it's there. Ctrl-click (Mac) or right-click (Windows) on the **intro_header** symbol icon and from the submenu choose Duplicate. See Figure 6–32.

8. In the Symbol dialog box, name the duplicate symbol **drawing_header** and be sure it's set to the movie clip type. Choose OK and the new symbol appears in the Library panel.

9. Double-click on the **drawing_header** symbol in the Library panel to enter editing mode (in the upper left corner of the document it should indicate drawing > drawing_header).

10. Double-click on the blue bordered box in the middle of the scene and change the words **introduction** to **drawing**. See Figure 6–33.

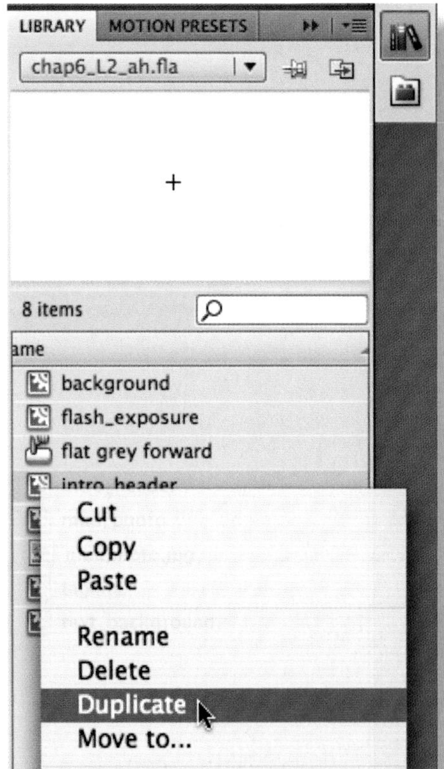

figure 6–32

Create a duplicate of the **intro_header** symbol from the Library panel.

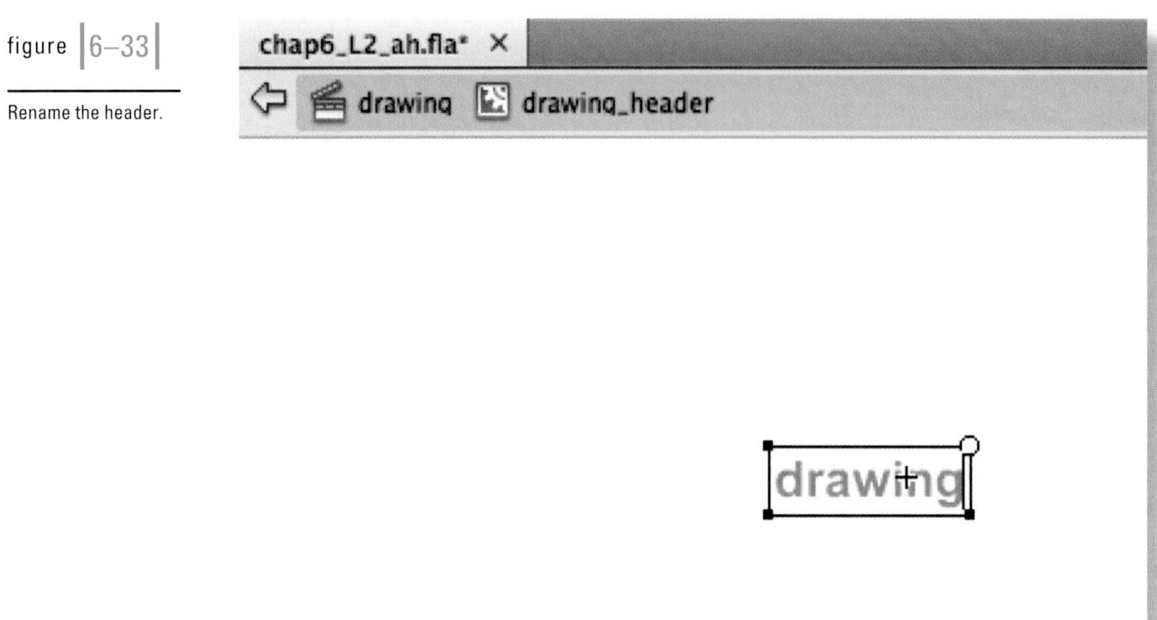

figure 6–33

Rename the header.

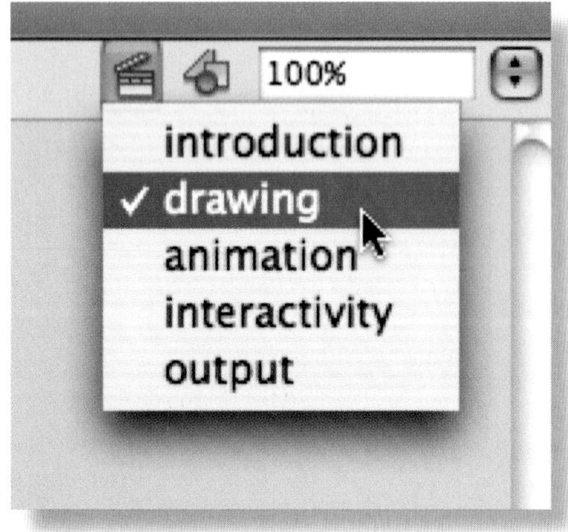

figure 6–34

Select a scene by clicking on the film-take clapper icon in the upper right of the Flash movie area.

11. Exit editing mode by clicking on the **drawing** scene name in the upper left of the document. Refer to Figure 6–33 again.

12. Create the headers for the other three scenes. Follow steps 6–10, naming each new duplicate to correspond with its scene name: **animation_header**, **interactivity_header**, and **output_header**.

13. Once all your scene header symbols have been created, let's update them in their respective scenes. Be sure you are still in the **drawing** scene, by clicking on the Edit Scene navigator (the film-take clapper) in the upper right of the document and choosing **drawing** from the list. See Figure 6–34.

14. Click on the **introduction** header instance on the scene, and in the Properties panel choose the Swap option. See Figure 6–35. In the Swap Symbol dialog box, browse for the **drawing_header** symbol and choose OK. An instance of the **drawing_header** is positioned in the same place as was previously the **introduction_header**. Mighty swift, indeed!

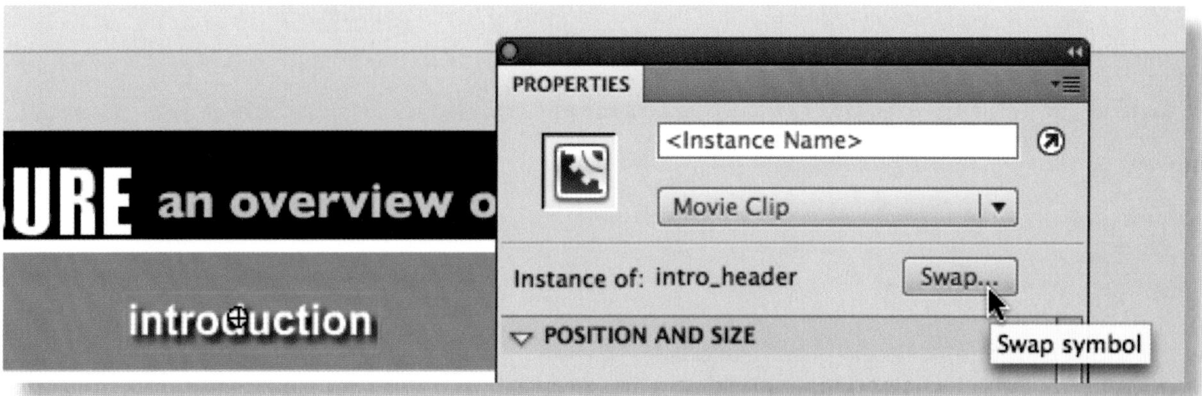

figure 6–35

Use the Swap option to exchange one symbol instance for another.

15. Using the Edit Scene navigator (see Figure 6–33 again), go to each scene and swap the **introduction_header** with the new header symbols you created to correspond with each scene.
16. Save your movie.

Adding Text and Color to Each Scene

1. Minimize the Flash program. Browse on your computer for the **chap06_lessons** folder and open the text file **scenes.txt**.
2. Copy the text in the section Graphics Scene Text. See Figure 6–36.
3. Minimize the text file and open up the Flash file again. Be sure the **drawing** scene is selected.
4. Double-click on the text block in the center of the movie. Select all the text and then Ctrl-click (Mac) or right-click (Windows) over the text and choose Paste. The new text should apply to the area.
5. Following steps 1–4, add the appropriate text to the other scenes.
6. Now make each scene a bit more unique—on each scene change the color of the cracked (exposed) mud photo instance on the left of each scene. Also change the movie background color. (Hint: to change the color of the instances, select an instance and in the Properties panel go to Color Effects > Tint and adjust the sliders so you can see the detail in the image.)
7. Choose Control > Test Movie and click on the forward button—each click should advance you to the next scene. Alright! But how do I go back to a scene? Let's add a back button to each scene in the next section. First, save your file.

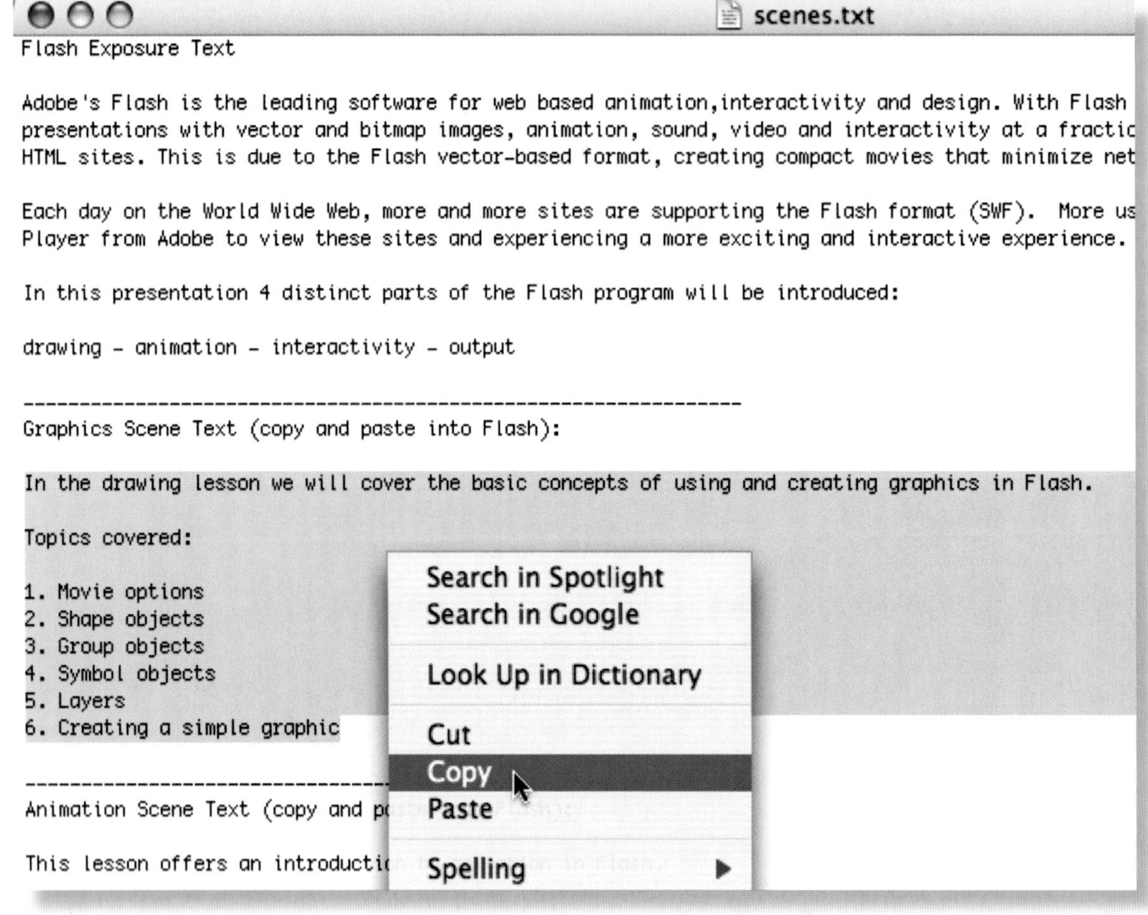
scenes.txt
Flash Exposure Text
Adobe's Flash is the leading software for web based animation,interactivity and design. With Flash
presentations with vector and bitmap images, animation, sound, video and interactivity at a fractic
HTML sites. This is due to the Flash vector-based format, creating compact movies that minimize net
Each day on the World Wide Web, more and more sites are supporting the Flash format (SWF). More us
Player from Adobe to view these sites and experiencing a more exciting and interactive experience.
In this presentation 4 distinct parts of the Flash program will be introduced:
drawing - animation - interactivity - output
Graphics Scene Text (copy and paste into Flash):
In the drawing lesson we will cover the basic concepts of using and creating graphics in Flash.
Topics covered:
1. Movie options
2. Shape objects
3. Group objects
4. Symbol objects
5. Layers
6. Creating a simple graphic
Animation Scene Text (copy and p
This lesson offers an introducti
Search in Spotlight
Search in Google
Look Up in Dictionary
Cut
Copy
Paste
Spelling

figure 6–36

Copy the text.

Adding a Back Button

1. Go to the **drawing** scene. Select the **buttons** layer.
2. Choose Window > Common Libraries > Buttons > playback flat. From the list, click and drag the **flat grey back** button into the scene, next to the forward button.
3. Close the Buttons library. Select the button and in the Properties panel give it an instance name of **backBtn**.
4. Select the first frame of the **actions** layer and choose Window > Actions.
5. In the script, place your cursor after the semicolon at the end of the script, and from the Actions toolbar, choose ActionScript 2.0 Classes > Movie > Button > Event Handlers, then double-click on the **onRelease** handler to place it in the script pane.
6. Select the red words **not_set_yet** and type **backBtn**.

7. Place the cursor after the first bracket of this action, and from the Actions toolbox choose Global Functions > Timeline Control and double-click on the word **prevScene**.

8. In the Timeline Control submenu also double-click the word **play** to add to the script. This action is important to play the animation you created on the **introduction** scene if you click back through the presentation to that scene.

> **Note:** If you eventually add animation to the other scenes, you might also consider adding the play action as part of the first action as well—after the **nextScene ( );** line.

9. Choose the Check Syntax option at the top of the Actions panel to have Flash verify that your script has no errors.

10. Your script should look like Figure 6–37 and as indicated below:

```
forwardBtn.onRelease = function() {
    nextScene();
};
backBtn.onRelease = function() {
    prevScene();
    play();
};
```

11. Choose the Auto Format option at the top of the Actions panel to align your script.

12. Let's add this new action to the first frames of the other scenes. In the Actions panel, select the action you just created from backBtn . . . to . . . the semicolon at the end of the script. Choose Ctrl-click (Mac) or right-click (Windows) and select Copy. See Figure 6–38.

13. Choose the **animation** scene from the Edit Scene navigator (move the Actions panel aside if necessary).

14. Select the first frame of the **actions** layer—the Actions panel updates with the script that is currently on that frame.

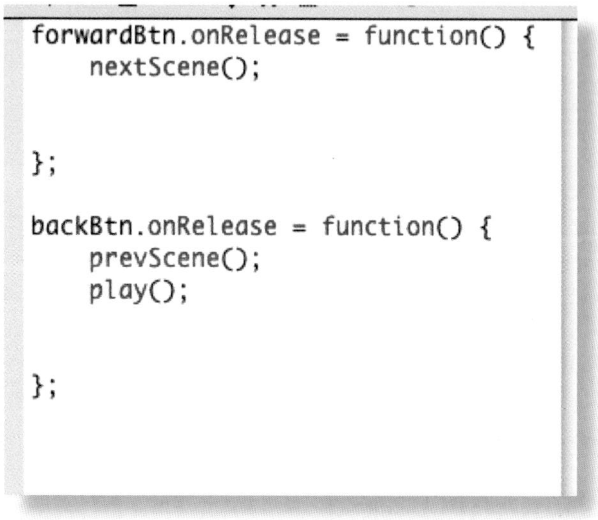

```
forwardBtn.onRelease = function() {
    nextScene();

};

backBtn.onRelease = function() {
    prevScene();
    play();

};
```

figure 6–37

The full script to execute the forward and back buttons on the presentation.

```
forwardBtn.onRelease = function() {
    nextScene();

};

backBtn.onRelease = function() {
    prevScene();
    play();
};
```

Select All
Undo
Redo
Cut
Copy
Paste

figure 6–38

Copy part of the script.

15. Click after the semicolon of the script and Ctrl-click (Mac) or right-click (Windows) over the script pane and choose Paste.

16. Select the check syntax option and the Auto Format option. The script should be the same as in step 10 or Figure 6–37.

17. Follow steps #13–#16, for the other scenes—**interactivity** and **output**.

18. Now add the back button object that will be called by the script to the other scenes. Go back to the drawing scene. Copy the back button object on the Stage.

19. Go to each of the other scenes—animation, interactivity, and output—select the first frame of the buttons layer and choose Edit > Paste in Place.

20. Choose Control > Test Movie and click through your presentation, and back.

> **Note:** Consider deleting the forward button object on the last scene, **output**, to indicate that's the end of the presentation.

21. Save your file.

Changing the Rollover Effect

1. This is for fun and practice—double-click on one of the forward buttons on the Stage in one of the scenes to enter its editing mode.

2. In the Timeline select the keyframe of the **outer circle** layer of the Over frame. See Figure 6–39.

3. Change the color of the outer circle from none to a color you can see when you rollover the button (I made mine green).

4. Exit editing mode.

5. Change the outer circle color of the back button as well (I made mine red).

6. Choose Control > Test Movie and test. Congratulations!

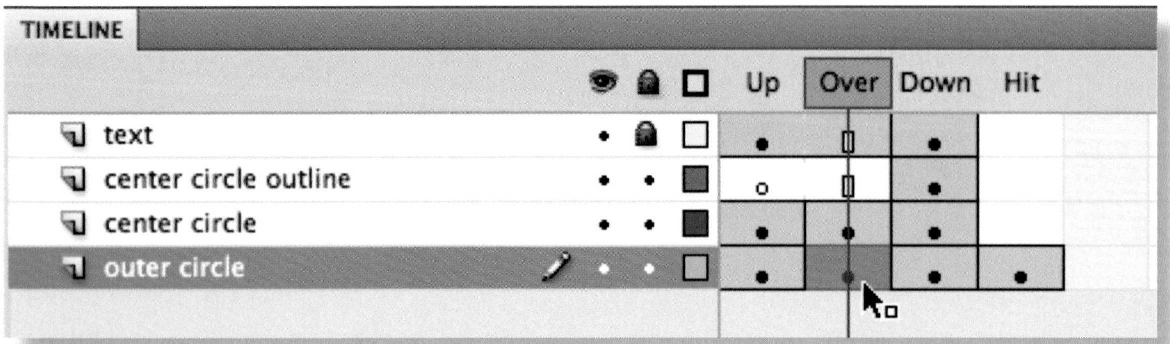

figure 6–39

Alter the color of the premade button.

SUMMARY

Whew! This chapter was packed full of the fundamentals of interactivity in Flash, including an introduction to Object Oriented Programming and ActionScripting, and then hands-on implementation of basic actions into an animated movie and scene-by-scene presentation.

in review

1. Why is Object Oriented Programming considered an intuitive way to approach programming?
2. What's the difference between a class and an object?
3. Name at least two visual objects (data types) that you can apply actions to within Flash.
4. What does the Behaviors panel contain that might be useful for designers?
5. Why is syntax important in ActionScripting?
6. Where should frame actions be placed in your Flash file?
7. What does it mean when you see a little "a" on a frame in the Timeline?
8. Where do you set an instance name?
9. What is the Hit state of a button?
10. Where does one go to add, delete, or copy scenes in Flash?
11. What does Swap symbols do?

exploring on your own

1. Want to learn more about OOP? Review the resources that I used to write the section, "An Overview of Object Oriented Programming."
   - *What is Object Oriented Software?* by Terry Montlick (*http://www.softwaredesign.com/objects.html*)?
   - *3.0 Coming from 2.0* by Bryan Grezeszak (*ActionScript.org* Flash, Flex, and ActionScript Resources at *http://www.ActionScript.org/resources*).

- *AS1 OOP: Object Basics* by Senocular (*http://www.kirupa.com*—a very useful resource for learning ActionScript).
- Search for terms "ActionScript," "Object Oriented Programming," and "Class-based Programming" on Wikipedia at *http://en.wikipedia.org*.
- *The Java Tutorials, Lesson: Object-Oriented Programming Concepts* (*http://java.sun.com/docs/books/tutorial/java/concepts/index.html*).
- *Just What is OO Programming* at *http://www.debreuil.com/docs/ch01_Intro.htm?* (This article is written for version Flash 5, but the section on the basics of OOP is very useful.)

2. Explore the Hit state of a button. Try this:
   a. Create a new Flash file.
   b. Create some bold text on the Stage that says "My Button."
   c. Convert the text to a button symbol, call it **mybutton**.
   d. Choose Control > Test Movie and rollover the button. Note when the little hand icon shows up—the clickable area of the button. The hand icon only shows up when you are hovering right over the filled area of the text. Move your cursor slightly away from the text and the hand disappears. Positioning the cursor just in the right spot to make it clickable can be very annoying for users. You can fix this by adding a Hit area. See Figure 6–40.

Hit area is activated:

My Button

Hit area is not activated:

My Button

figure 6–40

Activating the Hit area of a button.

figure 6–41

Create a larger Hit area for the button in the button's symbol editing mode.

e. Double-click on the **mybutton** instance on the Stage to enter its editing mode.

f. Copy and paste (or Alt/Option, click and drag) the keyframe on the Up frame to the Hit frame.

g. Select the Hit frame.

h. Draw a filled rectangle around the text on this frame. The color doesn't matter—it will be invisible in the final movie. See Figure 6–41.

i. Choose Control > Test Movie and rollover the button again. The clickable area is now defined by the area of the rectangle you just created in the Hit area of the button, but it's invisible, so as not to alter the design of your button.

Explorer pages

ELLIS NEDER

"View the Process" Flash presentation for TimeSlips Creative Storytelling Project (*http://www.timeslips.org/*). Designed and developed by Ellis Neder, Sway Design.

About Ellis Neder

Along with many graphic designers, Ellis began creating Web sites in the late 1990s completely unaware that this new medium we were all suddenly involved in would turn out to be such an ideal teaching tool. In 1999, he started his design studio, Sway Design (along with Annesa who moved on three years after), when he moved back to New York after living in Seattle for two years where he was the director of a children's art school and taught drawing and painting classes to teenagers. Ellis had done some marketing and graphic design for the school, including working with a design firm to launch the school's first Web site, and when he returned to New York, a number of his artist friends asked for help moving their film and theater projects online.

A year later he was asked by a Madison Avenue advertising firm to create branding projects in Flash and HTML for Sony and Sprint, so he quickly learned everything he could about how large companies were using interactive technologies. United Way saw his work and asked him to redesign their Web templates and also create an online manual that taught their local partner organizations how to build successful Web sites while correctly using the United Way brand. The project was a huge challenge and a great way to learn about the importance of Web standards because it forced him to explain everything he had learned up to that point about online content development "best practices".

Since 2000 Ellis has designed projects for non-profits, universities, and *Fortune 500* companies, and using the Web as an educational tool has been a constant theme throughout. The Web sites he has created teach people a variety of skills including how to use technology in the classroom, how to engage in the voting process, how artists go about creating their work, and how to be socially responsible when purchasing products online.

The two years Ellis spent in the classroom struggling to explain the mysteries of drawing and painting to a room full of restless teenagers honed his communication skills and, in a hands-on way, taught him the importance of clear, direct communication. Today he uses these same skills to help his clients educate the public about their brands, the products they sell, and the services they offer that make them unique.

Enjoy more of Ellis's work at *http://www.swaydesign.com*.

About the Work of Ellis Neder

> *"The first move in any creative process is to introduce constraints."*
> Alan Fletcher, *The Art of Looking Sideways*

In his own words, Ellis shares his work process . . . "We all begin a web design project with a few constraints; typography, the browsers and the tools we use like Flash and Photoshop to design with all limit us in some way at the outset. If you're creating work for a client, their initial content and their ideas about how a website should look also begin to constrain us. But there's one more constraint that plays a key role and it's one that often gets forgotten by younger designers. You aren't really designing for yourself and you aren't even designing for your client. You're designing for the client's audience and it's your job to define that audience and develop a visual language that connects with them."

"When people ask me what I do as a web designer I tell them—'I get paid to think like someone else.' This usually throws them off a little but I explain that, over the years, I've developed a solid understanding of the grid and the rules of typography and the roles they both play in creating a good design, but it's my ability to think outside of my own head that adds the most value to a project. It's key to imagine what the viewers of your sites will experience as they begin clicking links and scanning pages of text, and it's important to make that experience both easy and engaging, especially as faster and faster web technologies like mobile platforms become important. In his classic work on typography, *The Elements of Typographic Style*, the designer Robert Bringhurst called this 'the task of creative non-interference.' In all of my projects I strive for this approach of 'non-interference' with simple, clear design that lets my client's content say what it needs to say and connect with the audience as quickly as it can."

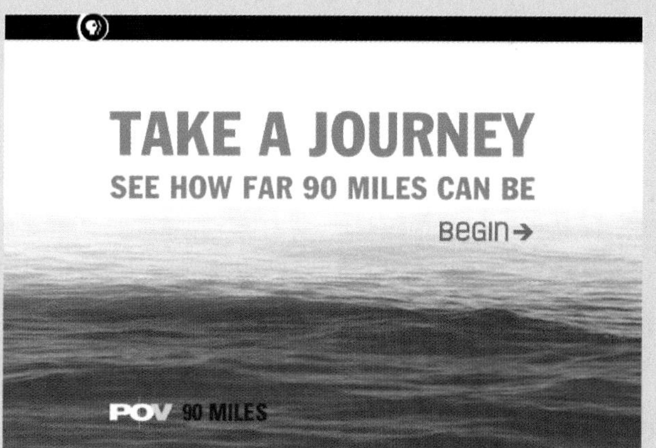

"The Journey Across 90 Miles" is a Flash mini-site for the documentary *90 Miles* that aired on P.O.V., a PBS showcase for independent non-fiction films (*http://www.pbs.org/pov/pov2003/90miles/*). Created by Ellis Neder, Sway Design.

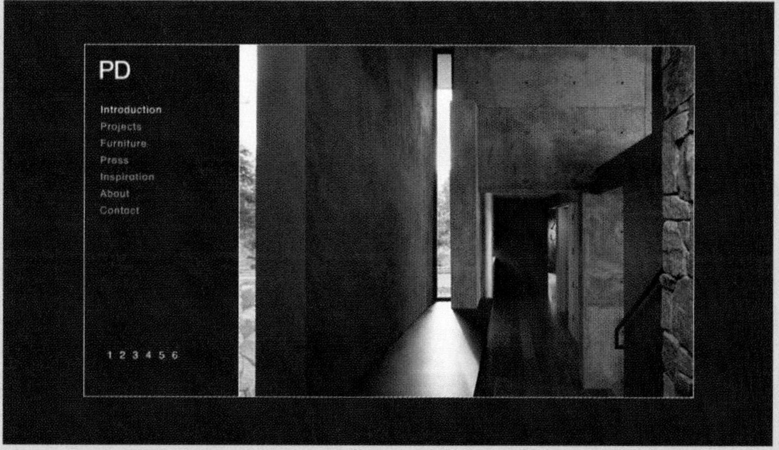

A Flash portfolio for Peace Design (*http://www.peacedesign.org*). Site designed and developed by Ellis Neder, Sway Design.

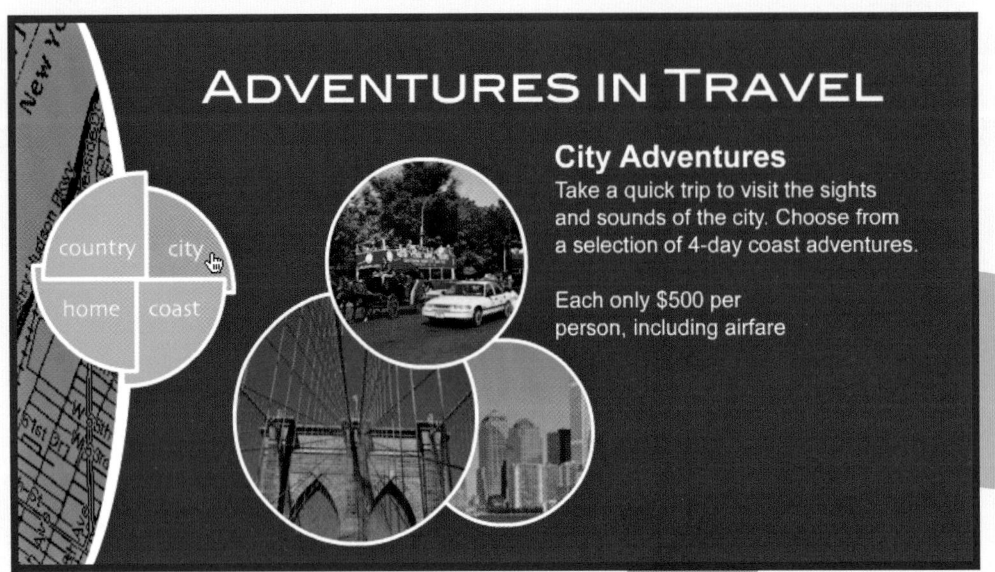
ADVENTURES IN TRAVEL
City Adventures
Take a quick trip to visit the sights and sounds of the city. Choose from a selection of 4-day coast adventures.
Each only $500 per person, including airfare
country
city
home
coast

| putting it all together |

7

charting your course

In the last chapter you assembled a simple presentation using scenes. In this chapter you learn an alternate and more versatile method for structuring your content using multiple SWFs. You will create a multi-SWF Web site and publish it for online delivery. Also, options for optimizing and testing your content, and an overview of the Web site design process will be presented.

goals

In this chapter you will:

- **Dissect the architecture of a multi-SWF movie**
- **Create a Flash Web site**
- **Discover some tips for optimizing a Flash document**
- **Get an overview of the Publish Settings panel**
- **Publish a SWF file into an HTML page**
- **Test the download speed of a Flash movie**
- **Gain some insight on the Web site design process**

OVERVIEW OF MULTI-SWF MOVIE CREATION

There are many innovative ways to construct an interactive Flash movie. In the last chapter, you used multiple scenes to differentiate sections of a simple presentation that was output as a SWF file. See Figure 7–1 for a visual representation of a scene structure within a Flash movie. Coming up you will use multiple SWFs to simulate the same function as using scenes, but as a better means for creating larger presentations and/or Web sites. External SWFs can be loaded into a scene of another SWF. They can be put on levels above and below each other (similar to layers in Photoshop, but much more interactive) and contain timelines that can run independently from each other. Because of these features, multi-SWF integration becomes an incredibly efficient and versatile way to build and update interactive content containing, for example, heavy graphics, audio and video, and complex navigation. See Figure 7–2 for a visual representation of the multi-SWF movie-making concept. This is a complex idea, so don't worry if you can't grasp it right away—it will become clearer as you work through the examples and lessons in this chapter.

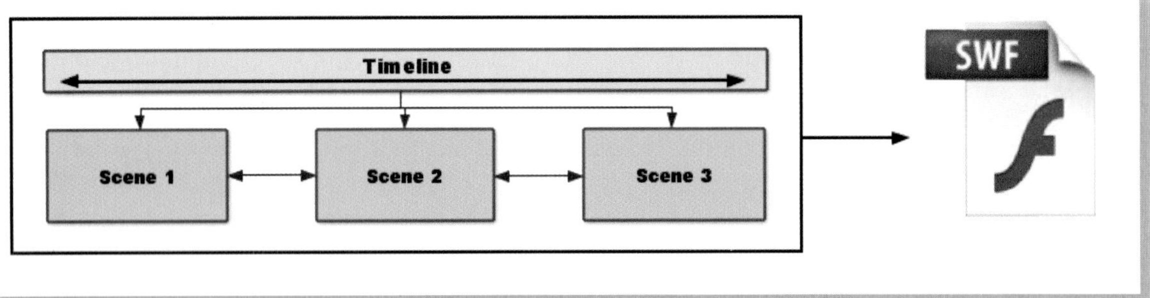

figure 7–1

Diagram of the multi-scene structure.

figure 7–2

Diagram of the multi-SWF structure.

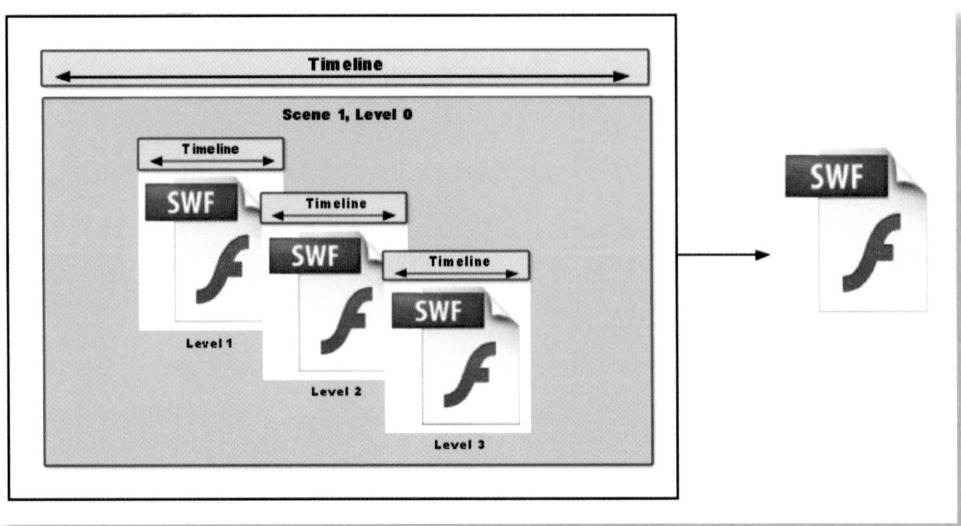

Note: I would like to provide a bit of more clarification here on how timelines work in scenes versus multi-SWFs. As you know from the last chapter, scenes have a timeline, but they are not independent from each other. They are actually part of the root or main timeline—when the playhead reaches the final frame of a scene, the playhead progresses to the next scene. When you publish a SWF file, the timeline of each scene combines into a single timeline in the SWF file. That makes using scenes to create long presentations disadvantageous; the movie must load all the frames on the one, big timeline before it can be played, resulting in increased wait-time for the viewer. With SWFs, each SWF and each timeline associated with that SWF can load and unload independently from the scene it's within, resulting in a more progressive download of information.

Often how this multi-SWF method works is that there is a base SWF containing actions that control the loading and unloading of other SWF's within it. Individual SWF's load on what are called *levels*. Levels are like layers with each level containing a SWF (movie) that can overlap or replace another SWF below or above it. Levels are numbered with zero (0) at the bottom of the stack on up. In ActionScript 2.0, you use the Load/Unload movie events to control these SWF's on different levels. See Figure 7–3.

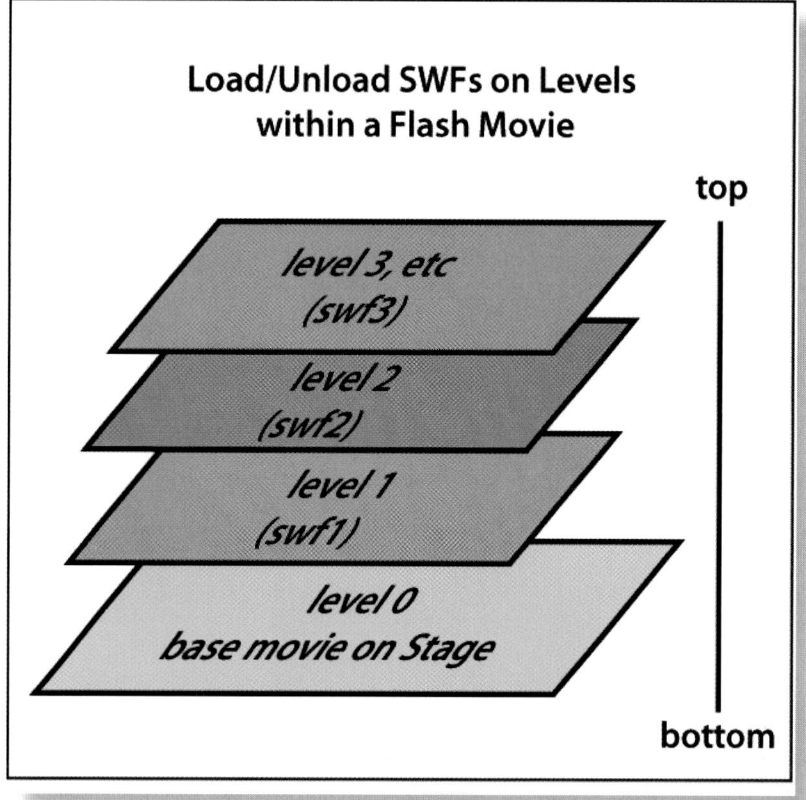

figure 7–3

Visual representation of how SWFs load and unload on levels in a Flash movie.

Let's view a series of screen shots from a site created with multiple SWFs by Justin Lerner of Jlern Design who is highlighted in one of the Explorer Pages of this book see Figure 7–4.

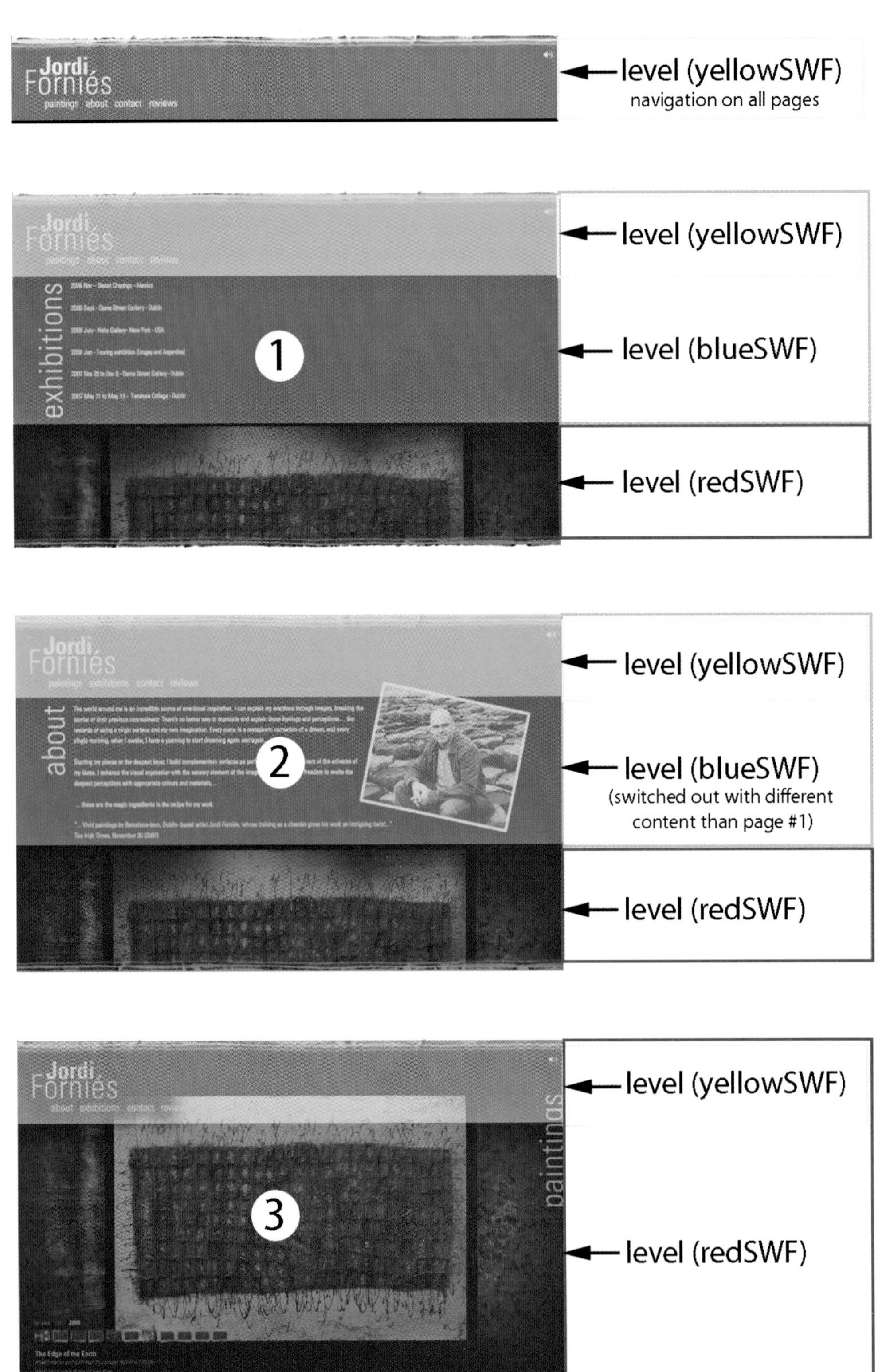

figure 7–4

Visual examination of how SWFs load and unload within a Flash site. Site screen shots compliments of Justin Lerner (Jlern Design).

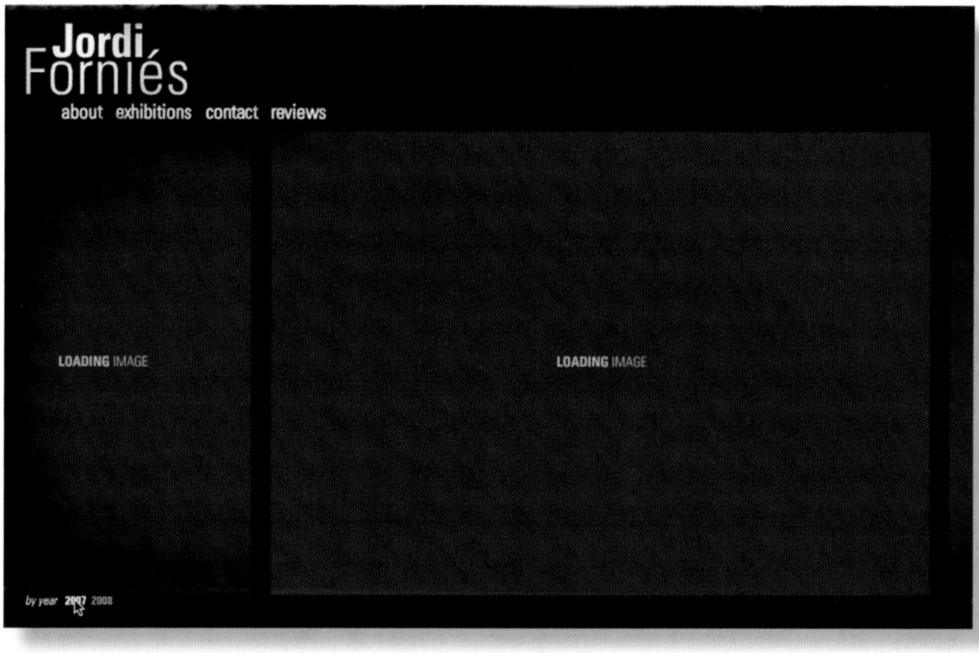

figure 7–5

The preloading screen of the Jordi Fornies site.

For reference in Figure 7–4, each SWF layered via levels into Web pages 1, 2, and 3 are color coded. The yellowSWF contains the navigation system for the site, which is visible on all three example pages of the site. Having the navigation on a single SWF is smart—it can be preloaded on each page and can contain all the button actions in one place—easy to update! The blueSWF and redSWF are other SWFs layered into some of the pages containing content that is loaded and unloaded from each page. See all this action by viewing the site itself—Jordi Forniés at http://www.jordifornies.com/. Note as you navigate through the pages which sections stay the same and which ones reload with new content. The sections of content being loaded in the page might contain what is called a preloader (an indicator that the content is being uploaded into the page). See Figure 7–5. More on preloaders later in this chapter and in the Adventures in Design: Making a Preloader after this chapter.

Note: Do an online search . . . can you identify other Flash-based Web sites using the multiple SWF structure?

From a user perspective you just explored the idea of multiple SWFs loading and unloading into levels within sections of a Web site. Now, let's dissect the process a bit more. In the next lesson you open up various SWFs and see how they are layered with one another. You'll discover that when all the pieces are put together you have the makings of a Web site, albeit simple in this example, but a start nonetheless. Then, from there, you will construct your own Web site (Project: Make Your Own Multi-SWF Movie site).

Lesson 1: Deconstruct a Multi-SWF Web Site

Examine the inner workings of a simple site using the multi-SWF structure for assembling Flash content.

Identifying the Level 0 and Level 1 Movies

1. On your computer locate your lessons folder that you saved from the book's CD. Open the **chap07_lessons/demos/multi_swf_final** folder. Inside the folder there are five FLA files—**index.fla**, **home.fla**, **country.fla**, **city.fla**, and **coast.fla**. See Figure 7–6. There are also five SWF files—**index.swf**, **home.swf**, **city.swf**, **country.swf**, and **coast.swf**. You will also see a file called **index.html**; this file contains Web-based code (HTML) that tells a browser (Firefox, Internet Explorer, Safari) what part of a Flash site to open and display first. You will create your own index.html file in the Flash Movie Optimization and Publishing section of this chapter.

figure |7–6|

Contents of the **multi_swf_final** folder.

2. Double-click on the **index.html** to open the Flash site in a browser. Click through the navigation. Note the navigation area on the left side of the page doesn't change, nor the "Adventures in Travel" header at the top.

3. Now, open the **index.fla** in Flash. In the file, note that what you see on the Stage are the same items that didn't change position when you clicked through the pages in the previous step. This **index.fla** is the base page—it sits at level 0 of the multi-SWF structure (refer to Figure 7–3 again).

4. Now, open the **city.fla** in Flash. Here, you see the same content that was in the **index.fla** (level 0), but with additional content specific to the city page. The content that is on level 0 is actually a template, a guide layer, to help properly layout the content for the city page. It will not output with the final city SWF movie. You will create your own template in this chapter's project. Choose Control > Test Movie to see that this is true; the template is not visible in the SWF.

5. In the Timeline, turn off the visibility of the template layer. See Figure 7–7. The content that is now visible is what will be layered (on level 1) over the content of the index page (level 0). The red background will actually become transparent.

figure |7–7|

Hide the template layer.

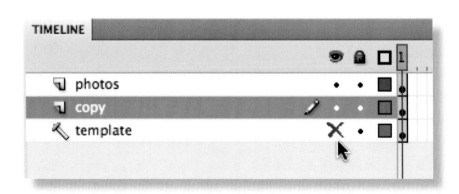

6. Open the **country.fla**, **home.fla**, and **coast.fla** and note that they are set up the same way—the level 0 content is a template for identifying where to put the content for each of the final SWFs that will load into the page.

7. Now, go back to the **index.fla** and let's look at the ActionScript that runs this whole thing. Select the first frame of the actions layer, and choose Window > Actions. See Figure 7–8.

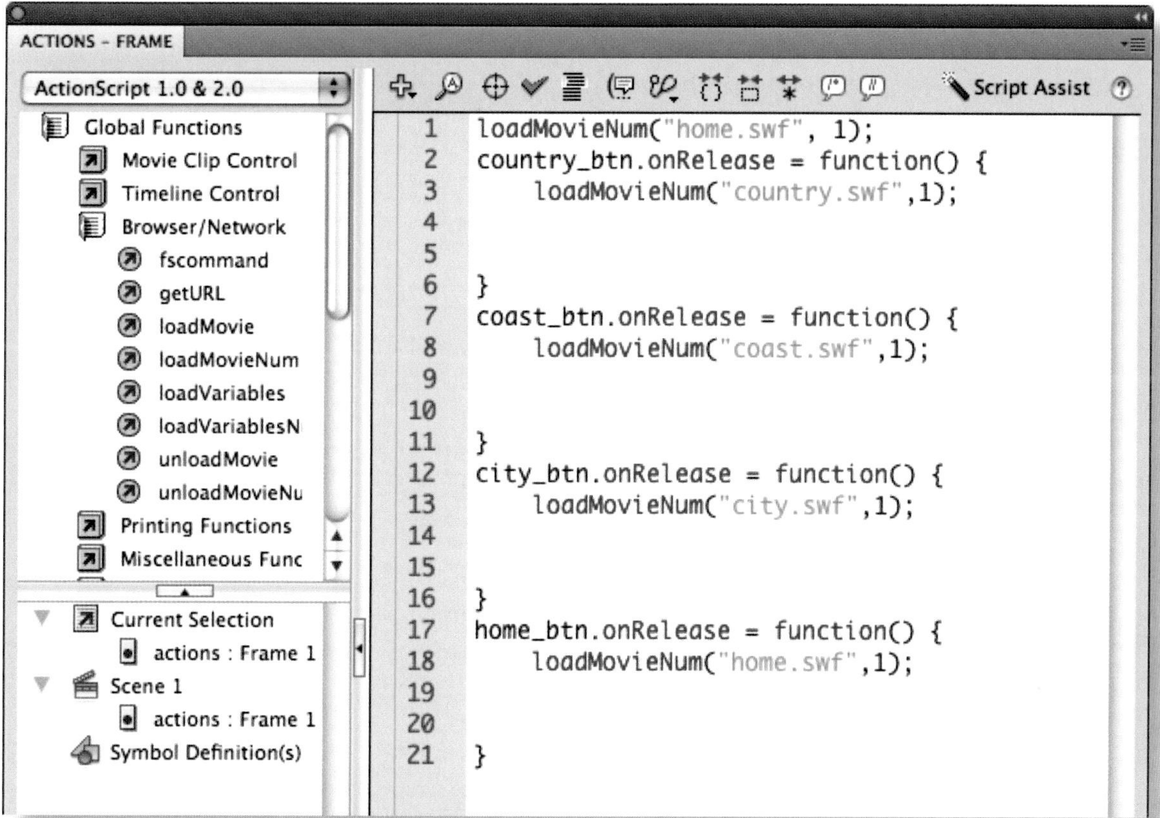

figure 7–8

Behind the scenes (the Actions panel) of a multi-SWF site.

8. Parts of this script should look somewhat familiar to you. Basically when a user clicks on one of the buttons on the nav bar, for example **city_btn**, on release the **city.swf** (the published version of the **city.fla**) is loaded into the **index.swf** on level 1. See Figure 7–9.

9. Close all the files. Hopefully, you have a better idea of how all the pieces of this site are designed and implemented. In the next section, practice creating this functionality step-by-step.

```
}
city_btn.onRelease = function() {
    loadMovieNum("city.swf",1);
```

figure 7–9

English translation of an action: On release of the **city_btn** the **city.swf** (the published version of the **city.fla**) is loaded into the **index.swf** on level 1.

Setting up the SWF Files

1. First, let's publish each of the premade FLAs into SWF files. In Flash, open the **city.fla** in the **chap7L1** folder. Choose File > Publish to publish the file into a SWF. File > Publish does the same thing as Convert > Test Movie, but instead of showing you the final SWF, it saves it automatically in the same folder as the original FLA. Minimize Flash for a moment and see if the **city.swf** was saved in the **chap7L1** folder.

2. Close the **city.swf**. Open the **home.fla**, **coast.fla**, and **country.fla** and publish each of those files into SWFs. Close all the files. Now you are ready to load these SWFs into the site.

> **Note:** Make sure you keep all the SWFs in the same folder, along with the index file, so Flash can find and display them through ActionScript.

Making the Load Actions

1. Choose File > Open and open the **index.fla** in the **chap7L1** folder. If you get a dialog box warning that "One or more fonts used by this movie are not available," choose the Use Default option. This file is the base movie of the Adventure Travel site. As you've learned, the base movie usually includes elements of the site that remain consistent, such as the site title, the navigation bar, and the background images, etc.; items that won't change from page to page.

2. Be sure the workspace is set to Classic.

3. Select the green country button on the Stage and in the Properties panel give it the instance name of **country_btn**. See Figure 7–10.

> **Note:** A generic button symbol with a rollover color has already been created for you in this example. Feel free to take a look in the Library's panel.

figure 7–10

Create a unique name for the generic button instance.

4. Select each of the other buttons and name them, respectively—**city_btn**, **home_btn**, and **coast_btn**.

5. Create a new layer, name it **actions** and move it to the top of the layer list. See Figure 7–11.

6. Select the first frame of the **actions** layer and choose Window > Actions (Alt/Option + F9) to open the Actions panel.

7. Be sure the ActionScript 1.0 & 2.0 option is selected in the upper left of the panel.

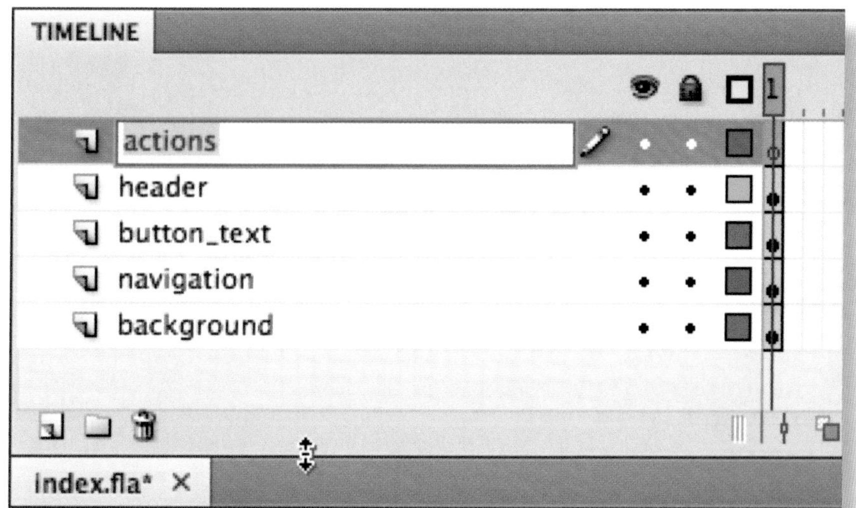

figure 7–11

Create an **actions** layer and place it at the top of the layers list.

8. The first action to add is one that will load the home page content (**home.swf**) into the base SWF right away. From the Actions toolbox choose Global Functions > Browser/Network > loadMovieNum. Between the parentheses type "**home.swf**", 1. The line of code should look like Figure 7–12 or as below:

```
loadMovieNum("home.swf",1);
```

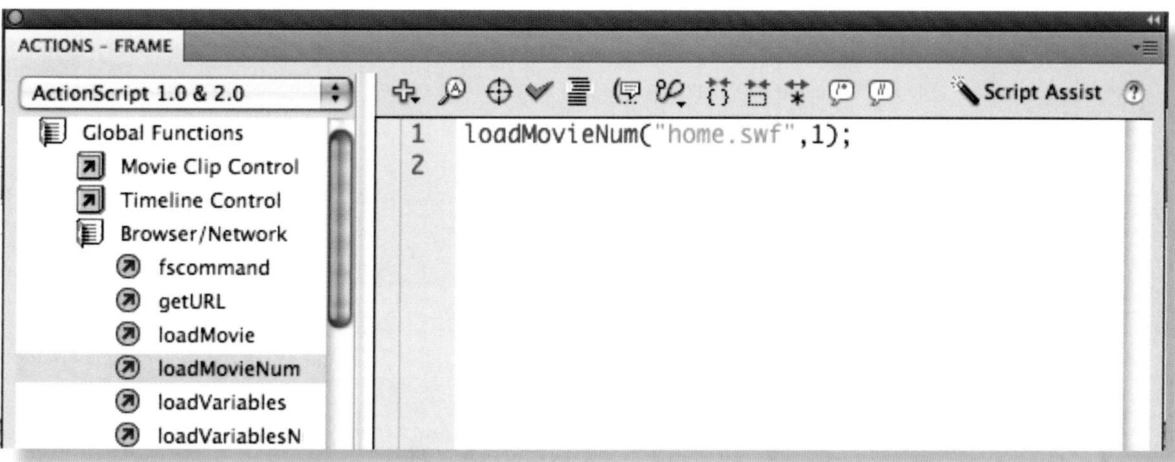

figure 7–12

The loadMovieNum action.

> **Note:** It's imperative that the **home.swf** in the line of code is surrounded by curly quotes or the action will not work.

9. Place the cursor after the semicolon in the script. From the Actions toolbox choose ActionScript 2.0 Classes > Movie > Button > Event Handlers > onRelease.

10. In the red **not_set_yet** area of the script, type **home_btn**.

11. Place the cursor after the first curly bracket and from the Actions toolbox choose Global Functions > Browser/Network > loadMovieNum.

```
loadMovieNum("home.swf", 1);
home_btn.onRelease = function() {
    loadMovieNum("home.swf", 1);


};
```

figure |7–13|

The complete loadMovieNum action for the **home.swf**.

12. Between the parentheses enter **"home.swf", 1**. Choose the Auto Format option (if you get an error message, check the syntax of your code carefully with the following example of the code). See below and the complete script so far in Figure 7–13.

home_btn.onRelease = function() {

loadMovieNum("home.swf", 1);

};

Note: Basically this new part of the script says: "When a user clicks the home button, open up the SWF called home.swf on level 1 (over the top of the index page, which is on level 0)."

Copy these new parts of the script (see also Figure 7–14):

home_btn.onRelease = function() {

loadMovieNum("home.swf", 1);

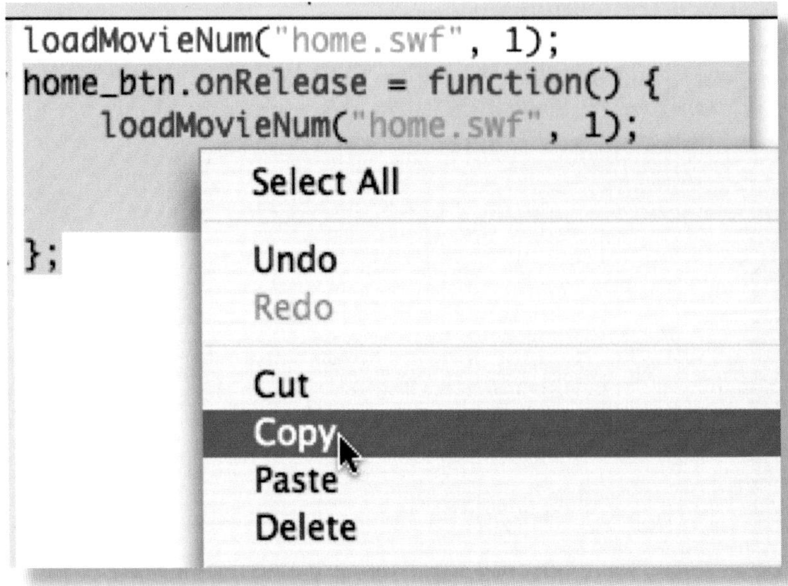

figure |7–14|

Select and copy part of the action.

13. Place the cursor after the last semicolon in the script and choose Paste. Choose Paste two more times. Choose Auto Format.

14. Change the code in the pasted versions to call the instance names and SWFs of the other parts of the site. See below and Figure 7–15.

```
city_btn.onRelease = function() {

    loadMovieNum("city.swf", 1);

};

country_btn.onRelease = function() {

    loadMovieNum("country.swf", 1);

};

coast_btn.onRelease = function() {

    loadMovieNum("coast.swf", 1);

};
```

15. Close the Actions panel and test the movie. Super cool!

```
loadMovieNum("home.swf", 1);
home_btn.onRelease = function() {
    loadMovieNum("home.swf", 1);


};
city_btn.onRelease = function() {
    loadMovieNum("city.swf", 1);


};
country_btn.onRelease = function() {
    loadMovieNum("country.swf", 1);


};
coast_btn.onRelease = function() {
    loadMovieNum("coast.swf", 1);


};|
```

figure 7–15

The completed script for loading the Adventures in Travel SWFs.

16. One more thing . . . close the SWF, then choose File > Publish Settings. Under Formats, select the HTML option along with the Flash option. (The HTML option and others are further explained in the Flash Movie Optimization and Publishing section of this chapter.) See Figure 7–16.

17. Choose Publish at the bottom of the Publish Settings window.

18. Open your **chap07L1** folder and double-click on the **index.html** page to open the Flash movie in a browser.

19. Save your **index.fla**. You are done with this lesson.

> **Note:** For fun, alter the level numbers in the load movie scripts you created on the actions layer of the **index.fla**. Change the level number on each of the SWFs. See Figure 7–17. Then test the movie—since each SWF is now opening on a different level they overlap each other rather than replace each other on level 1 as our original script indicated. You can also unload any of these movies using the unloadMovieNum event found in the Actions toolbox (Global > Functions > Browser/Network).

figure 7–16

Select the HTML publishing option in the Publish Settings panel.

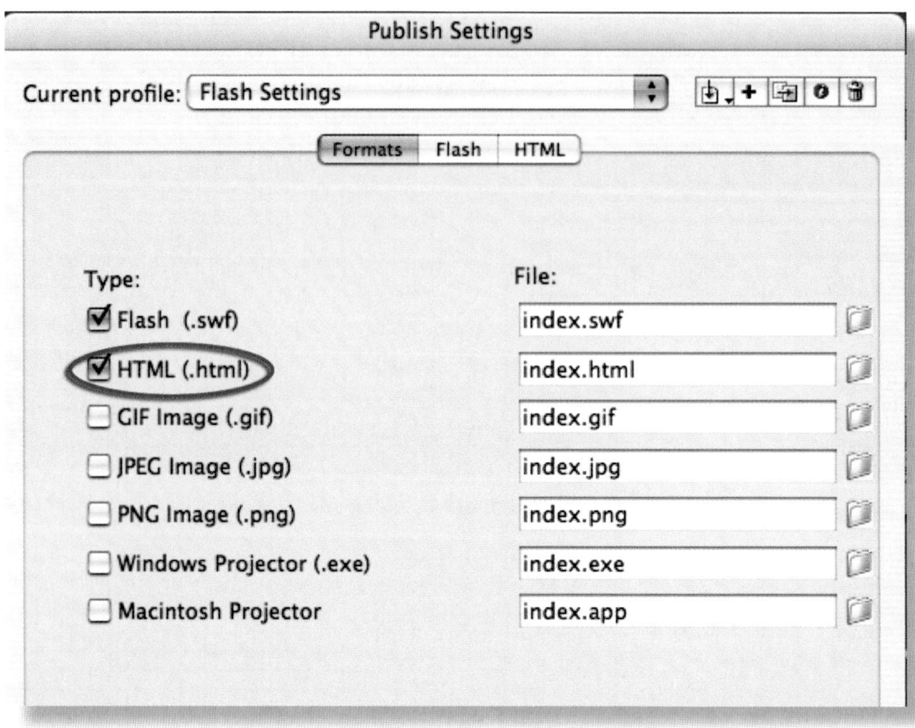

figure 7–17

For fun, alter the level numbers in the script, then publish the Movie and see what happens.

```
loadMovieNum("home.swf", 1);
home_btn.onRelease = function() {
    loadMovieNum("home.swf", 1);


};
city_btn.onRelease = function() {
    loadMovieNum("city.swf", 2);


};
country_btn.onRelease = function() {
    loadMovieNum("country.swf", 3);


};
coast_btn.onRelease = function() {
    loadMovieNum("coast.swf", 4);


};
```

> **Note:** For future reference . . . when you start building complex, many leveled SWF sites, it's best practice to place SWFs on levels in multiples of 10—level 1 would be level 10 in the code, for example, level 2, would be level 20, etc., so that if additional levels are needed to add new content there is room within the levels structure to accommodate it.

PROJECT: MAKE YOUR OWN MULTI-SWF MOVIE

Here's your chance to take all that you learned in the last lesson and design your own version of a site for the fictitious client, Adventure Travel. You will set up the site structure to be the same as the example lesson you created above, but with your added artistic flair. There are five sections:

- Index FLA—contains navigation and any other elements that will remain the same on all pages of the site.
- Home FLA—contains text that introduces the business and the purpose of the site.
- City FLA—contains photos (JPEG format) and text about a city adventure.
- Coast FLA—contains photos (JPEG format) and text about a coast adventure.
- Country FLA—contains photos (JPEG format) and text about a country adventure.

Sketching the Design

Grab a pencil and some paper and sketch a few interface design ideas. First, what will be the over-all feel of the site—fun and playful, corporate and business-like, funky and cool? What will the home page look like? How will it announce the purpose of the site? How will the navigation work? Will the site have background elements, texture? What is the color scheme? What kind of fonts will be used? Keep your ideas simple, but clear—you're under a tight deadline, so you can't go too crazy!

Constructing the Base File

1. Once you've got some idea of what the site will look like you're ready to jump into Flash. Create a new movie and set the size to 760 × 420, a standard site size.

2. Make a new layer and title it **background**. Create any background elements that will stay static and consistent throughout the site.

3. Next, create another layer and title it **navigation**. Design a navigation structure for the site—it needs to contain four buttons with the titles: home, city, country, and coast.

4. Create another layer titled **header**, and create a headline and/or company logo for the site. Be sure to leave plenty of blank space on the page to bring up the specific information for each SWF that will load.

5. Save this file in a folder titled **my_site**, and title it **index.fla**.

Creating a Template

1. Let's make a template image out of the **index** page so that you can use it as a guide to build your other pages. Choose File > Publish Settings and under Formats choose JPEG Image (.jpg). Then, choose Publish. See Figure 7–18.

figure 7–18

Create a JPEG image of a Flash frame to use as a template.

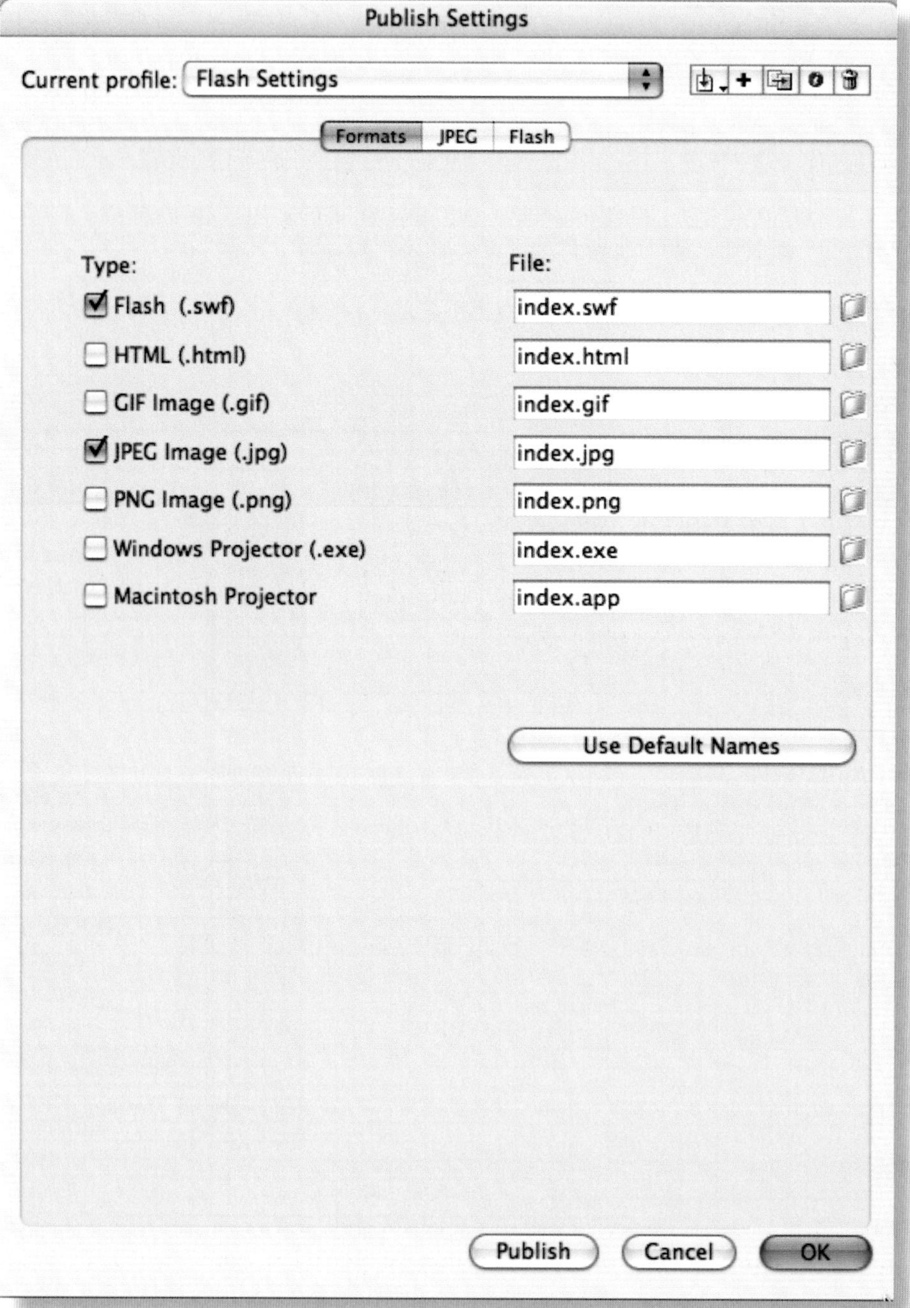

2. Create a new movie with the 760 × 420 dimensions—the same size as the index page.

3. Choose File > Import > Import to Stage and open the **index.jpg** you created in the last step. This is a flat image of the index page that will be used as a template. Be sure it's positioned right over the white movie area of the document.

4. Change the Layer 1 name to **template**. Then Ctrl-click (Mac) or right-click (Windows) over the layer name and choose Guide from the drop down menu. See Figure 7–19.

5. Lock the template layer and notice that the layer now has a different icon (a T-square) next to the layer name. See Figure 7–20.

6. Save this file as **city.fla** in your **my_site** folder.

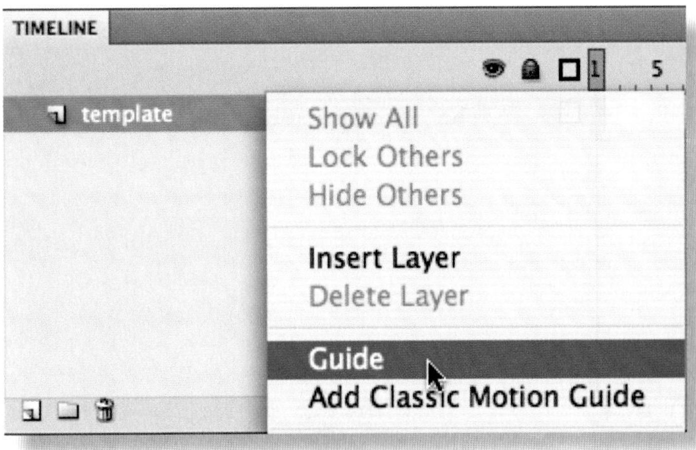

figure |7–19|

Convert a template to a guide layer, so it will not render in the final movie.

figure |7–20|

A guide layer is indicated by a T-square icon next to the layer name.

Creating the Pages

1. Design your city page. Create new layers for each element, including a block of text, and 2–3 images representative of a city scene. Feel free to add some animation too!

2. Save the FLA then publish a SWF version of the file.

3. Next, choose File > Save As and save a copy of the **city.fla** as **country.fla**.

4. In the **country.fla** repurpose the text and images used for the city page to reflect the country page. Save and publish the file.

5. Repeat steps #3 and #4 to create the **coast** and **home** pages.

Adding Interactivity

1. Close all files. Then, open the **index.fla** from your **my_site** folder.

2. Select each of the buttons you created and give them descriptive instance names, for example, select the **home** button and in the Properties panel give it the name **home_btn**.

3. Create a new layer with the name **actions**. Place it at the top of the layers list.

4. Select the first frame of this **actions** layer.

5. Open the Actions panel and enter in the load movie scripts for each of the buttons. To do this, review the section Making the Load Actions in the first lesson and see Figure 7–15. Be sure that the instance names you use in the ActionScript are spelled exactly how you named them in step #2 above.

6. Save the file. Go to File > Publish Settings and be sure under Formats the Flash (.swf) and HTML (.html) options are chosen and the file name for the HTML page is set to **index**. Choose Publish.

7. Inside your **my_site** folder open the **index.html** in a browser and click-through your first Flash Web site. Show off your creation to a friend.

FLASH MOVIE OPTIMIZATION AND PUBLISHING

Optimization and publishing (also called output) are important topics to understand as you start designing and developing more complex Flash movies. Knowing how to create a Flash movie that will play "nicely" in the real world (online and on other peoples computers) is critical. Let's review a list of tips for optimizing your Flash files, go through the options in the Publish Settings panel, and explore the Bandwidth Profile to test the download speed of your movies.

Flash Movie Optimization Tips

Optimization is a process that should be considered for any content that will be published to the online environment. It's the process of preparing functionally optimal multimedia elements—graphics (static and animated), audio, video, and text. It's the artful balance between finding the best visual or auditory quality of the element and its quantitative file size for efficient download and playback speed. Flash is very smart and performs some optimization automatically. You can also further compress a SWF file when you publish it. But before exporting the final document there is more you can do. The following is taken directly from the Flash Help files located at: http://help.adobe.com/en_US/Flash/10.0_UsingFlash/.

Optimize Documents

- Use symbols, animated or otherwise, for every element that appears more than once.
- Use tweened animations whenever possible when creating animation sequences. Tweened animations use less file space than a series of keyframes.
- Use movie clips instead of graphic symbols for animation sequences.
- Limit the area of change in each keyframe; make the action take place in as small an area as possible.
- Avoid animating bitmap elements; use bitmap images as background or static elements. (My note: also optimize and crop them to the dimensions you will use in your movie before exporting them into Flash.)
- Use mp3, the smallest sound format, whenever possible.

Optimize Elements and Lines

- Group elements.
- Use layers to separate elements that change during the animation from elements that do not.
- Use Modify > Shape > Optimize to minimize the number of separate lines that are used to describe shapes.
- Limit the number of special line types, such as dashed, dotted, ragged, and so on. Solid lines require less memory. Lines created with the Pencil tool require less memory than brush strokes.

Optimize Text and Fonts

- Limit the number of fonts and font styles. Use embedded fonts sparingly because they increase file size.
- For Embed Fonts options, select only the characters needed instead of including the entire font.

Optimize Colors

- Use the Color Effects menu in the Properties panel to create many instances of a single symbol in different colors.
- Use the Color panel (Window > Color) to match the color palette of the document to a browser-specific palette.
- Use gradients sparingly. Filling an area with gradient color requires about 50 bytes more than filling it with solid color.
- Use alpha transparency sparingly because it can slow playback.

For a video tutorial about optimizing SWF files, see: http://www.adobe.com/go/vid0140.

Overview of the Publish Settings Panel

The Publish Settings panel (File > Publish Settings) is where you go to prepare your file for output. Publishing a SWF file is the most common output format and the default option in the Publish Settings panel. There are other formats, however, that can be selected—see list below. Options for each selected format are also available in the Publish Settings area—once a format is chosen the options for the format appear as tabs next to the Format tab at the top of the panel. See Figure 7–21. We will not go through all the format options, but I encourage you to explore them and see the Flash help files for more detail.

- Flash (.swf)—The default setting, outputs the Flash movie into the SWF format for play back via the Flash Player.
- HTML (.doc)—Creates an HTML document required to playback Flash content in a browser; it activates the SWF file and specifies browser settings.

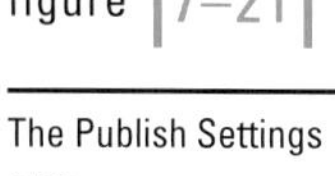

figure 7–21

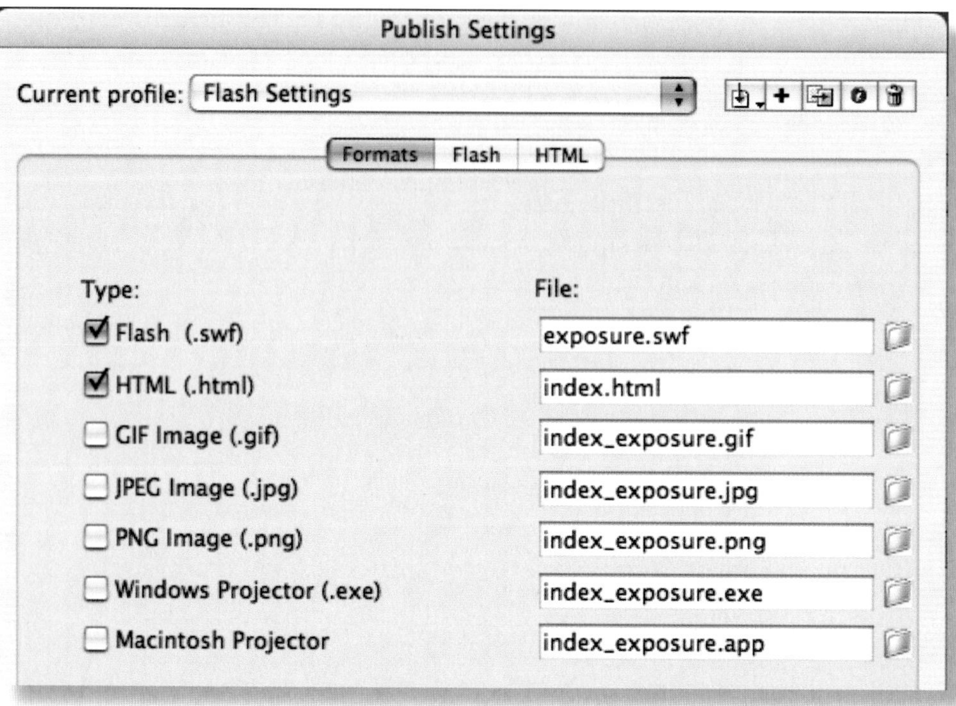

The Publish Settings area.

- GIF Image (.gif): Saves a Web-compatible GIF image of the currently selected frame in the Flash Movie.
- JPEG Image (.jpg): Saves a Web-compatible JPEG image of the currently selected frame in the Flash movie.
- PNG Image (.png): Saves a Web-compatible PNG image of the currently selected frame in the Flash movie.
- Windows Projector (.exe): Produces a stand-alone version of the Flash movie—runs without the use of the Flash Player—for the Windows platform. This format is not suitable for online delivery, and might not support all Flash features.
- Macintosh Projector: Produces a stand-alone version of the Flash movie—runs without the use of the Flash Player—for the Mac platform. This format is not suitable for online delivery, and might not support all Flash features.

Explore the HTML Publishing Option

It's likely that most of the Flash content you create will be viewed from a Web browser, so you will want to save your SWF file as well as an HTML document. Let's take a quick look under the hood of an HTML page generated by Flash and at how it works to call a SWF properly into a browser window.

1. Open **chap07_lessons/demos/HTML/exposure.fla**. This movie will look familiar—it's the presentation you created in Chapter 6.

2. Choose File > Publish Settings and under Formats select the Flash (.swf) and HTML (.html) options. Change the name of the HTML page to **index.html** ("index" is the default naming convention for the first page of any Web site). Refer to Figure 7–21 again.

3. Select the Flash tab and take a look at the various settings—change the version setting, if not already, to Flash Player 10 (or the latest version).

4. Now, select the HTML tab and take a look at its various settings. For now, leave the settings at the default.

5. Select Publish. The SWF and HTML files will be published in the **chap07_lessons/demos/ HTML** folder. Minimize Flash and find these files on your computer.

6. Check out the size of the SWF movie by Ctrl-clicking (Mac) or right-click (Windows) on the file (**exposure.swf**) and going to Get Info or Properties. The file is about 28K—wow, this is small! Flash does some really slick compression on the file as part of the SWF conversion process. Close the info.

7. Double-click on the HTML file (**index.html**) to open a browser window and view. Or, alternatively, open a browser (Internet Explorer, Firefox, etc.) and choose File > Open File, then browse for the HTML file.

8. In the browser window view the source code of the HTML file—for Firefox choose View > Page Source, for Internet Explorer choose View > Source.

9. There's a lot of important information in the source code, and lucky for you Flash writes the code for you. Also lucky are the comment tags indicated by a double slash (//) that tell what each section of the code does. Look, for example, for the comment that indicates the beginning of the code that checks for the type of Flash player a viewer is using (//Flash Version Player Detection).

10. Now, look at some of the code more closely; it's a section of the code that defines how the browser reads the SWF file and indicates the name of the SWF file that is being called by the document. This might be important if you need to change the name or parameters of your SWF file by directly updating it in the HTML page (i.e., if you have an HTML editor program in which to update it).

    Scroll down the page and locate the code between the <noscript></noscript> tags. There are two places where the SWF name is identified—each place is to fulfill the coding requirements for the possible browsers that will view the Flash movie. Explore the code and see if you can identify the two places where "**exposure.swf**" is being called. See also Figure 7–22.

```
<object classid="clsid:d27cdb6e-ae6d-11cf-96b8-444553540000"
codebase="http://download.macromedia.com/pub/shockwave/cabs/flash/swflash.cab
#version=10,0,0,0" width="760" height="420" id="exposure" align="middle">
        <param name="allowScriptAccess" value="sameDomain" />
        <param name="allowFullScreen" value="false" />
        <param name="movie" value="exposure.swf" /><param name="quality" value="high" />
        <param name= "bgcolor" value="#ffffff" />
<embed src="exposure.swf" quality="high" bgcolor="#ffffff" width="760" height="420"
```

name="exposure" align="middle"
allowScriptAccess="sameDomain" allowFullScreen="false"
type="application/x-shockwave-flash" pluginspage="http://www.adobe.com/go/getflashplayer" />
</object>

Note: If you build Web pages in Adobe Dreamweaver, the program supports the import and play back of SWF content within a Web page. Similar to what the Publish command does in Flash, it will create the necessary code to play your SWF properly in a browser.

```
</script>
<h3><noscript>
    <object classid="clsid:d27cdb6e-ae6d-11cf-96b8-444553540000"
    codebase="http://download.macromedia.com/pub/shockwave/cabs/flash/swflash.cab#version=10,0,0,0"
    width="760" height="420" id="exposure" align="middle">
    <param name="allowScriptAccess" value="sameDomain" />
    <param name="allowFullScreen" value="false" />
    <param name="movie" value="exposure.swf" />
    <param name="quality" value="high" />
    <param name="bgcolor" value="#ffffff" />
    <embed src="exposure.swf" quality="high" bgcolor="#ffffff" width="760" height="420"
    name="exposure" align="middle"
    allowScriptAccess="sameDomain" allowFullScreen="false"
    type="application/x-shockwave-flash" pluginspage="http://www.adobe.com/go/getflashplayer" />
    </object>
</noscript></h3>
</body>
</html>
```

figure 7–22

The HTML code that calls a SWF into a Web page.

Testing Playback Performance

By default the playback speed of a Flash movie is set to 24 frames per second, but you can set it to any amount. However, that doesn't mean the playback matches it exactly—the Flash Player attempts to meet the frame rate you set, but the actual frame rate during play back can vary on different computers. If a document that is downloading reaches a particular frame before the frame's required data is downloaded, the document pauses until the data arrives. This is actually a good thing if you have parts of your movie that need to play together—an animation with a voice over, for example, or a video with a transcript. Of course, as you've learned, optimizing the content before playback is important, but that might not completely alleviate the wait-time a user must experience to see your masterpiece. The wait-time of a Flash movie or parts of it (i.e., sections where SWFs are loading into other SWFs) is usually indicated by a preloader. Through ActionScript a preloader monitors the loading process and then plays the movie when enough of it (as determined in the code) has loaded. It also

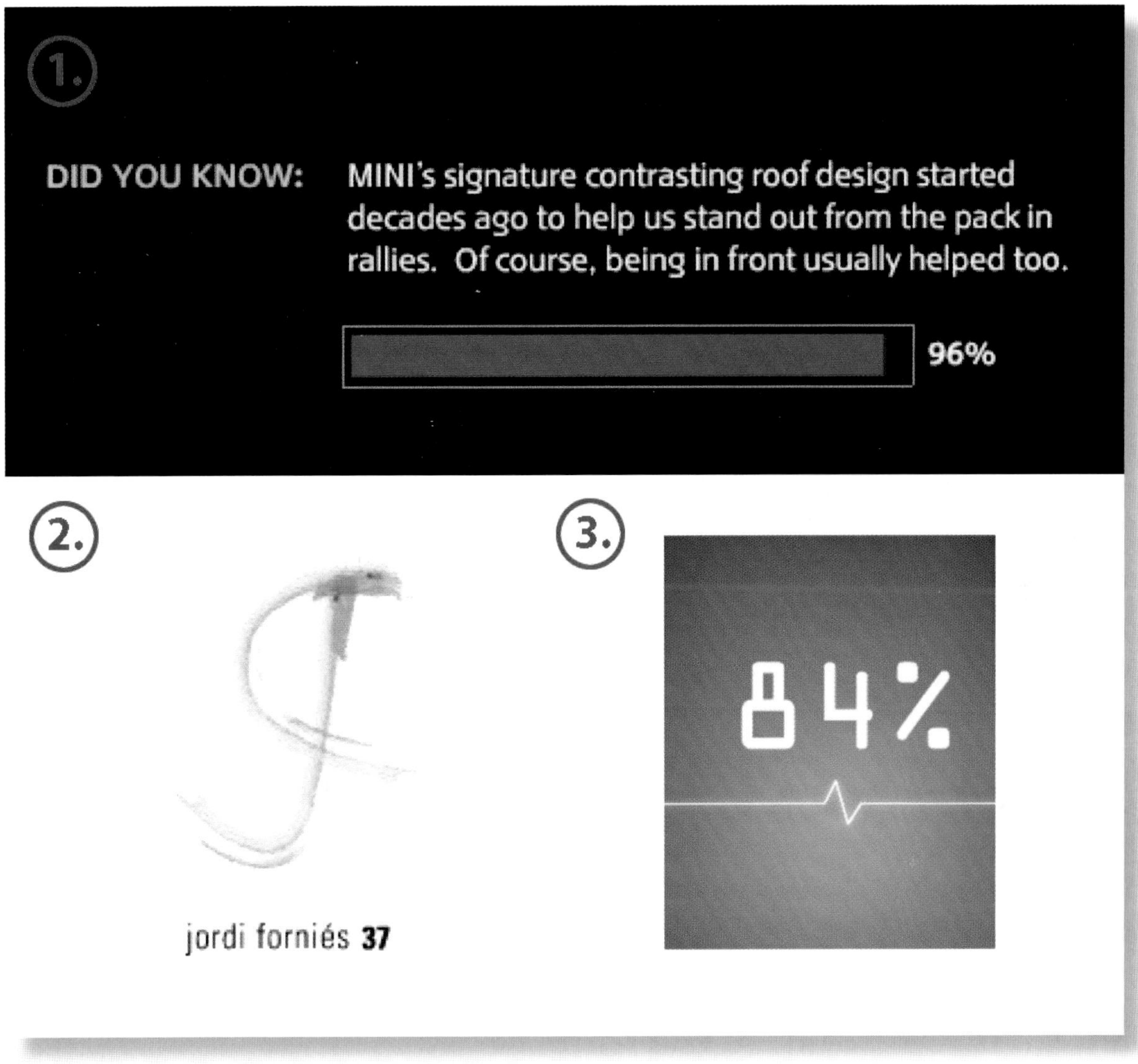

figure |7–23|

Three distinct visual examples of a preloader screen, each indicating the percentage of content that is loaded before the movie plays.

shows visitors the progress of the preload, so they will see how much is downloaded and hopefully will wait for it to finish (see Figure 7–23). There are many ways (scripts) for creating preloaders, some quite complex depending on how a Flash application is constructed. You will learn about one way in the Adventures in Design: Making a Preloader at the end of this chapter. See also some sensational example preloaders at: *http://www.smashingmagazine.com/2008/03/13/showcase-of-creative-flash-preloaders/*.

The best way to test the download and playback speed of your Flash movie is to run it on a variety of computers, operating systems, browsers, and Internet connections, but you can also

figure 7–24

Set the simulation download speed for the Bandwidth Profiler.

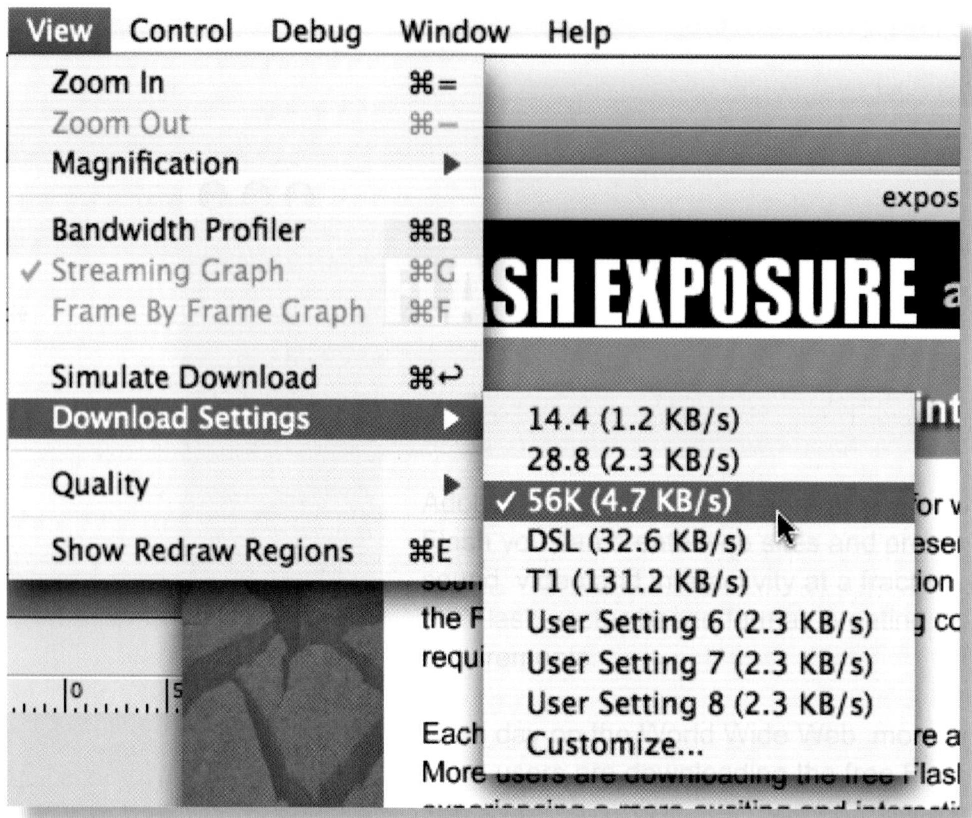

view the performance graphically using Flash's Bandwidth Profiler. The Bandwidth Profiler simulates how much data is sent for each frame according to the connection speed you specify. Let's give it a try:

1. Open the Flash Exposure presentation—**chap07_lessons/demos/HTML/exposure.fla**.
2. Select Control > Test Movie. Note that the menu options change at the top of the Flash interface.
3. Without closing the movie preview, select View > Download Settings, and select a download speed to determine the streaming rate that Flash simulates. (For purposes of this demonstration, I suggest choosing a slower connection speed—56K or less.) To enter a custom user setting, select Customize. See Figure 7–24.
4. Select View > Bandwidth Profiler to show a graph of the downloading performance. See Figure 7–25.

   The left side of the profiler displays information about the Movie—its dimensions (760 × 420), frame rate (24), file size (25 KB—very small), frame duration (125 fr), and the amount of frames to preload before the presentation will start (107 fr). It also shows the Settings chosen, which is the bandwidth you determined in step 3 under the Download Settings option. And,

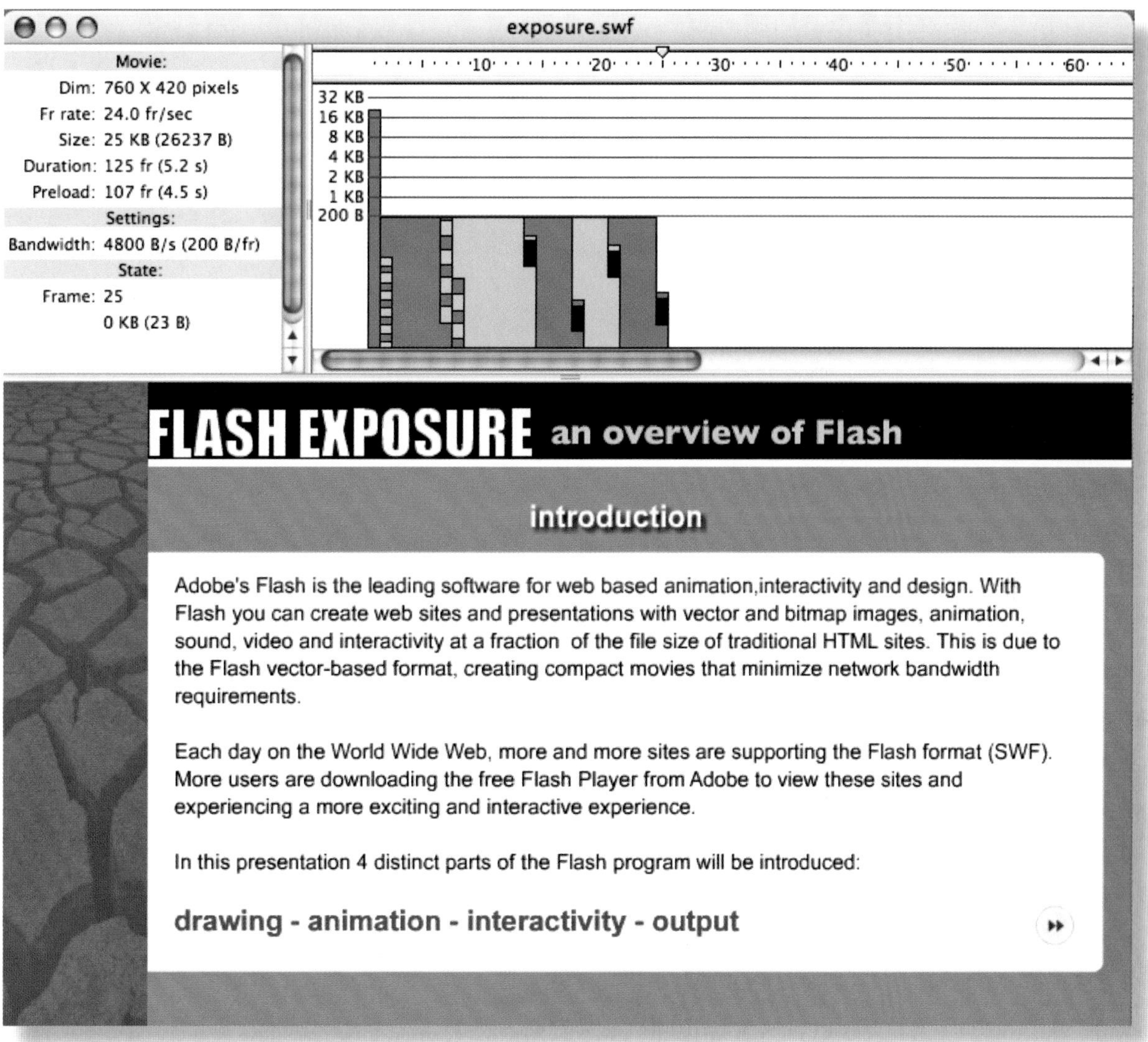
exposure.swf
Movie:
Dim: 760 X 420 pixels
Fr rate: 24.0 fr/sec
Size: 25 KB (26237 B)
Duration: 125 fr (5.2 s)
Preload: 107 fr (4.5 s)
Settings:
Bandwidth: 4800 B/s (200 B/fr)
State:
Frame: 25
0 KB (23 B)
32 KB
16 KB
8 KB
4 KB
2 KB
1 KB
200 B
FLASH EXPOSURE an overview of Flash
introduction
Adobe's Flash is the leading software for web based animation,interactivity and design. With Flash you can create web sites and presentations with vector and bitmap images, animation, sound, video and interactivity at a fraction of the file size of traditional HTML sites. This is due to the Flash vector-based format, creating compact movies that minimize network bandwidth requirements.
Each day on the World Wide Web, more and more sites are supporting the Flash format (SWF). More users are downloading the free Flash Player from Adobe to view these sites and experiencing a more exciting and interactive experience.
In this presentation 4 distinct parts of the Flash program will be introduced:
drawing - animation - interactivity - output

figure 7–25

The Bandwidth Profiler graph.

finally the State, which indicates where the movie is in time based on the playback location on the right section of the profiler.

The right section of the profiler shows the Timeline header and graph. In the graph, each bar represents an individual frame of the document. The size of the bar corresponds to that frame's size in bytes. You can click on each bar (it turns red) to show each section of the presentation in the movie window below. See Figure 7–26.

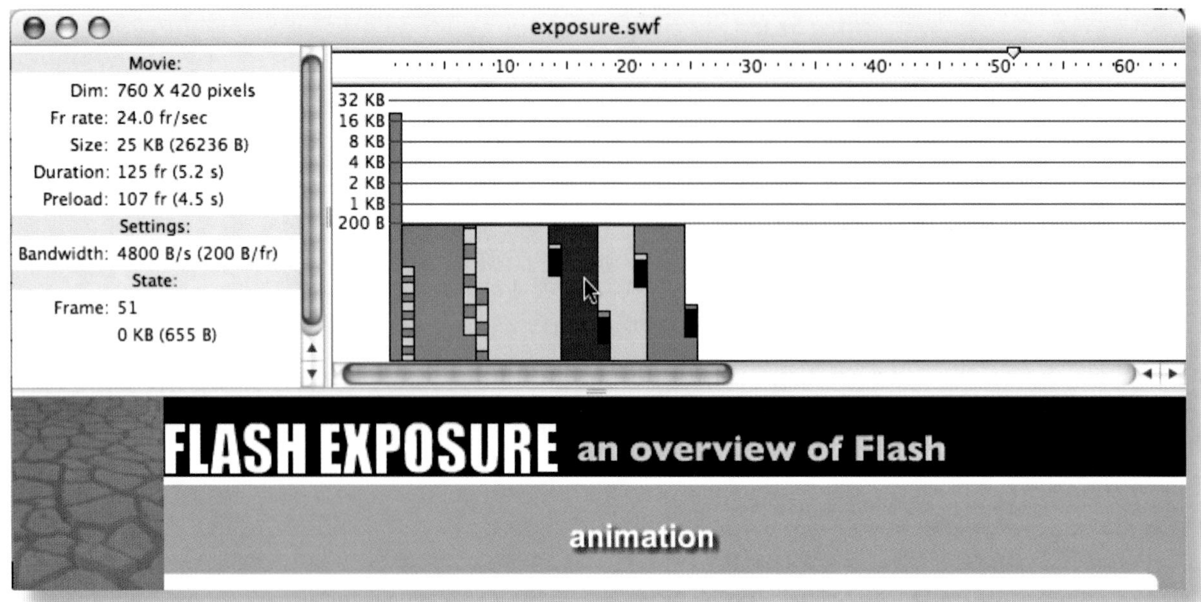

figure 7–26

View the profile of each section of a movie.

The thin, horizontal red line in the graph indicates whether a given frame streams in real time with the current connection speed set in the View menu. If a bar extends above the red line, the document must wait for that frame to load.

> **Note: The first vertical section in the graph that extends above the red bar is the preload amount for the movie.**

5. Select View > Simulate Download to simulate the document playback at the connection speed you chose in the Download Settings. Right away after choosing Simulate Download look at the playback head at the top of the document—it will hold while the preload frames download then start to play. See Figure 7–27.
6. Choose Simulate Download again and this time watch the load progression below the State area on the left side of the profiler (you might need to expand the window to see it).
7. Close the test window.

Flash can also generate a size report (a text file with the .txt extension) that lists the size of each frame, shape, text, sound, video, and ActionScript script by frame. This is good information to know what sections and elements of a movie might need to be better optimized. To generate a size report:

1. Open a Flash file.
2. Select File > Publish Settings, and click the Flash tab.

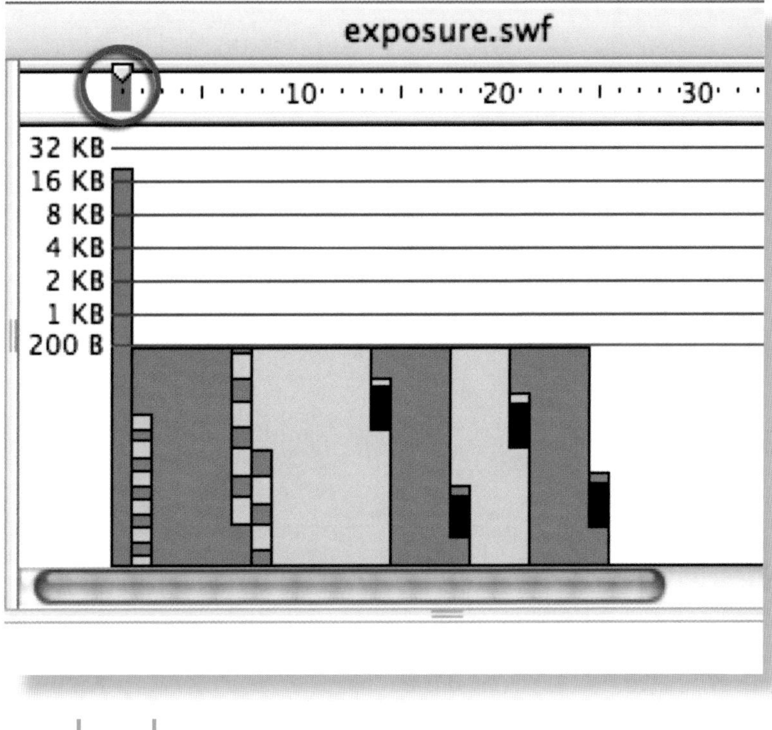

figure 7–27

Watch the playback head at the top of the document during a download simulation—it will hold while the preload frames download then start to play.

3. Select Generate Size Report.
4. Click Publish.
5. Minimize Flash and search for the report (yourfilename.txt) in the same location as the Flash file.

OVERVIEW OF THE WEB SITE DESIGN PROCESS

The fundamental steps of Web site creation, or any media related project are planning, developing, testing, and implementation. You have already learned many specifics in the design process. Now, let's take this opportunity to examine the bigger picture of how all these parts fit together.

Planning

Planning is the first phase. It's the time where your ideas for a project get mapped-out, either on paper, or perhaps drawn up on the computer. Planning includes site mapping, mocking-up, and user compatibility considerations.

Site Mapping

A site map is a diagram of what will be your site's navigation, usually in the form of a hierarchical tree that indicates each page of a site and how each page links to another. It's the visual

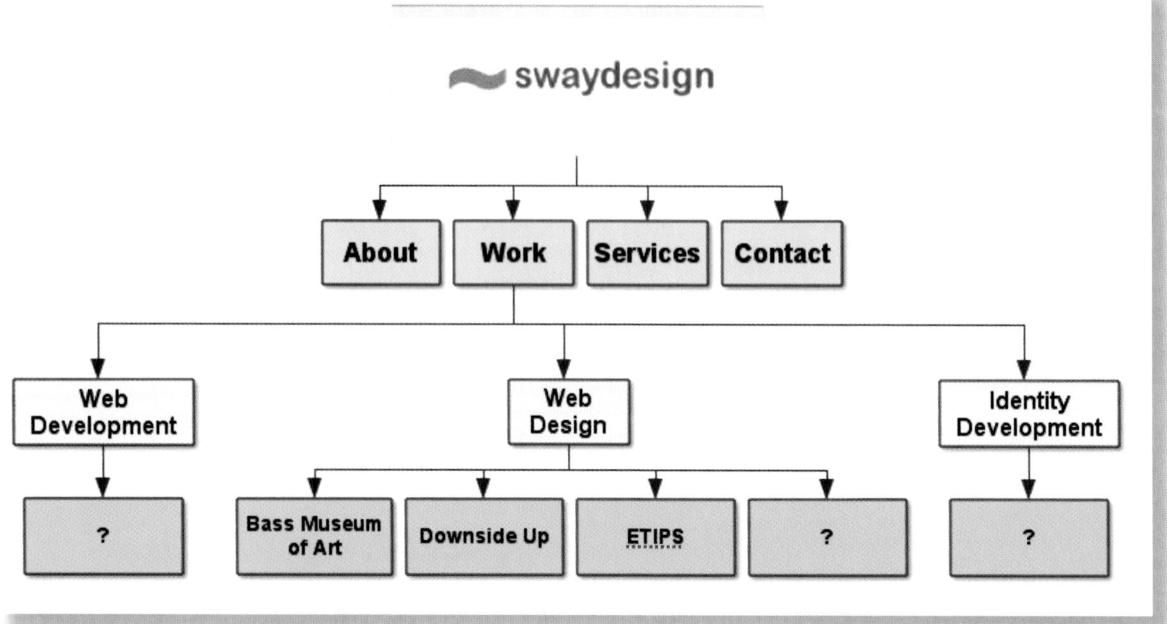

figure 7–28

An example site map.

representation of how a user might move through your site. Site maps are useful to help organize a site's content into a logical flow of information, as well as to give you (the designer) and your client a good sense of the site's size. I like to create my site maps in a concept mapping program called Inspiration. Try out a trial version at *http://www.inspiration.com*.

Figure 7–28 is a partial site map example of Sway Design's site at *http://www.swaydesign.com* created in Inspiration. Open the Sway Design site as you look through this map. Notice that the homepage links are indicated at the top level. Follow the link called "work" and add the titles of other links related to this section in the blank areas of the site map. In this example, we are visualizing the site map after the site is created, but in reality the site map is always created first in the Web design process. You should create a site map for any site you plan to develop.

Mocking-up

Additionally, part of the planning phase is determining the look, feel, and functionality of the site. Creating a visual mock-up or a series of thumbnail sketches of what the site might look like is always a good idea. Some designers often draw their designs by hand, scan the best one, import it into Flash, and use it as a guide to build each site page. You can also design your mock-ups in a program like Adobe Illustrator, Photoshop, or Fireworks.

User Compatibility

Designing for the Web is a tricky proposition—there are many variables on the user end that you have no control over. Unlike strictly HTML-based sites, Flash is considered a cross platform and browser compatible technology, as long as the user has the Flash player installed. The design and functionality of a Flash movie will not change whether viewed on a Mac or PC, or Firefox, Internet Explorer or other browser. However, there are other issues that need to be considered, such as site size and usability/accessibility, to meet the needs of a site's users.

- **Site size**—What will be the dimensions of my site? Where will it be viewed; on small laptop screens, large monitors, or via a mobile device? Recommendations for what might be the most universal size to make your site change as technology changes. I traditionally keep my sites at around 760 × 420 pixels or 800 × 600 pixels, but I revisit the research done on what are the most commonly set screen pixel widths of users each time I make a new site. Do a search online for the topic "browser size" and plenty of information will be made available. For starters see Jakob Nielson's article at: *http://www.useit.com/alertbox/screen_resolution.html.* The truth is you can't please everyone, so you should find a width that allows the vast majority of your site visitors to view your Web site without horizontal scrolling. I like to add that for the home page a user should not have to scroll the content vertically either. All important content should be "above the fold"; a term used in newspaper publishing, but just as well applies to Web pages—above the fold refers to the viewing area of a browser before one has to scroll down or expand the browser window.
- **Usability /Accessibility**—Does the design of my site meet the needs of the majority of users who will be viewing my site? Is the text legible? Is the navigation clear? Is the site purpose clearly stated? Can contact information be found quickly? Is it accessible to screen readers, and to users with visual or hearing impairments, or learning difficulties? All of these questions are vital to consider in the planning process, although the specifics of meeting all these needs go beyond the scope of this book. See Adventures in Design: Accessibility in Flash after Chapter 8 for a bit more insight on this important subject as it relates to Flash.

Development

Development is the second phase. It's the part of the process where you do all the work; you build the site based on the user considerations you have determined and tools and structures you have chosen to use in the planning phase. There are two main parts to the development phase—gathering content and assembling content.

Gathering Content

Gathering content for your layout can be the most time-consuming and challenging part of the process, so leave plenty of time for it in your project timeline. You may be in a situation where you must create all of the content—images and copy—yourself, or procure the content from other sources, such as your client or an outside resource (i.e., another artist or writer, photographer, illustrator, or image or font repository). At this point, you must consider the issues of copyright and content format.

- **Copyright Issues**—If you create your own content or use copyright-free material, don't worry about the permission process. However, to reuse others' material, such as a company's logo or a photo of a famous person, you need the correct permissions. As an example, every digital image in *Exploring Adobe Flash CS4* is protected by copyright law whether explicitly indicated or not. As soon as it is created, copyright is automatically implied; no copyright notices or procedures are required to protect the image from unauthorized reproduction. It certainly does not hurt, however, to register your work through the U.S. Copyright Office (i.e., if you made your creation in the United States) at *http://www.copyright.gov.* You should at least put a copyright notice (©, date, your name) on your work to deter individuals from using it without your permission. I requested permission and/or paid for the artwork and photographs used in this book that I did not create myself. I also had to acknowledge that permission was granted (i.e., "Printed by permission of . . ." or "Courtesy of . . .").

  With the proliferation of digital content in our society, copyright protections have come under renewed scrutiny. It has become easier than ever to procure and edit content without giving thought to the original artist. In regard to the protection of digitized content and its use for educational purposes, laws have been enacted, such as the Digital Millennium Copyright Act (for information, see Exploring on Your Own). You should also know about a provision in U.S. copyright law called "fair use." Fair use delineates the use of creative works for educational or nonprofit purposes, such as the photographs provided for the lesson project in this chapter. When determining whether to use someone else's work as part of your own, ask yourself, "Will copying this image—or text, font, music, video, or data—make me money or take money out of someone else's pocket?" If the answer is "yes," proceed with caution: get permission and credit the artist.
- **Format**—Another aspect of development is getting the content into the right format for your use. For example, if Flash is to be used as the medium for assembling your content you need be sure the content can be successfully imported into the program. Are the images and photos you want to use in the correct file format for Flash to use them properly? Are they optimized and cropped to the correct dimensions before importing? Is the written copy translatable in the digital environment? Is the video or audio you want to use optimized for online playback?

Assembling Content

Once you have gathered the content, you assemble it in your layout program, which in this case would be Flash. Everything you have learned thus far and continue to in the next chapters has been the "how" of assembling and organizing content into Flash from drawing, importing and animating objects, including images, audio and video, to adding ActionScript.

Testing

The next phase is testing. It seems that no one ever leaves enough time in project schedules to do testing, and it's the most important part. Testing is vital to making sure your site works properly and downloads efficiently on all types of computer platforms and browsers, and is successfully reaching your target audience. It's also the opportunity to fine-tune your creation. When I test a site I'm creating, I try to view it on a PC and a Mac, and on many different browsers (Safari, Internet Explorer, Firefox). I also set up opportunities for my site's targeted users to evaluate the site and provide feedback for further improvement. Testing can be a very time consuming part of your work, but the pay off can be substantial, especially if you're doing a site for a paying client where your utmost goal is to provide them the most functional product possible.

Implementation

The final phase is implementation. It's the moment when the site is done and you post it online for all to view. After this phase, a visit to the spa or a really nice restaurant is in order. After celebrating, however, remember you will need to maintain the site. An online creation is never really complete. There is always room for improvement—new technologies to stretch your talents, lots of glitches to be tweaked, and consistent updating.

SUMMARY

After this chapter you should be well on the way to putting together a simple, yet fully functional, Flash masterpiece. In the next three chapters, it's the icing on the cake as we get into the specifics of integrating text, sound, and video in Flash.

in review

1. Why is using the multi-SWF method to build Web sites more useful than using scenes?
2. How are levels used in Flash?
3. What does the loadMovieNum action do?
4. When is it important to publish an HTML page with your SWF?
5. Why do you save the first page of a Web site index.html?
6. Name at least three tips for optimizing a Flash document.
7. What does a preloader do?
8. What's the purpose of the Bandwidth Profiler?
9. Name the four parts of the Web site design process.
10. What's the purpose of a site map?

exploring on your own

1. Study about copyright online:
    - U.S. Copyright Office (copyright basics): *http://www.copyright.gov/circs/circ1.html*
    - Specifics of the Digital Millennium Copyright Act: *http://www.copyright.gov/legislation/dmca.pdf*
    - Copyright Web site: *http://www.benedict.com*
    - Stanford University Libraries, Stanford Copyright & Fair Use Center: *http://fairuse.stanford.edu/*
    - Copyright Clearance Center to access copyright permission for millions of publications worldwide: *http://www.copyright.com/*

2. A Web site can be designed and developed integrating Flash- and HTML-based content. A portion of an HTML constructed site could contain a Flash supported element—animated movie, navigation bar, etc. These sites are often referred to as hybrid sites and are a popular way to get the best of all that Web-based technologies can offer. Following are a couple hybrid sites to explore. Ctrl-click (Mac), or right-click (Windows) over an area of the site and if the drop down menu indicates use of the Flash player, that section of the site is developed in Flash.

   - Roxbury Latin School – their home page contains a Flash movie embedded within the HTML-based site – *http://www.roxburylatin.org/*
   - Second Story interactive firm – their portfolio of work is enhanced with Flash – *http://secondstory.com/*

3. There are so many Flash resources online, including free templates of Flash layouts that you can use to aid your site designs. For example, check out: *http://www.flashmo.com/*.

ADVENTURES IN DESIGN

Making a Preloader

As you learned in Chapter 7, a preloader monitors the loading process of a Flash movie and then plays the movie when enough of it (as determined by the ActionScript code) has loaded. As well, it shows visitors the progress of the preload, presenting them with how much has been downloaded, so they will know how long it will take before the full movie begins. There are many ways (scripts) for creating preloaders, some quite complex depending on how a Flash application is constructed and what version of ActionScript you are using. For example, in a Flash presentation or Web site created with multiple SWF files, each SWF—depending on how much content it contains—could have a preloader. You experienced this in Chapter 7 when viewing the sections of Jordi Forniés site (designed by Justin Lerner) at *http://www.jordifornies.com/*. Each SWF that was loaded into another SWF had its own preloader (refer to Figure 7–5 in Chapter 7). Another good example where you can see preloaders in action is on the Mini Cooper site at *http://www.miniusa.com*. In this Adventures in Design I show you one method using ActionScript 2.0.

PROFESSIONAL PROJECT EXAMPLE

Last year, as part of their annual online giving campaign, The Roxbury Latin School hired me to create a Flash-based, self running presentation with photos, text, and sound that highlights their school. See Figure B–1. The development challenge with this presentation was seamlessly animating and syncing content so that it ran efficiently. Inevitably, however, the amount of content that needed to load before it could run in a seamless manner required a preloader. See Figure B–2.

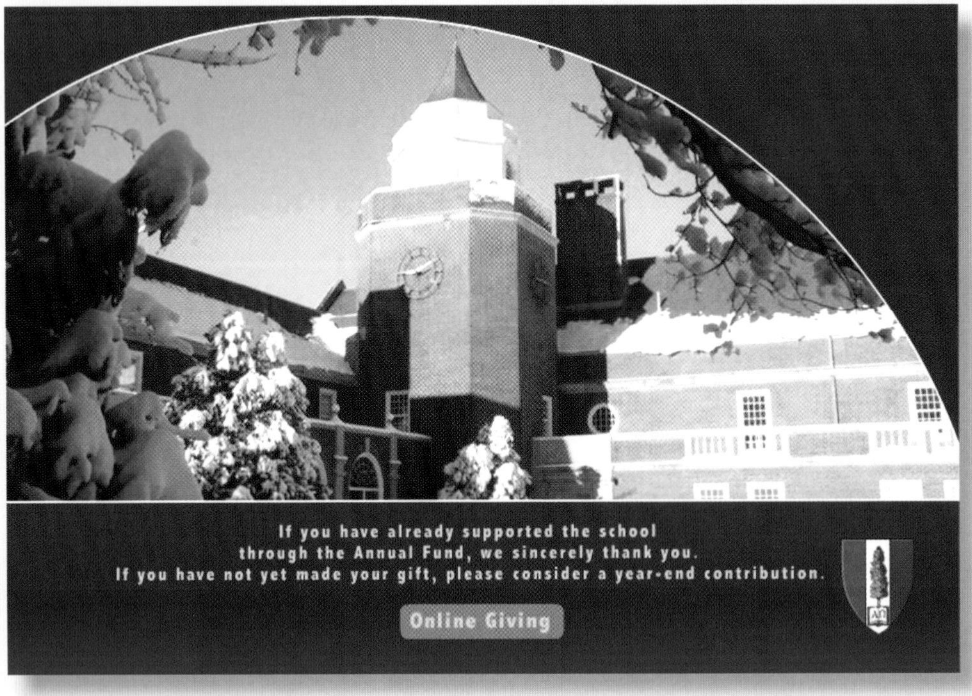

figure B–1 Example page of The Roxbury Latin School Flash presentation.

figure B–2 The preloader at the beginning of The Roxbury Latin School presentation.

YOUR TURN

Now, it's your chance to examine a preloader similar to the one I built for The Roxbury Latin School presentation. This preloader is part of a file you worked on in a previous lesson—the Flash Exposure presentation. There is quite a bit of code involved in making this preloader; admittedly I didn't write the code myself, but borrowed it from another Flash developer—Joshua Hirsch of Big Spaceship creative firm (*http://www.bigspaceship.com*). His sample files and article I found online, and are available in the **aid_examples/preloader/preloader_sample** folder. You will find borrowing code, adapted to your own needs, is a good way to acquire scripts that could otherwise be very difficult to write. It's OK to extract code from others who have willingly shared their ActionScripts with the public (see, for example, *http://www.adobe.com/devnet/flash*, *http://www.flashkit.com*, or *http://www.kirupa.com*). However, even with the coding provided for you, understanding all the pieces that make a preloader work can get complicated and for some overwhelming; the "Your Turn" section of this Adventures in Design is not for the faint of heart.

Introduction to the Preloader Scene

1. From Flash open the **aid_example/preloader/aid2_preloader.fla** file found on the back of the book CD.
2. Set the workspace to Classic.
3. Choose Control > Test Movie to view the preloader in action.

ADVENTURES IN DESIGN

Note: If you don't see the preloader, it's possible your computer has cached the file so quickly that the preloader is moot. Choose Control > Test Movie, and from the Menu bar choose View > Download Settings 56K or higher, and then View > Simulate Download.

4. Close the SWF movie file to go back to the FLA version.
5. From the scene drop-down menu (the film-taker icon in the upper right of the movie window) choose the **preloader** scene. I created this scene from the Scenes panel (Window > Other Panels > Scene). See Figure B–3.

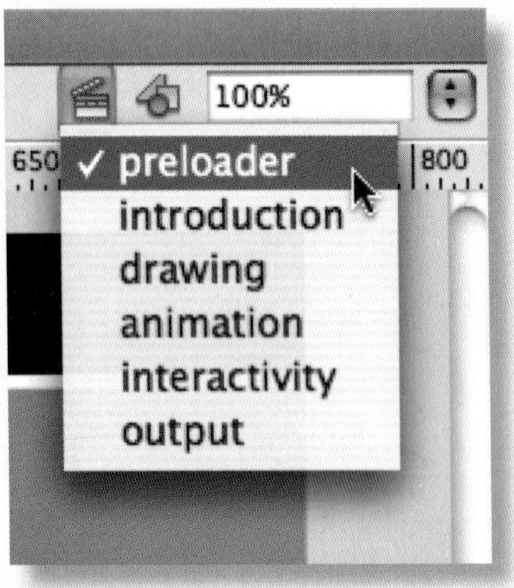

figure B–3 Choose the **preloader** scene.

6. Note the three layers on the Timeline—**background, preloader_mc**, and **actions**. Let's look at the elements on each one closely.
7. First, select the **background** layer. It contains the basic background objects of the movie. These are simple graphics that will load fast with the preloader graphic, so users know where they are. Keep this layer locked.

Exploring the Preloader_MC Layer

1. Now, select the **preloader_mc** layer. This layer contains the **preloader_mc** movie clip, which contains the preloader graphic and functionality. The instance name of the **preloader_mc** is also called **preloader_mc** (view the instance name in the Properties panel). The first frame of the movie clip is hidden—the only thing selected in the middle of the Stage should be a white dot with a crosshair. See Figure B–4.

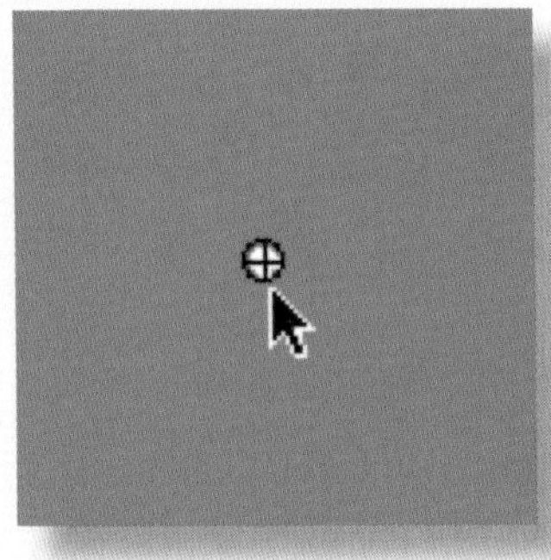

figure B–4 The **preloader_mc** movie clip is invisible in the first frame—a white dot indicates its location on the Stage.

2. Double-click on the white dot to enter the editing mode of the **preloader_mc**.
3. Hit Return/Enter on the keyboard to play back the animation in the movie clip.
4. Note there are two sections in the timeline labeled IN and OUT. The IN section is the part of the timeline and code that continues to loop until the content is loaded. Once loaded, an action is executed to go to the OUT section, which ends the preloading action and sends the user to the introduction (home) scene of the movie.
5. Within this **preloader_mc** there is dynamic text block (there is lots to learn about dynamic text blocks in Chapter 8) that on the fly creates the counting numbers that are entered within the circle graphic. Select frame 15 of the **dynamic text block** layer to see the dotted box on the Stage that will hold the numbers.

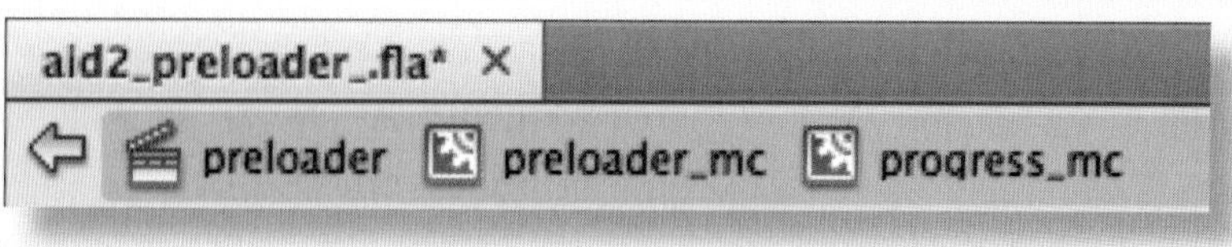

figure B–5 Inside the editing mode of the **progress_mc**.

6. Click (once) on the dynamic text block on the Stage to select it. Note in the Properties panel for the dynamic text that under Options there is a variable assigned called **pct_str** (percentage string). This variable, which can be named anything, is the name contained in the **Preloader.as** script (that you will explore in a later step) that executes the action within the dynamic text block.
7. Lock the **dynamic text box** layer, so you won't accidentally select it.
8. Within this **preloader_mc** is another embedded movie clip—select frame 15 of the **progress_mc** layer. Now, double-click on the white dot again in the center of the Stage. This should take you into the editing mode of the **progress_mc**. See Figure B–5.
9. Play back the animation. The green circle (if you don't see it, unlock the layers) is a mask that circles around and creates the animation graphic of the preloader.
10. Go back to the main Timeline by clicking on **preloader** up in the navigation bar for the editing modes (refer to Figure B–5 again). You will see once again the three layers we've been exploring in the Timeline—**background**, **preloader_mc**, and **actions**.

Examining the Actions Layer

1. OK, last layer to examine—the **actions** layer. Click on frame 2 of the actions layer (it has a little "a" on it).
2. Choose Window > Actions to view the actions on this frame. Whoa! There is a lot of code here, which we won't decipher step by step. However, there are comments indicated by a slash/slash (//) before each action to give you an idea of what the actions do. One thing I do want you to notice in the script is the code gotoAndPlay ("SITE")—where is this **SITE**? Let's find out. See Figure B–6.
3. Close the Actions panel.
4. From the film-take clapper in the upper right corner of the movie choose the **introduction** scene. Note on the **label** layer the frame label **SITE**. This label indicates where the "go to and play SITE" action that you just saw in the **preloader** scene goes.

> **Note: How do I create a frame label? To create a frame label, select a frame and in the Properties panel under Label type a label name. See Figure B–7.**

5. Go back to the **preloader** scene.

The Preloader Class

1. Test the movie again to view the preloader. Notice the counting action that occurs within the circular graphic. This is a nice feature to let a user know how long before the movie begins to play. We identified the

ADVENTURES IN DESIGN

```
stop();

// this will be called when the preloader finishes animating out
function onPreloaderOut(){
    preloader_mc.removeEventListener("onPreloaderOut", this);
    gotoAndPlay("SITE");
}

// add this timeline as a listener to listen for the 'onPreloaderOut' event
preloader_mc.addEventListener("onPreloaderOut", this);

// tell the preloader to start preloading this timeline
preloader_mc.startPreload(this);
```

figure B–6 The code that executes part of the preloader's functionality. Note the action to go to and play a frame action called **SITE**.

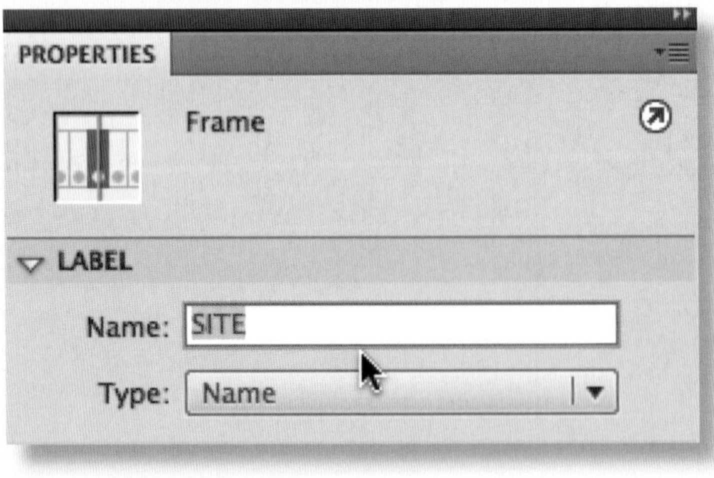

figure B–7 Frame labels are useful to call a specific point on a timeline via ActionScript.

dynamic text box that will visually show the numbers counting on the **preloader** scene, but where is the code to make it all work?

2. The code is actually external to the file—yes, you can create scripts outside of Flash that can be called into a SWF at run-time. This is convenient when you want to use the script document as part of other Flash files—just link to it—and/or need to update it without having to open and republish a FLA/SWF file.
3. Minimize the Flash program and search in your lessons folder or on the back of the book CD for the **aid_examples/preloader** folder. Double-click on the file titled **Preloader.as** (see Figure B–8) to open it.
4. There is a lot of scary ActionScript in this file; it's all necessary to get your preloader to work properly. Read through the comments (indicated by //) for descriptions of each section of the script. Once again, I didn't write all this code, but borrowed it from Joshua Hirsch (*http://www.bigspaceship.com*) and adapted it for use in my own projects. See his sample files and article in the **aid_examples/preloader/preloader_sample** folder.
5. That's a wrap for this Adventures in Design. Take the challenge and try to recreate this preloader in your own Flash movie.

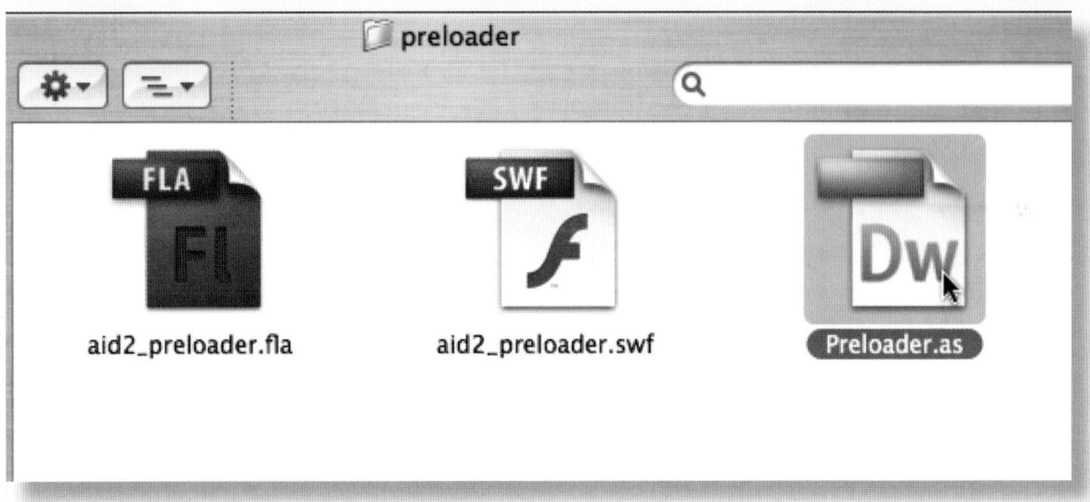

figure B–8 Because I have Adobe Dreamweaver on my machine the .as (actionscript) file is indicated by a DW icon—this file is actually a plain text file with the .as extension on the end that can be opened in any program that supports text files, such as Microsoft Word.

Explorer pages

JUSTIN LERNER

"There is no tipping point for knowledge in the field of web design. Everyday is a chance to do something you didn't do yesterday."

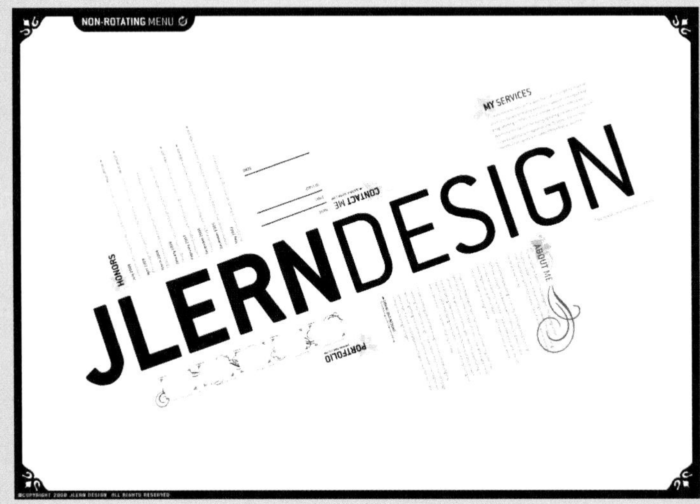

Justin Lerner's Web site home page, where Justin uses Flash to create an exploratory online experience. Courtesy of Justin Lerner.

About Justin Lerner

Justin Lerner was born and raised in East Brunswick, New Jersey. The youngest child of three in a family of artists, Justin was interested in drawing and painting at an early age. In high school, as the emergence of computers in art became more prevalent, he was turned on to the field of graphic design by his mother who had a friend in the industry. After that, he attended the University of Delaware from 1999 to 2003 to focus on graphic design in the very selective Visual Communications program. Knowing very little about Web site design, Justin took an elective course in the winter of 2001 on the basics of this emerging field and instantly fell in love with the concept of design using motion and interactivity. There had been no Web design major at the University at the time, so he created his own curriculum building Web sites in place of the print design projects that were assigned. Justin became a night owl and continued to teach himself everything he needed to know about building the flash Web sites he envisioned.

Justin's freelance business got started while he was still in school. He began taking on small jobs for friends, and as the word spread, more opportunities presented themselves. After graduating, he worked for five years at a small local design shop while keeping his freelance business growing on the side. Justin's ultimate goal was to work for himself, and he was finally able to achieve that goal in January 2008.

With the launch of a new Web site that received recognition from the likes of *Communication Arts*, *South by Southwest*, *The Pixel Awards*, and a handful of other design magazines, Justin's freelance business is off to a great start. Taking on projects for companies all over the world, he continues to build his portfolio with innovative work for clients such as M&M, Waterford Crystal, and Campbell's. Justin is truly doing what he loves everyday and gets excited every time he has the opportunity to create a new interactive experience for the Web.

See more of Justin's work at *http://www.jlern.com.*

About the Work of Justin Lerner

Justin shares with us his work process . . . "I think of every project as a chance to do something new. The idea of exploring new ground or getting myself into an unknown situation is what makes the field of art and design so exciting. The element of surprise is always there and I surprise myself a lot with what I accomplish. The first part of my process is researching the subject matter. If I am building a restaurant website, then I will go eat at the restaurant and really soak up the atmosphere. I take note of small details—such as a wall decoration that I can pull into the website to give the viewer a sense of what the restaurant is like, without having been there. Sometimes I like to think of my websites as a movie set, where I strive to create just the right lighting and effects. My goal is to produce a mood that will drive an emotional response, while informing the viewer. In my opinion, sharing information through a website is not enough—I want to engage the viewer with an online experience that leaves a lasting impression."

"I try my best to keep an open mind and set no boundaries for my creative visions. If I can think it up, then I will figure out how to produce it. I never let myself get intimidated by a concept that seems beyond my capabilities. If I don't know how to do it now, I will by the time the project is complete. With technology constantly evolving, this is a great field for someone who loves to learn. The motivation to create something innovative and new is a huge driving force that I thrive on, so I feel lucky that I get to incorporate that into my job everyday."

Flash site design for Postimpressions in Wilmington, Delaware. Courtesy of Justin Lerner.

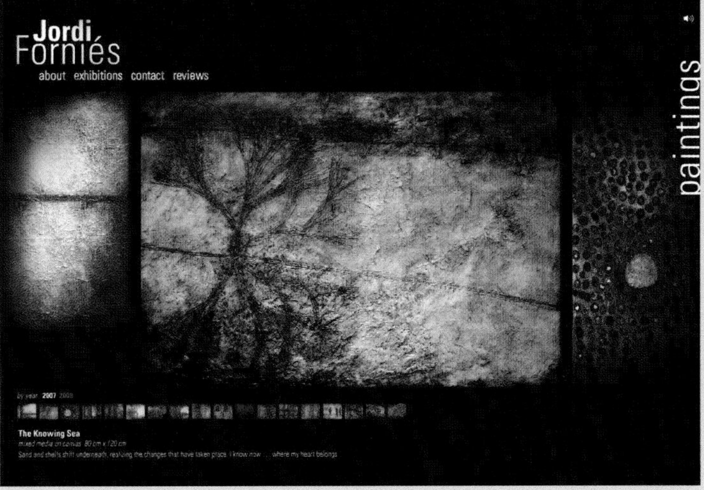

Artist Jordi Forniés Web site (*http://www.jordifornies.com*). Site designed and developed by Justin Lerner.

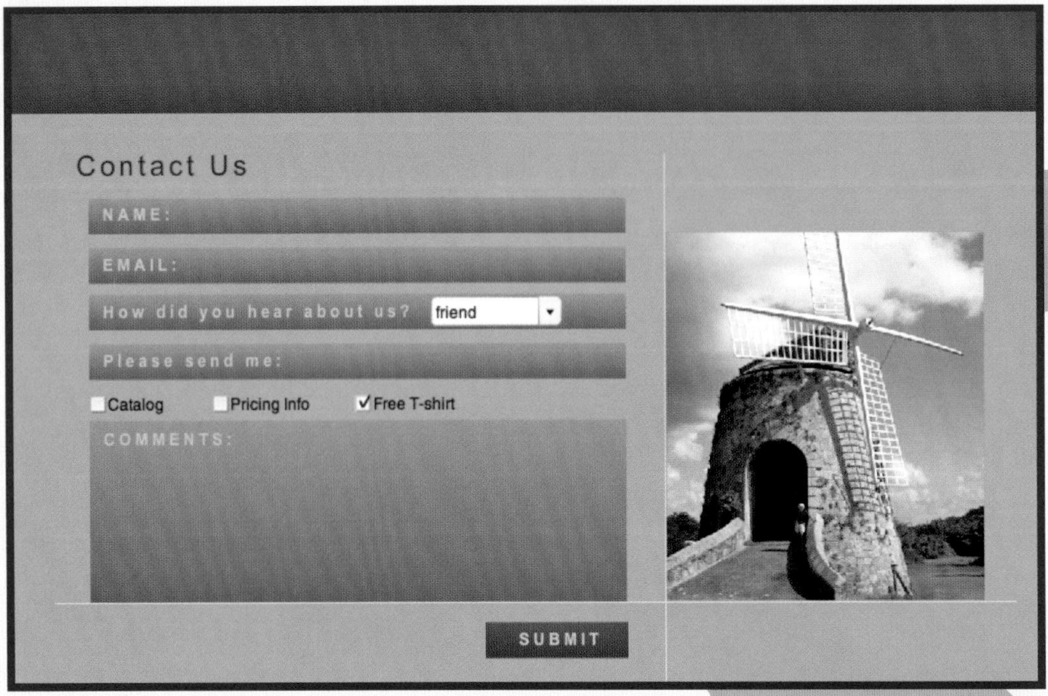

8

| working with text |

charting your course

Text plays an important role in Flash. To enhance the aesthetic and interactive elements of your Flash movie, in this chapter learn about the three text types—static, input, and dynamic—and their properties. Also, covered are important aspects and features related to text, such as embedded versus device fonts, anti-aliasing, font mapping, forms, scrolling and accessibility. Finally, you'll create a Flash form, scrolling text, and get an overview of designing with web-based text.

goals

In this chapter you will:

- **Explore static, input, and dynamic text properties**
- **Learn the differences between embedded and device fonts**
- **Understand the concept of anti-aliasing**
- **Create a Flash form**
- **Create a scrolling text block**
- **Discover best practices for designing with Web-based text**

TYPES OF TEXT

There are three types of text in Flash—static, input, and dynamic. Each is described in detail, as follows.

Static Text

Static text displays text that doesn't change within your Flash movie. It's embedded as part of the final SWF. So far, in this book you have only played with static text.

When creating static text, you can place text on a single line that expands as you type (called label text), or in a fixed-width (horizontal) or height (vertical) field that expands and wraps words automatically (called block text). Follow the steps to learn how to create each type.

To create label text:

1. Select the Text tool.
2. Be sure Static Text is the selected option in the Properties panel. See Figure 8–1.
3. Click once on the Stage and start typing. As you type the text line grows longer, until you hit Enter/Return on your keyboard to start a new line. This is called label text, as is indicated by a circle in the upper-right corner of the box. See Figure 8–2.

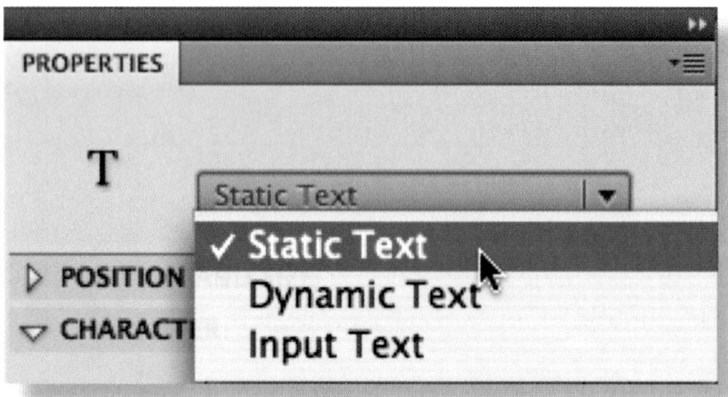

figure 8–1

Select the Static Text option.

To create block text:

1. Select the Text tool.
2. Be sure Static Text is selected in the Properties panel.
3. Click and drag on the Stage to determine the size of the text area you would like. Start typing in the block; when you hit the end of the first line, the text is automatically wrapped to the next line. This is called block text, indicated by the square in the top-right corner of the box. See Figure 8–3.

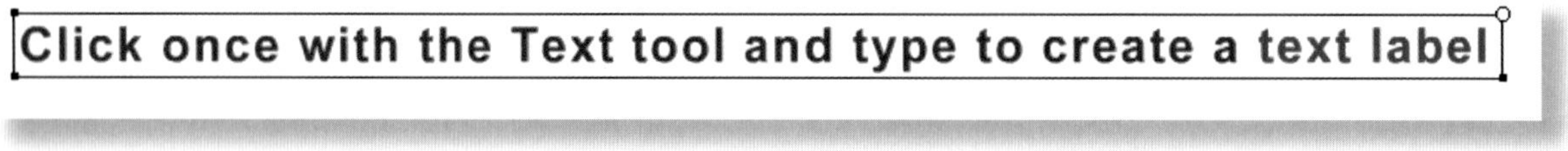

Click once with the Text tool and type to create a text label

figure 8–2

A text label is a long line of text.

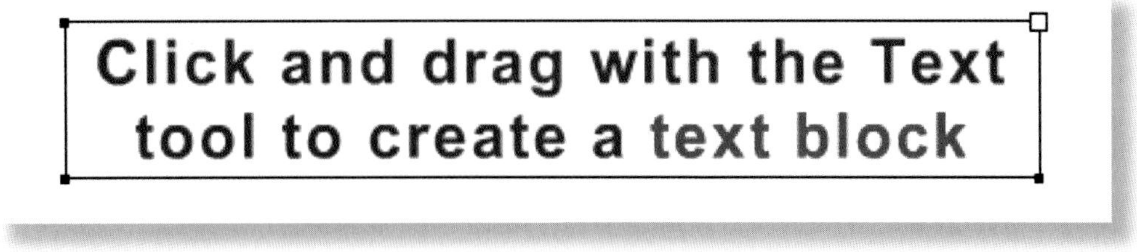

Click and drag with the Text tool to create a text block

figure 8–3

A text block is a confined area of text that wraps from line to line.

To adjust the size of the text block, click and drag on the square while the Text tool is selected.

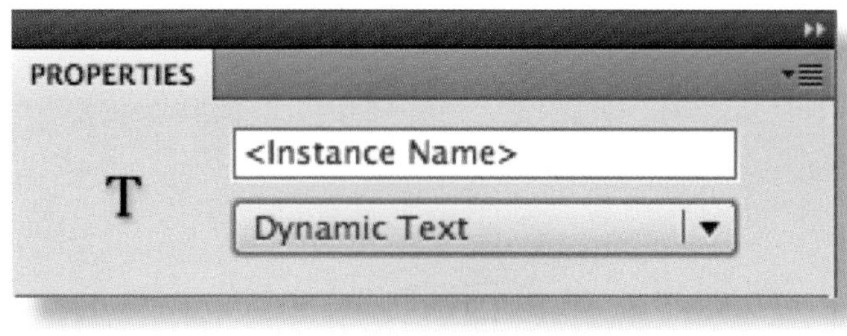

figure 8–4

An instance name can be defined for dynamic and input text.

Dynamic Text

Dynamic text displays text on the fly—it can be imported at the run time of a SWF from another source, such as a text (.txt) file external to Flash, or a database with continuously updated content like stock quotes or the weather report. Dynamic text can be updated outside of Flash, have HTML style properties defined within it, and can be made accessible to screen readers. Unlike static text, dynamic text can also have an instance name applied to it so that it can be called through ActionScript. See Figure 8–4.

Input Text

Input text allows you to create form fields in which users can enter text that can either be sent back to them or another receiving party (e.g., the owner of the Web site or the site administrator). Learn more about forms and make your own in the About Forms and Lesson 1 sections of this chapter. Like dynamic text, input text can also be made accessible and have an instance name applied to it so that it can be called through ActionScript.

Text Properties

There are many formatting options available in the Properties panel for static, input, and dynamic text. Some of these options you have already explored with static text throughout this book and most of them are probably familiar to you from working with text in word processing programs. Refer to Figure 8–5 as you go through the options that follow.

Position and Size

For precise placement of text you can adjust its position on the Stage (x and y) and block size (w and h) numerically in the Position and Size area of the Properties panel. To do this, either

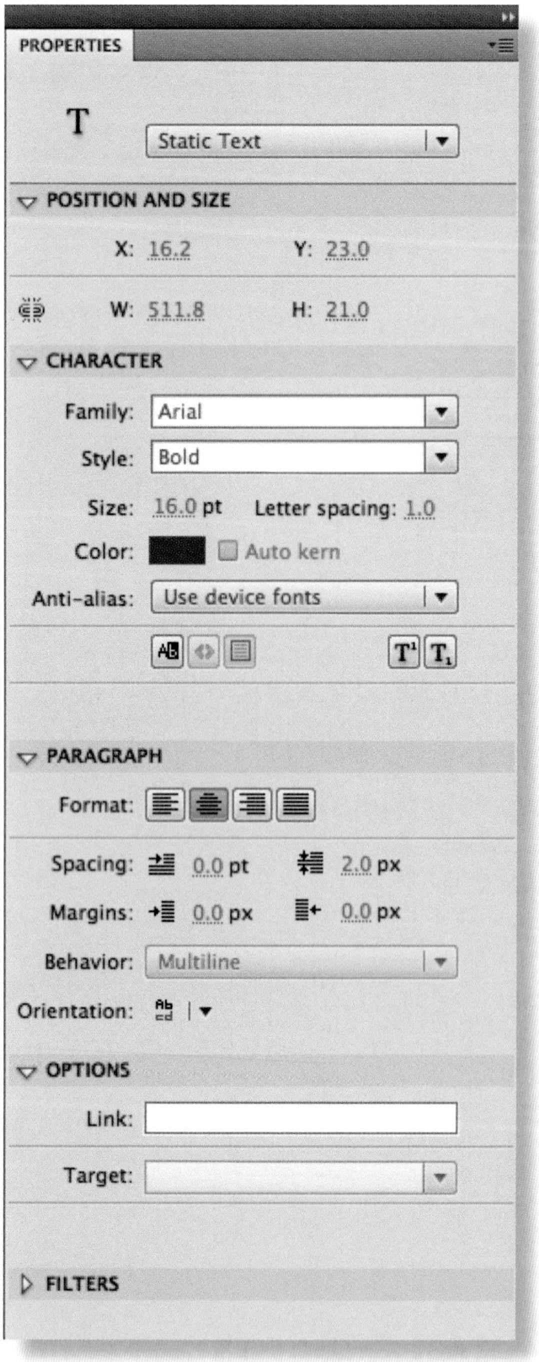

figure 8–5

The Properties for text.

click on a value to highlight it and type in the new value, or place your cursor right below a value until you see a hand icon with a double-sided arrow, then click and drag right or left to increase or decrease the value (this is called scrubbing). See Figure 8–6.

Character

Text character options include font, style, size, letter spacing, and color. Design tips for how best to use these formatting options within Flash are covered at the end of this chapter. There is also an option to adjust how text is displayed; it's anti-aliasing settings. Learn more about this in the section of this chapter titled "What is Anti-aliasing?"

Finally, there are several other options in this area depending on the type of text you are using, including whether or not the text will be selectable by the end user, rendered as HTML, have a border around it, or is formatted in superscript or subscript (characters that are set slightly below or above a text's base line, such as in the use of footnotes or mathematical or computing values). See Figure 8–7.

> **Note:** Grayed-out sections of the Properties panel indicate properties that are not available for the text type you have selected.

Paragraph

Paragraph settings are also available for the justification of text, its indention and line spacing and left and right margins. Depending on the type of text used, you can also adjust the behavior (line type) of a text block. For example, with an input text field you can restrict a user to write within a single line, multiple lines (multiline), or multiple lines with no wrap (multiline no wrap), or, when typing in a password, hide the password characters from view. Here, you can also adjust the horizontal or vertical orientation of static text. See Figure 8–8.

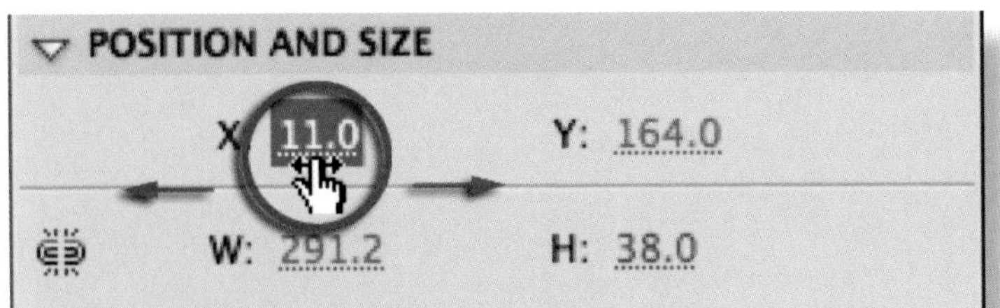

figure 8–6

Adjust the size of a text area by "scrubbing" right and left below the number field.

figure 8–7

Additional options for text in the Character area.

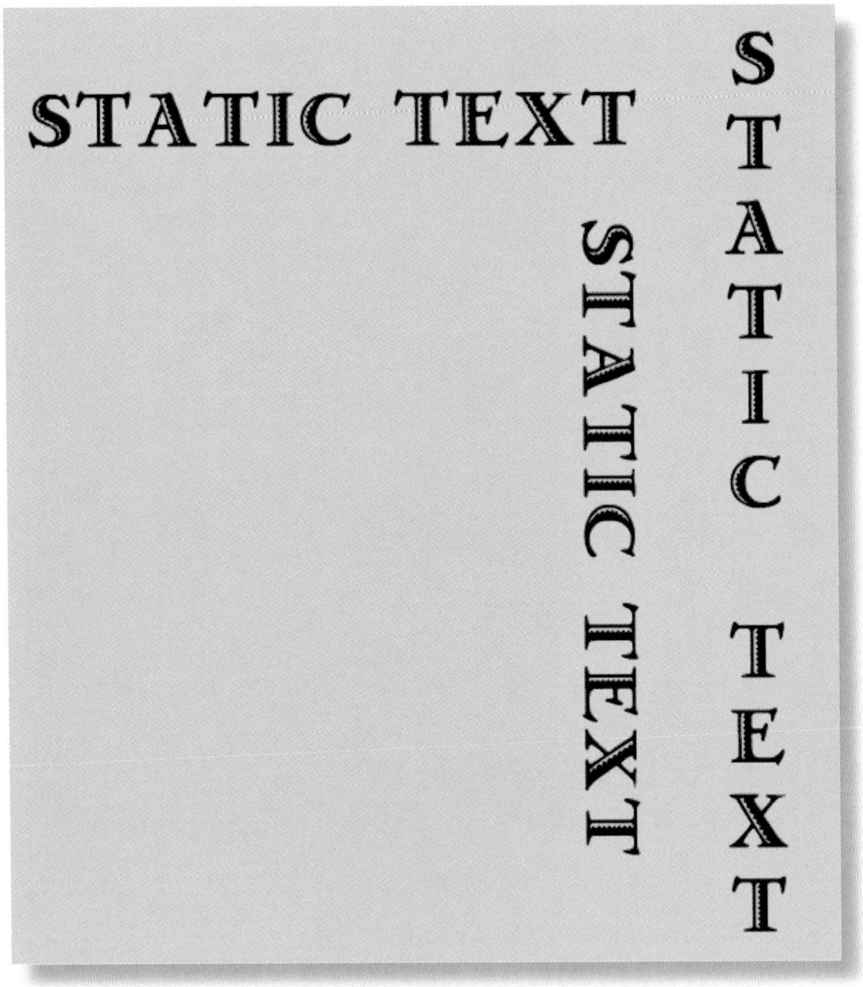

figure 8–8

Text can be set horizontally or vertically.

Options

For static and dynamic text, the Options area provides a quick way to create a hyperlink to an outside URL or a mailto: action within the text. See Figure 8–9. You actually did this in the first chapter. This is such a wonderful option, especially for those who have been using Flash for a while and previously had to code ActionScript on a button instance to get a hyperlink to work. However, keep in mind, this quick link option will only work on text, not on graphics. See Exploring on Your Own section at the end of this chapter on how to create a URL or mailto action on a graphic symbol using the bit more tedious method of entering the code in the Actions panel. For dynamic and input text, there is also a variable field in the Option area where you can enter in a name for the text block that can be identified by a back-end form script.

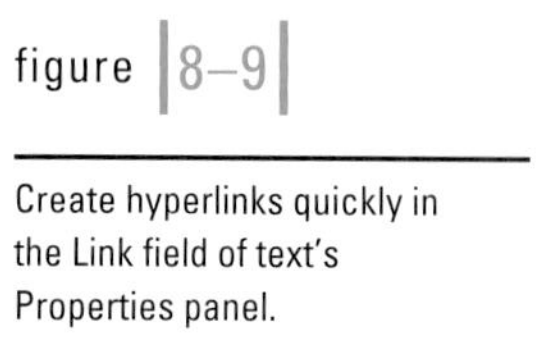

figure 8–9

Create hyperlinks quickly in the Link field of text's Properties panel.

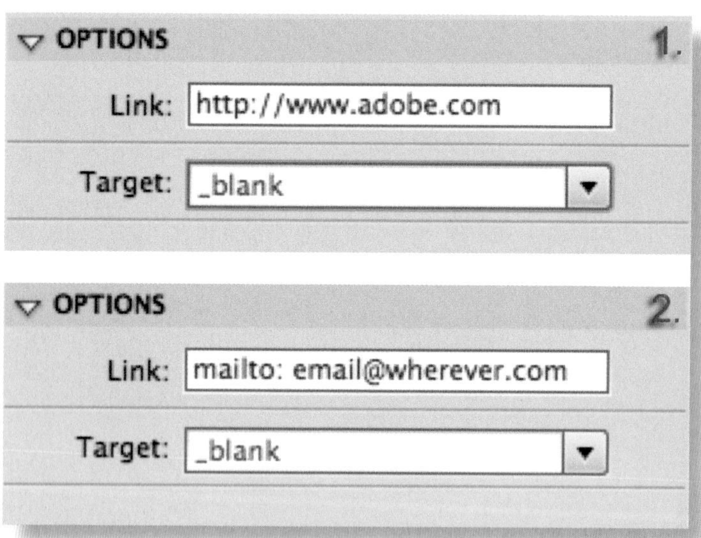

For input text, the Options area also contains the option to enter a maximum number of characters a user can type into an input field. See Figure 8–10.

figure 8–10

Options for input text.

Filters

From the filters area you can add and modify special effects on your text, such as drop shadows, bevels, and glows. Explore these variations on your own—create some text, select it, choose Add Filter at the bottom of the filters window (see Figure 8-11) and then modify the options in the Property and Value areas. See Figure 8-12 for examples.

EMBEDDED VERSUS DEVICE FONTS

Text in Flash is represented in two ways: (1) as font outlines (characters broken down into shapes) that are embedded within a published Flash document (SWF) or (2) by device fonts, which is when a font is determined by a specific font name (i.e., Arial, Verdana, Comic Sans, etc.) or general font type like serif or sans serif (see the Designing with Type section) that must be located on the end-users' computer. The advantage of embedded fonts is that the typographic design of a movie is uncompromised, maintaining the layout envisioned by the designer. The disadvantage is that it increases the size of the SWF file and, depending on the font style and size, can make the text less legible than if rendered as a device font. Device fonts are an alternative to embedded fonts and when used result in a smaller SWF file. They are also more legible at small

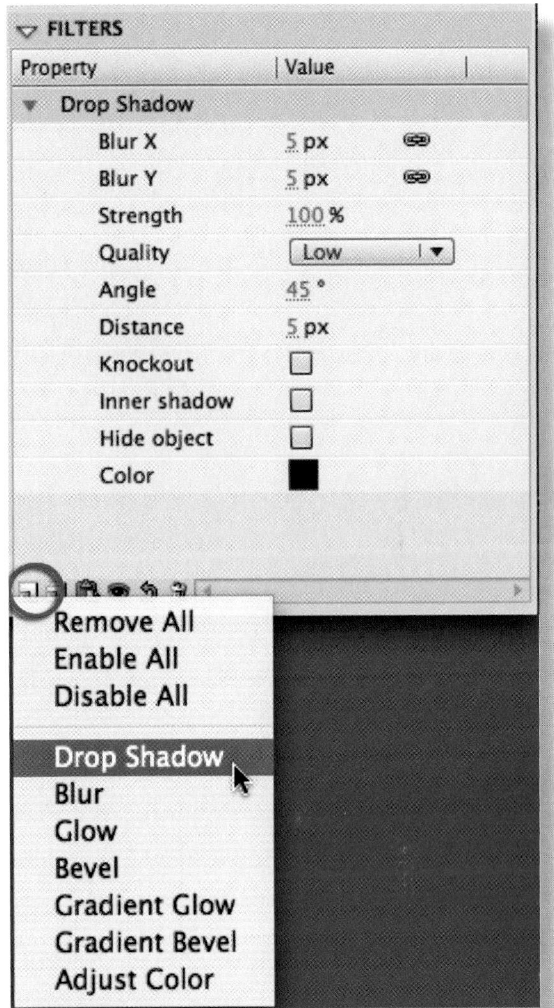

figure 8–11

Add filter effects to text.

figure 8–12

An example of the drop shadow effect on text.

point sizes (below 10 points). However, as mentioned previously, if a user's computer does not have an installed font that corresponds to the device font, text may look different than expected. Flash includes three generic device fonts, and when you specify one of these fonts and then export the document, the Flash Player uses the font on the user's computer that most closely resembles the generic device font. See Figure 8–13 for an example of the fonts that resemble each generic type.

- _sans (similar to Helvetica or Arial)
- _serif (similar to Times Roman)
- _typewriter (similar to Courier)

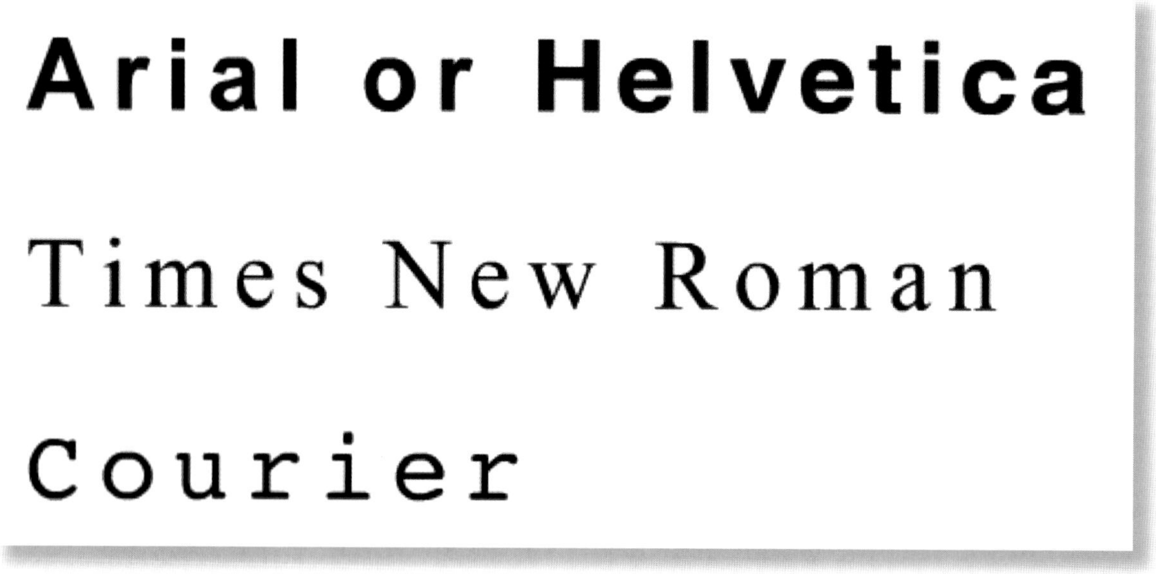

Arial or Helvetica

Times New Roman

Courier

figure 8–13

Examples of sans-serif, serif, and typewriter font styles.

Something to be aware of is that not all fonts displayed in Flash can be exported as outlines—often this is a restriction in the type of font that is available locally (for example, whether the font is designed for screen-based or print-based viewing), or its copyright restrictions preventing unauthorized use. To verify that a font can be exported, use the View > Preview Mode > Antialias Text command to preview the text; jagged type indicates that Flash does not recognize that font's outline and will not export the text.

FONT MAPPING

If you work with an FLA document that contains fonts that aren't installed on your system, Flash substitutes those fonts with fonts available on your system. This happens to me often when I open a student's Flash assignment—inevitably the student has used some funky font in

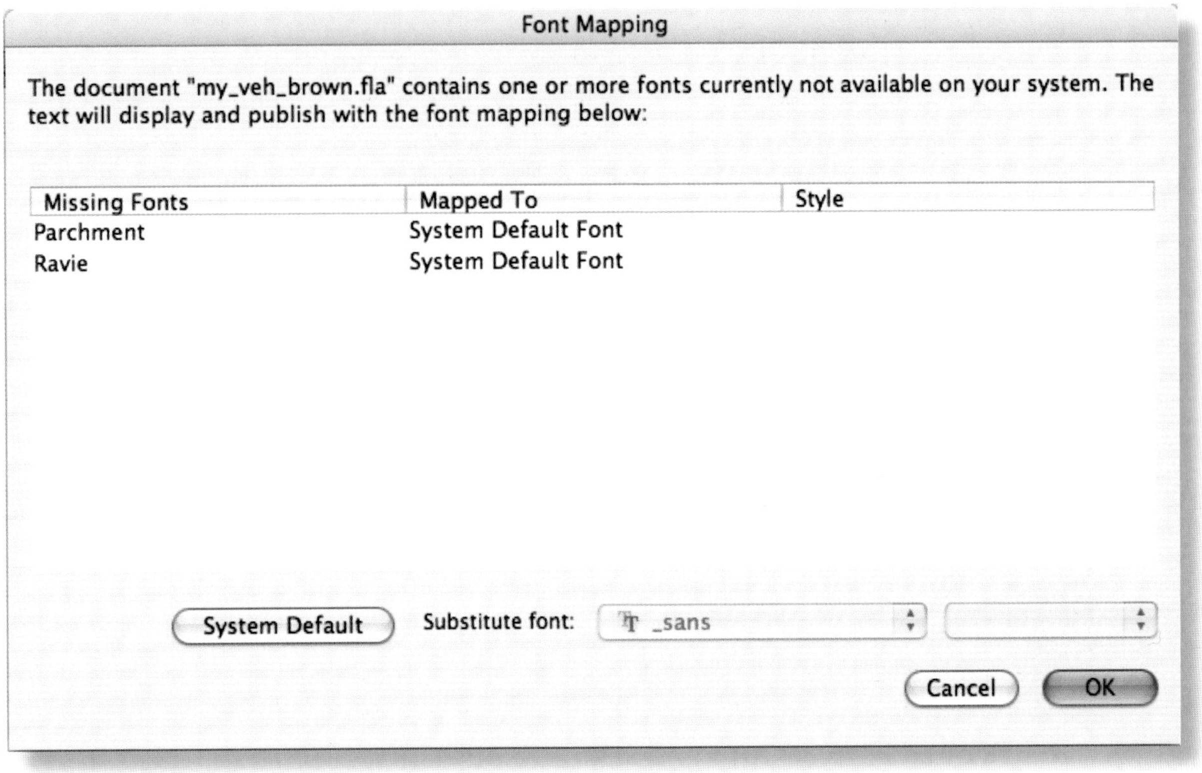

Font Mapping

The document "my_veh_brown.fla" contains one or more fonts currently not available on your system. The text will display and publish with the font mapping below:

Missing Fonts	Mapped To	Style
Parchment	System Default Font	
Ravie	System Default Font	

System Default   Substitute font: _sans

Cancel   OK

figure 8–14

In the Font Mapping window you can choose to have Flash use a default system font as a substitute for fonts that are defined in a Flash FLA file, but are not available on the computer that is opening the file.

their file that is not available even in my extensive font collection. When this happens, Flash opens the Font Mapping window and gives me the option to view the file using a substitute font, either my system's default font (see Figure 8–14) or a font selected from my own font repository (see Figure 8–15).

When a font is substituted, the text is displayed on your system using the substitute font, but the missing font information is saved with the document. That's a good thing because when the document is opened on a system that includes the missing font the text is again displayed in the correct font. When you work with a document that includes missing fonts, the missing fonts appear, enclosed in parentheses, in the font list in the Properties panel. When you select substitute fonts, the substitute fonts' names also appear. See Figure 8–16.

Also important to know is that if you apply formatting (such as font size or kerning) to the substitute font, the formatting when the text is displayed again with its missing font may not look as expected. You can change a substitute font you've chosen at any time by choosing Flash > Font Mapping (Mac) or Edit > Font Mapping (Windows).

Font Mapping

The document "my_veh_brown.fla" contains one or more fonts currently not available on your system. The text will display and publish with the font mapping below:

Missing Fonts	Mapped To	Style
Parchment	Arial	Regular
Ravie	Bell Gothic Std	Bold

System Default   Substitute font: Bell Gothic Std   Bold

Cancel   OK

figure 8–15

In the Font Mapping window you can also choose to substitute a missing font with another font in your local font folder.

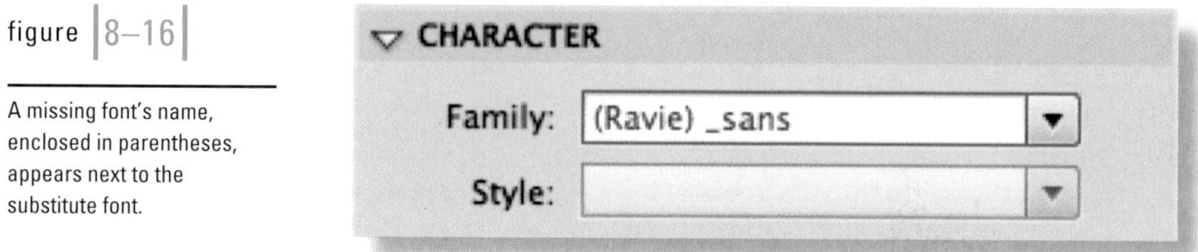

figure 8–16

A missing font's name, enclosed in parentheses, appears next to the substitute font.

WHAT IS ANTI-ALIASING?

As we learned a nice thing about SWFs is that they can embed the fonts used in a movie maintaining the typographic vision that the designer intended. However, this embedding process, while a windfall for the designer, has caused a common complaint from viewers of Flash-based Web sites—that they must squint to read the text because either the font is too small or it appears blurry and out of focus. The former issue (text too small) can be solved with some understanding of Web-based typography design and accessibility (see Designing with

Type in this chapter), and the later (blurry text) has been greatly improved with Flash's font rasterization system that lets you specify the anti-aliasing properties for fonts. Anti-aliasing simulates the smoothing of pixilated edges of bitmap rendered graphics and/or text characters through the gradation of color. See Figure 8–17 and Figure 8–18. The improved anti-aliasing capabilities are available only for SWF files published for Flash Player 8 or later.

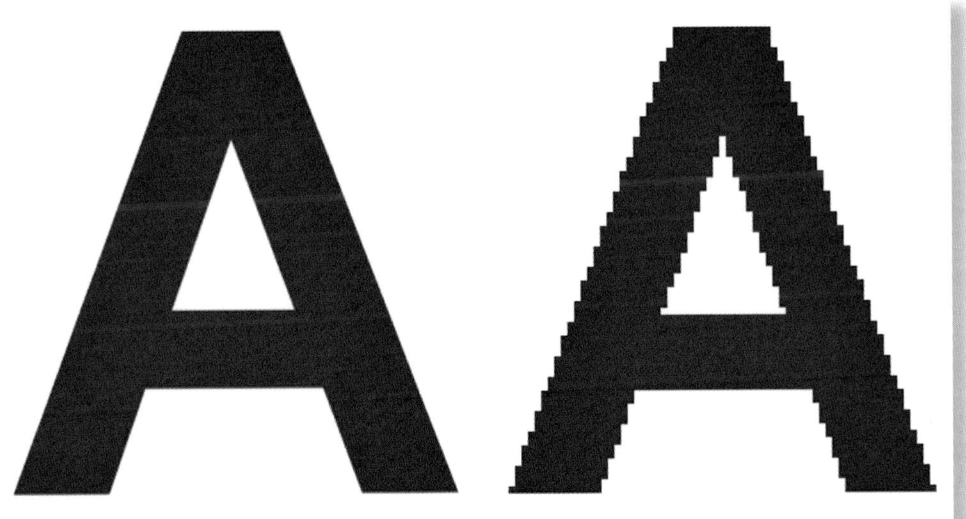

figure 8–17

An example of a letter with (smooth edges) and without (pixilated edges) anti-aliasing applied.

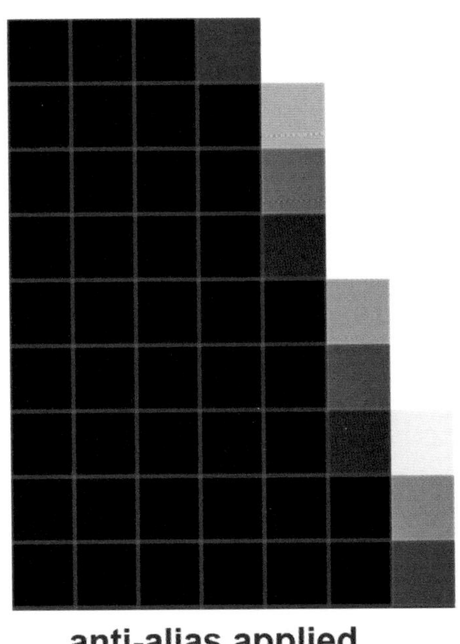

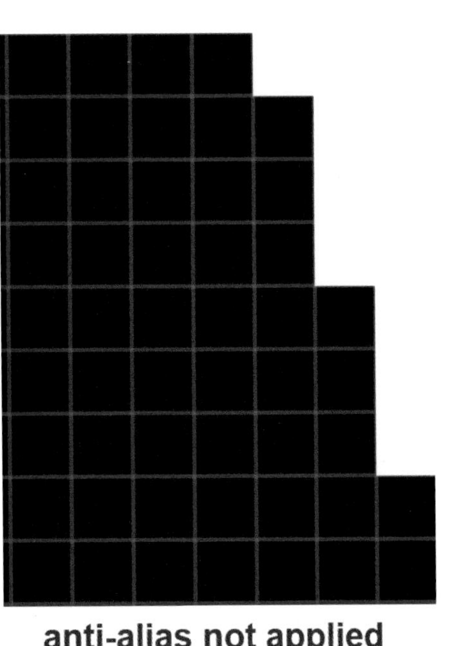

figure 8–18

A close-up view of how anti-aliasing is applied—an object with anti-aliasing has a gradation of colored pixels along the objects edge. Viewed from a distance, the edges of the object appear smoother.

Anti-aliasing options are in the Properties panel of selected text. Descriptions of each option are taken from the Flash help files:

- **Use Device Fonts**: Specifies that the SWF file use the fonts installed on the local computer to display the fonts. Typically, device fonts are legible at most font sizes. Although this option doesn't increase the size of the SWF file, it forces you to rely on the fonts installed on the user's computer for font display. When using device fonts, choose only commonly installed font families.
- **Bitmap Text (No Anti-Alias)**: Turns off anti-aliasing and provides no text smoothing. The text is displayed using sharp edges, and the resulting SWF file size is increased because the font outlines are embedded in the file. Bitmap text is sharp at the exported size, but scales poorly.
- **Anti-Alias For Animation**: Creates a smoother animation by ignoring alignment and kerning information. This option creates a larger SWF file because font outlines are embedded. For legibility, use 10-point or larger type when specifying this option.
- **Anti-Alias For Readability**: Uses the Flash text rendering engine to improve the legibility of fonts, particularly at small sizes. This option creates a larger SWF file because font outlines are embedded. To use this option, you must publish to Flash Player 8 or later. (Do not use this option if you intend to animate text, instead use Anti-Alias For Animation.)
- **Custom Anti-Alias**: Lets you modify the font's properties. Use Sharpness to specify the smoothness of the transition between the text edges and the background. Use Thickness to specify how thick the font anti-aliasing transition appears. (Larger values cause the characters to look thicker.) Specifying Custom Anti-Alias creates a larger SWF file because font outlines are embedded. To use this option, you must publish to Flash Player 8 or later.

OTHER TEXT FEATURES

There are several other features of Flash text that might be useful for you, including the spell checker, scroll bar component, break apart, accessibility panel, and input form elements.

Spell Checker

The Flash spell checker is easy to use—so use it! Simply choose Text > Check Spelling . . . from the menu bar and it will highlight and provide suggestions for any misspelled words (or what it thinks is misspelled) in any text blocks located on any scenes in your Flash movie. You can adjust spelling settings and create and edit a personal dictionary by choosing Text > Spelling Setup . . . from the menu bar. See Figure 8–19.

Scrolling

Most Flash movies are designed with an absolute document size unlike most HTML Web pages, which can contain a continuous stream of information that can be scrolled vertically within a browser window. A good solution to working with a large amount of text

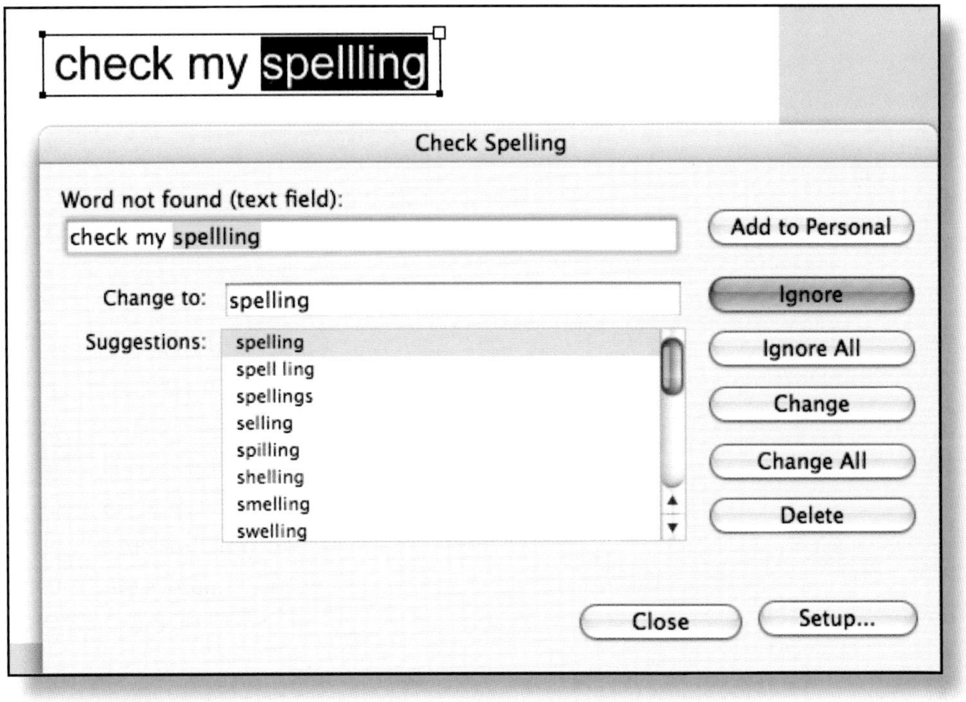

figure 8–19

Check Spelling—always a handy feature!

in a restricted (absolute-sized) movie area is to add a scroll bar along side a text block. See Figure 8–20. There are several methods for making scroll bars using ActionScript—some more or less complicated to construct. You will learn how to make a scroll bar using a Flash component in Lesson 2 of this chapter.

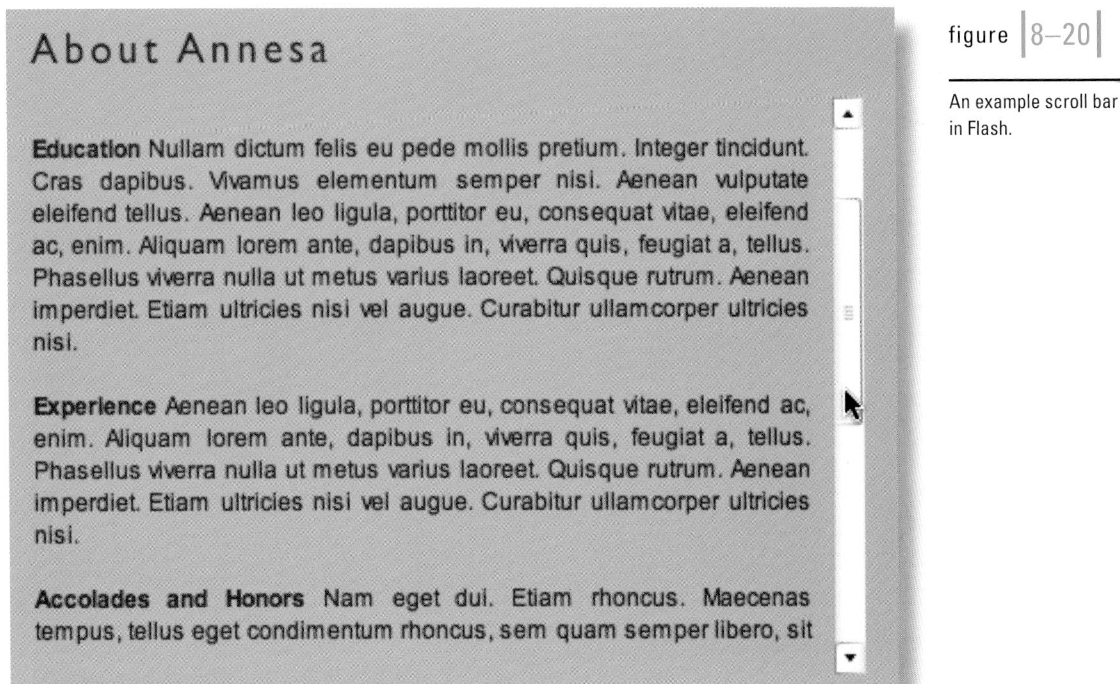

figure 8–20

An example scroll bar in Flash.

Break Apart

Break Apart (Modify > Break Apart) is a useful command to break text into shapes so that you can modify or add effects to the text as you can with any shape graphic (add gradients, shape animate, etc.). It's also useful if you want to ensure someone sees a font you've used if he/she doesn't have it installed on his/her system (this is recommended for only small amounts of text, however). To do this, select some text and choose Modify > Break Apart two times to convert the characters to shape objects. See Figure 8–21.

figure |8–21|

Text broken apart and with a gradient color effect applied.

Break Apart is also useful if you want to motion tween individual text characters. Try this:

1. Create some simple text.
2. Choose Modify > Break Apart to break the text apart as individually grouped objects. See Figure 8–22.
3. Select all the text characters and choose Modify > Timeline > Distribute to Layers. Each letter is automatically placed on an individual layer ready to be animated. See Figure 8–23.

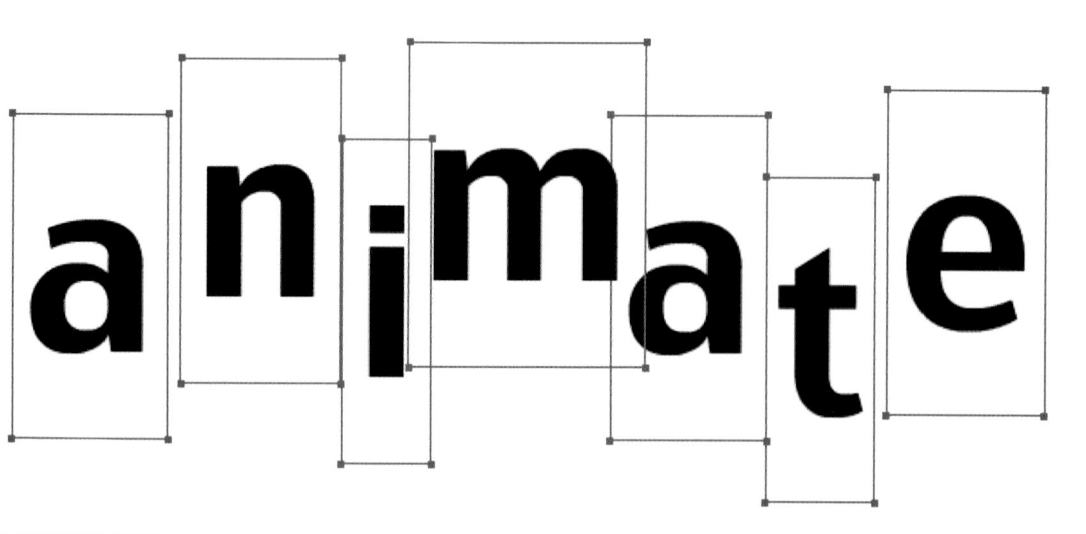

figure |8–22|

Text broken apart into individually grouped letters.

Text Accessibility

Because all the elements of a Flash movie are usually embedded in a single object (a SWF), adding accessible text equivalents (called ALT tags) for images or embedded text elements is important to support users accessing Web pages through screen readers or have chosen to turn off images from view. To add ALT tags to a graphic or embedded text element, first save the object as a symbol, select it, then choose Window > Other Panels > Accessibility and enter in a name and description. See Figure 8–24.

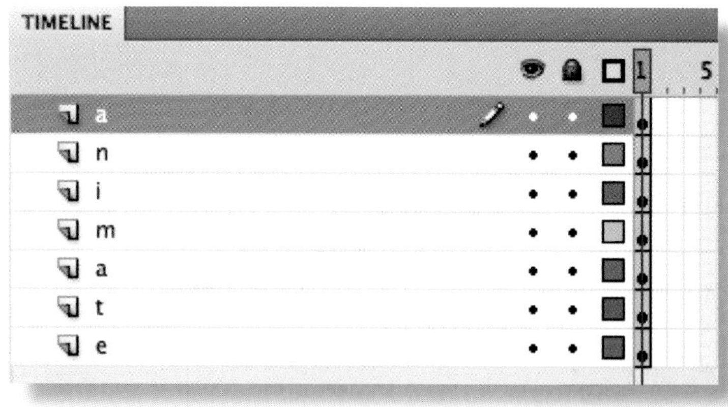

figure 8–23

Individual letters are distributed to layers, so you can easily animate each letter.

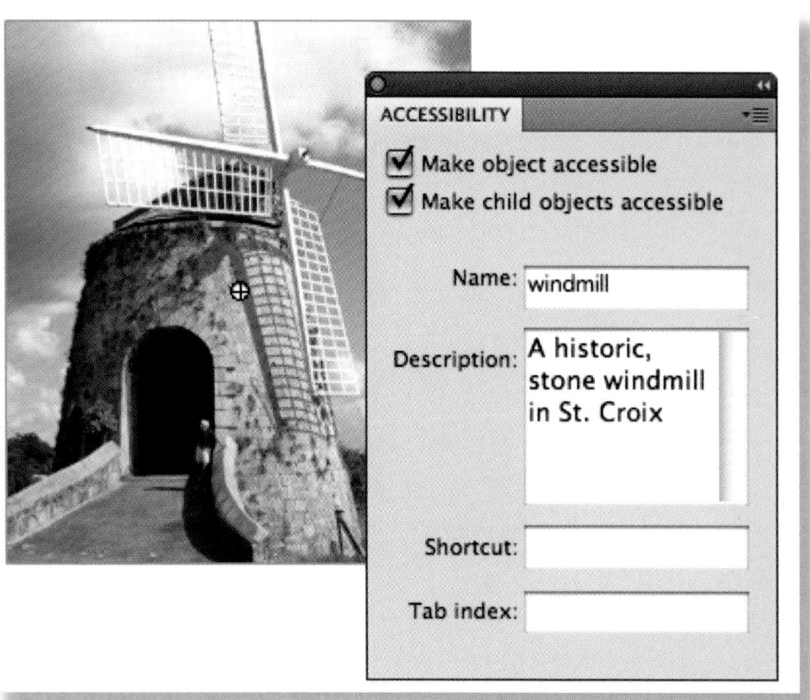

figure 8–24

Adding an accessible ALT tag to a Flash object.

About Forms

Web forms are a way for Web site owners to collect information, usually text-based, from a user. We have all filled out a Web form at one time or another. Forms provide two-way interactivity—instead of users just getting information sent to them they also can send information back. The development of this two-way functionality within a Web page can often be confusing to grasp for novice Web designers. The making of functional forms involves the creation and integration of two parts. The first part is the building of the front-end page with input text fields and elements—checkboxes, radio buttons, selectable lists—and a submit button that when clicked sends a message (method) to a script, the second part of this integration process. The script executes an action; it validates or determines the information being sent and instructs the Web server to send the information (via e-mail, for example) to the Web site owner. This script is written in a Web-based programming language, such as C, Java, PHP, or Perl. The first part of this process (building the form) is something you can create in Flash and that's what you will do in Lesson 1 of this chapter. The creation of the second part (the form script) is beyond the scope of this book and requires access to a Web server. However, in the Exploring On Your Own section I have provided online resources with further information on building forms and template scripts to get you started on integrating this second part.

Lesson 1: Creating a Form

Using Flash's input text and premade Components you will build the front-end design of a form.

> **Note:** Components are complex movie clips that have defined parameters, which are set during document authoring, and a unique set of ActionScript methods that allow you to change and add options at runtime.

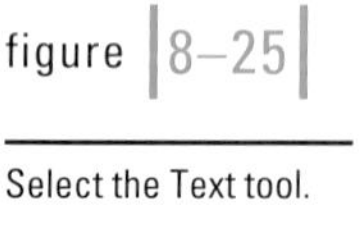

Select the Text tool.

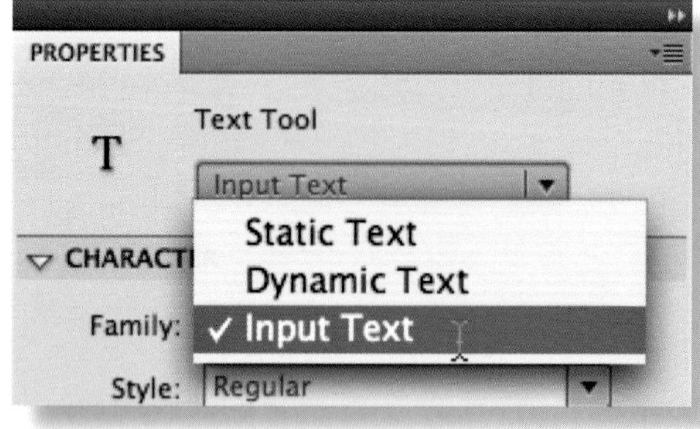

figure 8–26

Choose the Input Text option.

Looking Over the File

1. From Flash, open the **chap8_L1.fla** file in the **chap08_lessons** folder.
2. Be sure your workspace is set to Classic view.
3. To get you going on building a form, this file has been partially set up for you. Expand the Timeline panel and click on each layer to familiarize yourself with what's on the Stage.
4. Lock all the layers.

Creating Input Text Fields

1. Insert a new layer and name it **input_text_fields**.
2. Choose the Text tool in the Tools panel. See Figure 8–25.
3. In the Properties panel, set the text type to Input Text. See Figure 8–26.

4. In the Characters panel, set the following (see Figure 8–27):
    - Family: Arial (a familiar font that is available on most everyone's computer)
    - Style: Regular
    - Size: 12 pt.
    - Letter Spacing: 1.0
    - Color: Black
    - Anti-alias: Use device fonts
    - Note that the Selectable option is automatically chosen, so users can copy and paste content within the input fields.
5. Click and drag from left to right after the **Name:** title to create an input text field. See Figure 8–28.

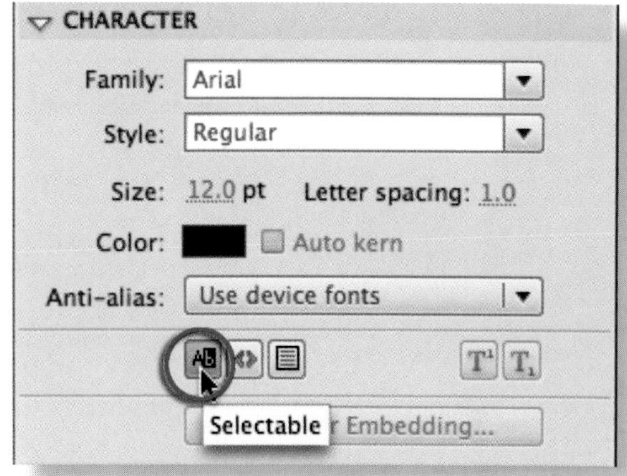

figure 8–27

Input text is made selectable by default.

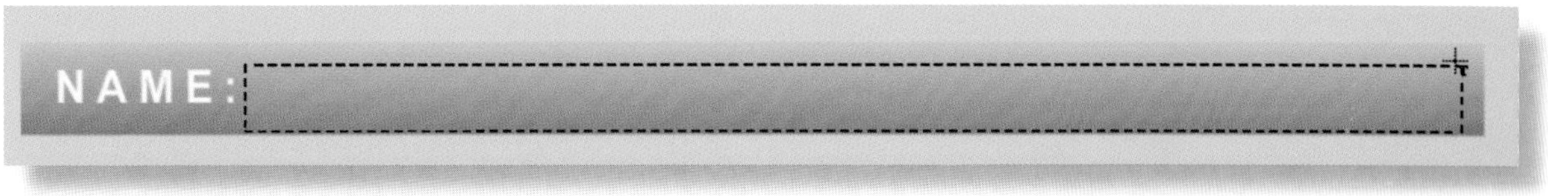

figure 8–28

An input text field.

6. Choose the Selection tool to see the blue bordered, empty text box. Adjust its position over the green field area if necessary.

> **Note:** If you don't see the text field, be sure you have Input Text selected in the Properties panel.

7. Deselect the text box and note that it has a dashed line around it—this indicates an input text field.
8. Choose Control > Test Movie to view the SWF.
9. Click the cursor right after the **Name:** title and type your name. See Figure 8–29. Hey, it works! Note also that you can select the text.
10. Close the SWF file. Select the input text field, hold down the Alt/Option key, and drag down to create a copy of the text field for the **Email:** area.
11. Select the Text tool and create another text field for the **Comments:** area. See Figure 8–30.

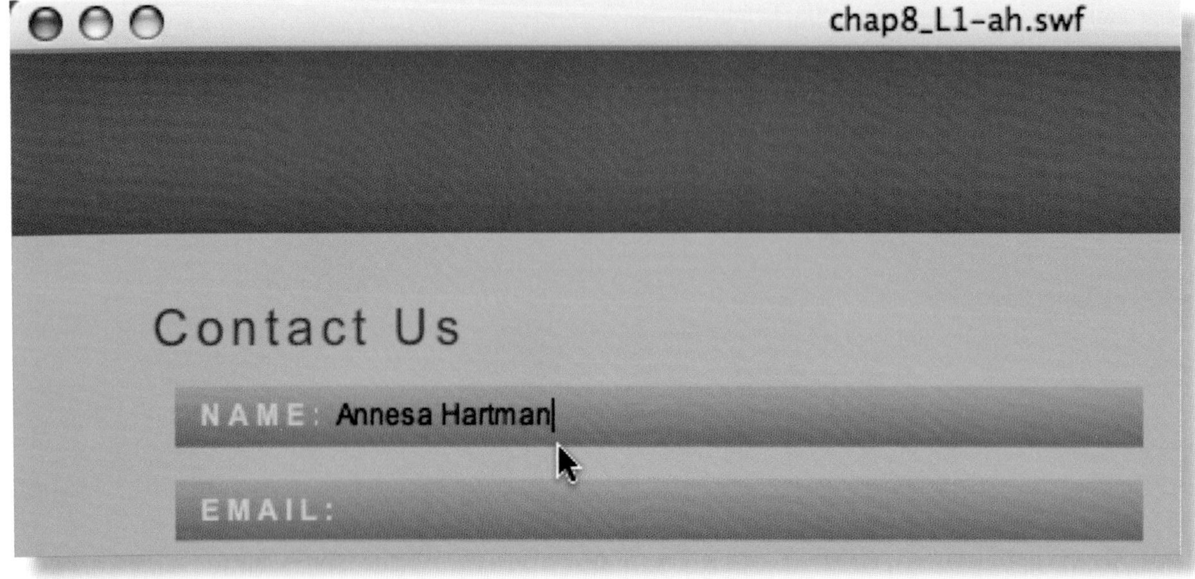

figure 8–29

Enter information in the input text field of a published SWF.

figure 8–30

Create a larger input text field.

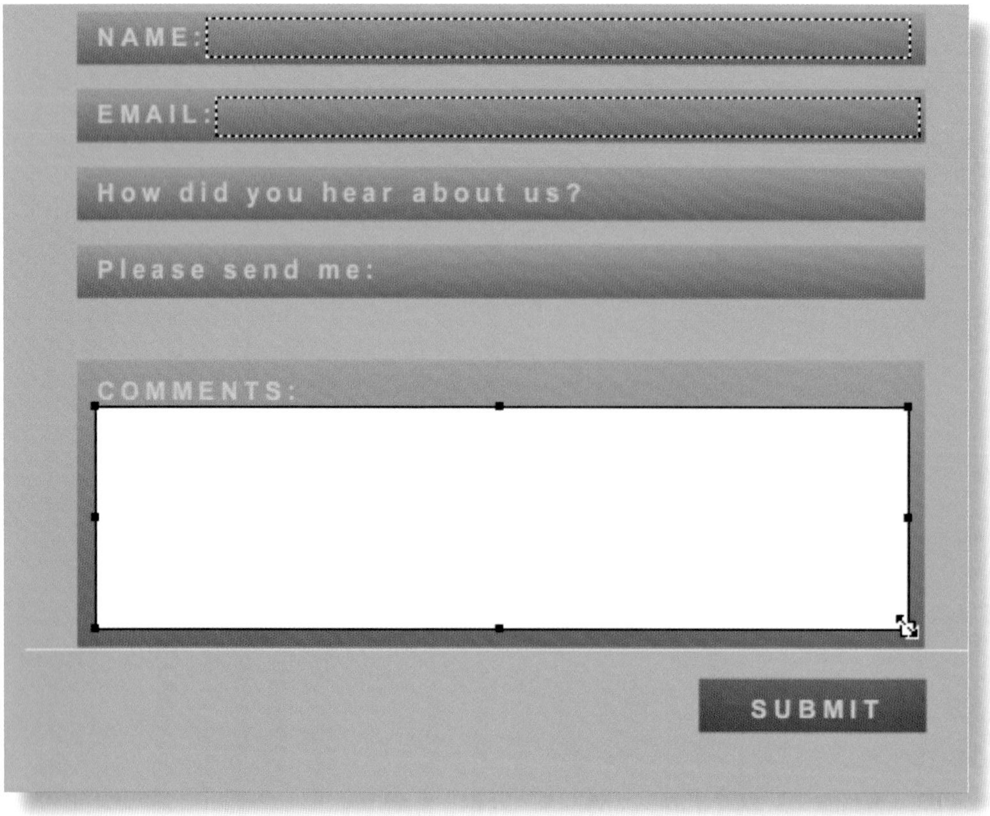

12. Select the **Comments:** area text field and under Paragraph in the Properties panel choose the Multiline behavior (see Figure 8–31).

13. Choose Control > Test Movie and type some text in the **Comments:** area to see that the multiline wrapping of the text works.

14. Close the SWF file and save your file in your lessons folder.

Adding Form Components

1. Create a new layer at the top of the layer list and name it **form_components**.

2. Be sure this layer is selected and choose Window > Components.

3. In the Components window, expand the User Interface list. Click and drag a copy of the ComboBox component to the Stage and place it after the **How did you hear about us?** line. See Figure 8–32.

figure 8–31

Choose the multiline option in the Paragraph properties for the input text.

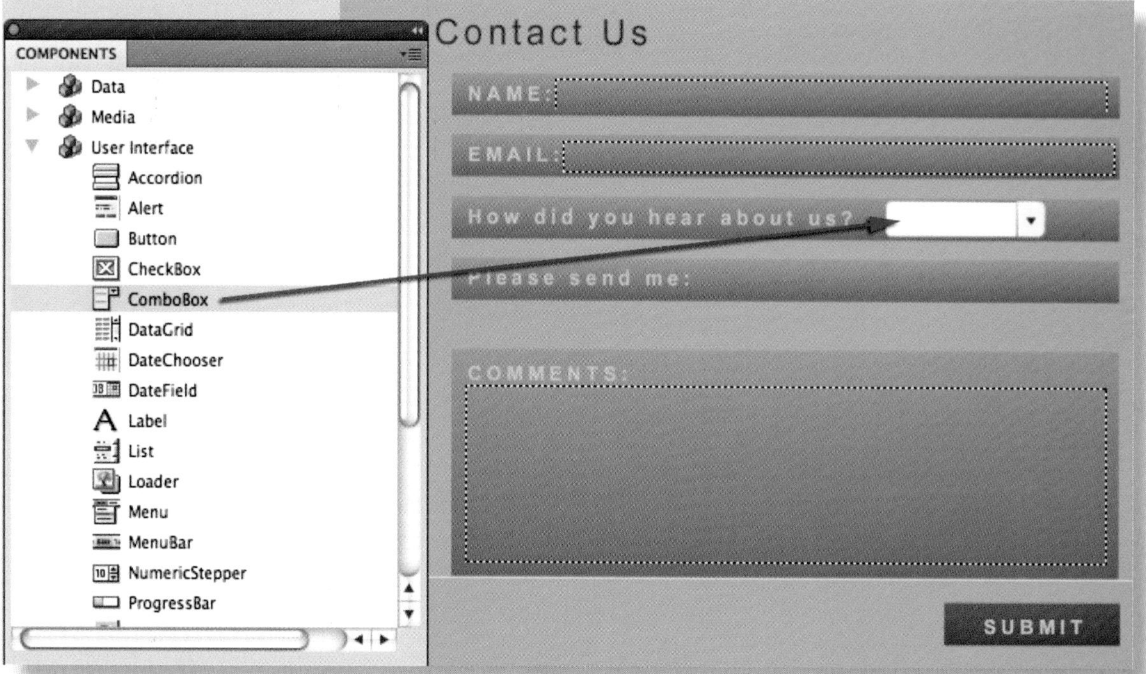

figure 8–32

From the Components panel, drag an instance of the ComboBox to the form.

4. Next, drag a copy of the CheckBox component below the **Please send me:** area. Make two more copies in the same area. Align the copies using the Align panel. See Figure 8–33 and Figure 8–34.

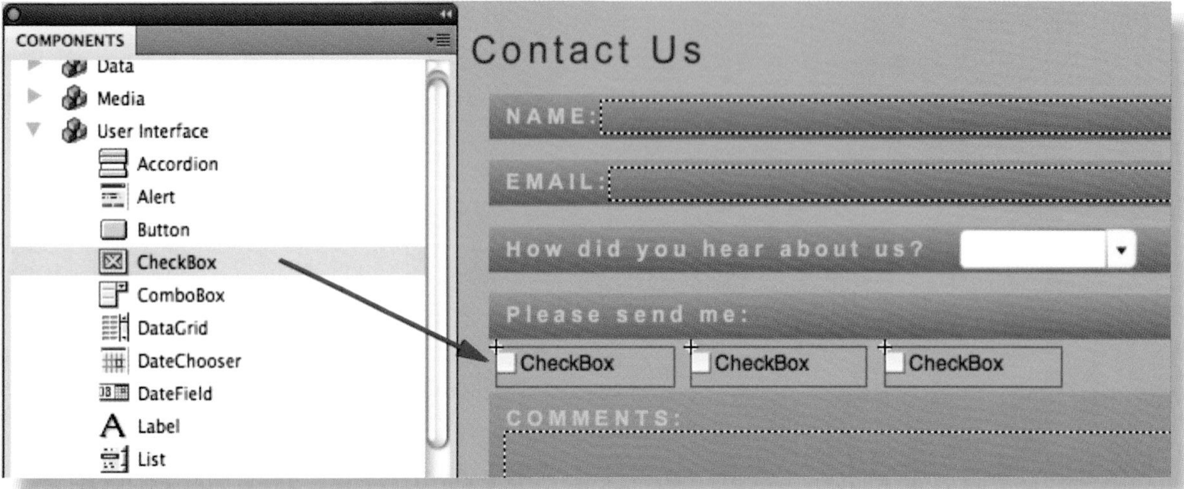

figure 8–33

Create CheckBox components on the form.

figure 8–34

Use the Align panel to align the form elements.

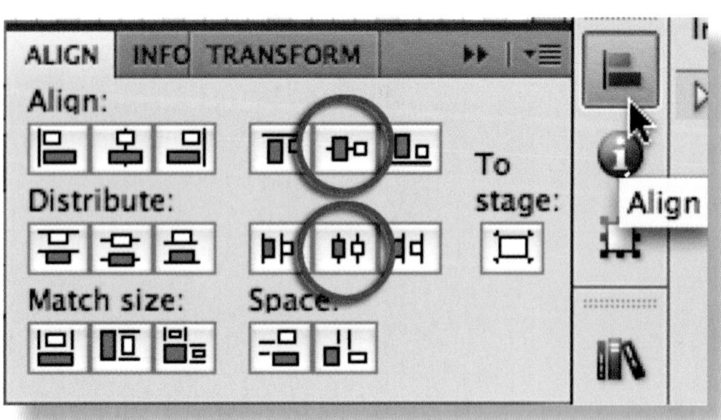

5. Close the Components window and choose Window > Component Inspector. The Component Inspector is where you set the parameters for your components, so they can be uniquely identified by the back-end form script that will receive the information. There are many options in this inspector, but for now let's only set label names that users can choose when answering the question on the form: **How did you hear about us?**

6. Select the ComboBox component. In the Component Inspector, be sure the Parameters tab is selected at the top.

7. Double-click in the Value area of the label's name (third in the list). See Figure 8–35.

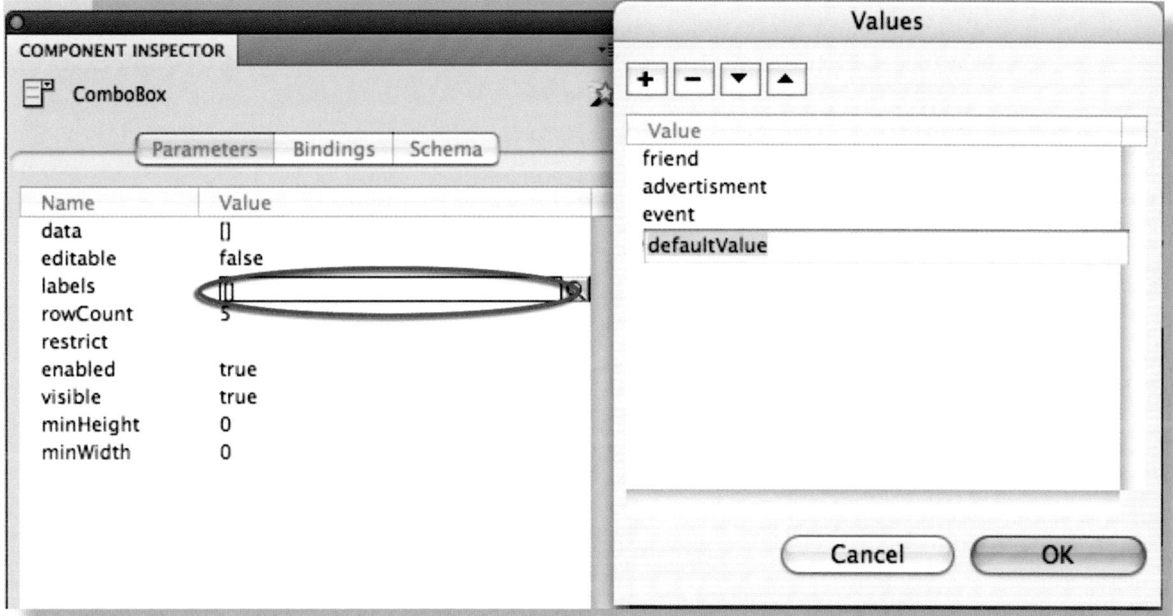

figure 8–35

In the Component Inspector, add the items that appear in the combo drop down box.

8. In the Values window, click the plus button four times to create four defaultValues. Double-click on one of the defaultValues and replace the default name with the word **friend**. For the other defaultValues, replace with **advertisement**, **event**, and **other**. Refer to Figure 8–35 again.

9. Click OK to close the Values window.

10. Now select a CheckBox component on the Stage. In the Components Inspector, click once in the Value area of the label's name and enter the word **Catalog**. See Figure 8–36.

figure 8–36

In the Component Inspector, add the labels for each check box.

figure 8–37

The labels for each check box shown on the form.

11. Select each of the other two CheckBox components and for their values enter **Pricing Info** and **Free T-shirt**. See Figure 8–37.

12. Publish the movie and test out the components. See Figure 8–38.

13. Save your file.

figure 8–38

Publish the movie and test the combo box and check box elements on the form.

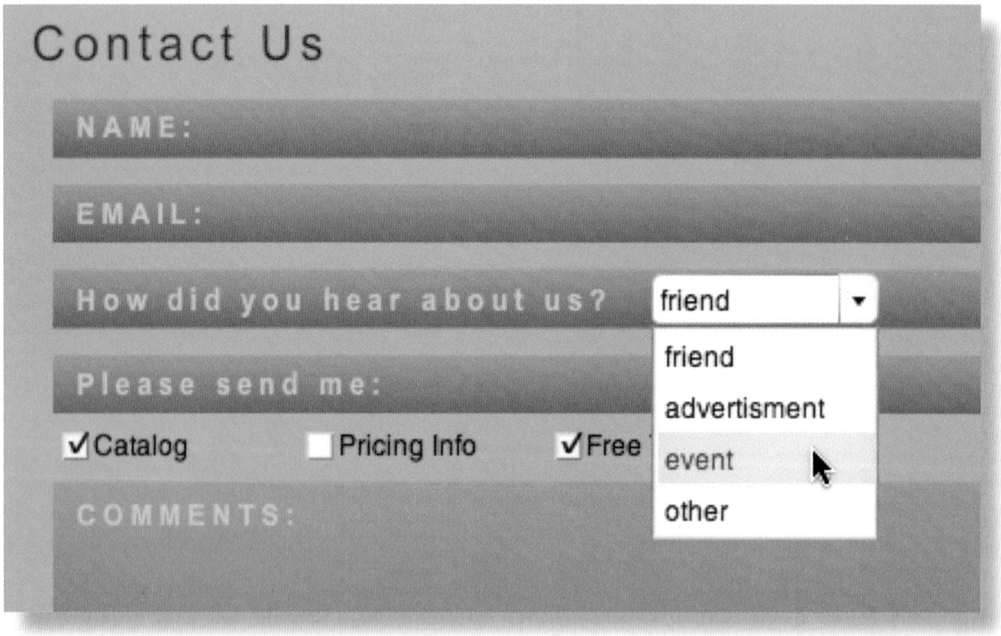

Creating a Thank You Message

After a form is filled out, a user clicks the Submit button and a thank you screen is usually presented to verify that the message has been sent to its intended receiver. As mentioned previously (see section above: About Forms), in this lesson you will not create the functionality of the information actually being sent to a back-end form. I will, however, show you an example of what the ActionScript might look like to do this, as well as steps for creating the "thank you" redirect message.

1. Create a new layer above the other layers and name it **thank_you**.

2. Expand the Timeline panel, so you can see all the layers.

3. Select frame 10 of all the layers and insert a frame. See Figure 8–39.

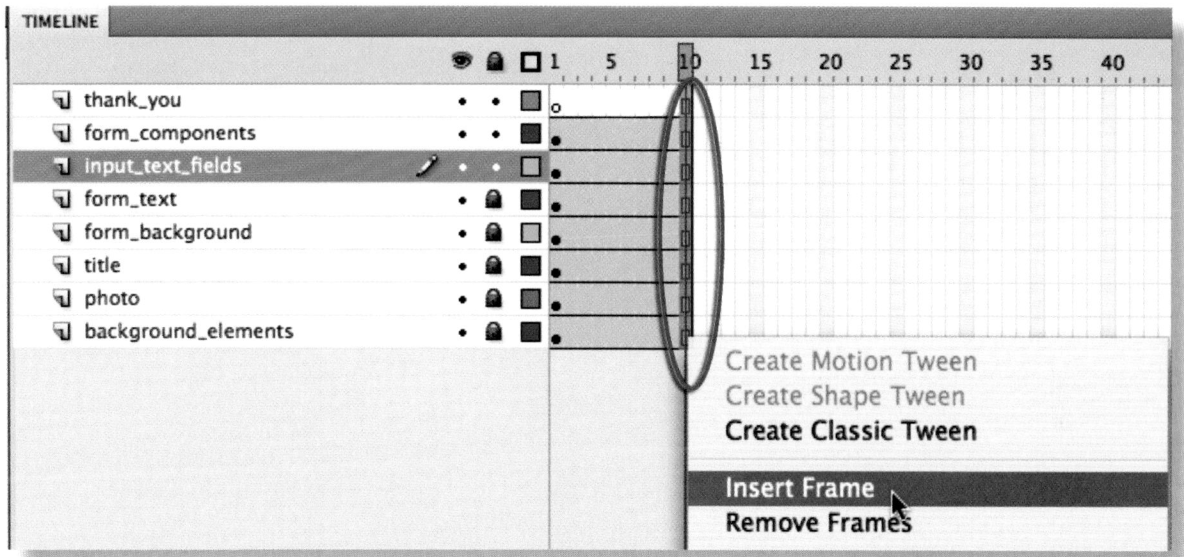

figure 8–39

Insert frames at frame 10 of all the layers.

4. Select frame 2 of **form_components**, **input_text_fields**, **form_text**, **form_background**, and **title** layers and insert a blank keyframe. This will hide these sections of the movie from frame 2 to frame 10, where you'll build the thank you message. See Figure 8–40.

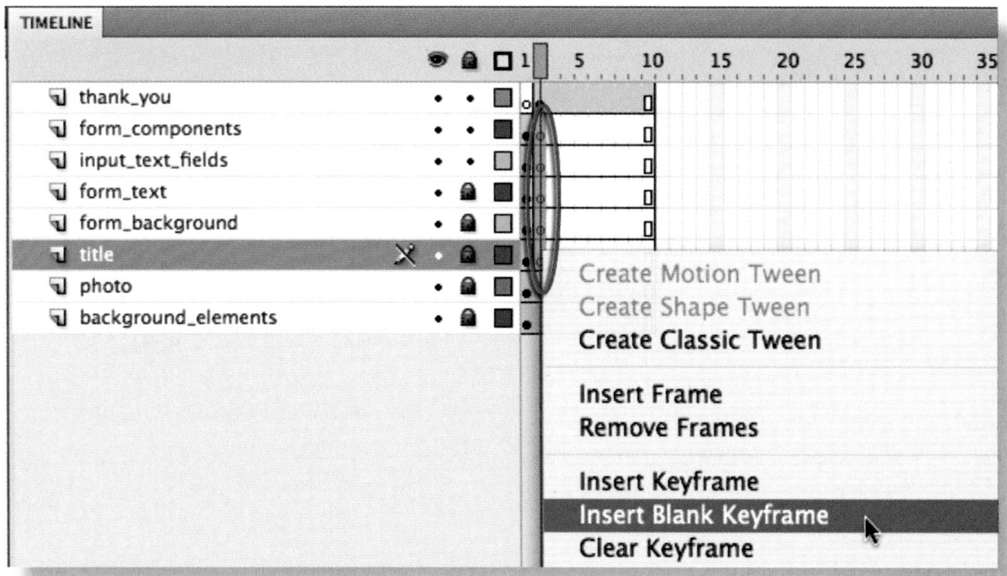

figure 8–40

Create blank keyframes.

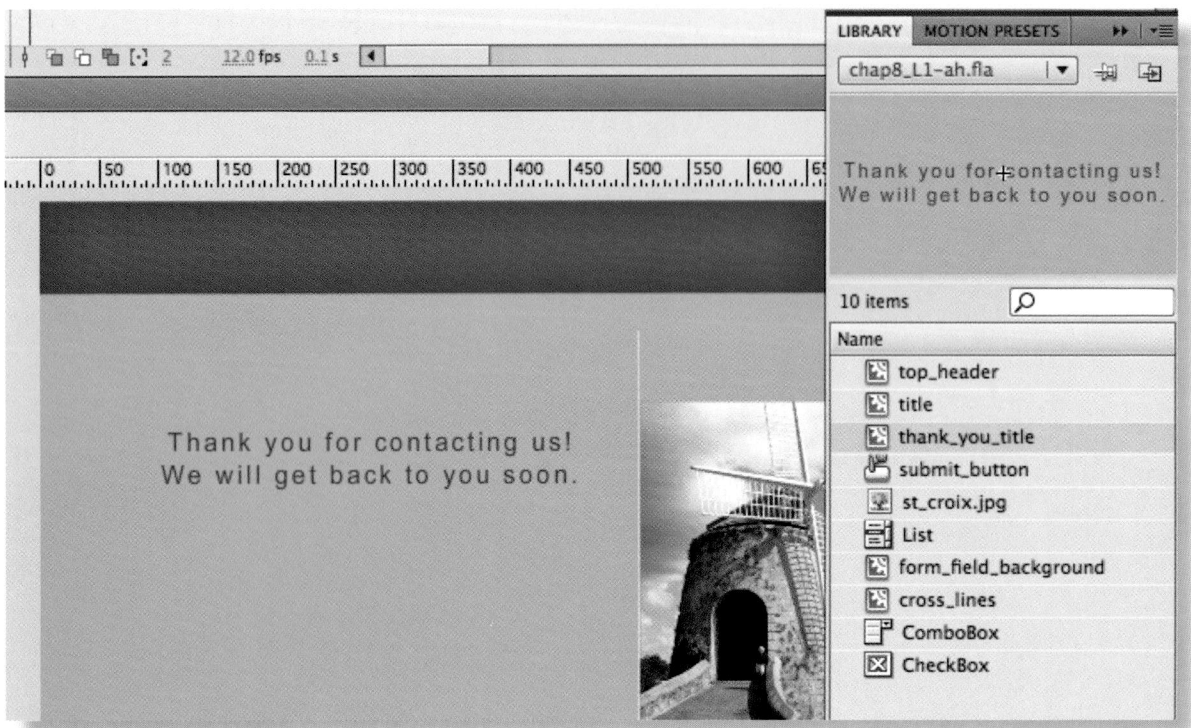

figure 8–41

Place an instance of the thank you title on the Stage.

5. Insert a keyframe at frame 2 of the **thank_you** layer. Be sure the keyframe is selected.

6. Open up the Library and drag an instance of the **thank_you_title** symbol to the center of the scene. See Figure 8–41.

7. Move the playback head back and forth from frame 1 to frame 2. On frame 1 should be the form and on frame 2 the thank you message.

8. Create a new layer called **actions**. Be sure it's at the top of the layer list, and then lock it.

9. Select the first frame of the **actions** layer.

10. Open the Actions panel (Window > Actions) and make sure the file is set to ActionScript 1.0 & 2.0.

11. Make a stop action—choose Global Functions > Timeline Control, and double-click on **stop** to enter it in the script pane.

12. Click on frame 1 of the **actions** layer, hold down the Alt/Option key and click and drag to make a copy of this frame to frame 2 (you might need to move aside or minimize the Actions panel momentarily to do this). Both frames 1 and 2 on the **actions** layer should now have a stop action on them.

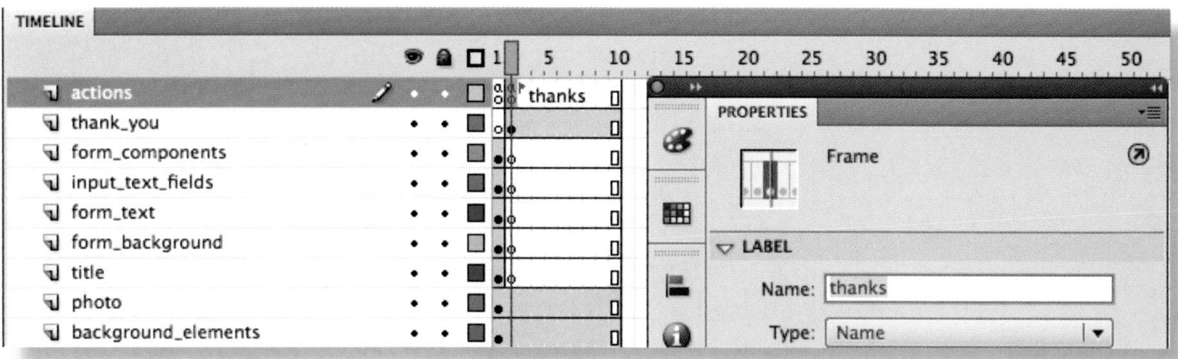

figure 8–42

Create a frame label.

13. Select frame 2 of the **actions** layer and in the Properties panel enter a label name for the frame—call it **thanks**. The label will appear next to the frame in the timeline. See Figure 8–42.

> **Note:** In ActionScript you can call a frame by the frame number or by a label name assigned to that frame. Best practice in ActionScript is to call a frame by a label name as it uniquely identifies the frame avoiding confusion with other frames that might have the same frame number within a movie.

14. Move the playback head to frame 1 of the scene.

15. Select the Submit button—the text, not the red graphic behind it. This button symbol has already been created for you and is located in the Library.

16. In the Properties panel, name the button instance **submit**. See Figure 8–43.

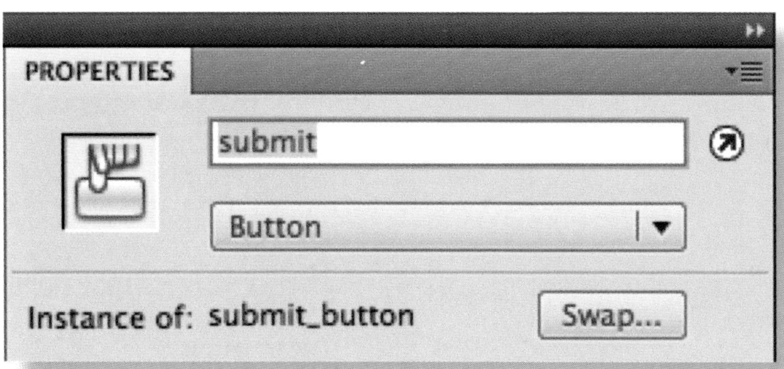

figure 8–43

Create a unique name for the submit button instance.

17. Select frame 1 of the **actions** layer. Open the Actions panel and enter in the following script after the stop action (see also Figure 8–44):

```
submit.onRelease = function() {
    gotoAndStop("thanks");
}
```

figure 8–44

The ActionScript to bring up the thank you page when someone chooses the submit button.

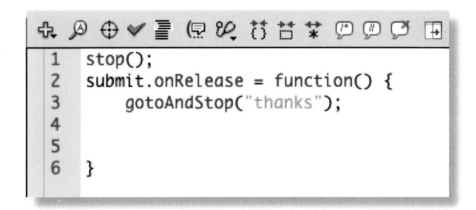

```
stop();
submit.onRelease = function() {
    gotoAndStop("thanks");


}
```

18. Publish the movie and test the Submit button. Are you sent to the Thank You message?

19. Save your file.

> **Note:** We will not add the action that calls the back-end form script, since we do not have a back-end script or a Web server setup to run it. However, for reference, here's an example process for doing this: first, save the form you built in Flash as a movie clip and give it the instance name **form**. Next, add the example script below to your submit button. Basically, this action takes the variables (text field information) from the instance **form** and sends (posts) it to the external form script (written in a Web-based coding language like PHP or Perl).
>
> ```
> on (release) {
>     // send variables in form movie clip (the text fields)
>     // to e-mail PHP page which will send the mail
>     form.loadVariables("your_script.php", "POST");
> }
> ```
>
> See also resources for setting up form mail scripts in the Exploring on Your Own section at the end of this chapter.

Lesson 2: Making a Scroll Bar

Inevitably you will run into the situation where you will want to include more text than there is available space in your Flash movie. This is where a scroll bar comes in handy. There are numerous ways to create scroll bars in Flash; let's cover the most "designer-friendly" version in this lesson. As well, discover the two methods for placement of text within a scrollable text block—internally and externally to Flash.

Looking Over the File

1. From Flash open the **chap8_L2a.fla** file in the **chap08_lessons** folder.
2. Be sure your workspace is set to Classic view.
3. To get you started right away, this file is partially set up for you. Expand the Timeline panel and click on each layer to familiarize yourself with what's on the Stage.
4. Lock all the layers.

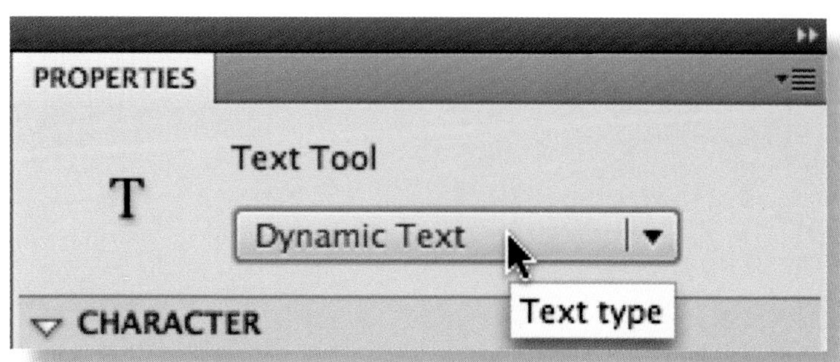

figure 8–45

Select the Dynamic Text type.

Creating a Dynamic Text Block

1. Create a new layer above the other layers called **dynamic_text**.
2. Choose the Text tool in the Tools panel.
3. In the Properties panel, set the text type to Dynamic Text. See Figure 8–45.
4. In the Characters panel, set the following (see Figure 8–46):
   - Family: Arial Style: Regular
   - Size: 12 pt.
   - Letter Spacing: 1.0
   - Color: A dark green
   - Anti-alias: Use device fonts
   - Check the Selectable option, if you would like users to copy and paste the content within the text field.

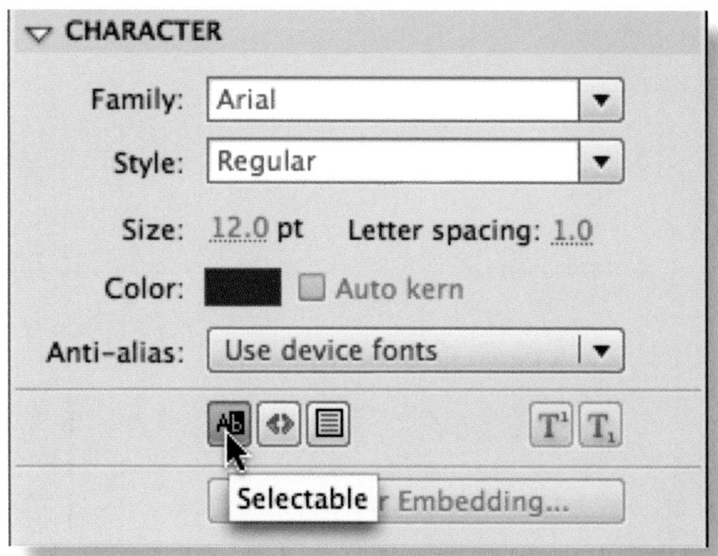

figure 8–46

You can choose to make the dynamic text selectable or not by the end user.

5. Under the **About Annesa** title, click and drag from left to right to create a dynamic text field. See Figure 8–47.

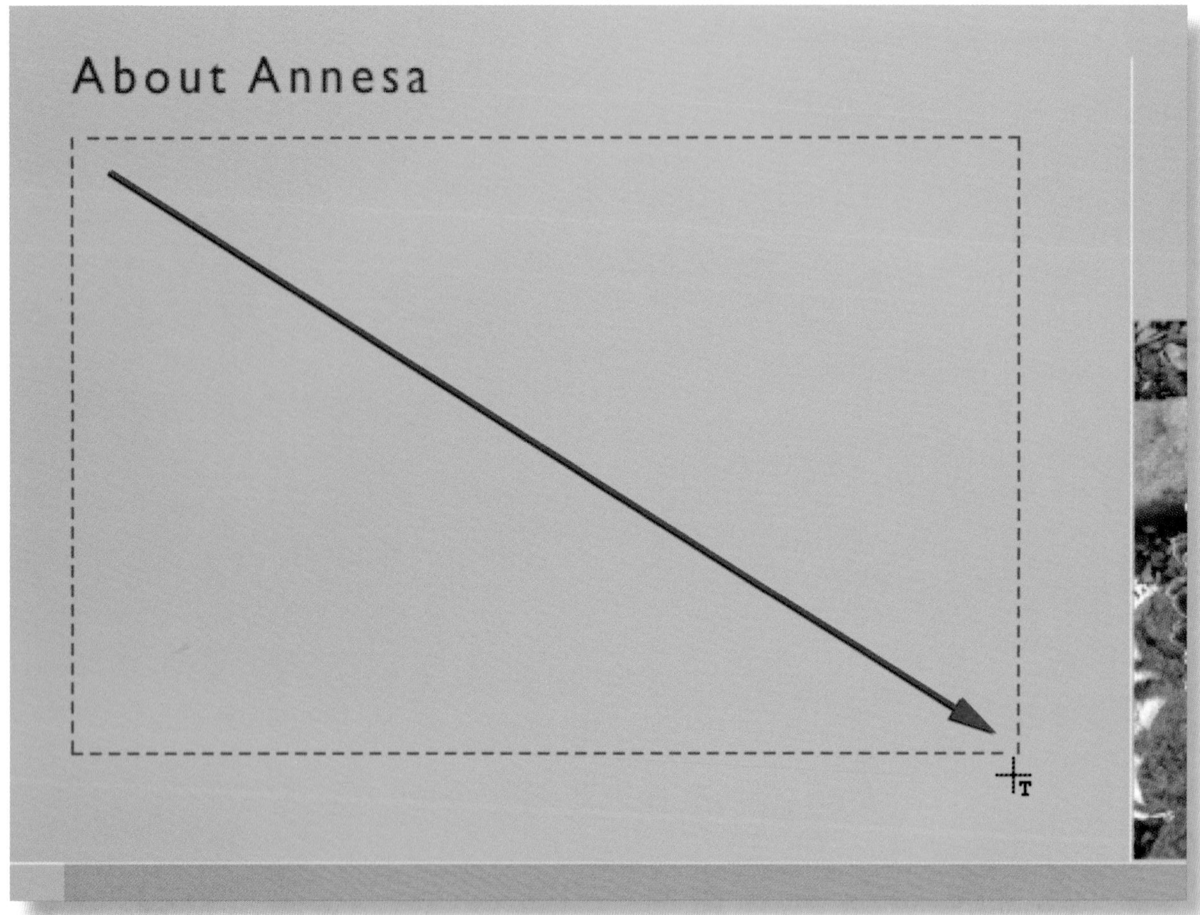

figure 8–47

Create a text block.

6. Choose the Selection tool to see the blue bordered, empty text box. Adjust its position by entering in the following values in the Position and Size area of the Properties panel (see also Figure 8–48):

   - X: 60.0
   - Y: 140.0
   - W: 415.0
   - H: 280.0

7. In the Properties panel, under Paragraph choose the Multiline behavior. See Figure 8–49.

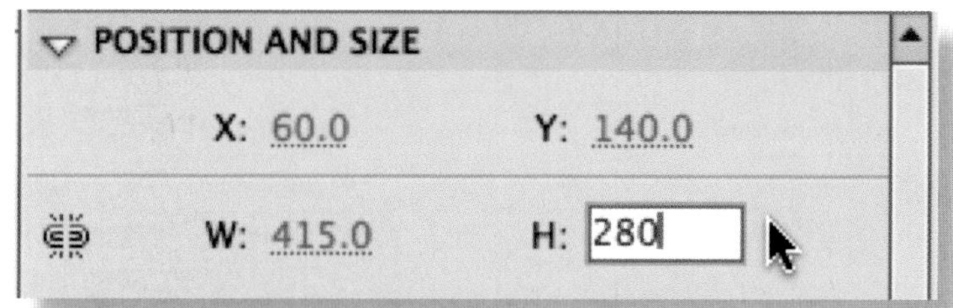

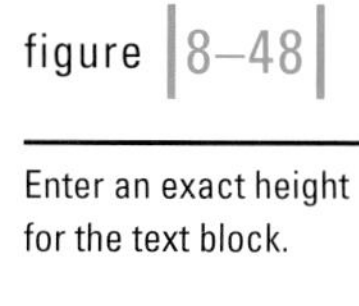

figure 8–48

Enter an exact height for the text block.

figure 8–49

Choose the Multiline option for the text block.

8. Deselect the text box and note that is has a dashed line around it—like an input text block, this indicates a dynamic text field.

9. Save your file.

Adding the Scroll Bar and Internal Text

1. Flash is particular with the order in which you build a scrollable text block. Before adding the text into the text block, you need to create the scroll bar. Choose Window > Components.

2. In the Components panel under the User Interface list, click and drag a copy of the UIScrollBar to the right, inside edge, of the text block (see Figure 8–50).

> **Note: The scroll bar component must be placed within the text block so that it is properly assigned to that text block. Once assigned, you can then reposition the scroll bar (more on that soon . . .).**

3. Close the Component panel.

4. Now, we need some text to put in the dynamic text block. Let's make some placeholder text—nonsensical text usually made up of Latin words (called lorem ipsum)—that mimics the positioning of real content until it is available. Amazingly, but not surprising, there are many placeholder, dummy, lorem ipsum text generators available on the Web. If you have access

figure 8–50

Place a UIScrollBar component on the Stage.

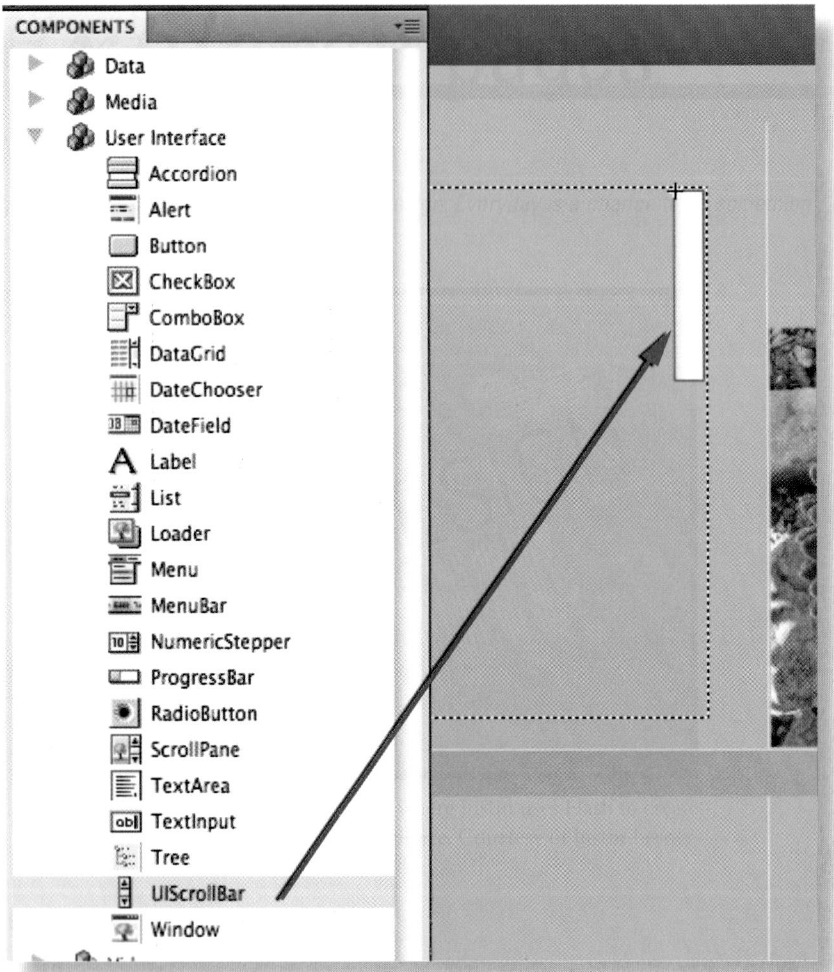

to the Web go to: *http://www.blindtextgenerator.com/*. See Figure 8–51. On the page, under Options choose the lorem ipsum dummy text, 200 words, 4 paragraphs. The text is generated on the right. Select and copy the text.

> **Note:** If you do not have access to the Internet, you can use the dummy text provided in the **chap8_lessons/text_files** folder, **lorem_ipsum.txt**.

> **Note:** Resources for more text generators are in the Exploring on Your Own section at the end of this chapter.

5. Go back to your Flash file. Select the Text tool and click in the text block on the Stage. Paste the lorem ipsum text. Click away from the text block to deselect it. The formatting of the text should be set to the options you created in the Character panel—Arial, dark green color, etc. See Figure 8–52.

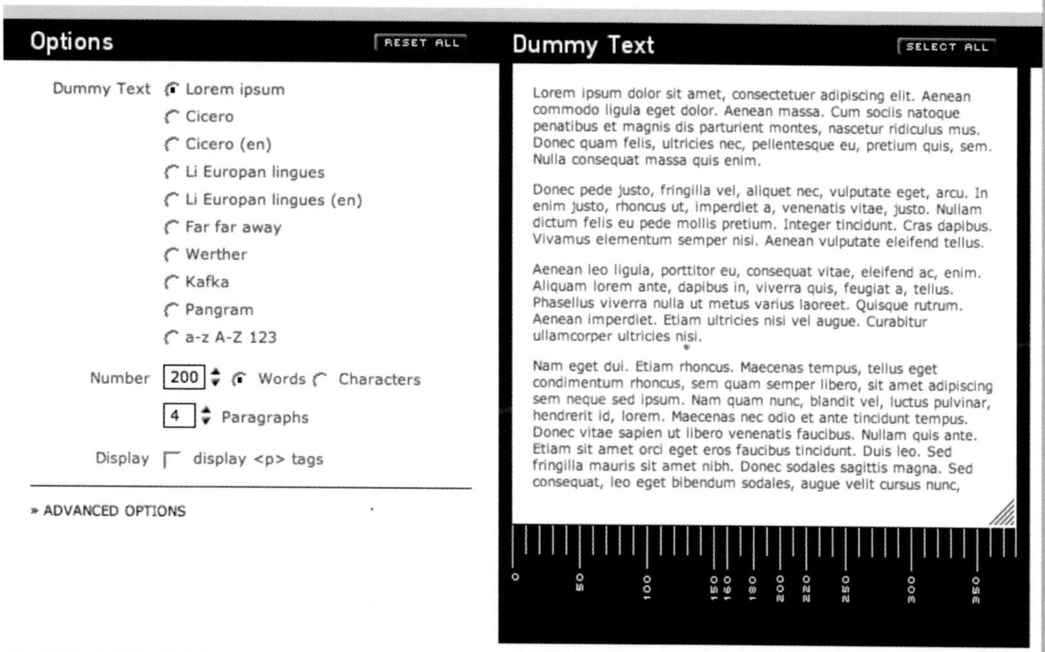

figure 8–51

A text generator Web site, see: *http://www.blindtextgenerator.com/*

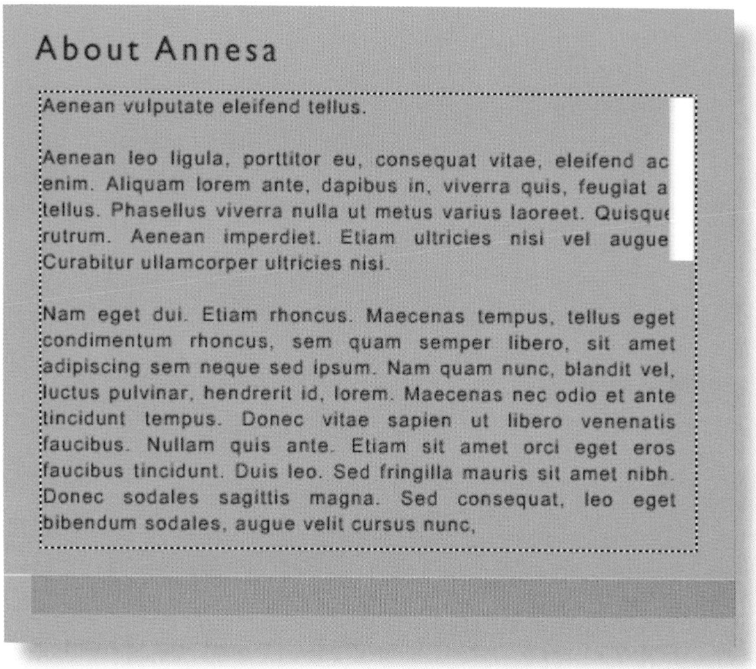

figure 8–52

Copy the lorem ipsum text into the text block.

figure | 8–53 |

Test the movie and try the scroll bar.

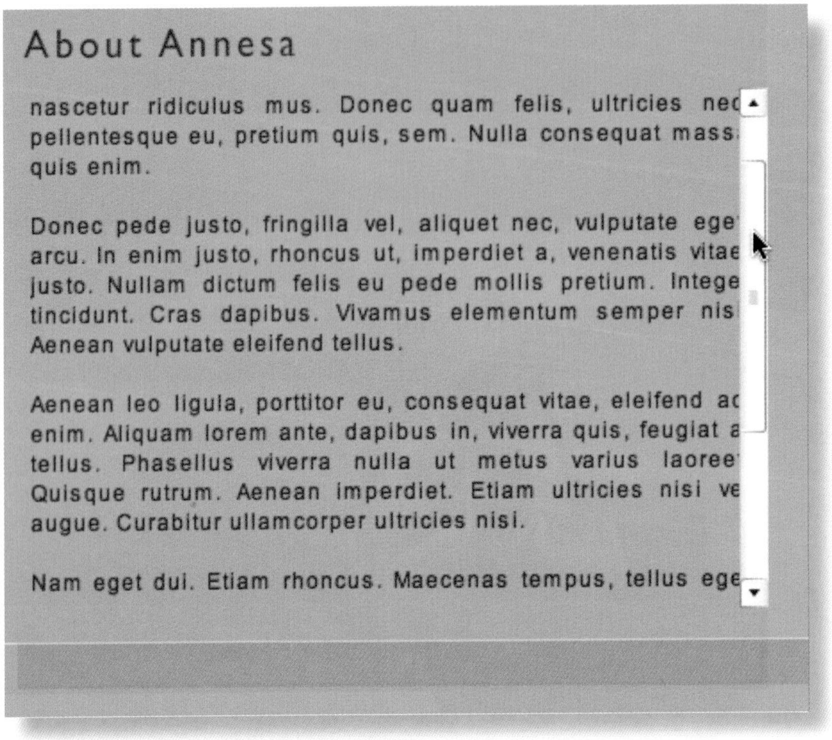

6. Publish the SWF and try out the scrolling action. Is the scroll bar overlapping the text? Let's fix this. See Figure 8–53.

7. Close the SWF movie. Select the scroll bar component. Using the page up and page down arrow keys on your keyboard, incrementally move the scroll bar component to the right, outside edge of the text block, but still touching the dashed line of the block. See Figure 8–54. Publish the movie again and test the result. See Figure 8–55.

> **Note: I have found that that while adding the scroll component to a text block is quite easy—basically click and drag—making it work can be very touchy if not done in the correct order. Suggestions for order:**
>
> **a. Add your scroll bar component *before* adding the text into the text block.**
>
> **b. Be sure the scroll bar component is placed in the upper *inside* right corner of the text block to initiate itself with the text block.**
>
> **c. Copy the text into the text block.**
>
> **d. Publish the SWF *before* repositioning the scroll bar. Then reposition the scroll bar carefully, otherwise it has a tendency to detach itself from its associated text block. Use the arrow keys on the keyboard to move the scroll bar incrementally to the right *outside* edge of the text block—still touching the text block, but not overlapping the text.**

8. Save your file in your lessons folder. Now, let's explore another option for how your text is rendered in the scrolling text block.

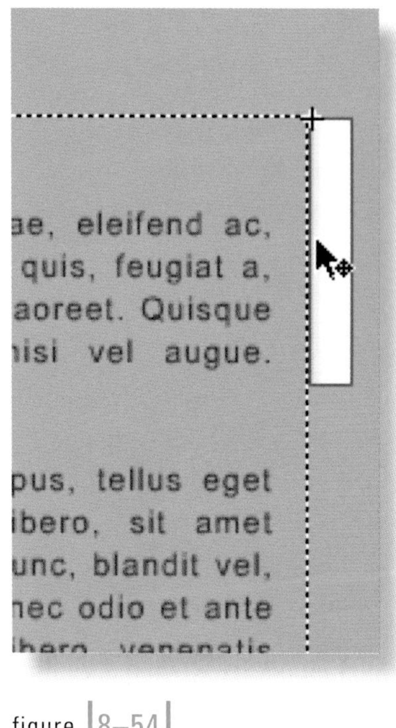

figure 8–54

Adjust the scroll bar.

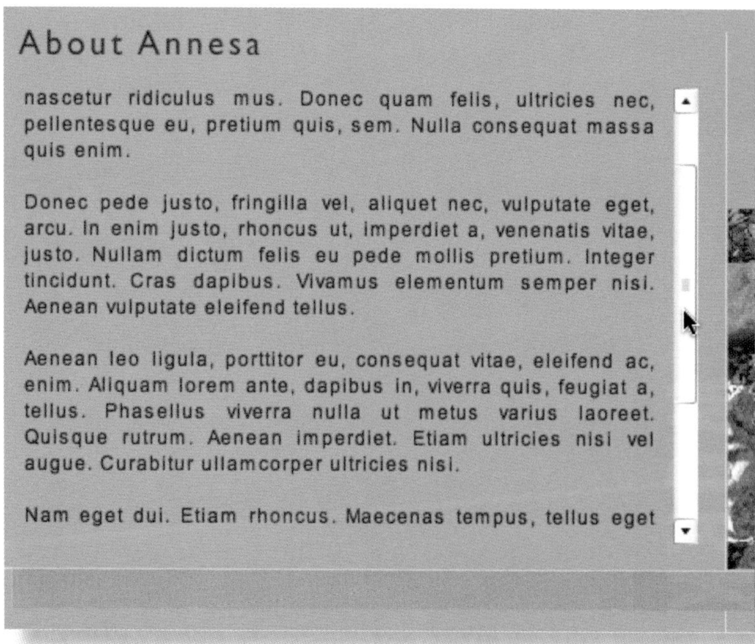

figure 8–55

Test the scroll bar.

Adding the Scroll Bar and External Text

In the last section of this tutorial you copy and pasted text directly into your dynamic text box within Flash. Now, the text will be called into the text block from a text file external to Flash. This method is useful for quick updating of textual content without having to open Flash—you open the external TXT file, make changes, and it's automatically (dynamically!) updated in the SWF. The ActionScript to execute this method can seem a bit daunting, but it's already provided for you in the file—you just need to understand how all the pieces come together to create the final result.

1. From Flash, open the **chap8_L2b.fla** file in the **chap08_lessons** folder. A dynamic text block is already created for you, as you learned in steps #1–9 in the section of this tutorial called **Creating a Dynamic Text Block**.
2. Select the dynamic text block and in the Properties panel enter **my_txt** for the instance name. See Figure 8–56.
3. Choose Window > Components.

figure 8–56

Enter an instance name for the text block.

4. In the Components panel under the User Interface list, click and drag a copy of the UIScrollBar anywhere on the Stage. Now, delete it. What? It's roundabout, but we just created a copy of the UIScrollBar component in the Library—open the Library panel to see it. With this method, we don't need the scroll bar component on the Stage because in the ActionScript—which you will examine shortly—the scroll bar is being called at run time (when the file is published) directly from the Library and into the Scene. Very slick!

5. OK, the dynamic text and the scroll bar are all set—next let's examine the external text file (called **annesa_bio.txt** in this example) that will be loaded into the Scene. Minimize Flash.

6. In your lessons folder, go to **chap08_lessons/text_files** and open the file **annesa_bio.txt**. See Figure 8–57. This is an example of how a text file should be set up to load properly into a dynamic text block. The **content** = line at the top is required and the HTML tags define text formatting <p> (paragraph return), <b> (bold), and
 (line break).

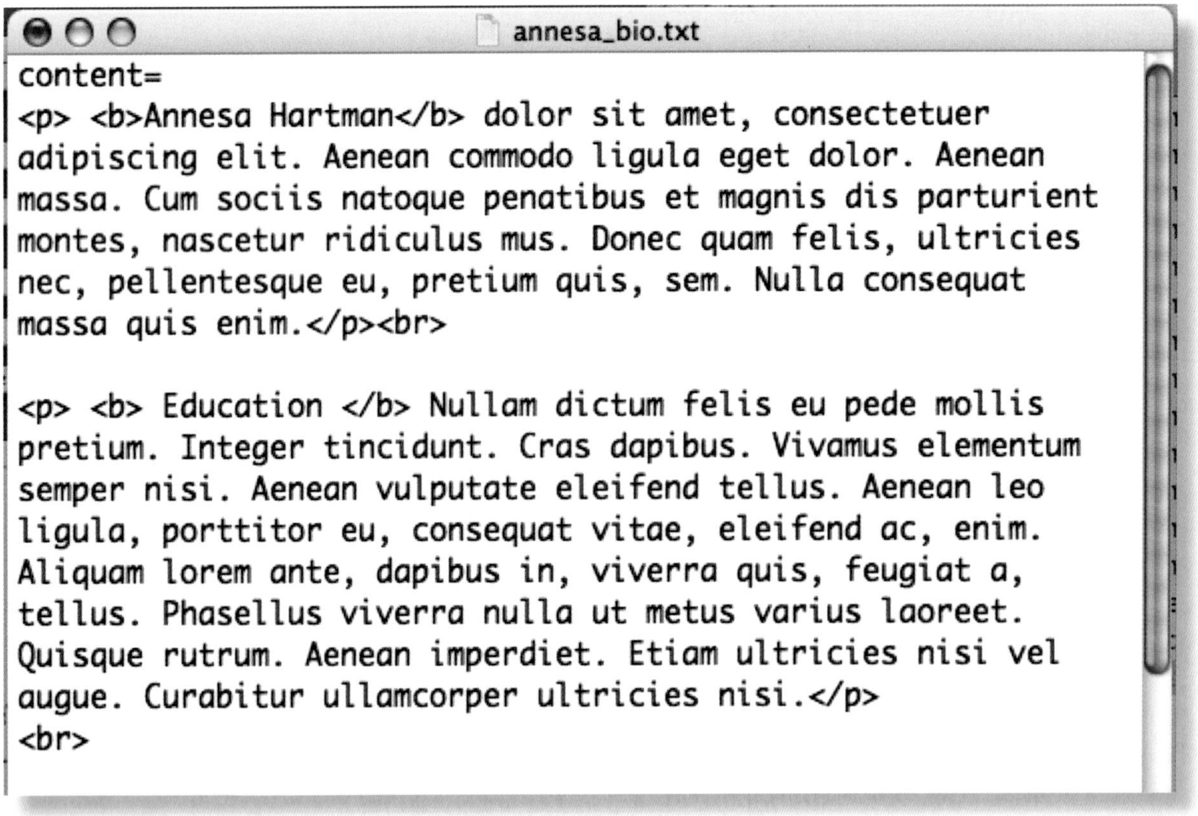

annesa_bio.txt

```
content=
<p> <b>Annesa Hartman</b> dolor sit amet, consectetuer
adipiscing elit. Aenean commodo ligula eget dolor. Aenean
massa. Cum sociis natoque penatibus et magnis dis parturient
montes, nascetur ridiculus mus. Donec quam felis, ultricies
nec, pellentesque eu, pretium quis, sem. Nulla consequat
massa quis enim.</p><br>

<p> <b> Education </b> Nullam dictum felis eu pede mollis
pretium. Integer tincidunt. Cras dapibus. Vivamus elementum
semper nisi. Aenean vulputate eleifend tellus. Aenean leo
ligula, porttitor eu, consequat vitae, eleifend ac, enim.
Aliquam lorem ante, dapibus in, viverra quis, feugiat a,
tellus. Phasellus viverra nulla ut metus varius laoreet.
Quisque rutrum. Aenean imperdiet. Etiam ultricies nisi vel
augue. Curabitur ullamcorper ultricies nisi.</p>
<br>
```

figure 8–57

A view of the text file that will be called into the Flash movie.

Note: Flash can support only a subset of standard HTML tags (the code that defines formatting in Web pages), including:

- Anchor: <a href="/support/flash/ts/documents/url">
- Bold: <b>
- Font: < font [color="#xxxxxx"] [face="Type Face"] [size="Type Size"]>
- Italic: <I>
- Paragraph: <p [align="left"|"right"|"center"]>
- Underline: <u>
- Break:
- Image: <img src="/images/flash/dogs.jpg"/>. The <img> tag lets you embed external image files (JPEG, GIF, PNG), SWF files, and movie clips inside text fields and TextArea component instances.
- List Item: <li>
- Ordered and unordered lists (<ol> and <ul> tags) are not recognized by Flash Player, so they do not modify how your list is rendered. All list items use bullets.
- Span: The <span> tag is available only for use with CSS text styles.
- TextFormat: The <textformat> tag lets you use a subset of paragraph formatting properties of the TextFormat class within HTML text fields, including line leading, indentation, margins, and tab stops. You can combine <textformat> tags with the built-in HTML tags.

7. Close the text file, and go back to your Flash file.
8. Select the first frame (with the little "a") of the **actions** layer and choose Window > Actions (F9).
9. In the Actions script pane is the code necessary to put all this together. There are plenty of new things in this script, but in general what it does is that it creates a scroll bar (called **my_sb**) for the dynamic text block (**my_txt**) and then loads the external text file (**text_files/annesa_bio.txt**) into the **my_txt** text block. See Figure 8–58 on the next page.
10. Close the Actions panel, then save your file—be sure it's saved in a folder that also contains the **text_files** folder, which contains **annesa_bio.txt**.
11. Publish the file, and scroll!

DESIGNING WITH TYPE

Like other elements of design, such as color, shapes, and textures, type evokes a look and feel. Type can be used as a decorative enhancement to a design, but in most cases it's meant to be read. Let's cover some best practices of type design that take into account a text's readability and visual impact, specifically its spacing and alignment and font selection and size.

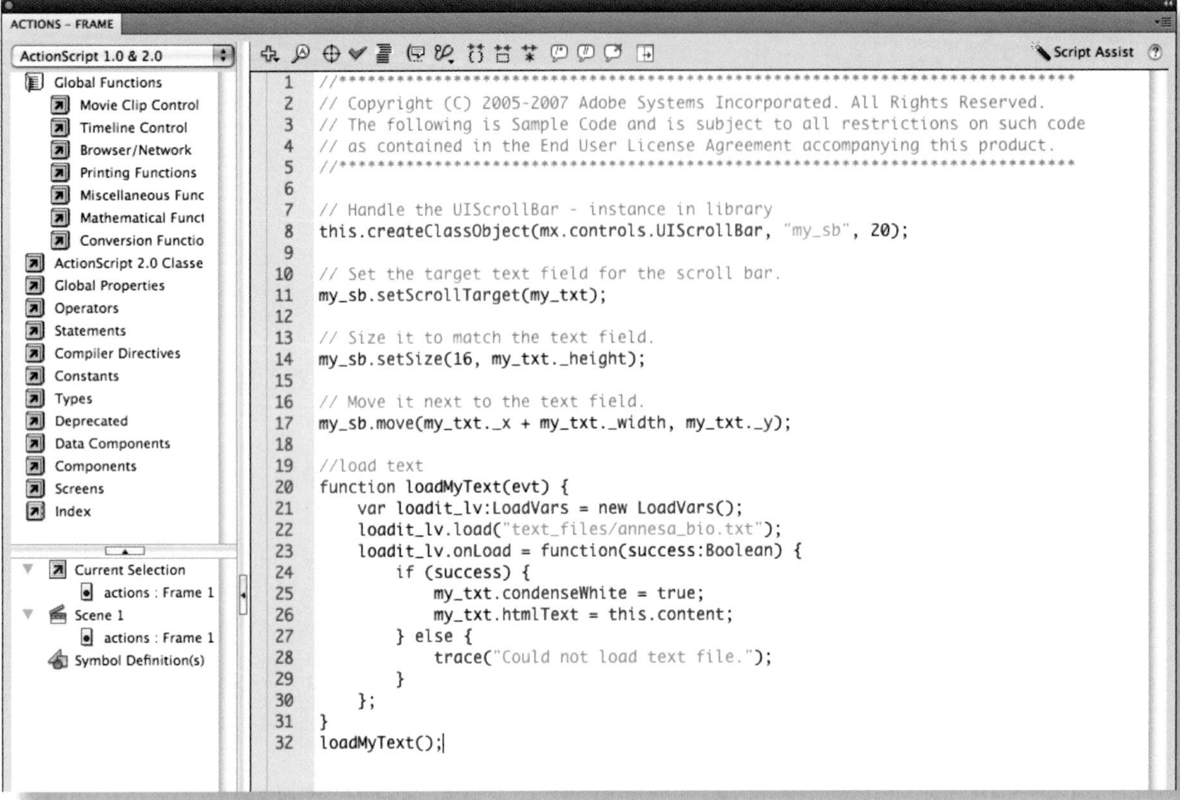

figure 8–58

The ActionScript created by the UIScrollBar component.

Spacing and Alignment

Line Length

Long lines of text are no fun to read, and short lines of text can break up the text flow, so you need to find the right balance. A general rule is that a line should have 55–60 characters, or approximately 9–10 words, for optimal readability.

Leading or Line Spacing

Leading refers to the air—the space—between lines of type. It is measured in points from baseline to baseline. Depending on the font type used, leading can vary for optimal readability. Line spacing can be found in the Paragraph area of the Properties panel for text. See Figure 8–59 and Figure 8–60.

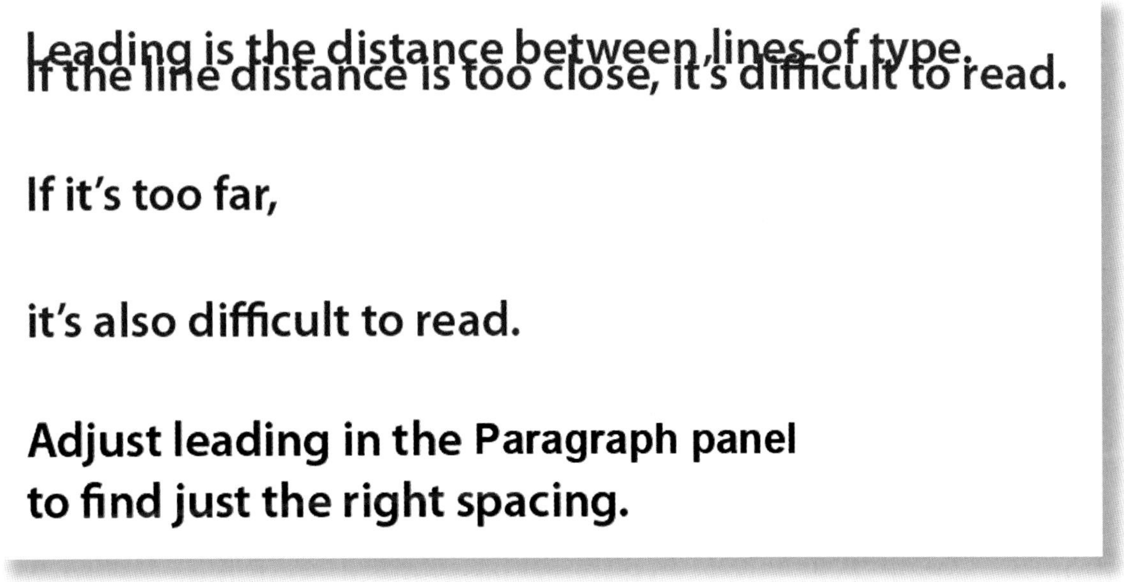

Leading is the distance between lines of type.
If the line distance is too close, it's difficult to read.

If it's too far,

it's also difficult to read.

Adjust leading in the Paragraph panel
to find just the right spacing.

figure 8–59

Example of text leading (line spacing).

figure 8–60

Adjust line spacing (leading) in the Paragraph options for the Properties panel for selected text.

Word and Letter Spacing

Although subtle, minor variations in word and letter spacing can make a huge impact on text legibility.

- **Tracking**: Tracking is the process of adjusting the space between selected characters (words or letters) or entire blocks of text. See Figure 8–61. Most typefaces available today are designed with correct spacing between characters. However, you might find yourself wanting to adjust these defaults if, for example, you want to work with ALL CAPS. Tracking (letter spacing) is in the Characters area of the Properties panel for text. See Figure 8–62.

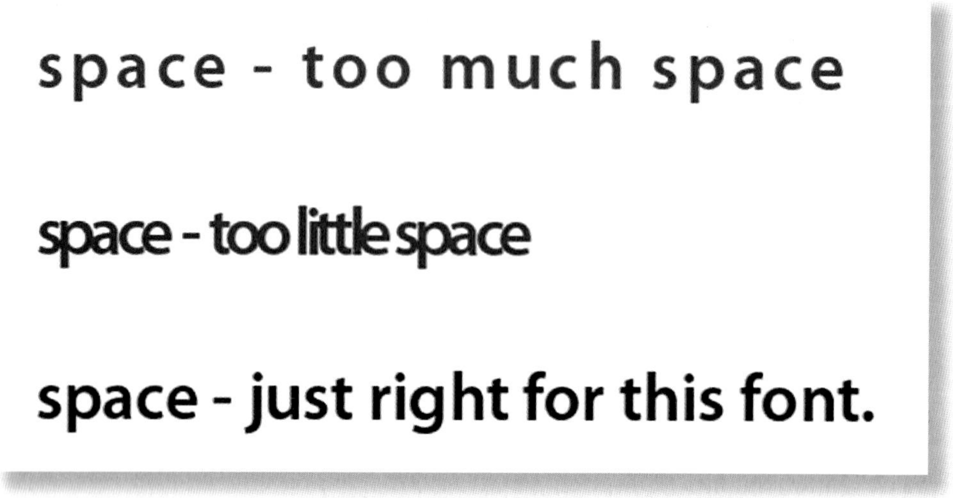

figure 8–61

Examples of letter spacing (tracking).

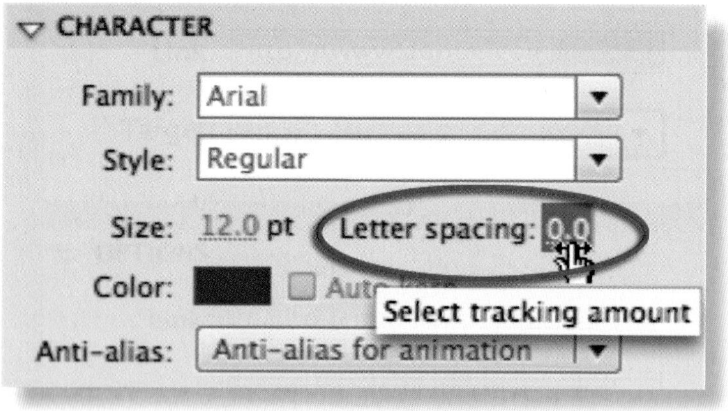

figure 8–62

Adjust letter spacing in the Character options of the Properties panel for selected text.

- **Kerning**: An even subtler variation of character spacing, kerning refers to how space appears between two letters. For most letters, kerning is relatively uniform, but in some cases, such as with A and V, kerning must be adjusted so spacing looks consistent and more readable. See Figure 8–63. Kerning is also very useful when working with decorative type in a large headline. Flash offers an Auto Kern option for static text in the Characters area of the Properties panel of text. See Figure 8–64.

> **Note:** The differences between tracking and kerning are so subtle that novice designers often get the two terms confused. Tracking provides a more global spacing of selected words and letters, whereas kerning works between two specific characters, depending on how they are placed next to each other.

Justification

Justification is the alignment of lines of text or text blocks. Documentation with lots of text is usually formatted with a left justification—aligned to the left margin (flush left) and ragged on the right.

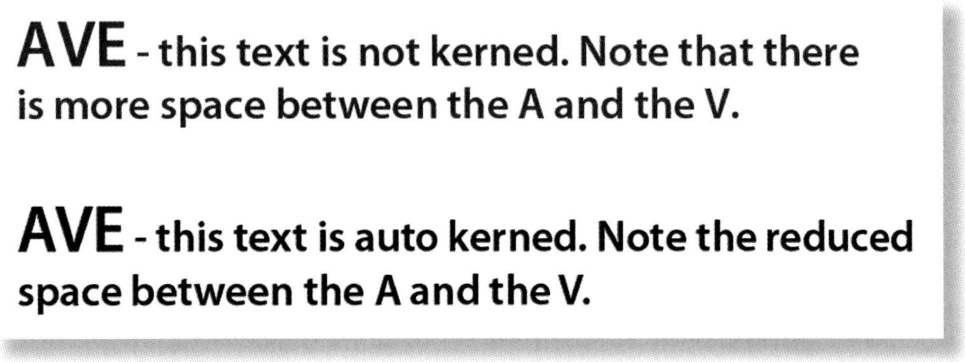

AVE - this text is not kerned. Note that there is more space between the A and the V.

AVE - this text is auto kerned. Note the reduced space between the A and the V.

figure 8–63

Examples of kerned and nonkerned letters.

You can also choose to align text to the right margin (flush right) with the left side ragged, but the resulting text is not as easy to read. For a more formal look, all lines might be justified on both the right and left sides (no ragged edges), such as in this book. Often, newspaper or magazine articles have this type of look. Centered justification works well with small amounts of copy. See Figure 8–65. Justification options are found in the Paragraph area of the Properties panel for text. See Figure 8–66.

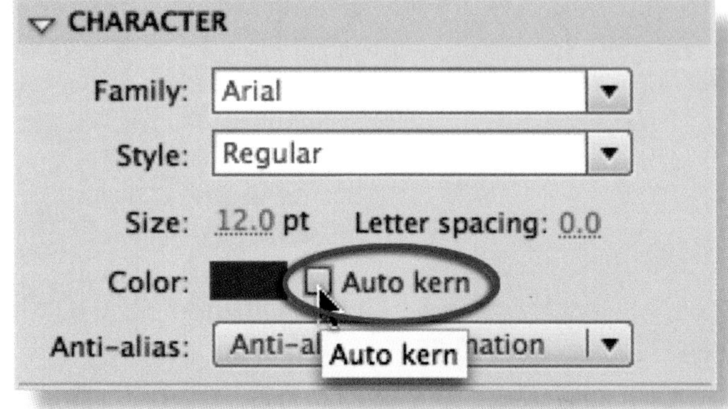

figure 8–64

Set kerning in the Character options of the Properties panel of selected static text.

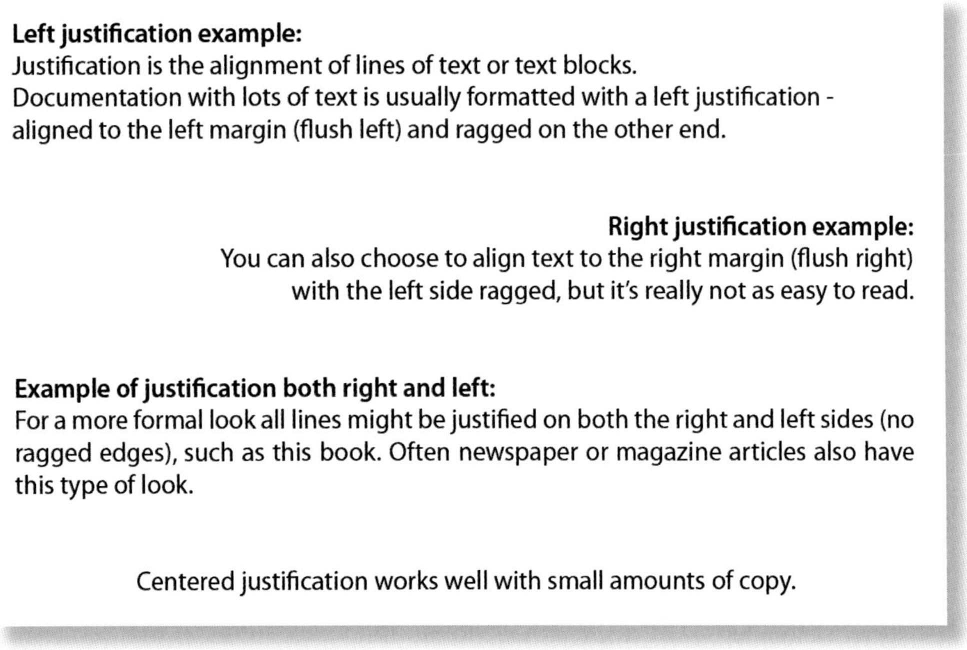

Left justification example:
Justification is the alignment of lines of text or text blocks.
Documentation with lots of text is usually formatted with a left justification - aligned to the left margin (flush left) and ragged on the other end.

Right justification example:
You can also choose to align text to the right margin (flush right) with the left side ragged, but it's really not as easy to read.

Example of justification both right and left:
For a more formal look all lines might be justified on both the right and left sides (no ragged edges), such as this book. Often newspaper or magazine articles also have this type of look.

Centered justification works well with small amounts of copy.

figure 8–65

Examples of each justification option.

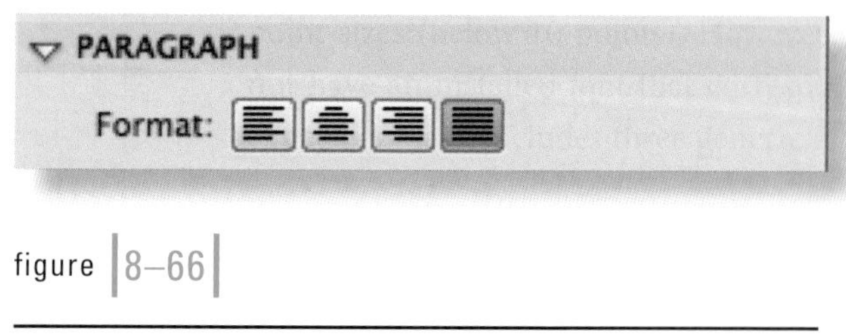

figure 8–66

Set justification in the Paragraph options of the Properties panel for selected text.

Font Selection and Size

Proportional versus Fixed Pitch

Fonts are distinguishable by their style and the way in which their individual letters and characters are spaced. Spacing of a font can be either fixed pitch (mono-spaced) or proportional. A fixed-pitch font is usually defined as a typewriter font, where each character takes up the same amount of space from left to right and is representative of how old-style typewriters used to reproduce letterforms. Modern digital type and printable text are generally designed using proportional spacing, where each letter is given just the amount of space it needs to look visually appealing and legible. Proportional fonts can be formatted better on a page and actually improve readability over fixed-pitch fonts. See Figure 8–67.

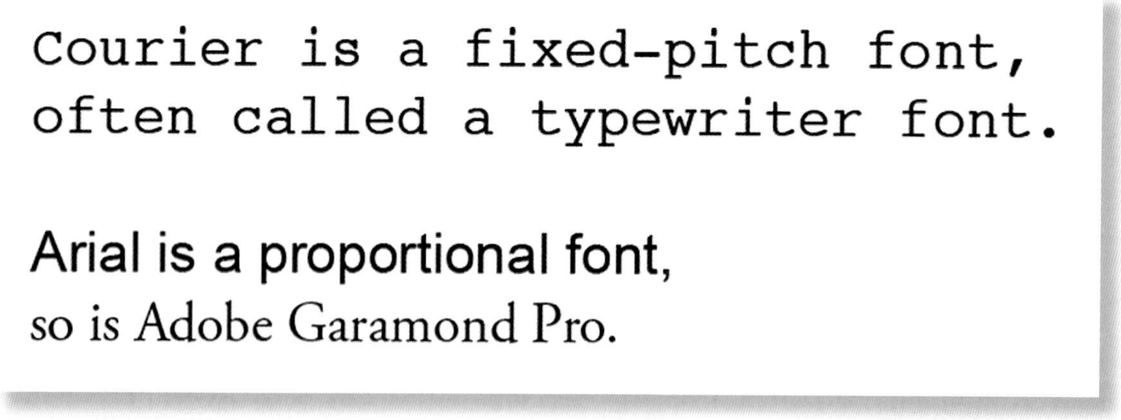

Courier is a fixed-pitch font,
often called a typewriter font.

Arial is a proportional font,
so is Adobe Garamond Pro.

figure 8–67

Fixed pitch versus proportional fonts.

Serif versus Sans Serif

It is important to know the difference between serif and sans-serif fonts because both types play a vital role in the readability of either print or Web-based documents. Serif fonts are letterforms with tails or cross lines at the ends of each letter stroke. Sans-serif fonts do not have these tails—evolutionally speaking, they have been removed. Serif fonts usually have a more formal look, whereas sans-serif fonts often look bolder and more modern. See Figure 8–68.

For printed documents containing lots of text, serif fonts, such as Times New Roman, are easier to read. This is why newspapers traditionally use serif fonts for their copy.

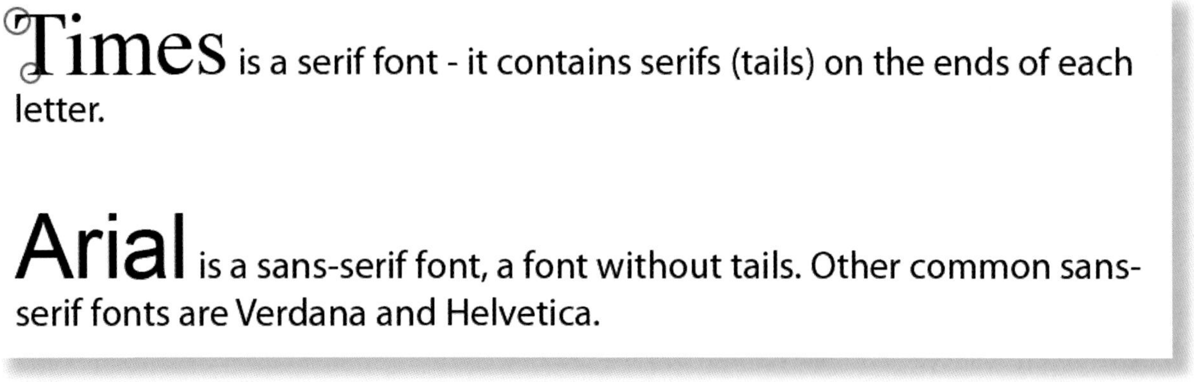

Times is a serif font - it contains serifs (tails) on the ends of each letter.

Arial is a sans-serif font, a font without tails. Other common sans-serif fonts are Verdana and Helvetica.

figure |8–68|

Serif versus sans-serif fonts.

For screen-based text, like in your Flash movie, sans-serif fonts are recommended, such as Arial, Helvetica, or Verdana. This is especially true when working with type sizes that are less than 12 points (the little tails of certain serif fonts get lost when the text is viewed on a lit screen). I like to use a combination of serif and sans-serif fonts in my designs, and stick with just two or three font families or typefaces (any more gets distracting). For Flash page designs, for example, you might use a serif font family for the topic headings and a sans-serif font family for the body copy (main text areas).

Contrast

To really put some "oomph" in your type design, the principle of contrast is a must-know. Contrast as defined by the Oxford American Dictionary, is "the state of being strikingly different from something else, typically something in juxtaposition or close association." Contrast is commonly used in design to heighten visual impact. Here are six characteristics of type that can be manipulated to create contrast.

- **Size**: Big-size versus small-size type offers contrast, such as a 20-point headline above 10-point body text.
- **Weight**: Most font families and font formatting options come in varying weights for the purpose of providing contrast, such as medium, light, italic, bold, or condensed versions. See Figure 8–69.
- **Structure**: Within a layout, a combination of serif and sans-serif fonts offers contrast.
- **Form**: Form implies a font's shape. For example, a good contrast of form would be an uppercase type set against lowercase type.
- **Color**: The color of type can make a huge impact on a design, especially how it might contrast with a colored background or other colored objects. Be sure there is sufficient

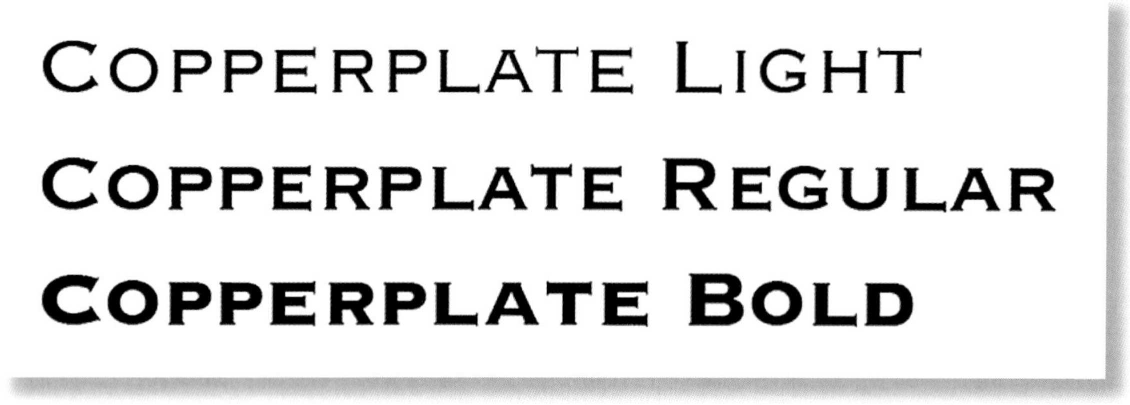

COPPERPLATE LIGHT
COPPERPLATE REGULAR
COPPERPLATE BOLD

figure 8–69

Example of the various styles within a font family.

contrast when working with colored copy, such as white text on a black background or dark blue text on a white background. Avoid combinations like yellow text on a white background, or dark blue text on a black background.

- **Direction**: You can change the direction, orientation, of text to provide contrast. The option to change the direction of static text from a horizontal to vertical orientation is found in the Paragraph area of the Properties panel for text. See Figure 8–70.

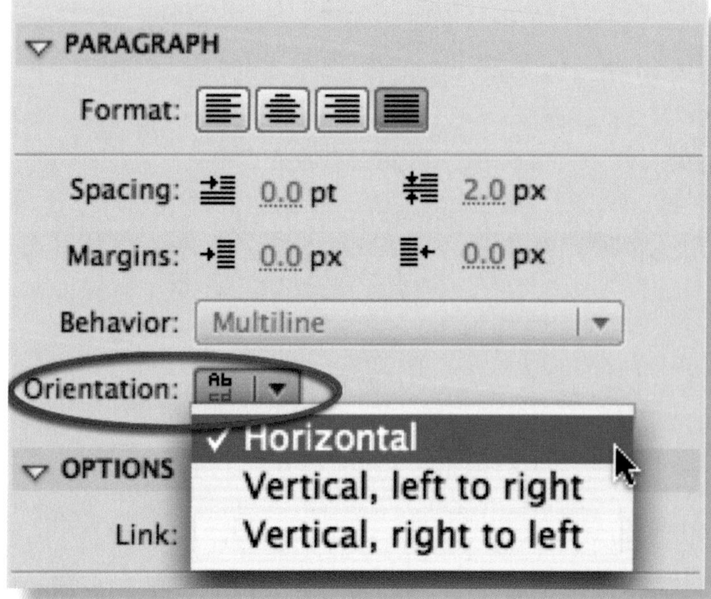

figure 8–70

Set the orientation of text.

SUMMARY

Often overlooked as an important design element, text plays a critical role in providing an effective, functional, accessible, and aesthetically pleasing experience for Flash content viewers.

in review

1. Describe the three types of text in Flash.
2. What is an advantage of embedded fonts? A disadvantage?
3. What is an advantage of device fonts? A disadvantage?
4. Define anti-aliasing.
5. What's the purpose of font mapping?
6. What does the Break Apart command do?
7. What's an ALT tag?
8. Which two parts are required to be integrated for the making of functional forms?
9. What is a Component?
10. What is lorem ipsum? How is it used in design?
11. What are at least three type design best practices when working with Web-based text?

exploring on your own

1. Visit some fun online sites that use typographic design with Flash animation—*http://www.ni9e.com/typo/*—select the sites with the word "typo" in the title.
2. Some more Flash site inspiration: *http://www.webdesignerwall.com/trends/30-artistic-flash-sites/*
3. In this chapter, you learned a quick way to create a hyperlink on text using the Link option in the Properties panel of either static or dynamic text. To create the same action on a graphic instance (like a filled button shape, for example) you need to write the code in the Actions panel. Here are the steps to create an ActionScript 2.0 supported hyperlink on a graphic button

that either links to an outside Web page or opens up a mail program and puts a contact's e-mail address in the To: field.

a. Create a generic button symbol.

b. Place two instances of the buttons on the Stage.

c. Give each button an instance name in the Properties panel.

d. Create a layer called "actions."

e. Select the first frame of the **actions** layer and enter the code seen in Figure 8–71 in the Actions panel, but replace the instance names I used (**webpage_btn** and **contact_btn**) with the instance names you used. Hint: Choose the ActionScript 1.0 & 2.0 option, and the getURL action is found under Global Functions > Browser/Network on the toolbox.

f. Check the Auto Format and Syntax options for your code.

g. Test the movie. For an example file see: **chap8_lessons/demos/getURL_mailto_example.fla**

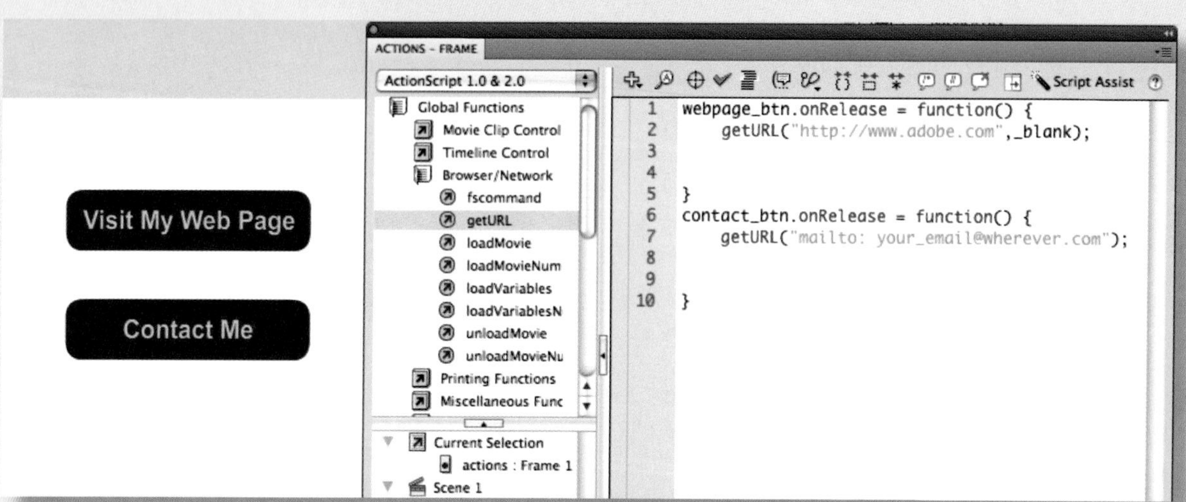

figure 8–71

Use the getURL action to create hyperlinks that open pages outside of a Flash movie.

4. Review these resources on form mail and form mail script templates:

   - Kirupa.com offers a tutorial on how to implement a Flash-based e-mail form using PHP: *http://www.kirupa.com/developer/actionscript/flash_php_email.htm.*
   - Gary Beene's Information Web site offers a great explanation of the form creation process: *http://www.garybeene.com/vb/tut-frm.htm.*
   - Matt's Script Archive, under the section FormMail, offers a sample CGI form mail script: *http://www.scriptarchive.com/*
   - Web Page Design for Designers offers a Flash form building program and other great resources: *http://www.wpdfd.com/software/*

5. Check out these placeholder text generators:

   - Lorem ipsum Generator3 can translate lorem ipsum (nonsensical Latin words) in English, German, and Spanish: *http://www.lorem-ipsum.info/generator3.*
   - Blind Text Generator: *http://www.blindtextgenerator.com/* is a simple to use generator and offers a good read on the history of "dummy or filler" text.
   - Discover more about the history of lorem ipsum text on Wikipedia: *http://en.wikipedia.org/wiki/Lorem_ipsum.*

ADVENTURES IN DESIGN

Accessibility in Flash

A drawback of Flash content has always been its inability to be accessible for all users. With each new version of Flash some improvements in this important area have been made; however, options for full accessibility are yet to come. Julie Strothman, an exceptional Web developer and my fellow colleague, shares with us what we can do to make Flash as accessible as possible.

Julie Strothman, M.S., is a user researcher, interaction designer, and project manager with the Landmark College Institute for Research and Training (LCIRT). At LCIRT, Julie works on NSF-funded projects, providing project management on a grant to broaden participation of underrepresented groups in computing fields, and performing user research and interface design on a grant to improve math education. Julie works closely with a group of students in LCIRT's Universal Design and Usability Lab. Together, they run and analyze usability tests, write usability and accessibility recommendations, and create design prototypes. Recent usability testing projects include evaluations of: community college Web sites, algebra learning resources, online courses for educators, course Web sites, and textbook ancillaries.

MAKING ACCESSIBLE CHOICES IN FLASH
By Julie Strothman

In general, Web producers want the broadest possible audience to use our content. Audiences affected by accessibility issues may be broader than you think: people with disabilities are the third largest minority group in the United States. Each release, Adobe has incorporated some additional accessibility options into Flash. While the Flash player is a cross-platform plug-in, many accessibility features are only available to people using Internet Explorer on Windows computers with Flash 6 or greater. We'll look here at how to use accessibility techniques, as well as the browsing behaviors these techniques support. It is essential to understand potential issues in order to truly accommodate user needs.

People who are blind may use a screen reader to listen to an audio version of the content. People with vision impairments may use a screen magnifier to zoom in on a particular area of the screen. People with cognitive difficulties may struggle with short-term memory requirements. People with reading difficulties may need to replay time-sensitive content. All of these people may struggle with small clickable areas. People with hearing loss and people who are deaf benefit from captions of audio content. People with mobility difficulties may be using input devices other than a mouse to navigate, such as their keyboard, their voice, or a switch. Many accessibility choices are helpful to people in challenging environments, regardless of ability: captions are useful in areas that are too noisy or too quiet for listening, increased clickable areas are useful for people dealing with sun glare, and a logical tab order is helpful when a laptop trackpad is not responding. Wise use of accessibility options can also enhance search engine ability to index Flash content.

PROFESSIONAL PROJECT EXAMPLE

In early 2008, Annesa and I worked with a group of students to explore computing careers. They were new to Web site planning and Flash design, and successfully created a Flash-based Web site demystifying learning disabilities and suggesting strategies for academic success. The site included Flash elements such as navigation buttons, animations, audio, video, and some animated text. Before making the site available online, I made some adjustments to make the site more accessible. (Using these techniques throughout your design process is the most efficient way to ensure accessibility.)

First, I set a tab order on all of the links for people who use a keyboard to navigate so that links receive focus from left-to-right and top-to-bottom. When these are not set, the order is quite random, adding to the user's cognitive load. Using the Accessibility panel in Flash, one can add a tab index to dynamic text, input text, buttons, movie clips, components, and screens. Tab order must be set for *all* accessible objects in a frame, in order for the player to follow the custom order at all. Further, each object assigned a tab order must have an instance name assigned in the Properties panel. You can reveal the tab order using the View > Show Tab Order, though it is important to test using the keyboard as well. See Figure C–1.

Some text is made available to screen readers by default in Flash (including dynamic text, input text fields, buttons, and movie clips), but graphic images need to have a description added. I added text descriptions of the images used so that people who are blind and listening with a screen reader would be aware of the meaning conveyed by the images. In the case where a group of graphics convey a single concept, I converted the group of images to a movie clip, gave it a name and longer description, and unchecked "make child objects accessible." See Figure C–2.

I converted all static text objects to dynamic text so the Flash player will expose them to screen readers.

The Web site's myths and truths page displays text that fades from the word myth to a myth statement, to the word truth, to a statement of truth. It includes forward and back controls to move back and forth between the myths/truths pairs. I added a pause control for people who read slowly and would benefit from keeping the text on the screen for a longer time. See Figure C–3.

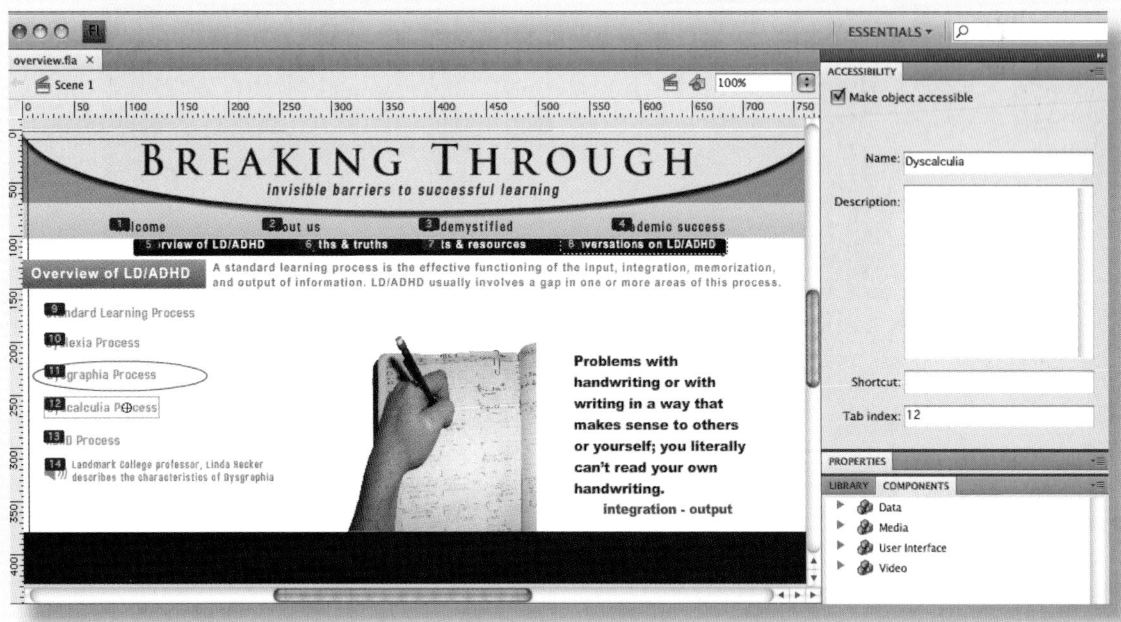

figure C–1 In the Accessibility panel (Window > Other Panels > Accessibility Panel, shown on the top right), a tab index has been added to each button. A name has been added in the panel because Flash will use the text inside the button for a label but will also add the word "button" to the words for each link. The tab order has been revealed (View > Show Tab Order—available in ActionScript 2.0 files at this time) in order to check for missing or redundant numbers.

ADVENTURES IN DESIGN

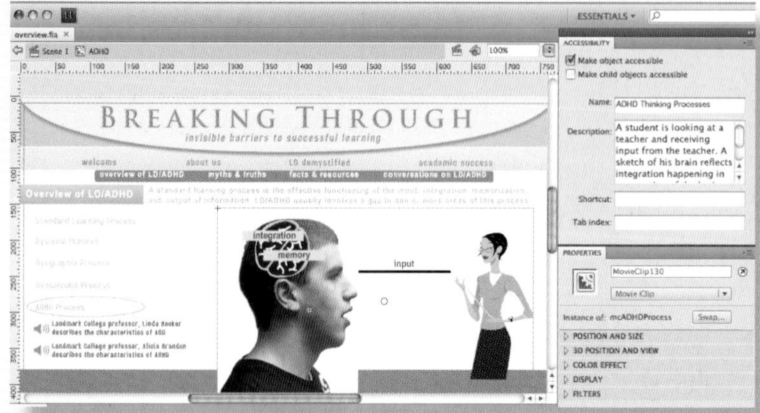

figure C–2 The graphic images were all selected and converted to a movie clip symbol. In the Accessibility panel, a name and longer text description of the image are entered and "Make child objects accessible" is *unchecked* so they are not read individually, which would be redundant.

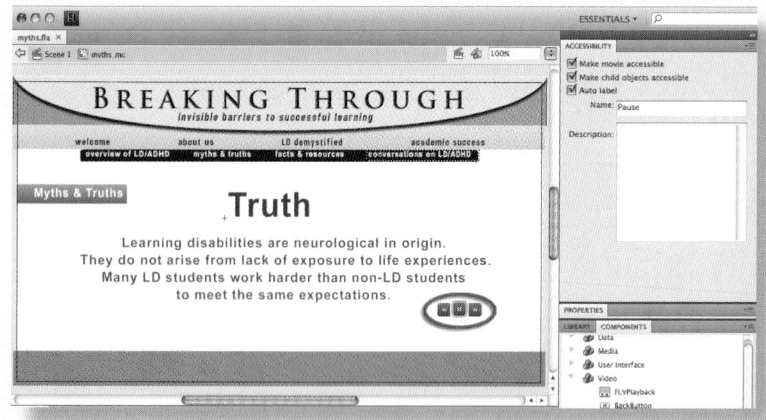

figure C–3 The text content in this page is animated, fading from a myth to a truth. I added a pause button for people who need longer to read, and stretched the timeline to keep the words "myth" and "truth" visible above their corresponding statement, to accommodate problems with short-term memory.

YOUR TURN

Using the sample file **accessibility/aid3_accessibility_practice.fla** in the **aid_examples** folder on the back of the book CD, use the accessibility techniques above and test out the results. (The file **aid_examples/accessibility/aid3_accessibility_practice_final.fla** has the accessibility techniques applied.)

Accessibility Practice Guidelines

1. Open Window > Other Panels > Accessibility Panel.
2. Decide which objects Flash should present information to screen readers. For each, make sure accessibility is turned on (in the Accessibility panel). For any objects that should be ignored by screen readers, turn accessibility off.
3. Convert text that should be accessible from static to dynamic text (in the Properties panel).
4. Group any graphics that convey a single concept and convert to a movie clip symbol (Modify > Convert to Symbol), then add a name in the Accessibility panel.

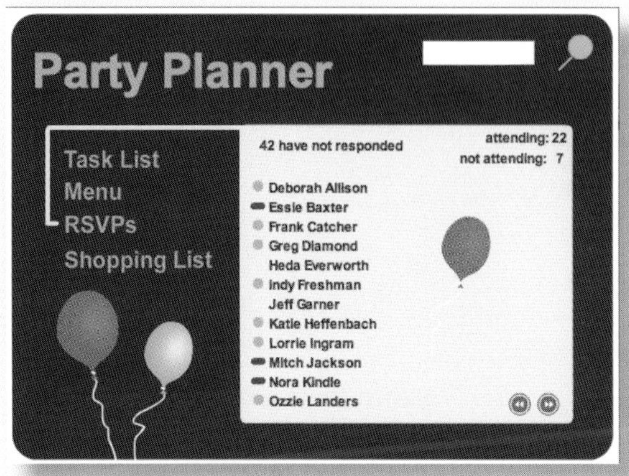

figure C–4 Use the Accessibility panel to enhance the accessibility of the Party Planner Flash file.

5. Add a tab index in the Accessibility panel to all accessible objects. Turn on View > Show Tab Order (at this time this option only works with files set to ActionScript 2.0).
6. Try testing the tab order and reading order in a browser. If you do not have the JAWS screen reader and you have a Windows machine, download the JAWS demo and try listening to the page (http://www.freedomscientific.com/fs_products/software_jaws.asp).

Things to Consider

There is a great deal more to explore regarding accessibility of Flash output. Below is a list of techniques to investigate further:

- **Assign text equivalents** Some images do not convey meaning and can be hidden from screen readers. Other images should be described in text for people who cannot see them or interpret their meaning.
- **Enable control over reading order** The order in which elements will be read is related to tab order, but slightly more complicated. Try listening to your SWF files with a demo version of JAWS software to see whether reading order needs to be adjusted. Test frequently throughout development!
- **Facilitate keyboard access** Avoid using empty movie clips as buttons. Screen readers will miss these areas.
- **Provide captions** Captions are essential for audio and video content. Flash can display caption content. Captions are added using third-party software.
- **Enable control over audio playback** Include audio play and pause buttons so that users can eliminate conflict between the sound of the Flash file and their screen reader.
- **Expose state of controls** Sometimes a control button will change function, such as a toggle of play and pause. The accessibility information should change when the button changes.
- **Test it: With real tools and with real people!** The best way to discover problems is to watch how people who use screen readers or navigate differently interact with your content.
- **Learn about general Web accessibility issues** Examples of Web accessibility issues might include color contrast, what constitutes good alternative text, techniques for good readability, etc.

Resources on Flash Accessibility

- WebAIM: *http://www.webaim.org/techniques/flash/*
- Adobe: *http://www.adobe.com/accessibility/index.html*

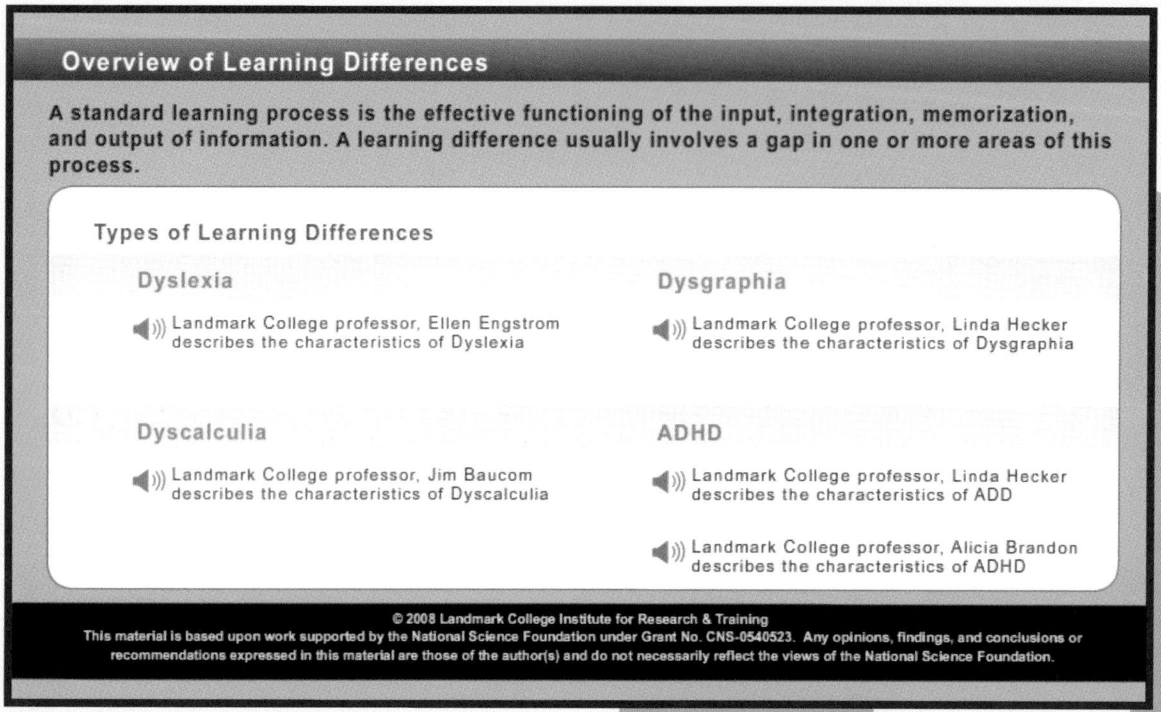

Overview of Learning Differences

A standard learning process is the effective functioning of the input, integration, memorization, and output of information. A learning difference usually involves a gap in one or more areas of this process.

Types of Learning Differences

Dyslexia

Landmark College professor, Ellen Engstrom describes the characteristics of Dyslexia

Dysgraphia

Landmark College professor, Linda Hecker describes the characteristics of Dysgraphia

Dyscalculia

Landmark College professor, Jim Baucom describes the characteristics of Dyscalculia

ADHD

Landmark College professor, Linda Hecker describes the characteristics of ADD

Landmark College professor, Alicia Brandon describes the characteristics of ADHD

This material is based upon work supported by the National Science Foundation under Grant No. CNS-0540523. Any opinions, findings, and conclusions or recommendations expressed in this material are those of the author(s) and do not necessarily reflect the views of the National Science Foundation.

9 | working with sound |

charting your course

By now you've got plenty of skills to integrate images, animation, text, and interactivity into a worthy Flash experience. Now, it's time to supplement it with sound (and in Chapter 10, video). This chapter covers an overview of sound reproduction, basic audio terminology and concepts, the sound options available in Flash, and the practices of working with sound within a movie.

goals

In this chapter you will:

- **Get an overview of sound reproduction basics**
- **Explore Flash's sound features**
- **Import a sound**
- **Attach a sound using ActionScript**
- **Create on/off buttons for sound**
- **Optimize and publish a movie with sound**

OVERVIEW OF SOUND REPRODUCTION

In Chapter 2, you learned about bitmap images—images that comprise of pixels, and whose quality and size are dependent on resolution (a measurement based on pixels per inch). The process of setting the resolution, compression, and dimensions for an image for its particular application is called optimization (see Chapter 7). For example, Flash is intended for screen-based content that quite possibly will be downloaded from the Web, so the resolution of images you use in the program—such as JPEG photos or GIF illustrations—should remain low, around 72–96 pixels per inch (ppi). This optimization process is also required of sound that will be used in Flash. However, instead of working with image pixels and their resolution, with sound you work with sample and bit rates.

figure |9–1|

The waveform of a sound selected in Flash's Library is shown in the preview window.

When reproducing sound digitally, the quality of the sound is determined by its sample rate—the number of times audio is measured (sampled) per second. This measurement is calculated by the number of cycles in a sound's sine wave or waveform. See Figure 9–1. A single wave cycle (the range from one peak to another peak of a sine wave) in one second is known as a hertz. A thousand wave cycles in one second is called a kilohertz (kHz). Samples of sound can also have different resolutions determined by bit depth—the amount of computer numbers that make up the complexity of that sound. Like images, sound is represented on the computer by a series of 0s and 1s known as bits. The larger the series of bits, the higher the bit depth and, in terms of sound, the higher the fidelity, quality, and file size of the sound—music played from a CD will most likely have a higher quality sound than the same sound heard via the Web. In short, sound has varied sample rates and bit depths, resulting in varied levels of sound quality and overall file size (see Figure 9–2)—important to know when you are determining the best sound solution for your Flash movie. In working with sound in Flash, common sample rates are 11, 22, and 44 kHz, and bit rates are 8 and 16 bits. More details on these sample and bit rates are provided later in this chapter.

Note: For a point of reference, sound reproduction and optimization can once again equate to bitmap images. The amount of kilohertz and bits in a digital sound could be thought of as the amount of kilobytes and bits in a digital image. For sound these elements determine the richness of the sound, while for images they determine the amount of color and visual detail. Consider this: if you were to paint a visual representation of Vivaldi's Four Seasons concerto (a complex and rich musical masterpiece), the painting would most likely demonstrate a vivid display of color. On the flip side, if you were to paint a representation of a professor's lecture (voice only), it might invoke a more achromatic, monotone art piece.

Approximate file size/memory required for 1 minute of digital audio:

File Type	44.1 KHz	22.05 KHz	11.025 KHz
16 bit Stereo	10.1 MB	5.05 MB	2.52 MB
16 bit Mono	5.05 MB	2.52 MB	1.26 MB
8 bit Mono	2.52 MB	1.26 MB	630 KB

figure 9–2

The sound quality of an audio file is dependent on its sample rate and bit depth.

AUDIO IN FLASH

Let's go over the various aspects of working with sound in Flash, including audio preparation, importing, Flash sound properties, and publishing. Then, you can practice these aspects and discover two ways to execute sound within the program—via the Timeline or from the Library—in the lessons that follow.

Preparing Audio for Flash

Flash has some capability for manipulating and optimizing sound, but it's not designed to offer the flexibility and features of programs that are specifically made for sound editing. After studying this chapter, if you find yourself really getting into sound in your Flash movies, you will want to prepare and tweak your audio in a program like any of the following. With these programs, you can better resample, clip, crop, equalize volume, mix multiple tracks, and add effects to your sound before importing them into Flash.

- Audacity (*http://audacity.sourceforge.net/*)—popular, low-end, cross-platform audio editor; and best of all, it's free.
- GoldWave (*http://www.goldwave.com/*)—low end, about $50 for the Windows platform.
- Sony's Sound Forge (*http://www.sonycreativesoftware.com/soundforge*)—a professional audio solution for the Windows platform, about $300.
- Adobe® Audition or Soundbooth™ (*http://www.adobe.com/products/*)—both products designed for cross-platform use. Audition is geared toward audiocentric professionals and Soundbooth toward the novice sound designer or developer. Costs range from $200 to $350.

- Cubase from Steinberg (*http://www.steinberg.net/en/products/musicproduction/cubase4_product.html*)—for advanced music production for Mac or Windows, ranging from $150 to $600.

Sound Import

When sound is imported into Flash, it is stored in the same Library as bitmaps and symbols. It can be placed on the Timeline, loaded into a SWF file at run time, or placed on the various states of a button. Flash supports the import of many sound formats (from the Flash Help files):

- ASND (Windows or Macintosh)—the native sound format of Adobe Soundbooth
- WAV (Windows only)
- AIFF (Macintosh only)
- MP3 (Windows or Macintosh, recommended for Web playback)

If you have QuickTime® 4 or later installed on your system, you can import these additional sound file formats:

- AIFF (Windows or Macintosh)
- Sound Designer® II (Macintosh only)
- Sound Only QuickTime Movies (Windows or Macintosh)
- Sun AU (Windows or Macintosh)
- System 7 Sounds (Macintosh only)
- WAV (Windows or Macintosh)

The format and compression scheme (called the codec, an acronym for encoder/decoder) of a particular format will make a big difference in the file size of the sound. At publish time, Flash has options for how an imported sound will be compressed within a SWF (see the Publishing Sound section later in this chapter). Practice the steps for importing a sound into Flash:

1. Open Flash and create a new document (Flash File, ActionScript 2.0).
2. Choose File > Import > Import to Library, and from the **chap09_lesson/audio_examples** folder, choose the **jazz.mp3** sound file.
3. Open the Library panel and drag an instance of the sound file—**jazz.mp3**—to the Stage. You will not see the sound on the Stage, but you can see a representation of its waveform and its length in Layer 1 of the Timeline—go to frame 105 of the Layer 1 timeline and insert a keyframe (F6) to see the full audio track. See Figure 9–3.
4. Be sure you have the volume turned up on your computer, and then hit Return or Enter on the keyboard to hear the sound.
5. Save this file as **sound_test.fla** in your lessons folder. Keep the file open for further practice in the next section—Sound Properties.

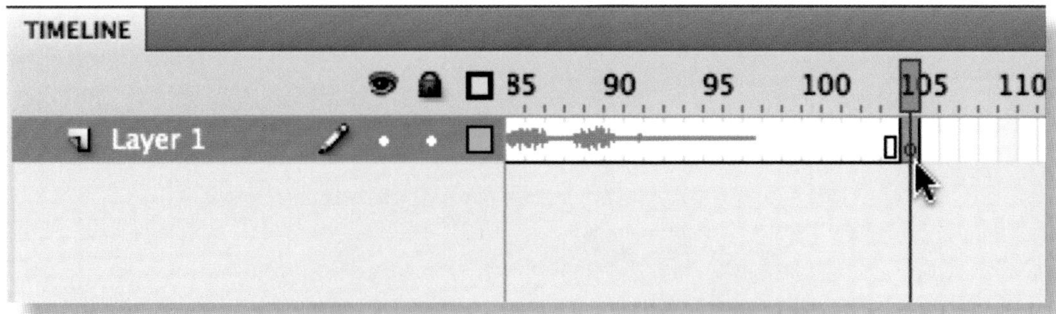

figure 9–3

Extend the time on the Timeline to see the frame length of the sound clip.

Sound Properties

Each sound that is imported into Flash has sound properties associated to it that can be viewed from the Library panel. See Figure 9–4. Check them out:

1. If not already, open the **sound_test.fla** you created in the Sound Import section above (or open the sample file **sound_test.fla** in the **chap09_lessons** folder).
2. Open the Library panel and Ctrl-click (Mac) or right-click (Windows) on the **jazz.mp3** sound file. From the drop down menu, choose Properties. You can also double-click on the sound icon in the Library to open its Properties.
3. In the Properties for the sound, notice the following (see Figure 9–5): the file name (**jazz.mp3**), its location on your computer and creation date, its sample rate and bit depth (44 kHz Stereo, 16 bit), and the compression setting (MP3). You will explore items under the Advanced/Basic toggle tab, such as Linkage, in a later lesson.
4. Choose the Test button to play the sound. Choose OK to close the Properties windows.
5. Keep your file open for further practice in the next section—Sound Settings.

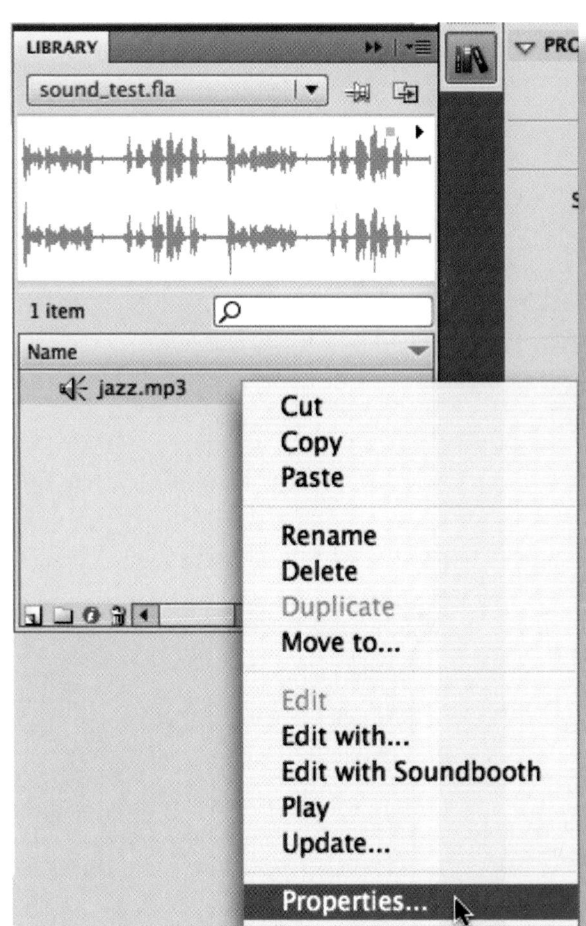

figure 9–4

Choose Sound Properties from the Library.

figure | 9–5 |

Explore options in the Sound Properties window.

Sound Settings

There are two types of sound synchronization in Flash: event and stream. An event sound downloads completely before it begins playing, and it continues playing until explicitly stopped (such as the end of the sound, or through a stop action). Looping ambient music or sounds that you want to play in the background of your movie or that are initiated by a button click are best saved as the event type. Stream sounds begin playing as soon as enough data for the first few frames have been downloaded; stream sounds are synchronized to the timeline for playing on a Web site. Stream sounds are great if you have a character, for example, in which its mouth movements are animated to specific words or sounds (see Figure 9–6). These sound types, along with some simple editing options, can be set in the Properties panel for an explicitly selected sound. See Figure 9–7. Associate the numbers in Figure 9–7 with the following descriptions adapted from the Flash help files:

1. **Name**—from the name drop down list, select an imported sound file to apply its settings.
2. **Effect**—choose from the Effects drop down menu any of the following options:
   - *None*: applies no effects to the sound file. Select this option to remove previously applied effects.
   - *Left Channel/Right Channel*: plays sound in the left or right channel only. (See note on channels below.)
   - *Fade Left To Right/Fade Right To Left*: shifts the sound from one channel to the other.

figure 9–6

An example Flash movie where mouth shapes were synced to voice-over.

figure 9–7

Sound options can be found in the Properties panel of a selected sound object.

- *Fade In*: gradually increases the volume of a sound over its duration.
- *Fade Out*: gradually decreases the volume of a sound over its duration.
- *Custom*: lets you create custom in and out volume points of sound using the Edit Envelope (see step 3).

Note: What is a channel and how does it relate to stereo or mono sound? I found a useful definition of this concept on the Basic Car Audio Electronics Web site: *http://www.bcae1.com/stermono.htm*:

> The terms stereo and mono are often used when referring to amplifier connections. A stereo amplifier has two independent channels, one left and one right. The left and right signals of the stereo signal are similar but not exactly the same. The two channels are used to give the audio a sense of depth. If one instrument or voice is only produced in the left channel, it will seem to originate from the left side of the listening area. If a particular sound is only slightly louder in one of the channels, that sound will seem to originate off center slightly toward the channel in which the sound is louder. If you have two speakers but supply mono signal to both of them, there will be no sense of separation or depth. If a mono signal is fed to both channels of a stereo amplifier, with a speaker on each channel, the output will mono.

This leads us to another question: what is the best channel setting for sound played back in Flash? To preserve some of the subtle qualities in instrumental music, I usually keep it in stereo, even if this increases the file size of my Flash movie. However, if it's being played as an ambient background, you might get away with setting it to mono, which will reduce its file size, but could have a noticeable effect on its sound quality. For voice, a mono setting usually works fine and will create a more optimized file. You can play with the mono and stereo settings of sound when you publish your SWF (see the Publishing Sound section).

3. **Edit Envelope**—click on the pencil icon next to the Effect settings to create custom adjustments to the volume of your sound. To make adjustments, move the start or end points (empty box shapes) of each channel up or down. You can even add volume adjustment points along each of the channels waveforms by clicking and dragging up or down on the envelope line. See Figure 9–8. Editing the envelope has been helpful for me when I needed to quiet a section of music that was jarringly too loud.

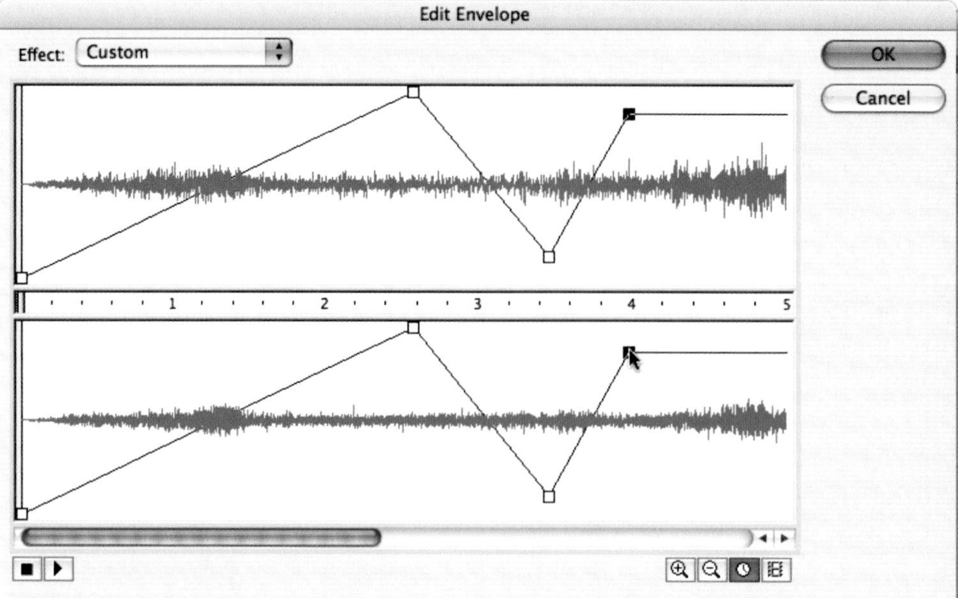

figure 9–8

Edit the volume of sections of sound with the Edit Envelope.

4. **Sync**—as mentioned previously, with this option you can set a sound to the event or stream type, and its variations start and stop. See Figure 9–9.
   - *Event:* synchronizes the sound to the occurrence of an event (e.g., movement of the timeline or when a user clicks a button). Important to know is that once an event sound is initiated, it plays in its entirety, independently of the timeline, even if the SWF file stops playing. If an event sound is playing and the sound is instantiated again (e.g., by the user clicking the button again), the first instance of the sound continues to play and another instance begins to play simultaneously.
   - *Start:* has the same function as Event, except that if the sound is already playing, no new instance of the sound plays.
   - *Stop:* silences the specified sound.
   - *Stream:* synchronizes the sound for playing on a Web site. Flash forces animation to keep pace with stream sounds. If Flash can't draw animation frames quickly enough, it skips frames. Unlike event sounds, stream sounds stop if the SWF file stops playing. Also, a stream sound can never play longer than the length of the frames it occupies.

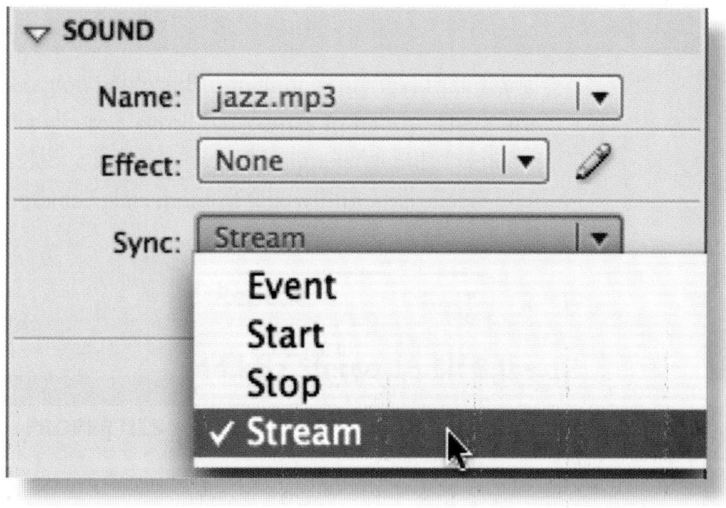

figure 9–9

The Sync options in the Properties panel for a selected sound.

5. **Repeat**—set the amount of times a sound repeats or continuously loops.
6. **File Compression**—indicates the sample rate, channels (stereo or mono), bit depth, and bit rate (an audio stream's size, over time) of the sound.

Play with these sound settings using the file you've been working on in the previous sections:

1. If not already, open the **sound_test.fla** you created in the Sound Import section above (or choose the **sound_test.fla** in the **chap09_lessons** folder).
2. Choose Control > Test Movie—by default it will keep looping the sound.
3. On **Layer 1** of the timeline, select the last keyframe. Then, click and drag on the last frame and move it to frame 40.
4. In the Properties panel, choose Event under the Sync option, if not already chosen.

5. Select the first frame of **Layer 1,** and choose Return (Enter) on the keyboard. Watch the playback head, and notice that even though the sound looks like it has ended at frame 40, it actually keeps playing. An event sound is independent of the timeline.

6. Select the first frame of **Layer 1** again, and now under the Sync setting, choose Stream. Play back the sound. It stops at frame 40—with streamed sound, the sound is synced with the timeline.

7. Now, keep the Stream option selected, and choose the Loop option, rather than Repeat. See Figure 9–10. Play it back to hear the result.

figure 9–10

Choose to loop a sound continuously.

8. Change the Sync option back to Event, and under Effect, select Fade In. Play back the sound. The sound will start soft and build in volume.

9. Feel free to play with the other options, and keep your file open for further practice in the next section—Publishing Sound.

Publishing Sound

When publishing a SWF file, you can set compression properties that will apply globally to all the sounds in your movie, or you can set properties for each individual sound.

If, for example, you have imported a WAV or AIFF formatted sound file, you can choose to have it published into the MP3 compressed format for better Web playback. It's important to understand, however, that a sound file cannot be sampled up—if a sound file was imported as an MP3, for example, it cannot be sampled up to the uncompressed RAW format. Once the detail—quality—of a sound file is removed, it cannot be added back again—the same concept goes for images. That's why it's a good idea, if you have the option, to always save the uncompressed versions of your files.

The global publishing settings for audio are found in the Publish Settings panel—choose File > Publish Settings and select the Flash tab at the top. See Figure 9–11.

You can create different settings for sounds synced as stream or event by choosing the Set button for each option. Under the Set option, you can choose a compression type, change stereo to mono, and determine bit rate and quality. See Figure 9–12.

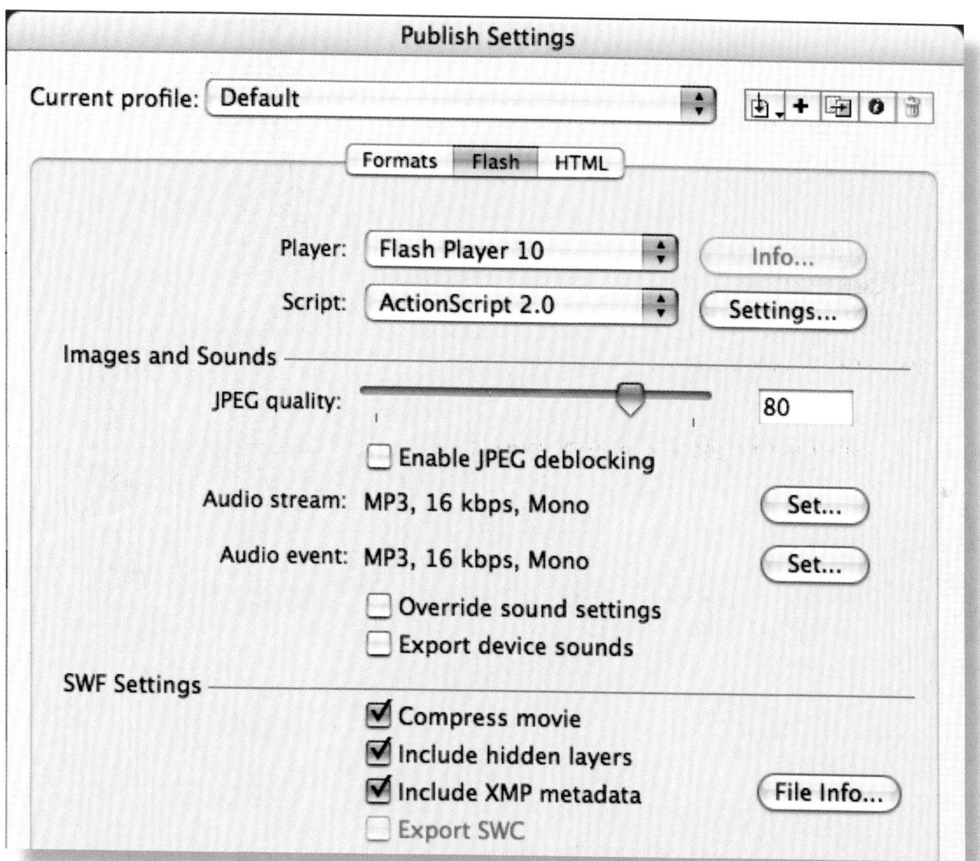

figure 9–11

Under the Flash tab in the Publish Settings area, you can find options for global sound output.

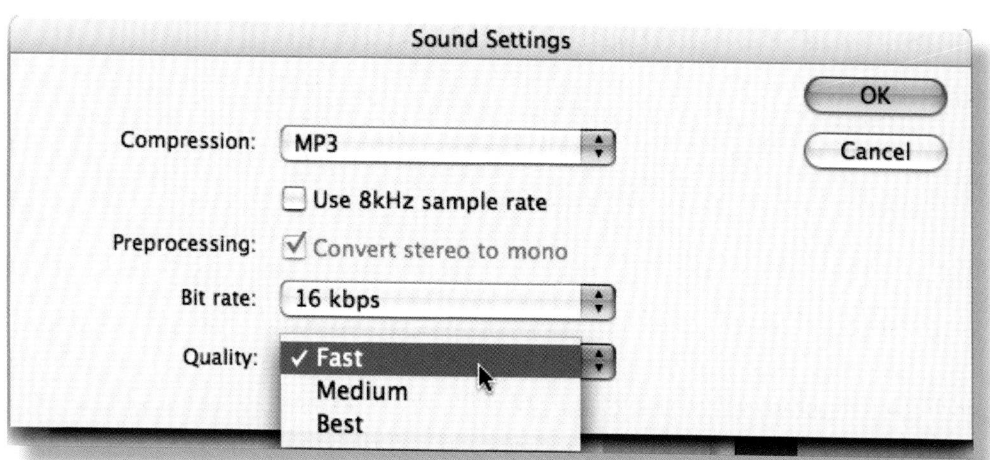

figure 9–12

The Sound Settings found in the Publish Settings area of Flash.

To set the publishing options for an individual sound, go to its sound properties—double-click the sound icon in the Library panel or preview pane, or Ctrl-click (Mac) or right-click (Windows) a sound file in the Library panel and select Properties from the sub menu.

In this panel, explore the following with the **sound_test.fla** file:

1. If the sound file has been edited externally, click Update. For Compression, select Default, ADPCM, MP3, Raw, or Speech (see descriptions below).
2. Set export settings, such as sample and bit rates.
3. Click Test to play the sound once. Click Stop if you want to stop testing the sound before it finishes playing.
4. Adjust export settings if necessary until the desired sound quality is achieved. Note how your decisions affect the final size of the exported sound—in the lower part of the Sound Properties window, watch how the percentage (based on the size of the original file) changes with each different setting. See Figure 9–13. Click OK.

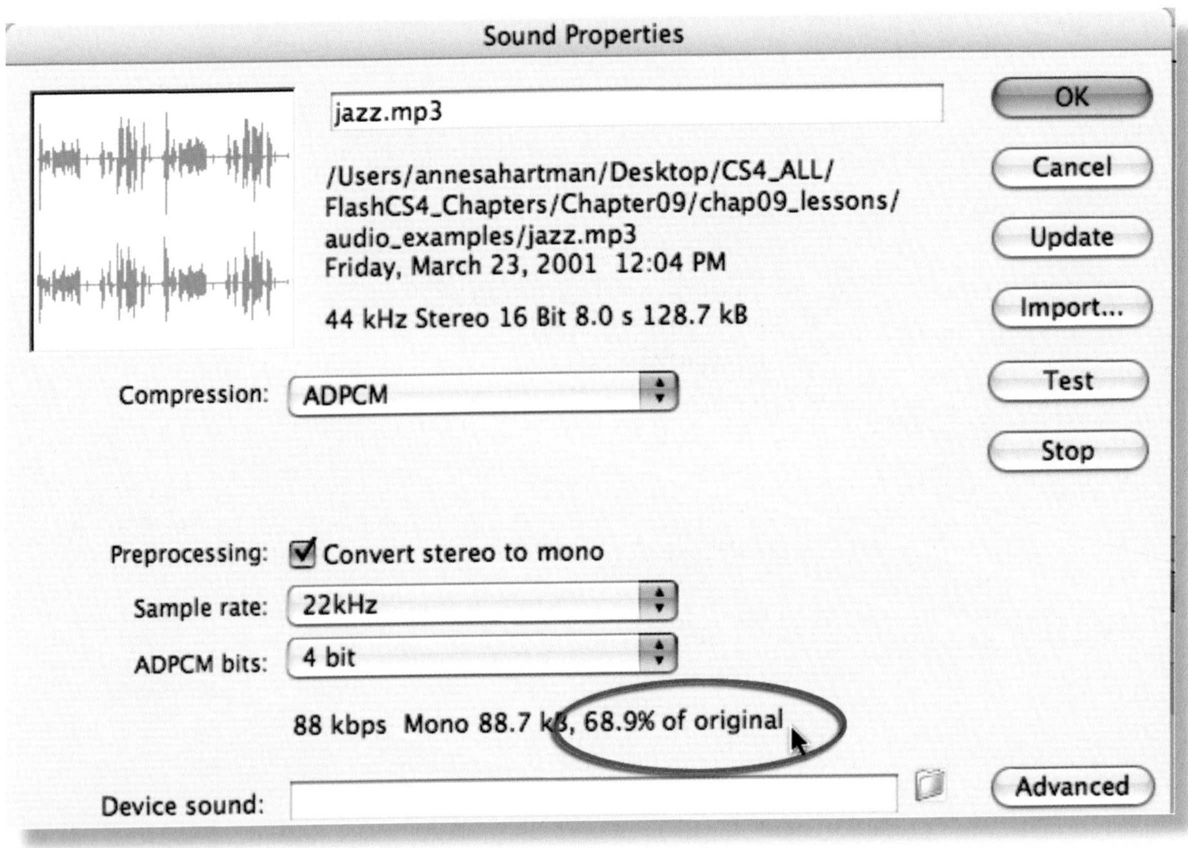

figure 9–13

Alter compression schemes of individual sound files in the Library and note the change in a sound's file size with each selection.

In both the global and individual sound settings, it's important to understand the meaning of each setting, so you can choose the best ones for your particular sound file. Review the following terminology taken, in part, from the Flash Help files.

Default Compression

The default compression setting is available in the sound properties for individual sound files—double-click on a sound file in the Library to open these properties. The Default compression option uses the global compression settings in the Publish Settings dialog box when you export your SWF file. If you select Default, no additional export settings are available.

ADPCM and Raw Compression and Options

ADPCM and Raw compression and their options are in the Publish Settings dialog box—choose File > Publish Settings, and then select the Flash tab at the top. Under Images and Sound, choose the Set option for either stream or event sounds. See Figure 9–14. You can also find this option in the sound properties of an individual sound file (double-click on the sound icon in the Library).

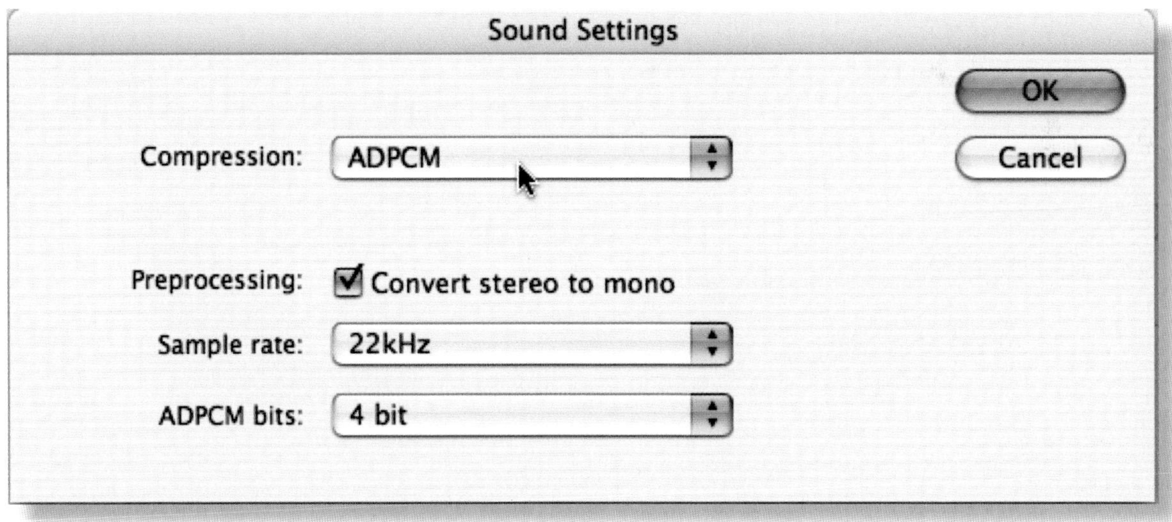

figure 9–14

The ADPCM compression settings found in the Publish Settings area of Flash.

ADPCM compression sets compression for 8- or 16-bit sound data. Use the ADPCM setting when you export short event sounds such as button clicks. Raw compression exports sounds with no sound compression.

Preprocessing

Preprocessing converts mixed stereo sounds to monaural (mono) when you select Convert stereo to mono (mono sounds are unaffected by this option).

Sample Rate

Sample rate controls sound fidelity and file size. Lower rates decrease file size but can also degrade sound quality. Rate options are as follows:

- 5 kHz: barely acceptable for speech
- 11 kHz: the lowest recommended quality for a short segment of music and one-quarter the standard CD rate
- 22 kHz: a popular choice for Web playback and half the standard CD rate
- 44 kHz: the standard CD audio rate

> **Note: Flash cannot increase the kilohertz rate of an imported sound above the rate at which it was imported.**

ADPCM Bits (ADPCM only)

ADPCM Bits specifies the bit depth of the sound compression (between 2 and 5 bits). Higher bit depths produce higher quality sound.

MP3 Compression and Options

The MP3 compression options are located in the Publish Settings dialog box, under the Flash tab. Under Images and Sound, choose the Set option for either stream or event sounds. MP3 is Flash's default publish setting for sound. Use MP3 when you are exporting longer stream sounds such as music sound tracks. You can also find this option in the sound properties of an individual sound file (double-click on the sound icon in the Library).

Use Imported MP3 Quality

The Use imported MP3 quality option is the default setting. Deselect to select other MP3 compression settings. Select to export an imported MP3 file with the same settings the file had when it was imported (note that, with this setting, Flash will not recompress the file—a good thing!).

Bit Rate

Bit rate determines the bits per second in the exported sound file. Flash supports 8 through 160 kbps CBR (constant bit rate). When you export music, set the bit rate to 16 kbps or higher for best results.

Preprocessing

Preprocessing converts mixed stereo sounds to monaural (mono sounds are unaffected by this option).

> **Note: The Preprocessing option is available only if you select a bit rate of 20 kbps or higher.**

Quality

Quality determines the compression speed and sound quality:

- Fast—yields faster compression but lower sound quality.
- Medium—yields somewhat slower compression but higher sound quality.
- Best—yields the slowest compression and the highest sound quality.

Speech Compression and Options

Speech compression exports sounds using a compression that is adapted to speech. The Speech compression options are located in the Publish Settings dialog box, under the Flash tab. Under Images and Sound, choose the Set option for either stream or event sounds. You can also find this option in the sound properties of an individual sound file (double-click on the sound icon in the Library).

Sample Rate

Sample rate controls sound fidelity and file size. A lower rate decreases file size but can also degrade sound quality. Select from the following options:

- 5 kHz: acceptable for speech
- 11 kHz: recommended for speech
- 22 kHz: acceptable for most types of music on the Web
- 44 kHz: the standard CD audio rate—however, because compression is applied, the sound is not of CD quality in the SWF file

Lesson 1: Stop and Play a Sound File

In Chapter 6, you made stop and go buttons to control the playback of an animated airplane. You will use the same lesson to import a sound and set the stop and go buttons to control that sound. There are numerous options to control sound in Flash, and you can find lots of tutorials on these many ways online. In this section, however, you learn the most basic sound actions—stop and play. Providing this option for viewers of your Flash movie is highly recommended.

Importing a Sound

1. Open **chap9L1a.fla** in the **chap09_lessons** folder.
2. Be sure the Classic workspace is selected.
3. Choose Control > Test Movie and test out the stop and go buttons. Close the SWF file.
4. Choose File > Import > Import to Library, and in the **audio_examples** folder, choose one of the following: **airplane.aiff** (if you are on a Mac) or **airplane.wav** (if you are on Windows).
5. Open the Library panel and click on the airplane sound file to highlight it in the Library preview area (if you don't see the viewing area, you might need to expand it by clicking and dragging down on the bottom of the preview—see Figure 9–15.)

figure 9–15

Expand the Library preview area, and from there, choose the play button to hear a selected sound.

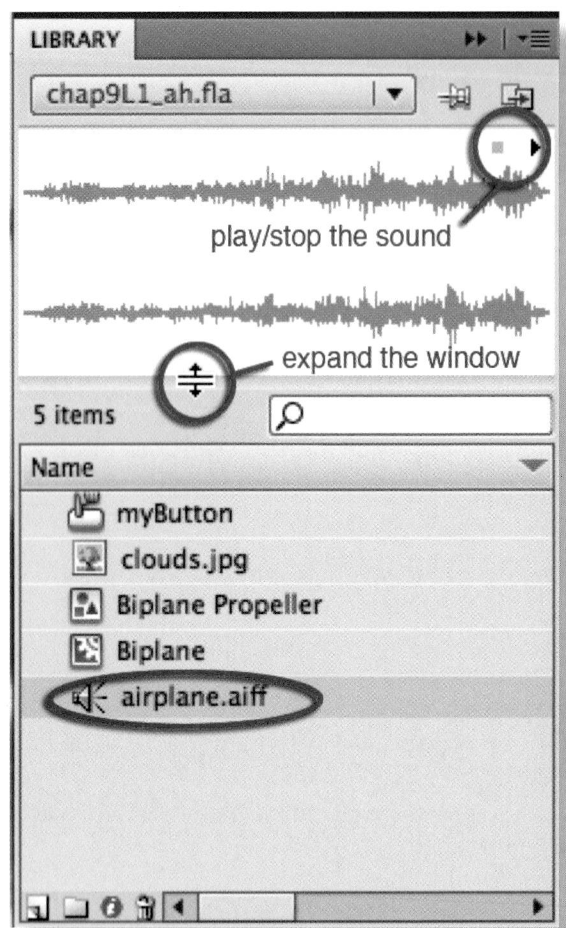

6. Click the play button in the upper right corner of the viewing area to hear the sound—don't forget to turn up the volume on your computer! See figure 9–15 again.

7. Create a new layer and name it **sound**. Place it below the **actions** layer.

8. On the **sound** layer, drag an instance of the airplane sound from the Library to the Stage. Note the waveform visual of the sound on the **sound** layer. See Figure 9–16.

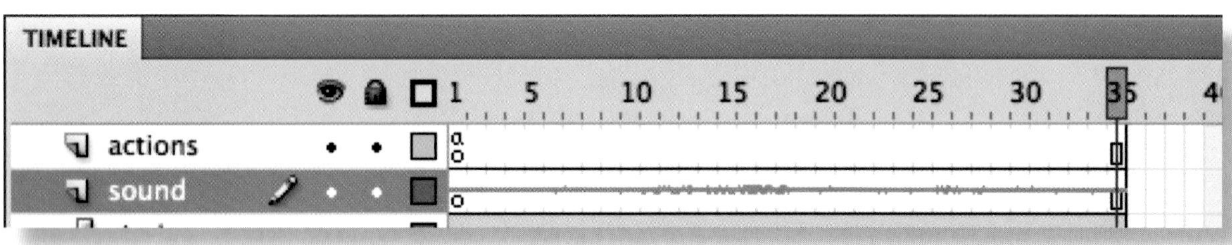

figure 9–16

The waveform of a sound on the Stage appears on a layer in the Timeline.

9. Select the **sound** layer, and in the Properties panel, be sure the Sync option is set to Stream, so that the sound is synced to the animation on the Timeline. See Figure 9–17.

10. Test the movie to play back the sound and animation. Notice that both the sound and the animation continue looping by default. However, if you hit the stop button, the animation stops, but not the sound. Let's fix this in the next section.

11. Save your file.

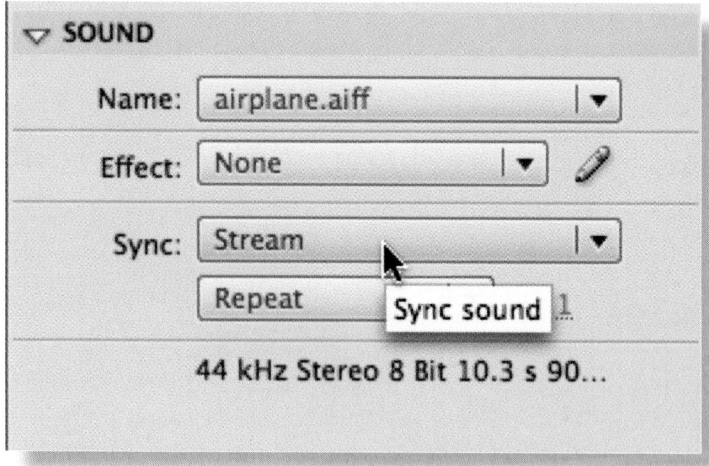

figure 9–17

Set the Sync option to Stream.

Adding a Stop All Sounds

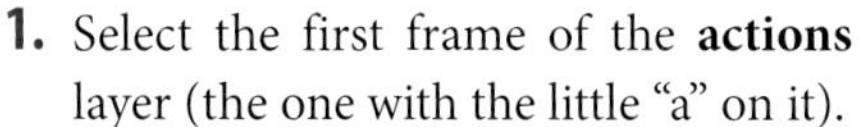

1. Select the first frame of the **actions** layer (the one with the little "a" on it).

2. Choose Window > Actions to open the Actions panel. Located in the script panel is the ActionScript that describes the stop and play functionality of the animation (you defined this script in Lesson 1: Stop and Play an Animated Movie in Chapter 6)

3. Place your cursor after the semicolon of the first stop action in the script, and then hit Return (Enter) to create a new line. Enter the following script (see also Figure 9–18):

    stopAllSounds();

ACTIONS - FRAME

```
myBtnStop.onRelease = function() {
    stop();
    stopAllSounds();

};

myBtnPlay.onRelease = function() {
    play();

};
```

figure 9–18

In the Actions panel, enter the script to stop all sounds in a Flash movie.

4. Close the Actions panel and choose Control > Test Movie. Test the buttons. In this example, the stopping and playing of the sound is explicitly linked to the stopping and playing of any animation that is on the Timeline. This works great in this example, but what if you want your sound to be more independent from its surroundings, such as the option for a user to mute a sound without affecting what's going on in the rest of the movie? Let's explore this in the next section.

5. Save and close this file.

Controlling a Background Sound

1. Open the **chap9L1b.fla** file from the **chap09_lessons** folder. This is similar to the file you have been working with, but the **sound** layer and the stop and go buttons for the animation have been removed. Also, the animation for the plane is now within a movie clip symbol, so it too can run independently of the timeline and unaffected by multiple things happening within the movie.

2. Choose File > Import to Library and open the **flying.mp3** found in the **chap09_lessons/audio_examples** folder.

3. Open the Library panel, select the **flying.mp3**, and play the sound by clicking on the play button in the Library viewing area. See Figure 9–19.

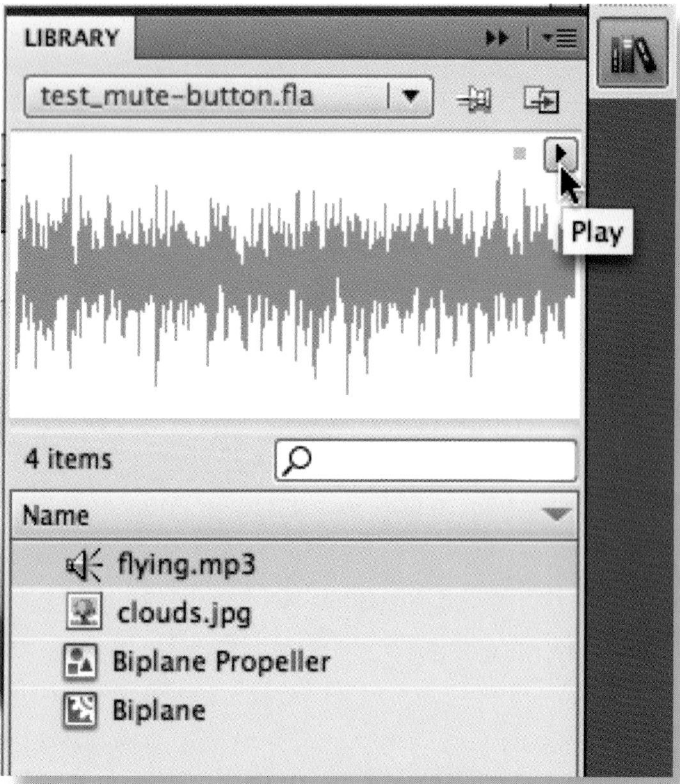

figure 9–19

Play the sound from the Library panel.

4. Create a unique identifier for this sound, so that it can be identified by ActionScript in a later step—double-click on the sound's icon in the Library to open its properties.

5. In the Properties panel, click on the Advanced tab at the bottom of the window to open more options (if the window is already open, the tab will be set to Basic).

6. In the Linkage area, choose the **Export for ActionScript** option, and for the Identifier, replace the file name with **flying_sound**. Refer to Figure 9–20. Click OK.

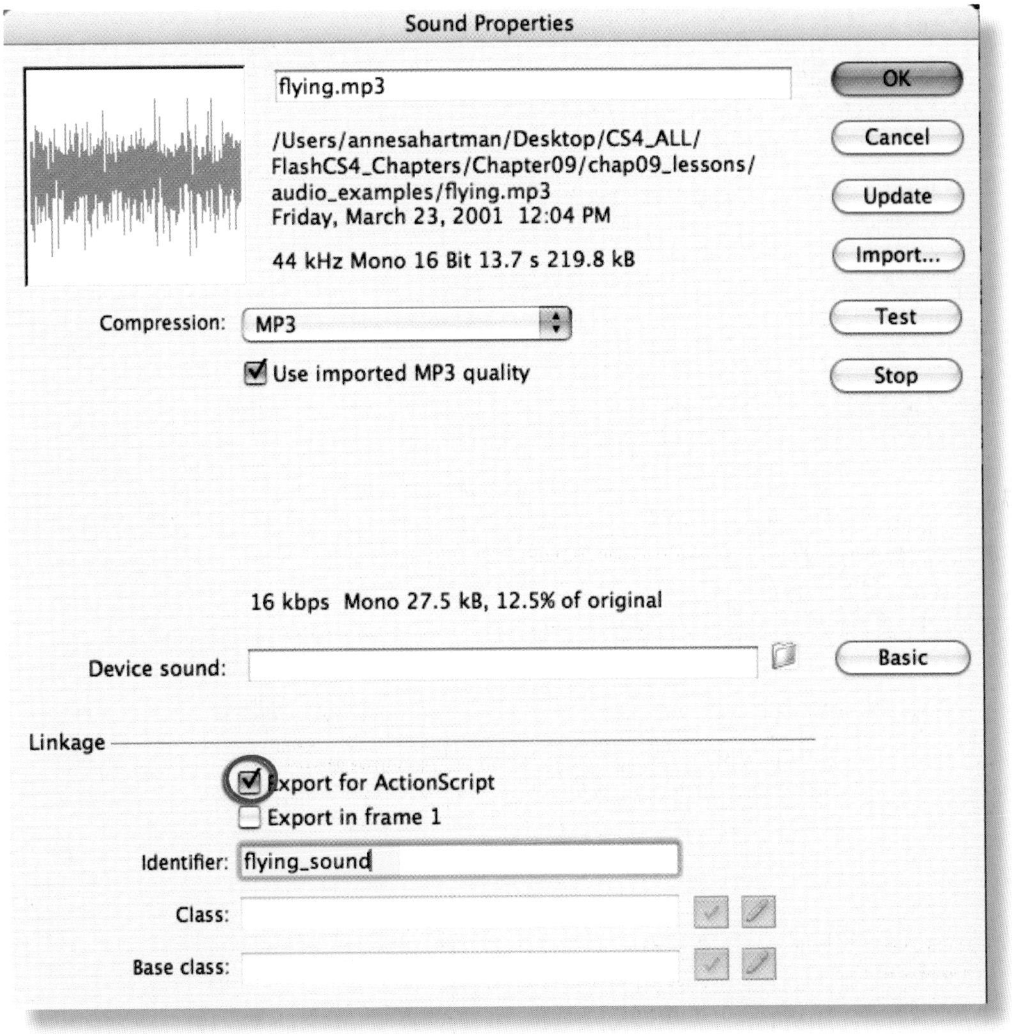

figure 9–20

Create an identifier for the sound file in its Sound Properties area.

Note: A linkage identifier can be named whatever you choose, just like when you set an instance name on a symbol object. Best practice is to keep your identifier names short, in lowercase, and intuitive, so they can easily be identified within an action script.

7. Using a Behavior, lets call this music into the movie. Select the first frame of the **actions** layer. Then, choose Window > Behaviors.

> **Note:** **Behaviors make the coding part of an action easier to execute; however, they are only supported by ActionScript 2.0 (not 3.0). An alternate method—involving more coding, but compatible with ActionScript 2.0 and 3.0—is covered in the next lesson.**

8. In the Behaviors window, click the plus button in the upper left corner, and from the drop down menu, choose Sound > Load Sound from Library. See Figure 9–21.

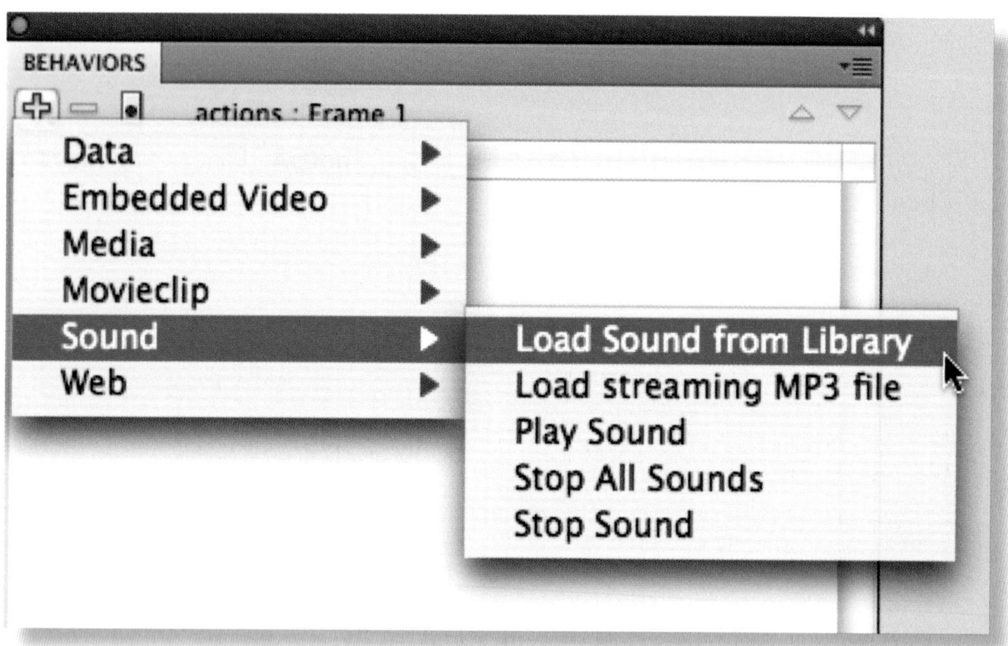

figure 9–21

Load a sound from the Library using a Behavior supported by ActionScript 2.0.

9. In the Load Sound from Library window, enter **flying_sound** for the Identifier and **background1** for the instance name. Keep **Play this sound when loaded** checked. See Figure 9–22. Select OK, and close the Behaviors panel.

10. Choose Control > Test Movie to play the sound.

11. Save the file.

Controlling the Sound with Stop and Play Buttons

1. Create a new layer called **buttons.**

2. Choose Window > Common Libraries > Buttons, scroll down the panel and open the **playback flat** folder. Drag an instance of the **flat blue play** and **flat blue stop** buttons to the upper right corner of the movie. See Figure 9–23. Close the Common Libraries window.

3. Select the stop button on the Stage. Choose Window > Behaviors, and from the Behaviors drop down menu, choose Sound > Stop Sound.

figure 9–22

Enter the identifier and instance names for the sound file to be loaded.

figure 9–23

From the Common Libraries in Flash, place an instance of the playback buttons onto the Stage.

4. In the Stop Sound window, enter **flying_sound** for the Identifier and **background1** for the instance name. See Figure 9–24. Click OK.

figure 9–24

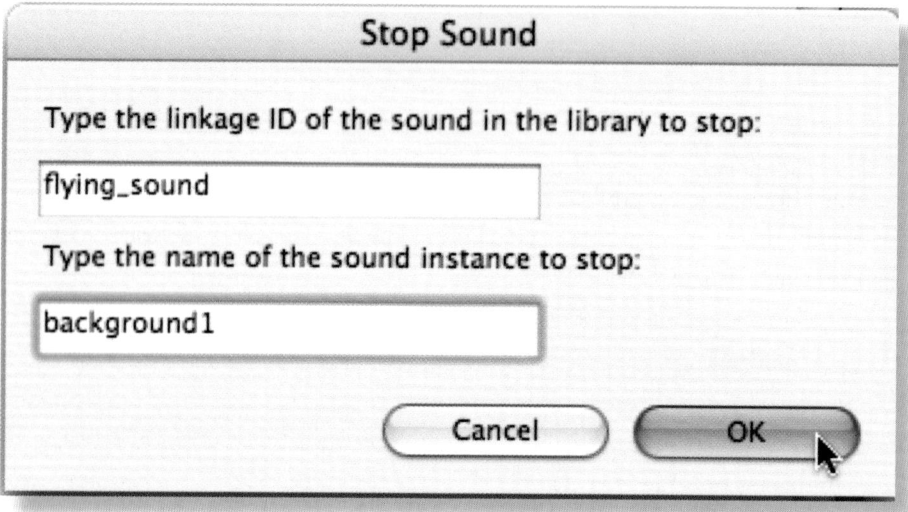

Using a Behavior, create a stop action for the sound.

5. In the Behaviors panel, be sure the On Release event is selected. See Figure 9–25.

figure 9–25

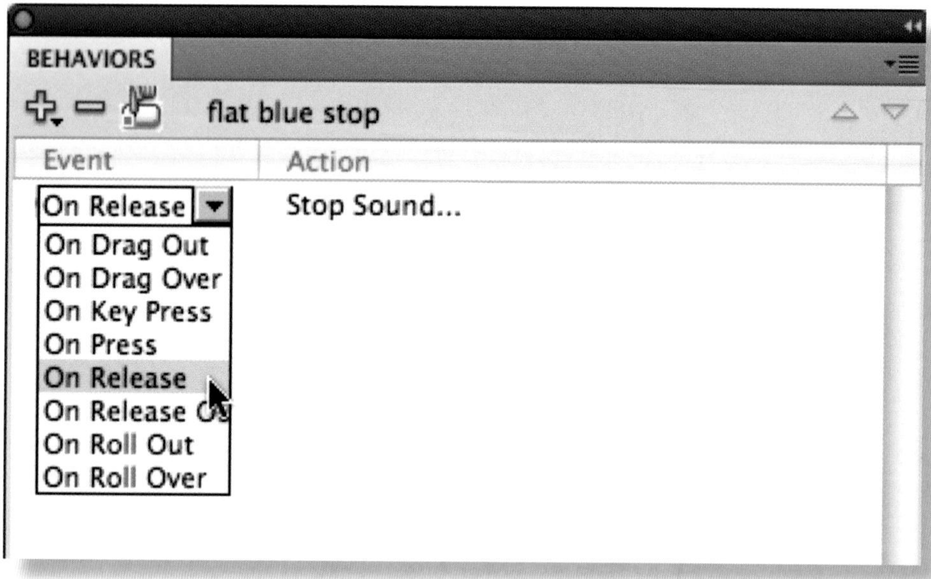

Choose the On Release event for the button.

6. Select the play button on the Stage. From the Behaviors drop down menu, choose Sound > Play Sound.
7. In the Play Sound window, enter **background1** for the instance name. Click OK.
8. Be sure the On Release event is selected in the Behaviors panel.

9. Close the Behaviors panel and test the movie.

10. Save your file. You did it!

Lesson 2: Attaching Sound from the Library

In the last lesson, you played with controlling a single sound synced (stream type) with an animation on the Timeline, and then again synced independently (event type) on the Timeline. In this next example, we take it a bit further—attaching a sound by creating an ActionScript using the attachSound method rather than a Behavior. And you'll attach not just one sound, but many sounds that are controlled through button actions. This method creates much more flexibility with what you can do with sound, especially when you are ready to venture into more advanced sound techniques beyond the scope of this book.

The example used for this lesson is a section of a Flash movie created by students at Landmark College in Vermont as part of a National Science Foundation grant. The sound clips contain voice narrations by Landmark College instructors, all of whom I credit for allowing me to use their voices in this lesson. Each of these sound clips that you will trigger from each of the buttons on the page was recorded and exported as MP3 files by a student, using the free Audacity audio editing program (*http://audacity.sourceforge.net/*).

Importing and Identifying the Sounds

1. Open the **chap9L2.fla** in the **chap09_lessons** folder.

2. Be sure the Classic workspace is selected.

3. First, let's import the sound files. Choose File > Import > Import to Library, and in the **chap09_lessons/audio_examples** folder, open **add.mp32**, **adhd.mp3**, **dyscalculia.mp3**, **dysgraphia.mp3**, and **dyslexia.mp3**.

4. Expand the Library panel, and play each of the sound files.

5. In the Library panel, double-click on the **add.mp3** file, and in its Sound Properties, expand the Advanced tab (if already expanded, the tab will be set to Basic). Under Linkage, select the Export for ActionScript option, and for the Identifier, replace the file name with **sound01**. See Figure 9–26. Choose OK.

6. Next, open the properties for the **adhd.mp3**. Under Linkage, select the Export for ActionScript option, and for the Identifier, replace the file name with **sound02**.

7. Open the properties for the **dyscalculia.mp3**. Under Linkage, select the Export for ActionScript option, and for the Identifier, replace the file name with **sound03**.

8. Open the properties for the **dysgraphia.mp3**. Under Linkage, select the Export for ActionScript option, and for the Identifier, replace the file name with **sound04**.

9. Open the properties for the **dyslexia.mp3**. Under Linkage, select the Export for ActionScript option, and for the Identifier, replace the file name with **sound05**.

10. Save your file.

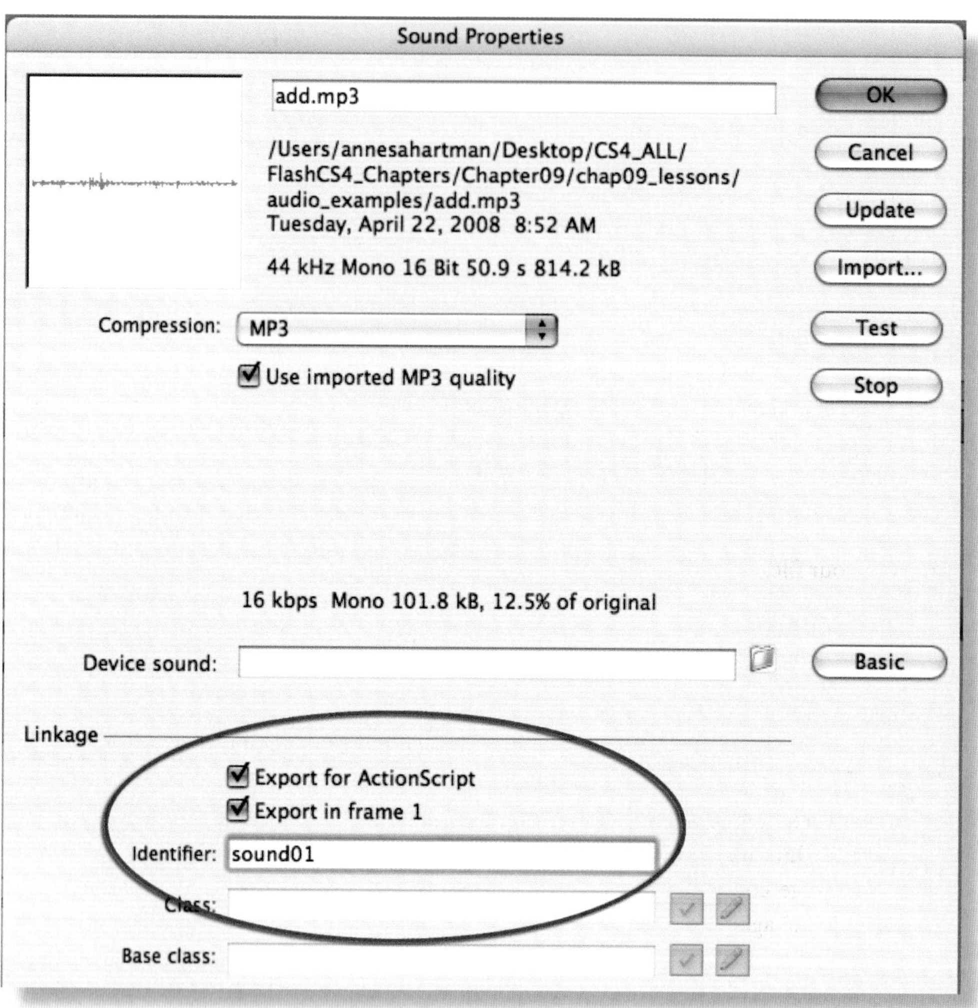

figure 9–26

Create an identifier for a selected sound.

Attach the Sounds in the Library to the Timeline

1. Create a new layer at the top of the layers list and name it **sound_actions**.
2. Click on the first frame and open the Actions panel.
3. Type in the following actions exactly as shown (see Figure 9–27):

```
stop();

firstSound = new Sound(this);

firstSound.attachSound("sound01")

secondSound = new Sound(this);

secondSound.attachSound("sound02")
```

thirdSound = new Sound(this);

thirdSound.attachSound("sound03")

fourthSound = new Sound(this);

fourthSound.attachSound("sound04")

fifthSound = new Sound(this);

fifthSound.attachSound("sound05")

4. Choose the Check Syntax option. If there are errors, carefully check the spelling of each part of the ActionScript (lowercase and uppercase) and that the unique identifiers for each sound are surrounded in quotes.

5. Save your file.

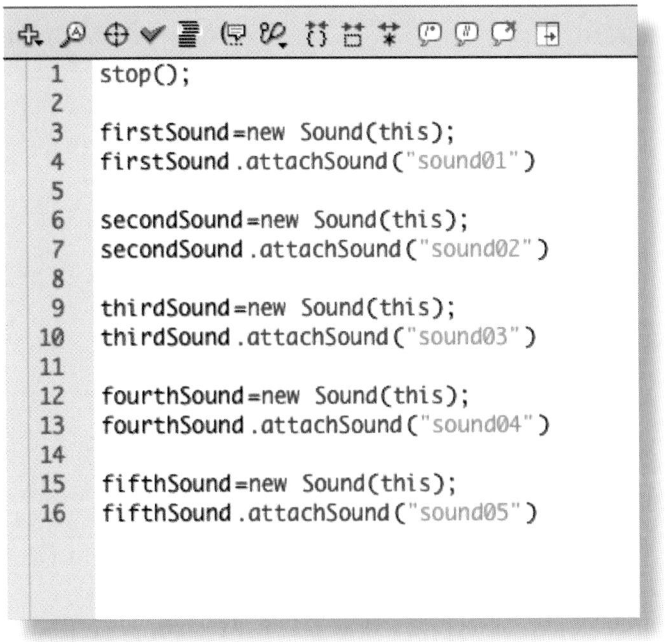

```
stop();

firstSound=new Sound(this);
firstSound.attachSound("sound01")

secondSound=new Sound(this);
secondSound.attachSound("sound02")

thirdSound=new Sound(this);
thirdSound.attachSound("sound03")

fourthSound=new Sound(this);
fourthSound.attachSound("sound04")

fifthSound=new Sound(this);
fifthSound.attachSound("sound05")
```

figure 9–27

Enter the script that will attach the sound to the movie.

Call the Sounds from the Buttons

1. Let's call the sound that will play when someone clicks the audio button under the Dyslexia header. First, however, remind yourself what the identifier and instance names are for that audio. To do this, open the Library panel and drag the left side of the panel open (see Figure 9–28). Under the Linkage column for the **dyslexia.mp3**, note the identifier name—**sound05**. Refer to Figure 9–28 again.

> **Note: At this time, you might also jot down the identifier names for the other audio files as well, since you will need to have them for reference in the next step—dysgraphia.mp3, sound04; dyscalculia.mp3, sound03; adhd.mp3, sound02; and add.mp3, sound01.**

2. Collapse the Library panel.

3. Select the first frame of the **sound_actions** layer. Jot down the instance name of each of the sound files that correspond to its unique identifier:

dyslexia.mp3, sound05 = fifthSound;

dysgraphia.mp3, sound04 = fourthSound;

dyscalculia.mp3; sound03 = thirdSound;

adhd.mp3, sound02 = secondSound;

add.mp3, sound01= firstSound

figure 9–28

Identify the identifiers for each sound in the Library panel.

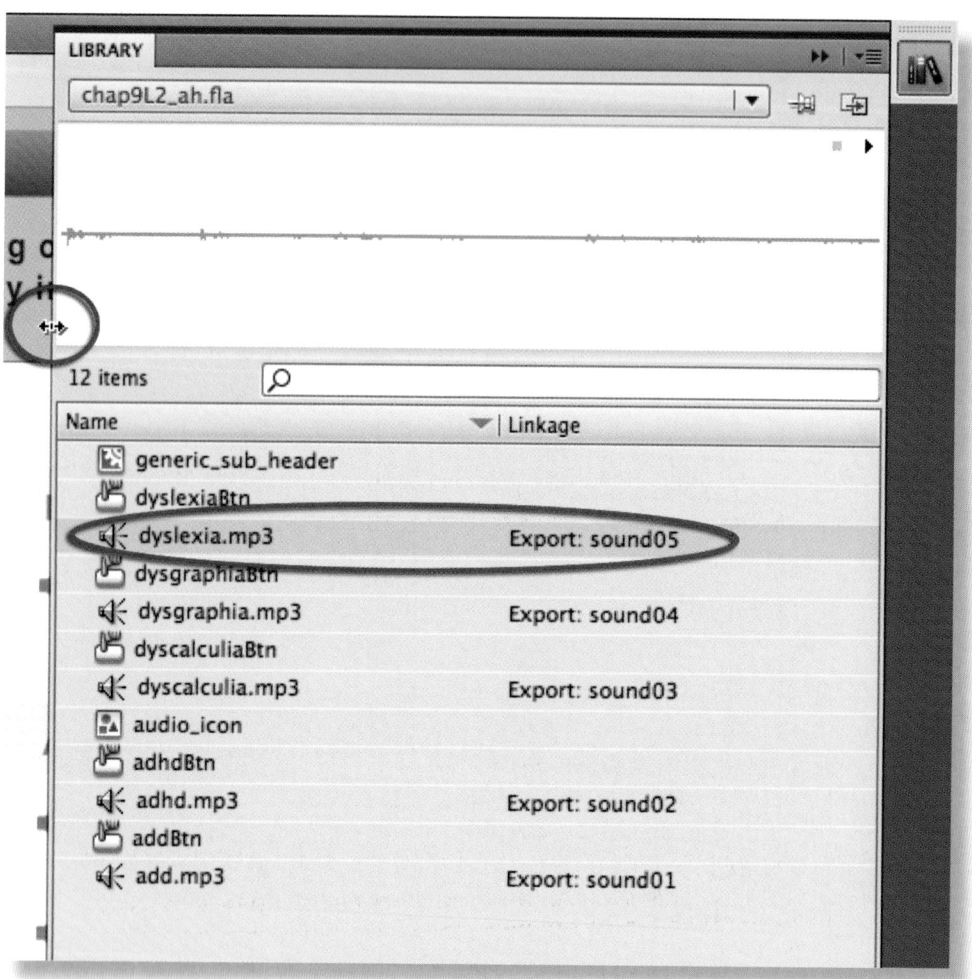

Note: As you can see, the names and places where numerous sounds and or other elements that are being called into a movie can get very confusing. This is where file organization is crucial! But remember, when you go to create identifier and instance names for sounds in your own projects, you can name them whatever is most intuitive for you. Just be aware of the standard syntax (lowercase, no spaces, no funky punctuation) when you name the files.

4. Select the button under the Dyslexia header. See Figure 9–29.
5. Choose Window > Actions and enter in the following action:

```
on (press) {
    stopAllSounds();
    fifthSound.start();
}
```

Types of Learning Differences

Dyslexia

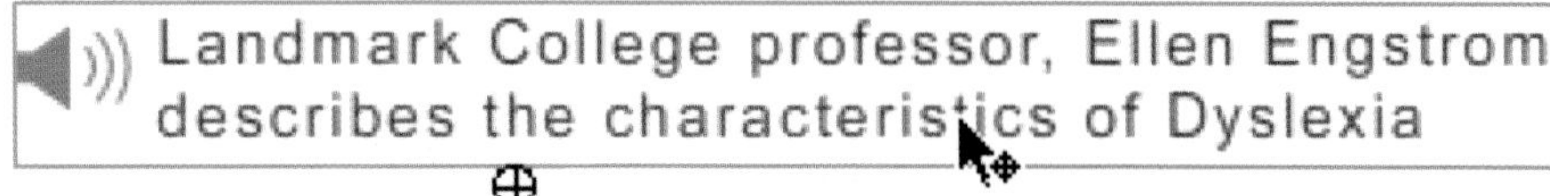

figure 9–29

Select a button.

6. Select the Dyscalculia button and enter (or copy and paste) the same action as above, but replacing the start action with its instance name that we figured out in step 3 above—**thirdSound** [i.e., thirdSound.start();]
7. Ditto on step 5 for the other buttons, but replacing the instance name for each corresponding sound.
8. Play back the movie and test each of the buttons.
9. Save your file.

Explore the Publish Settings Options

The sound files you imported into the Learning Differences Flash movie were saved as MP3, 44 kHz, 16-bit Mono. When published with these audio settings, the final SWF file is about 3.1 MB—kind of big! Let's see if they can be compressed further without any loss of quality in the final output of the movie.

1. In the **chap9L2.fla** file you've been working on, open the Library panel. Double-click on the **dyslexia.mp3** sound file to open its Sound Properties. Test the sound and note its sound quality.
2. Under Compression, choose the Speech option, and for Sample rate, choose 11 kHz. See Figure 9–30. Test the sound again. Is the sound quality still adequate? Close the Sound Properties.
3. Open the Sound Properties for each of the other sound files in the Library and change the settings to Compression: Speech and Sample rate: 11 kHz. Test each sound, and then click OK.
4. Choose Control > Test Movie to publish the file.

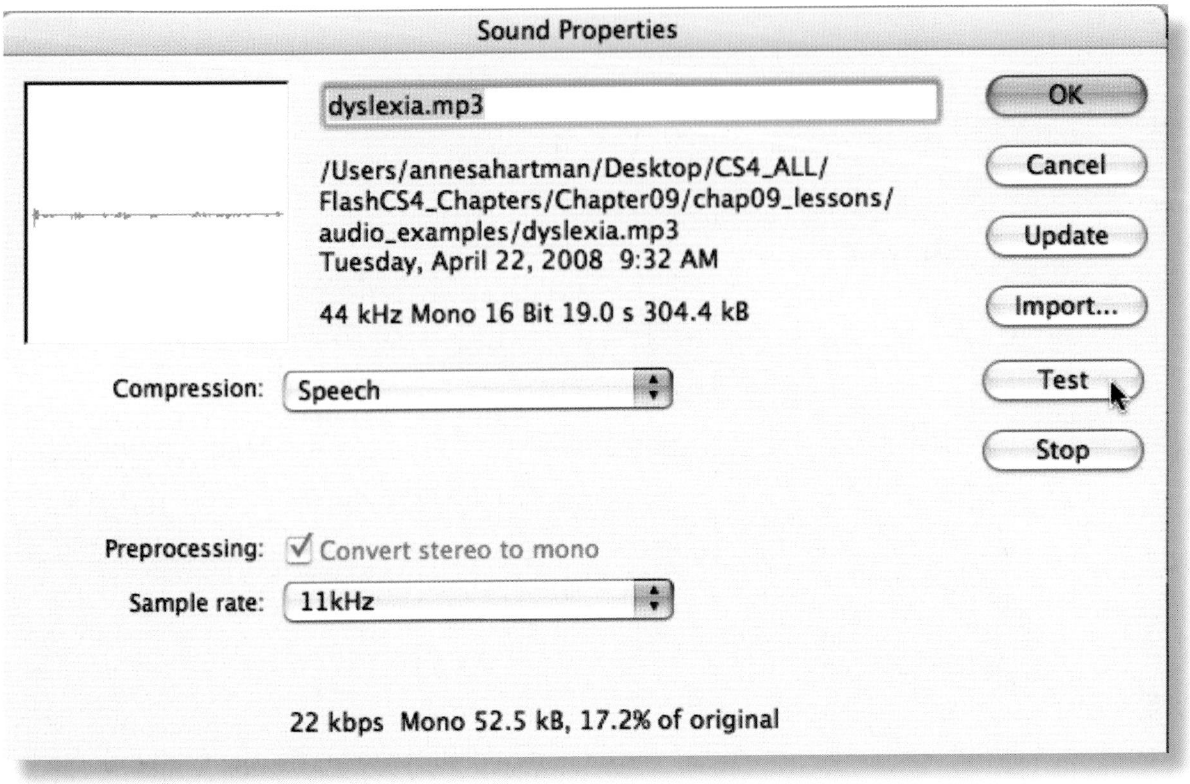

figure 9–30

Choose a compression option for the selected sound.

5. Minimize Flash and find the SWF you just published in the same folder as the FLA file. Ctrl-click (Mac) or right-click (Windows) over the SWF file icon, and choose Get Info or Properties from the drop down list. Note the size of the file—568 KB—is much smaller than the original 3.1 MB size, and the sound quality is still sufficient. See Figure 9–31.

figure 9–31

Note the compressed size of the SWF file that contains audio content.

SUMMARY

Sound reproduction basics, and importing and controlling sound within Flash, is now at your fingertips, and how you might use it to enhance your Flash creations is up to your imagination. Just don't go too overboard—remember sound files are big and can contribute to heavy downloads. Always optimize and edit your sound before importing in Flash, and then use the sound settings available within Flash to ensure the best quality and smallest file size. Consider, as well, making sounds that are accessible to your users—provide a mute option and/or offer text transcripts of sound lyrics and/or vocal presentations.

in review

1. What are the factors that determine the sound quality when reproducing sound digitally?
2. Name at least three sound file formats that Flash supports.
3. What's useful about the MP3 format for Web playback?
4. What might be a good sample rate for speech?
5. If you want to record sound or edit the length of your sound file, what program(s) might you use?
6. What's the difference between event and stream sound synchronization?
7. Where do you go to set a unique identifier for a sound file?
8. What does the stopAllSounds action do?
9. What does the attachSound action do?
10. What options will make sound more accessible?

exploring on your own

- Do a search online for "royalty-free sounds," "free audio," or variations thereof. Download a couple of audio files that you have found and practice importing and playing them back in Flash.
- Check out the site for the Freesound Project at: *http://www.freesound.org/*. What is the Freesound Project? What is Creative Commons and why is it important for artists?

ADVENTURES IN DESIGN

Game Play

One of the most useful ways I have learned more about how to create some of the cool Flash goodies you see on the Web, in addition to better understanding the interconnectedness of objects, timelines, and ActionScripts within the program, is to do a digital dig on someone else's completed Flash movie. The Internet is abundant with FLA files that Flash aficionados have posted for others to learn from and create their own adaptations. One favorite resource of mine is Kirupa.com (*http://www.kirupa.com*), but there are many more. The key to being able to properly decipher the inner-workings of a Flash file is knowing where to look; this comes from having a solid introduction to Flash (which you should have after completing this book) and practice with the process. In this Adventures in Design, let's dig into a Flash file that was created by one of my students.

STUDENT PROJECT EXAMPLE

Not but a week after his first introduction to ActionScripting, one of my Flash students, Edvin Eshagh, challenged himself to come up with his own simple Flash game. What he came up with is an inspiration to all first learning Flash; it's an excellent example of what can be done with even the most basic understanding of Flash objects and ActionScripting. Let's decipher Edvin's FLA file step by step. Then, you might try to make your own version of his little game.

YOUR TURN

In Flash open the **game_play/aid_game_play_final.fla** file in the **aid_examples** folder on the back of the book CD. Test the movie and try out the game—the goal is to shoot (click) the yellow circle on the moving target. When the circle is clicked (not as easy as it looks!), the target vanishes into smoke. Give it a try and then follow the steps below for a guided tour into how the game was made.

Note: This game is created using ActionScript 2.0. When you learn more about ActionScript 3.0 in your future Flash studies, consider coming back to this Adventures in Design and trying to recreate this same game using ActionScript 3.0 syntax only.

Exploring the Two States of the Game

1. If not already, open the **game_play/aid_game_play_final.fla** file in the **aid_examples** folder.
2. Set the workspace to Classic.
3. Open the Timeline panel so you can view all the layers and frames. See Figure D–1.
4. Frame 1 to frame 30 contains the elements and action of the game before the target is hit—the moving target and the crosshair mouse object. This is the first state of the game.

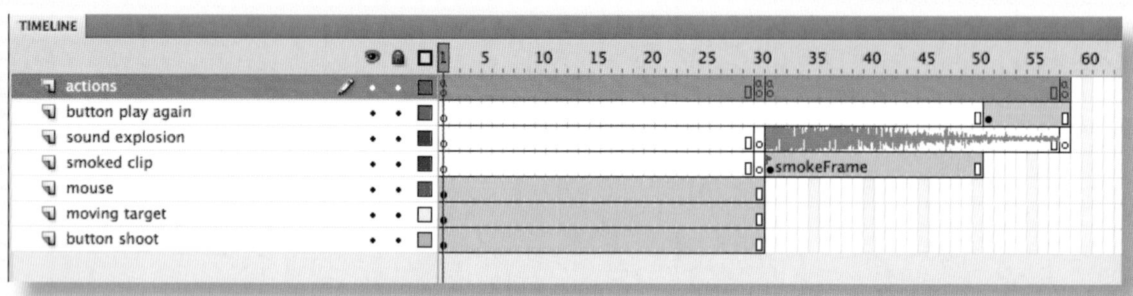

figure D–1 Get a good view of the file—its layers, objects, and frames.

5. Click on the action (the little "a") on frame 30, and view the action in the Actions panel:

   ```
   gotoAndPlay(1);
   ```

   Once the Timeline hits this frame, the first state of the game is repeated; it goes back and plays frame 1 again until the target is hit.

6. Move the playback head to frame 31 (note one of the layers is labeled "smokeFrame"). From frame 31 to frame 58 are the elements and actions that occur when the target is finally hit—the object animates into a smoke effect, an explosion sound occurs (visible waveform on the **sound explosion** layer), and the Play Again button appears at the end. This is the second state of the game.

Setting up the Mouse Drag Event

1. Let's now dig a bit deeper into the file—first, at how to change the mouse cursor to the "crosshair" target. See Figure D–2.

figure D–2 The crosshair object replaces the default cursor object that follows a user's mouse navigation.

2. Open the Libraries panel and notice the **sCrossHair** symbol that was created.

3. Now click on the instance of the **sCrossHair** object on the Stage and note the instance name in the Properties panel—**crossHair**.

4. Select the first frame of the **actions** layer (it has a little "a" on it). Now open the Actions panel and check out the ActionScript:

   ```
   Mouse.hide();
   startDrag(crossHair, true);
   ```

   Basically this code says: hide the current cursor icon and when a user starts to drag the mouse replace the icon with the **crossHair** instance.

5. Select the **mouse** layer and note that the mouse/crosshair object is visible in the first part of the game—disappearing at frame 31.

6. Click on frame 31 of the **actions** layer (the little "a") and view the actions in the Actions panel:

   ```
   startDrag(crossHair, false);
   Mouse.show();
   ```

   This action sets the crosshair icon to false—turns it off for the second state of the game—and resets the mouse to its default icon.

Examining the Button Movie Clips

1. The buttons in this game are what creates the interactivity of this game—click on the blue background on the Stage (the **button shoot** layer should be highlighted and in the Properties panel the Button type is indicated with the instance name **bShoot**).

2. Double-click on the **bShoot** button (anywhere on the blue area of the Stage) to enter editing mode. The Up position of this button is actually invisible (empty frames), the Down position contains a sound effect that is executed each time a user clicks (shoots), and its Hit area covers the complete Stage making the whole area in essence "hit-able".

3. Exit out of the **bShoot** editing mode.

4. Now, let's look at the code on the yellow circle button—this is the button that when finally targeted creates the smoke effect. Double-click on the moving

ADVENTURES IN DESIGN

target with the yellow circle (**sMovingTarget**) to enter its editing mode. Note the circular animation of the target within the movie clip.

5. Now, double-click on the moving target again—you are now in the **sTarget** symbol. Note the path in the upper left of the document window—**Scene1 > sMovingTarget > sTarget**.
6. Now, click (once only!) on the yellow circle to select it.
7. Open the Actions panel and note the action that is on the yellow circle button:

```
on(press) {
_root.gotoAndPlay("smokeFrame");
}
```

The code translates that on the press of the yellow circle button (when the target is hit); go back to Scene 1 (the root timeline) and start playing at the frame labeled **"smokeFrame"**.

8. Now, double-click on the yellow circle button. You should be inside the button symbol called **heart**. See Figure D–3.
9. In the Timeline for the **heart** symbol note the sound clip located on the Down frame; this is the audio that plays when the target is hit.
10. Exit completely out of the editing modes; go back to Scene 1.
11. One more button to examine—go to frame 58 (the last frame) of the game. Note on this last frame, there is a **stop** action on the **actions** layer; this is so this game won't keep looping over an over until the user wants it too—the Play Again button is clicked.
12. Select the Play Again button and view its actions in the Actions panel.

```
on (release) {
gotoAndPlay(1);
}
```

Basically on release of the button, the user goes back to frame 1 of the game (the first state) to start over.

Creating the Smoke/Explode Effect

1. Last thing—how to make the effect of the target fading up in smoke when it's hit. It's easy! On Scene 1, click on the frame labeled **smokeFrame** to select it.

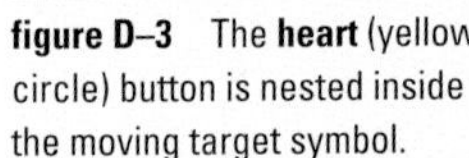

figure D–3 The **heart** (yellow circle) button is nested inside the moving target symbol.

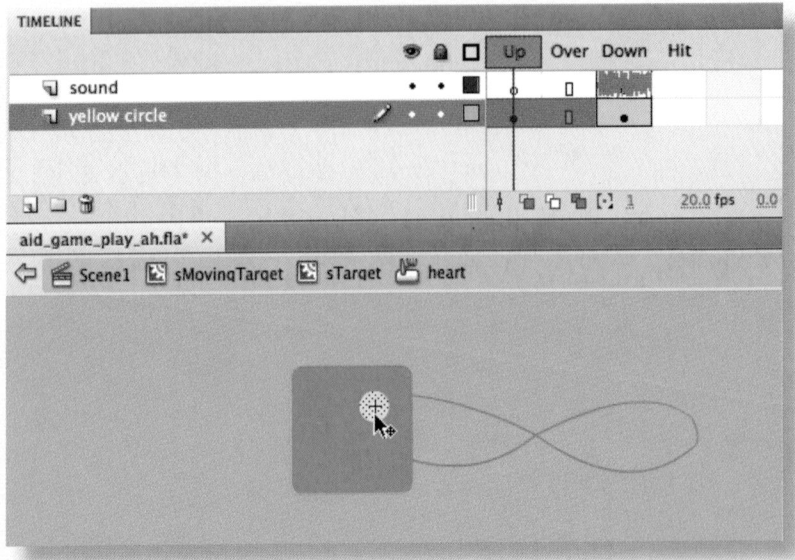

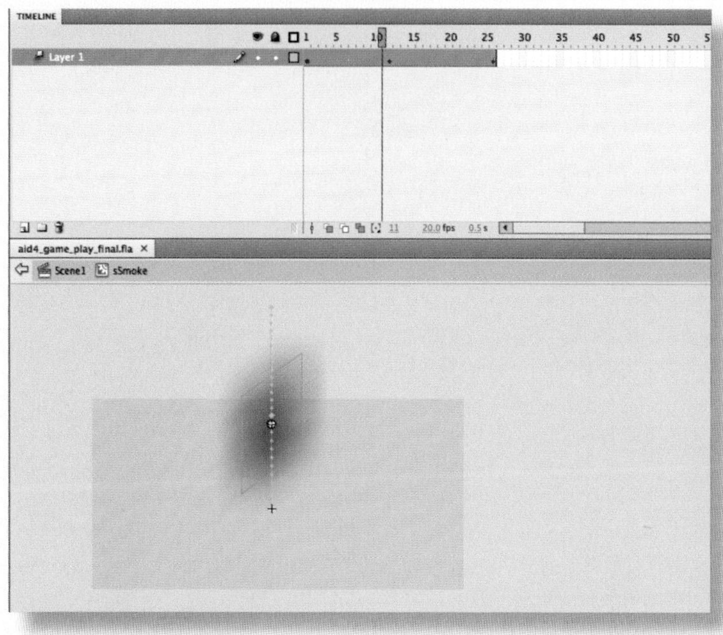

figure D–4 The smoke animation inside a movie clip.

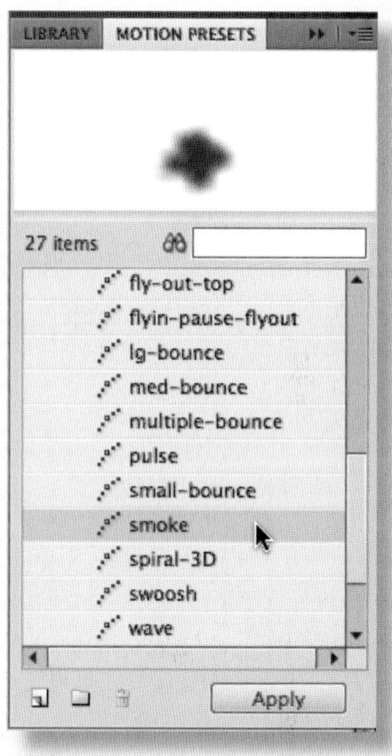

figure D–5 The Motion Preset panel—lots of fun pre-made animations to play with!

2. Double-click on the target object on the Stage—this is a duplicate of the **sMovingTarget** symbol, but with the animation removed. It is named **sSmoke**. Play back the animation. See Figure D–4.

3. This animation was created using a Motion Preset—a new goodie to play with. The symbol was created, selected, then under Window > Motion Presets > Default Presets the **smoke** preset was chosen. See Figure D–5.

> **Note: There are many cool presets—fly-in, fly-out, bounce, etc. Play with these preset options on your own. Create a symbol, and select it. Then, open the Motion Preset panel and select and apply any of the default presets. Play back the movie.**

4. Your Flash interactive "dig" is complete. Would you be able to create this same type of game on your own? Even if you don't understand how all the parts fit together, making some connections can only improve your continued understanding of this complex program. Try deciphering other Flash files—they are abundant online (*http://www.flashkit.com, http://www.kirupa.com, http://www.actionscript.org*—to name a few).

Explorer pages

JAMES COUTURE

"I'm constantly reminding myself that video doesn't need to be 'in a box.' Increasingly we're seeing that video can be heavily integrated into the design of a web page or a program."

About James Couture

James is an interactive designer for a video production company that films predominantly surgical videos. He creates interactive programs that mix surgical and testimonial clips with marketing messages or graphic data to create an informative package for the viewer. His job requires that he be able to take a large set of assets and create an environment where the viewer can explore them in the easiest, most intuitive way possible.

James has worked with Flash for eight years, and increasingly enjoys each new version. No other program gives him the extreme flexibility to take the concepts he envisions and rapidly build a unique interface customized for the task at hand. He can share pieces and elements across programs, or fashion something entirely new quickly and efficiently. For the first couple of years, James was building games with Flash 5 as a hobby. Video in Flash didn't exist yet, and he spent more time with the programming than the design tools. However, he was always excited to flip back and forth between the programming and design. Not only did it break up his work, but when he got stuck with a coding issue, he could usually find a design solution, and vice versa.

"Since bandwidth is steadily increasing, video will increase in quality and continue to be a valuable addition to any site," says James, "Luckily, Flash is there to make sure it's easy and looks great when it's done."

James can be contacted at: james.couture@capturedlightstudio.com.

About the Work of James Couture

In his own words, James shares with us his work process… "Flash continues to make everything video-related easier and more flexible. Originally, the net streams, buffering, error-correction were cumbersome. The addition of the FLVPlayback component changed a lot of that, and it keeps improving with every version. I normally shy away from packaged components since I always customize my programs for the client as much as possible. However, now that the control bar skin has moved away from a small number of color options to the full color wheel and its appearance is easy to alter, I can give the client a unique product and also save time."

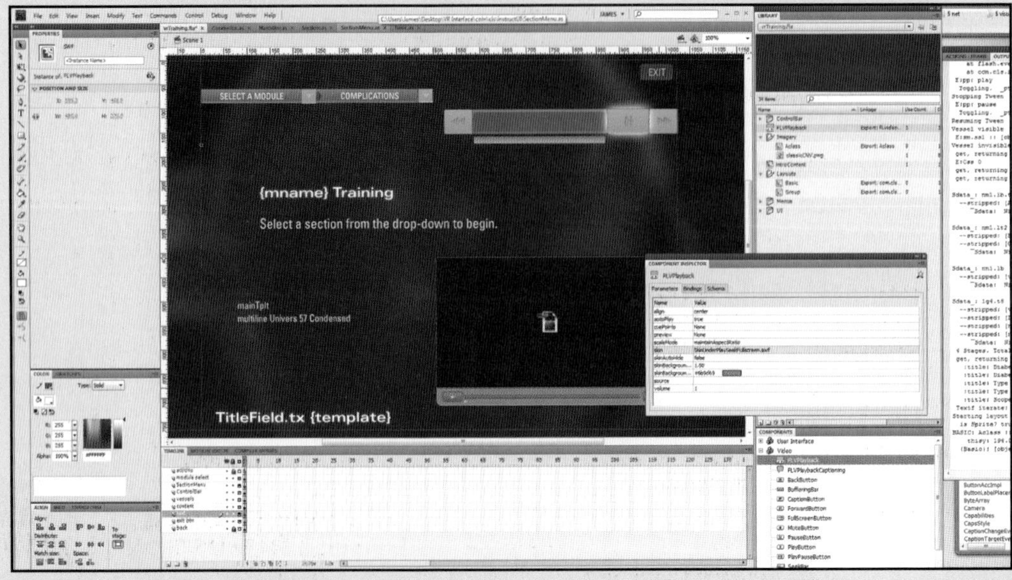

Screen shot of Flash CS4's video features. Courtesy of James Couture.

"Most other forms of video on the web require it to be in a box, with a certain control bar, as a single element on the page. With Flash's tools, I can treat a video stream almost exactly like I treat any graphic. I can blur it, mask it, scroll it, blend it—nearly anything you can think of can probably be done. Zip it onto the screen with a motion blur, for example, or display semi-transparent video streams for a selection menu."

"Cue points are a great feature for instructive programming. As the video progresses, my program can display accompanying information, links, or other selling points right alongside the video. It makes for an easy presentation tool since the cue points can be added into the video or with minimal ActionScript."

"Small videos as accent elements in a page are often very compelling. It keeps the user's experience much more coherent: he or she is more likely to click on the video if it doesn't involve a trip to another page, which will be more time-consuming. The viewer can investigate multiple topics or supporting information seamlessly. Videos that are small can benefit from not needing any significant time to load up; the Flash player is very efficient at anticipating when it can start playing."

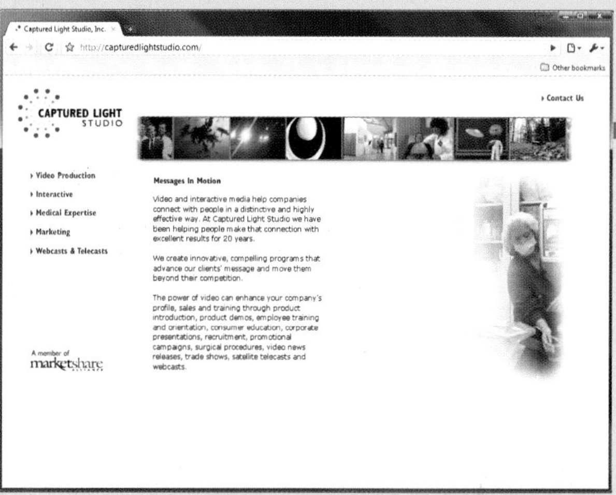

Example of video used as a graphic element on a Web page. Courtesy of James Couture and Captured Light Studio.

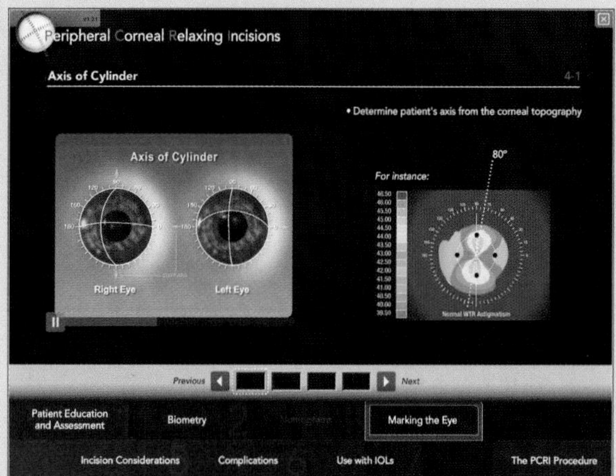

Example use of video in an instructional presentation. Courtesy of James Couture and Captured Light Studio.

Video enhancements within a Web page can engage a viewer. Courtesy of James Couture and Captured Light Studio.

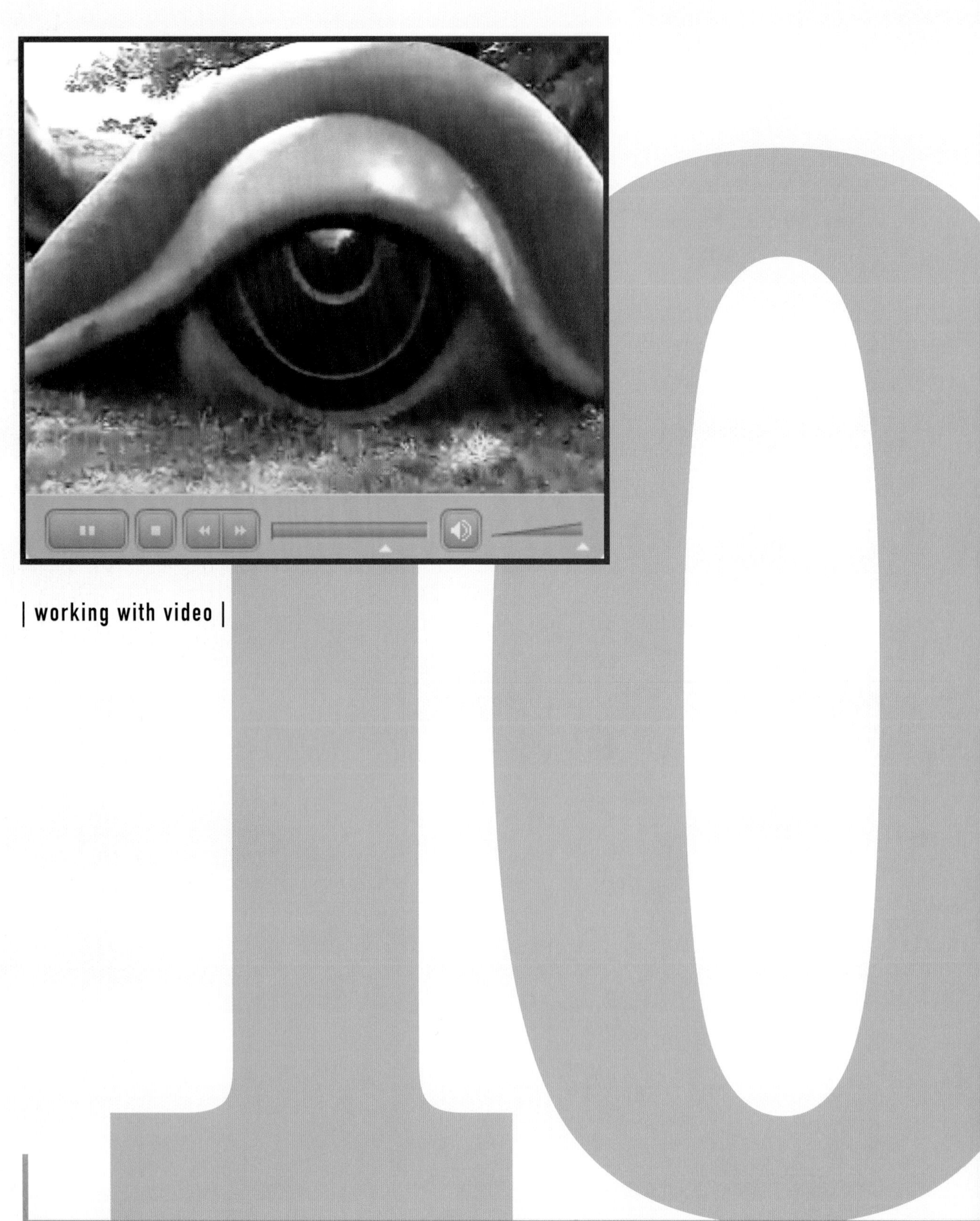

10

| working with video |

charting your course

Video has become a ubiquitous feature on the Web. YouTube (*http://www.youtube.com/*), for example, is a revolutionary online platform where even the most novice videographer can post and share video clips and millions can search and view them. As bandwidth expands and more and more people gain access to higher Internet connection speeds, the amount of video available online is bound to increase—in online learning materials, in real-time networking, for marketing, and for entertainment. The developers of Flash are keen on this evolution and have improved the integration and encoding capabilities of video with each new version of the program.

goals

In this chapter you will:

- **Get an overview of video characteristics**
- **Explore Flash's video features**
- **Import and embed video**
- **Load an external video clip into a SWF file**

OVERVIEW OF VIDEO CHARACTERISTICS

We are already quite familiar with the basic components of what make up video from previous chapters—bitmaps (Chapter 2) and audio (Chapter 9). Digital video is simply a series of bitmap images that when played back create the illusion of movement and, like a single bitmap image, must depend on resolution, bit depth, and dimensions to determine its quality and overall file size. Additionally, the sound quality of a video depends on the sound's sample rate and bit depth. There are a few other characteristics specific to video; we will cover frame rate, screen size, bit rate, and encoding—aspects that all interrelate in determining a video's quality and overall file size.

Frame Rate

Like animation, the frame rate of a video is measured in frames per second (fps). The higher the frame rate, the smoother and better the quality of the video appears, and the more data it contains. A standard TV video runs at about 30 fps. For a film, the frame rate is 24 fps. For Web videos, standard frame rates are 12–15 fps—this is the average amount of frame playback when a video is being downloaded from the Web. Of course, this rate varies by a user's connection speed. Someone with a dial-up connection will most likely get video playing back anywhere from 5 to 15 fps, for DSL or cable users, 15 fps, and for Broadband users, up to 30 fps is possible.

Video Screen Size

The frame rate of a video is linked to its dimensional size. Most online video players display video via the standard video 4:3 aspect ratio and range in size from small 320 × 240 pixels to larger 640 × 480 pixels. Becoming more common, however, are players that will display video in the 16:9 wide-screen ratio. See Figure 10–1. A best practice is to provide video in various sizes for users with various Internet connections and that matches the viewing aspect ratio of the player. The most current version of the Flash player supports both the standard and wide-screen modes. In the Flash Help files, there is a list of standard frame sizes that can be used as a guideline. You can experiment to find the best setting for your project.

Frame sizes for 4:3 aspect ratio video:

- Modem (56k): 160 × 120
- DSL: 320 × 240
- Cable: 512 × 384
- Cable/corporate LAN: 640 × 480

Frame sizes for 16:9 aspect ratio video:

- Modem (56k): 192 × 108
- DSL: 384 × 216
- Cable: 448 × 252
- Cable/corporate LAN: 704 × 396

figure | 10–1 |

The most current version of the Flash player supports both the standard and wide-screen video modes.

Bit Rate

"In telecommunications, bit rate or data transfer rate is the average number of bits, characters, or blocks per unit time passing between equipment in a data transmission system. This is typically measured in multiples of the units bit per second or byte per second," from *http://www.wikipedia.com*. The bit rate of a video is the average amount that the video streams or downloads over time (audio downloads are based on bit rates as well). It is measured in kilobits per second (kbps)—a unit of data transfer rate equal to 1000 bits per second. Bit rates vary with the screen size of the video. See Figure 10–2 for a chart of video screen sizes, bit rates, and the average download amount per minute.

Output size	Bitrate	File size download per minute
320 x 240 pixels	400kbps	3MB/minute
480 x 360 pixels	700kbps	4MB/minute
720 x 540 pixels	1000kbps	7.5MB/minute

figure | 10–2 |

Bitrates and file sizes vary with the screen size of the video.

Encoding/Compression

"In video editing and production video encoding is the process of preparing the video for output, where the digital video is encoded to meet proper formats and specifications for recording and playback through the use of video encoder software. Also called video conversion," from *http://webopedia.com*. Video encoding can be performed with a video editing program (Apple iMovie or Windows Movie Maker, for example) and also with the Adobe Media Encoder (AME), which comes with the Flash program (more on the AME, later in this chapter). Depending on the use, a video can be encoded using any number of video codecs—methods by which digital video (data) is compressed and decompressed—and many different formats. For example, and also more on this later, the compression scheme or codec of video used by Flash's video (FLV) formats is either On2 or Sorenson Spark, and for Flash's F4V format, it's H.264. These formats and their codecs produce more highly compressed (optimized) video for online delivery than video in a standard DVD or HD format.

> **Note:** There are many different video formats and compression schemes. There is no need for you to know them all, but you should be aware they exist and have different characteristics, depending on where they are to be output. We will work with video in the QuickTime and FLV formats.

VIDEO IN FLASH

Let's go over the various aspects of working with video in Flash, including video preparation, video import and playback methods, and the AME. Then, you'll get some hands-on practice in the lessons.

> **Note:** For fun, view some excellent examples of Flash video in the form of movie trailers at: *http://www.dreamworksanimation.com/*. Go to the Movies link and choose Trailers.

Preparing Video for Flash

Flash is not a video creation or editing program. It's great at compressing video for online delivery, but the production of the video is done elsewhere—either by a professional videographer or perhaps by yourself using a mini DV recorder and off-the-shelf video software programs such as Apple iMovie, Windows Movie Maker, or more sophisticated ones—Adobe Premiere or Apple Final Cut Pro. Flash prefers imported video in its proprietary FLV or F4V formats. The FLV with the On2 video encoder is supported by Flash Player 8 or above. The F4V with the H.264 video encoder is supported by Flash 9.0.r115 Player or higher.

Luckily, the Flash program includes the AME—a stand-alone application that can convert, encode, video as stated in the Flash Help files "into a variety of distribution formats for different applications and audiences," such as common formats like QuickTime (.mov) or Windows (.avi or .wmp) into the FLV or F4V formats. See Figure 10–3. It also has custom export settings for filters and formats for both video and audio. See Figure 10–4. You will try out the AME in the first lesson of this chapter.

> **Note: When installed with Flash CS4, the AME provides export formats for FLV and F4V video only. When installed with other Adobe products (i.e., Adobe Premiere or After Effects), additional export formats are made available for use within those specific applications.**

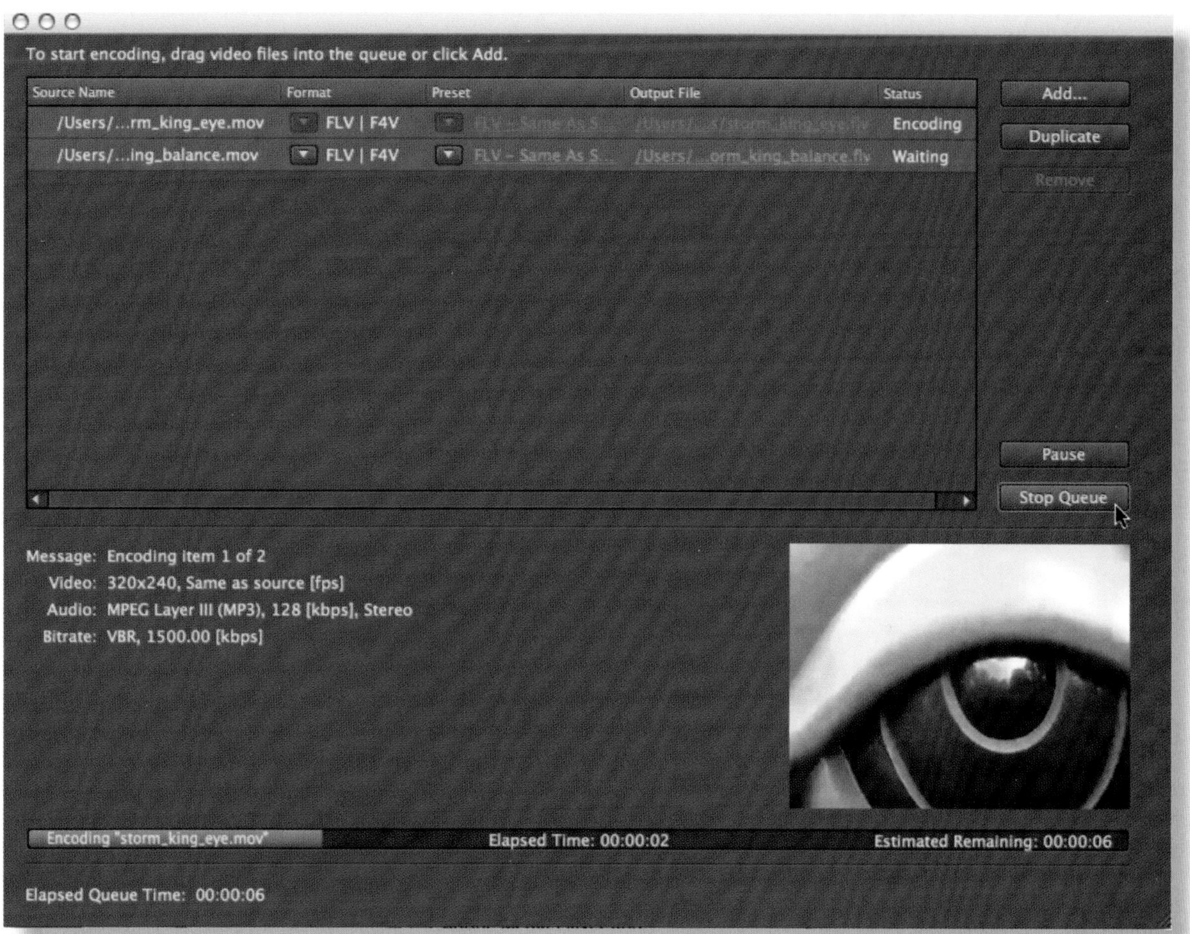

figure | 10–3 |

The Adobe Media Encoder (AME) in action.

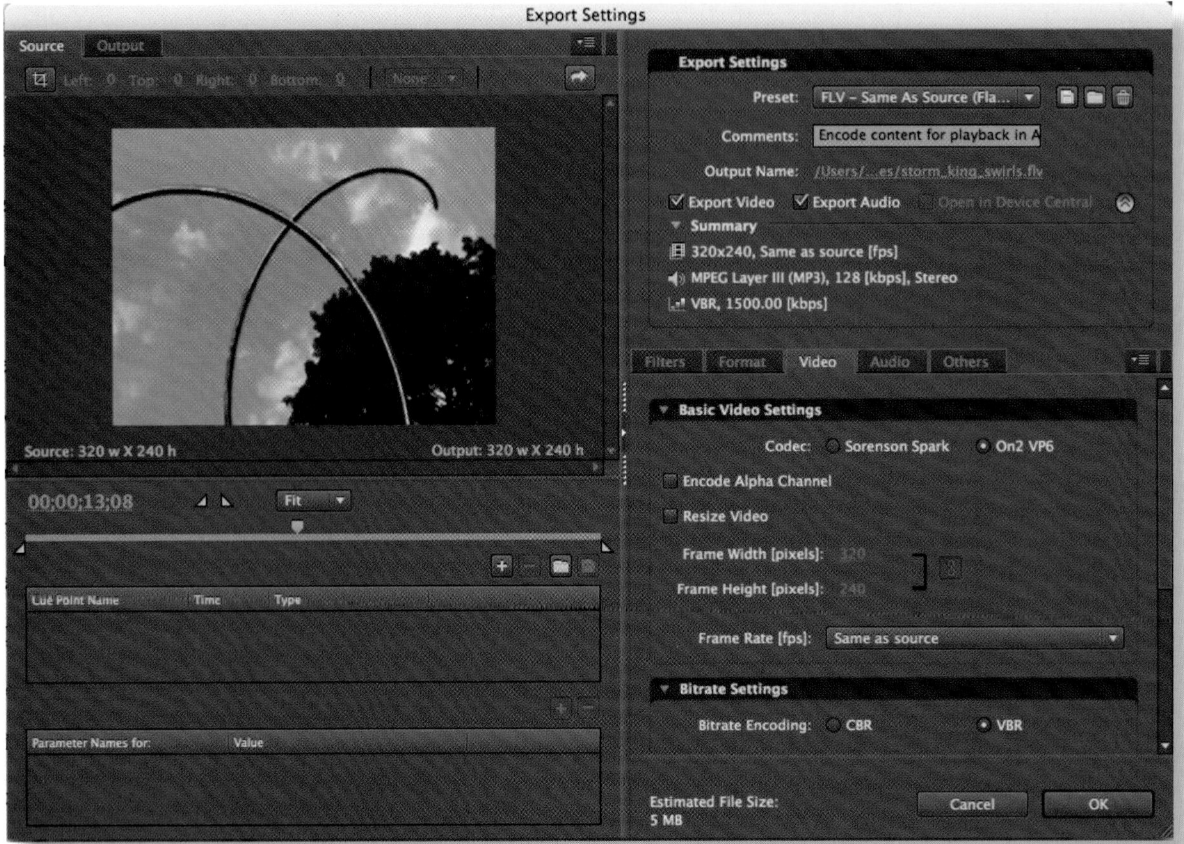

figure |10–4|

The custom Export Settings area of the Adobe Media Encoder.

Video Import and Playback

Flash provides several methods by which you can import video into Flash, incorporate the video into your Flash document, and play it back for users. Like audio, you can either embed a video clip directly into your Flash movie or have it load into the SWF file at run time through a Web server, or the Adobe Flash Media Server or Flash Video Streaming Service (FVSS). Flash takes you step-by-step through the import process using its Import Video wizard (explored in Lessons 1 and 2).

Video Embedded in a Flash Document

Embedded video, like embedded audio, is imported directly into a Flash document's timeline. The individual frames of the video are visually represented on the timeline. The video is published as part of the final SWF file, which can significantly increase the movie's size. Embedding video is a good option for short video clips (10 seconds or less in length) with no audio.

Larger video clips might experience playback problems with the synchronization of any audio within the video.

Video Progressively Downloaded from a Web Server

Unlike embedded video, video progressively downloaded from a Web server keeps the overall SWF file size smaller until the video is called into the SWF. It is easier to update since the video is external to the SWF file, and during delivery on the user end, it begins playing as soon as the first segment is downloaded and cached to the local computer's hard drive (progressive downloading).

> **Note:** Loading a video from an external source into a SWF uses a similar method of delivery as you learned in the last chapter with audio—when you called the audio into the SWF file using the attachSound ActionScript.

Video Streamed with Flash Media Server or FVSS

Flash video deployed by a Flash Media Server or FVSS uses a true streaming solution that provides the most optimized delivery of the video to the client downloading the video—making a better viewing experience, no matter what the connection speed is. A Flash Media Server or FVSS solution is expensive, but if lots of Flash video are to be delivered to users with varied Internet connections, or many users at one time, it's the most efficient way to go. For more about Flash Media Server, visit: *http://www.adobe.com/go/flash_media_server*, and for FVSS, visit: *http://www.adobe.com/go/fvss*.

For your initial learning and the practicality of it all, you will learn how to integrate video that is stored locally on your computer, and prepare it as if you were going to deliver it through a Web hosting service.

Lesson 1: Embedding a Video

Let's embed a short video into a Flash file, convert it to a movie clip, and add some functionality and an accessible Alt tag.

Importing the Video

1. Open Flash and create a new Flash file (ActionScript 2.0).
2. Choose File > Save and save your file as **my_video.fla** in your lessons folder.
3. Be sure the Classic workspace is selected.
4. Choose Import > Import Video (see Figure 10–5) to open the Import Video wizard.
5. Choose the **Embed FLV in SWF and play in timeline** option. See Figure 10–6. Note the warning at the bottom of the dialog box.

figure 10–5

Import Video from the File menu.

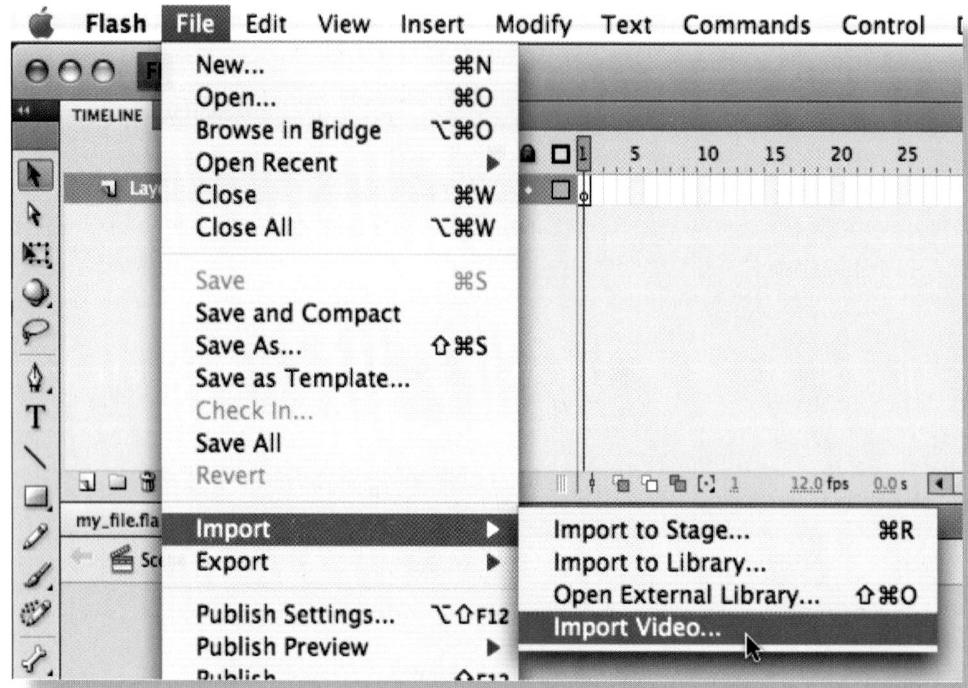

figure 10–6

The Import Video wizard.

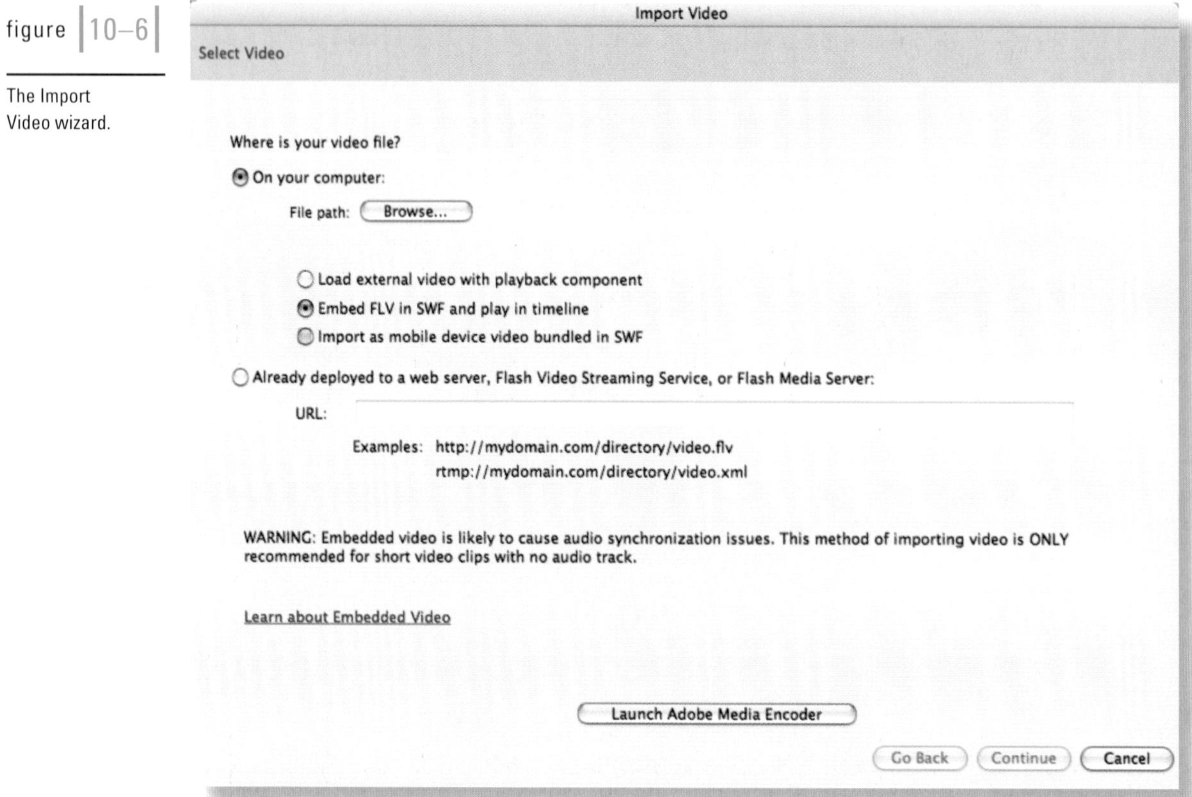

6. Next, choose Browse and open the **storm_king_swirls.mov** in the **chap10_lessons/video_examples** folder. A warning comes up: "The video format you have selected is not supported for embedded video. Please select an FLV file." See Figure 10–7. What's up? Let me explain: I shot this video clip of a moving sculpture at the Storm King Art Center, in Mountainville, NY, with my Sony DV recorder. I then imported and compressed the video clip in iMovie, and converted it to the QuickTime (.mov) format. This video can be viewed via Apple's QuickTime player, but to be used by Flash, it must first be converted into the FLV format via Adobe's stand-alone program, the AME. Let's do this next.

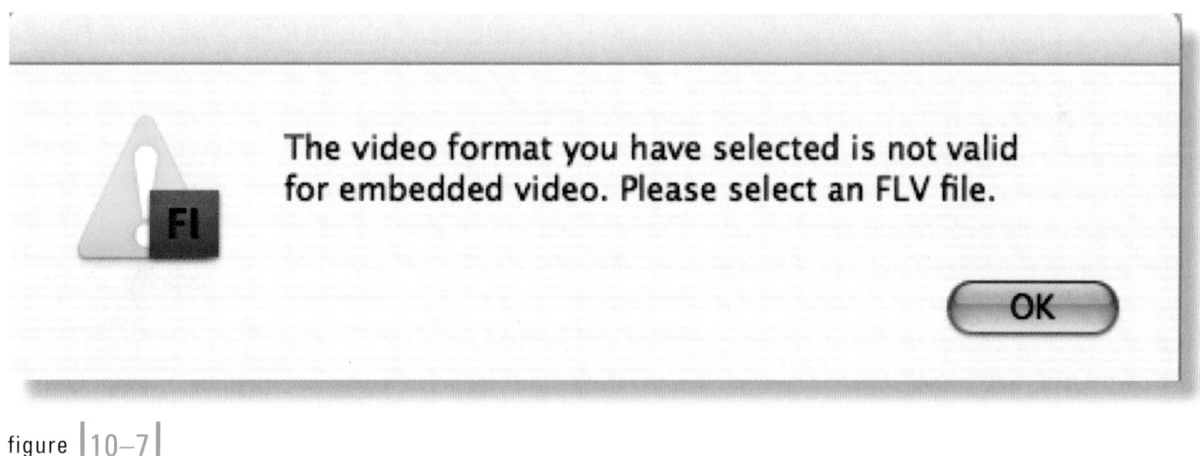

figure | 10–7 |

A warning for embedded video. Use the AME to convert the video into the format desired.

7. Click OK to close the warning message. In the Import Video wizard, choose the **Launch Adobe Media Encoder** button at the bottom of the window. See Figure 10–8. A reminder comes up that after you have converted the file into the proper format, you'll need to click the Browse button again to import the newly encoded file (see Figure 10–9). Then, the AME launches.

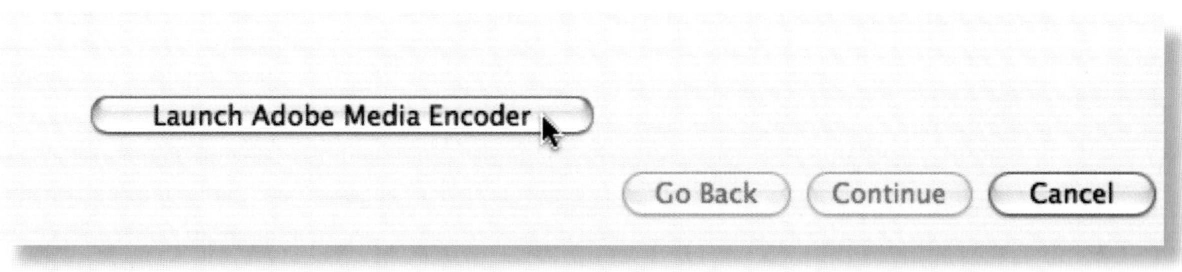

figure | 10–8 |

Launch the Adobe Media Encoder from the Import Video wizard or from your Applications folder on your local hard drive.

figure |10–9|

The Import Video wizard tells you exactly what you need to do to import your video properly into Flash.

8. The file appears in the encoders queue list.

> **Note:** If the file doesn't appear in the queue list, in the AME window, choose Add (see Figure 10–10) and open the **storm_king_swirls.mov** in the **chap10_lessons/video_examples** folder.

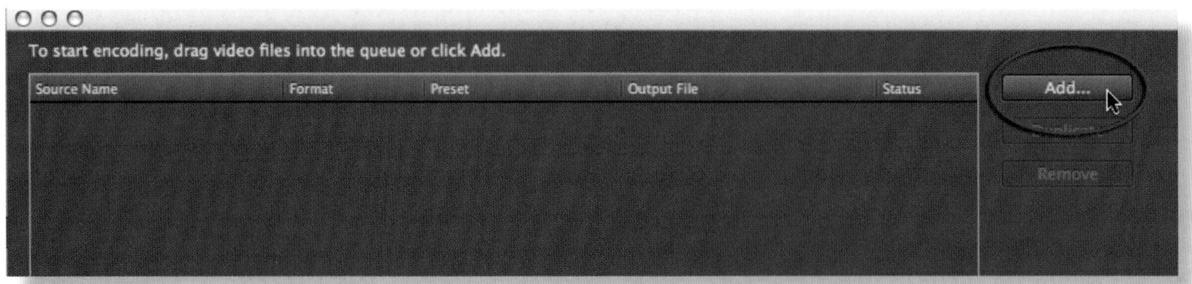

figure |10–10|

Add any number of video clips that you need to convert into the AME.

9. Under Preset, choose the **FLV—Same As Source (Flash 8 and Higher)** option. See Figure 10–11.

> **Note:** There are many preset export settings for various delivery scenarios, and you can even customize your own. The FLV—Same As Source (Flash 8 and Higher) is the required preset to convert the QuickTime video used in the lesson, so it can run properly as an embedded FLV file.

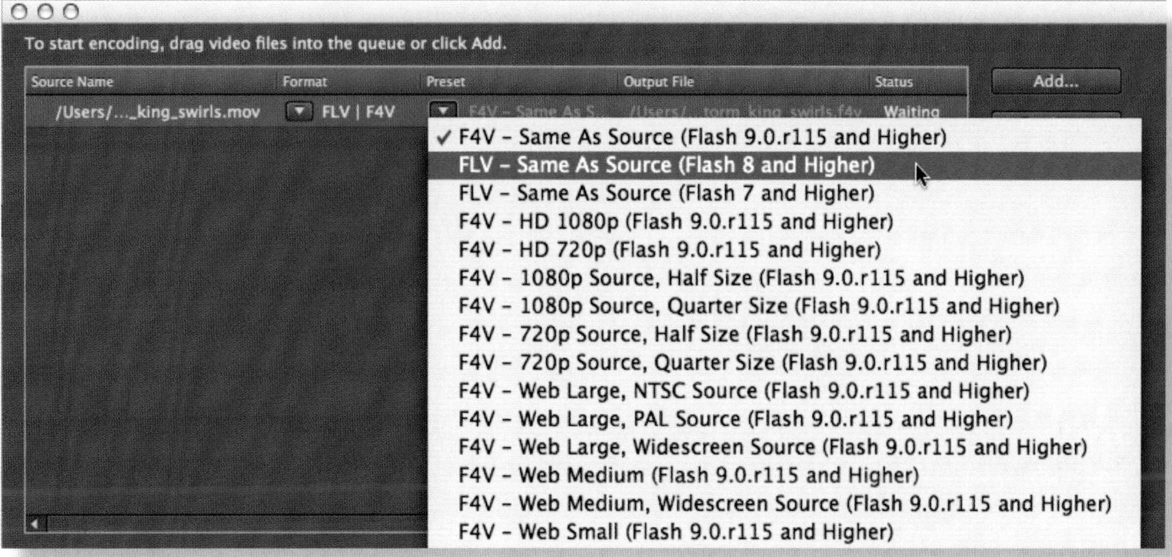

figure 10–11

In the AME, you can select a preset for the video conversion or customize your own. For the lesson, choose FLV—Same As Source (Flash 8 and Higher).

10. Choose the Start Queue button to convert the file. See Figure 10–12. The file can be seen going through its encoding process in the lower part of the AME window.

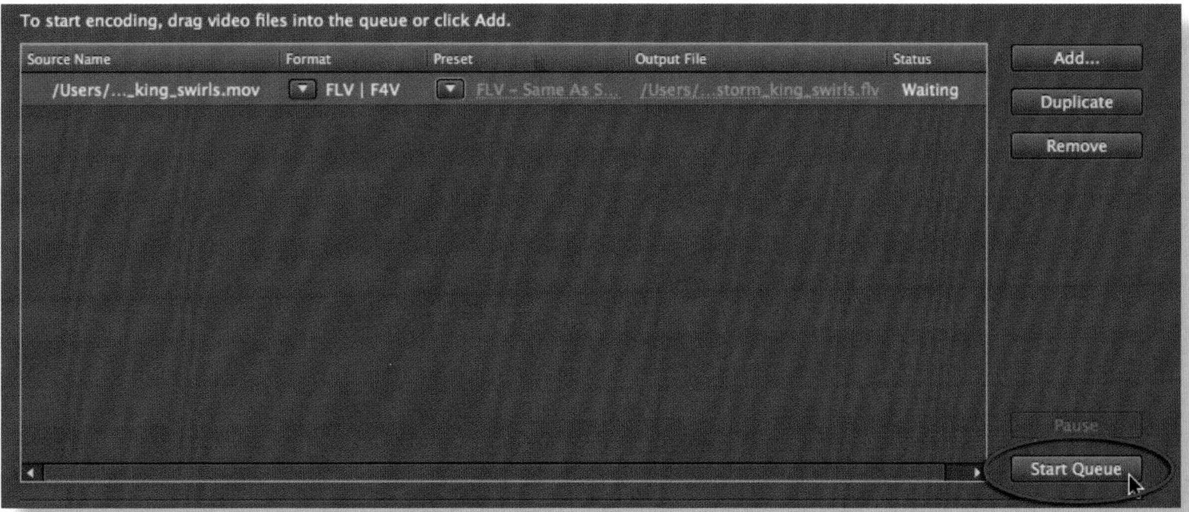

figure 10–12

Start the encoding process.

11. Once the file is encoded, close the AME program. See Figure 10–13.

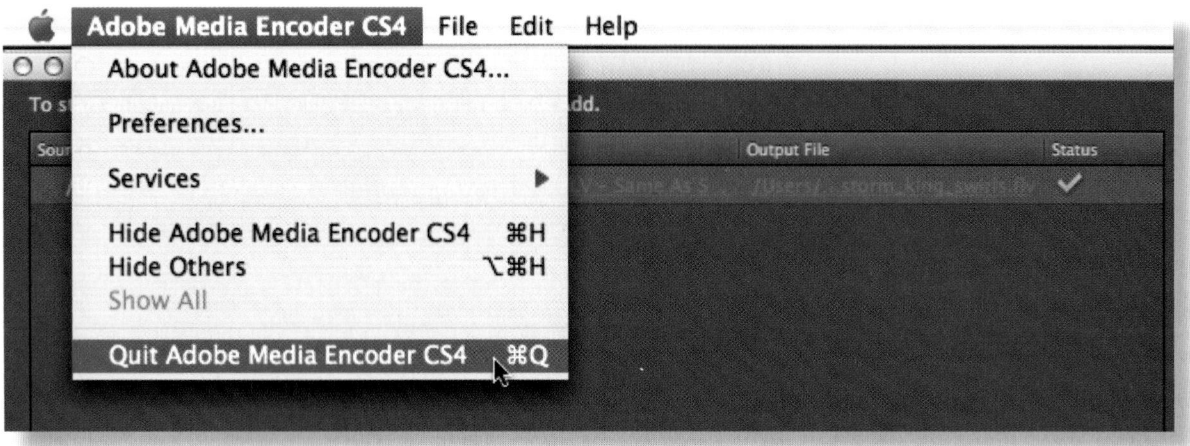

figure | 10–13 |

Close the AME.

12. The Import Video wizard window should still be open. Choose the Browse button again, and search for the FLV file you just created—it should be located in the same folder as your lesson, **my_video.fla** (if not there, check to see if it's in the same folder as the original QuickTime movie—**chap10_lessons/video_examples/storm_king_swirls.flv**).

13. Be sure the **Embed FLV in SWF and play in timeline** option is selected, and then choose Continue at the bottom of the window.

14. In the Embedding options window, choose Symbol type: Movie Clip. This will place the video in a movie clip with an independent timeline for better control. Leave the other settings as they are. See Figure 10–14.

15. Choose Continue again and read the notes in the Finish Flash Import section.

16. Click Finish. An instance of the movie clip video will be placed on the Stage.

17. Rename Layer 1 to **video**.

18. Choose Control > Test Movie to view the video. It repeats by default—just like an animation on a movie clip timeline.

> **Note:** To view the amount of frames that make up the video, double-click on the movie clip video to enter the editing mode. Drag the playback head along the top of the timeline of **Layer 1** (where the video is placed) until you get to the end of the frames. The Storm King video is 339 frames in length, which, downloading at 15 fps, is about 20 seconds long.

19. Save the file.

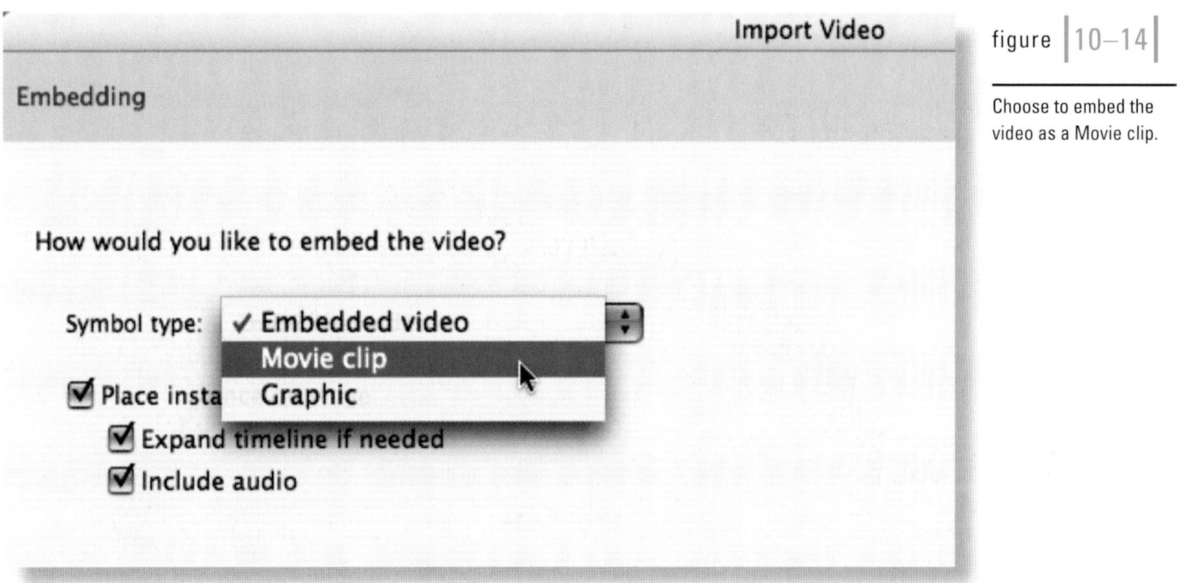

figure 10–14

Choose to embed the video as a Movie clip.

Create a Pause and Play Button with ActionScript

1. For fun and practice, let's create a pause and play button for the video using ActionScript.
2. First, exit out of the editing mode for the **storm_king_swirls.flv** by clicking on Scene 1 in the upper left corner of the movie window.
3. Select the video, and in the Properties panel, give it the instance name **storm_king**. See Figure 10–15.
4. Create a new layer and call it **buttons**.
5. Choose Window > Common Libraries > Buttons, and from the **playback rounded** folder, place an instance of the **rounded green pause** and **rounded green play** button to the lower right corner of the video. See Figure 10–16.

figure 10–15

Assign the video an instance name.

> **Note:** If you prefer to choose a different pause and play button from the Library or make your own, go for it!

figure | 10–16 |

Position the pause and play buttons.

6. Click the pause button on the Stage to select it and open the Actions panel (Alt/Option F9). Enter the following code (watch your syntax!) in the Actions panel (see Figure 10–17):

```
on (release) {

this.storm_king.stop();

}
```

> **Note:** The word "this" is actually a reserved word in the ActionScript language. It is a global property that is often used in ActionScript to reference an object or movie clip instance on the Stage.

figure | 10–17 |

```
on (release) {
    this.storm_king.stop();

}
```

Create an action on the pause button.

7. Keep the Actions panel open and select the play button. Enter the following code carefully (see also Figure 10–18):

```
on (release) {

  if(this.storm_king._currentframe == this.storm_king._totalframes){

          this.storm_king.gotoAndPlay(1);

  } else {

          this.storm_king.play();

  }

}
```

```
on (release) {
    if(this.storm_king._currentframe == this.storm_king._totalframes){
        this.storm_king.gotoAndPlay(1);
    } else {
        this.storm_king.play();
    }

}
```

Script Assist

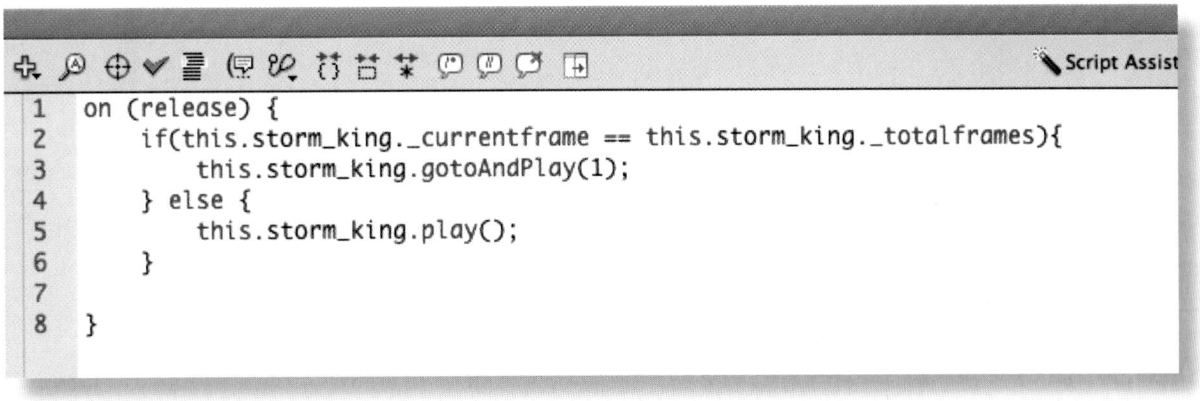

figure |10–18|

Create an action on the play button.

Note: Why so much code for the simple action—play? This is what is termed a conditional statement, or "if. . .then" statement. Basically, the action translates as follows: on the release of the play button, if the current frames of the video (called "storm_king") equals the total frames in the video (it's at the end of the video, in other words), go back to frame one of the video and play. Otherwise, just start playing from the frame where it was paused.

Note: A cautionary warning here is that in this lesson, we named the video instance **storm_king**, but just like on instance objects in previous lessons, you can choose any instance name you'd like. If you do, however, be sure that the instance name you choose is also the same one (with the same, exact spelling) that is being coded into any ActionScript that is calling that instance.

8. Close the Actions panel and test the movie.

9. Create an accessibility text description (Alt tag) of the video movie clip, so that users who are unable or choose not to view the video will have some indication that a video element exists on the page. Select the video movie clip on the Stage.

10. Choose Window > Other Panels > Accessibility and enter a short description name in the Name area, and then a more detailed description in the Description area. See Figure 10–19. Close the panel.

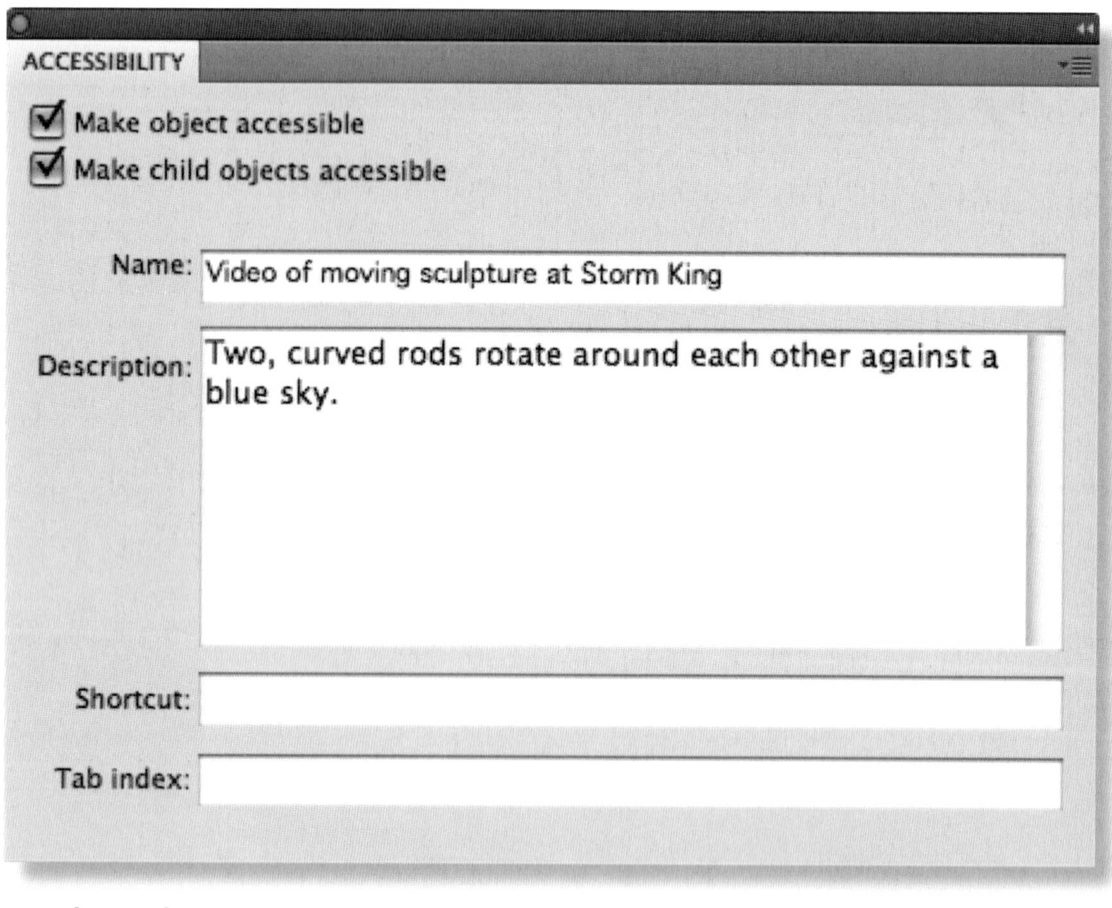

figure 10–19

Create a text equivalent for the video to be read by those with screen readers or who choose to turn off images from view in their browser.

> **Note:** For more information on accessibility in Flash, see Adventures in Design: Accessibility in Flash after Chapter 8.

11. Finally, make the movie stand out—create a colorful background frame for the movie. See my final version in the **chap10_lessons** folder—**chap10L1_final.fla**—and Figure 10–20.

12. Save your creation and close the file.

figure |10–20|

Create a background frame for the video and test out its functionality.

Lesson 2: Externally Loading Video Using a Component

In this lesson, let's explore a different method for implementing video into a Flash movie. First, you will set up your file structure as if you are preparing your movie and video to be uploaded to a Web site, use the Import Video wizard to call in the video from an external location, and then adjust options using the FLVPlayback Component.

Setting up the File Structure

1. Before getting into Flash, you want to set up a folder that will contain all the elements necessary to make your video presentation run properly on the Web. In your lessons folder (or somewhere on your computer), create a new folder and call it **My_Flash_Video**.

2. From the **chap10_lessons/video_examples** folder on the back of the CD, place a copy of the **storm_king_balance.flv** and **storm_king_eye.flv** files into your **My_Flash_Video** folder.

> **Note:** The video files have already been converted to the FLV format using the AME you explored in Lesson 1.

3. Now, open Flash and create a new Flash file (ActionScript 2.0).
4. Choose File > Save and save your file as **my_video_external.fla** in your **My_Flash_Video** folder.
5. Be sure the Classic workspace is selected.

Importing the Video

1. Choose Import > Import Video to open the Import Video wizard.
2. Choose Browse and open the **storm_king_balance.flv** in your **My_Flash_Video** folder.
3. Choose the **Load external video with playback component** option. See Figure 10–21.

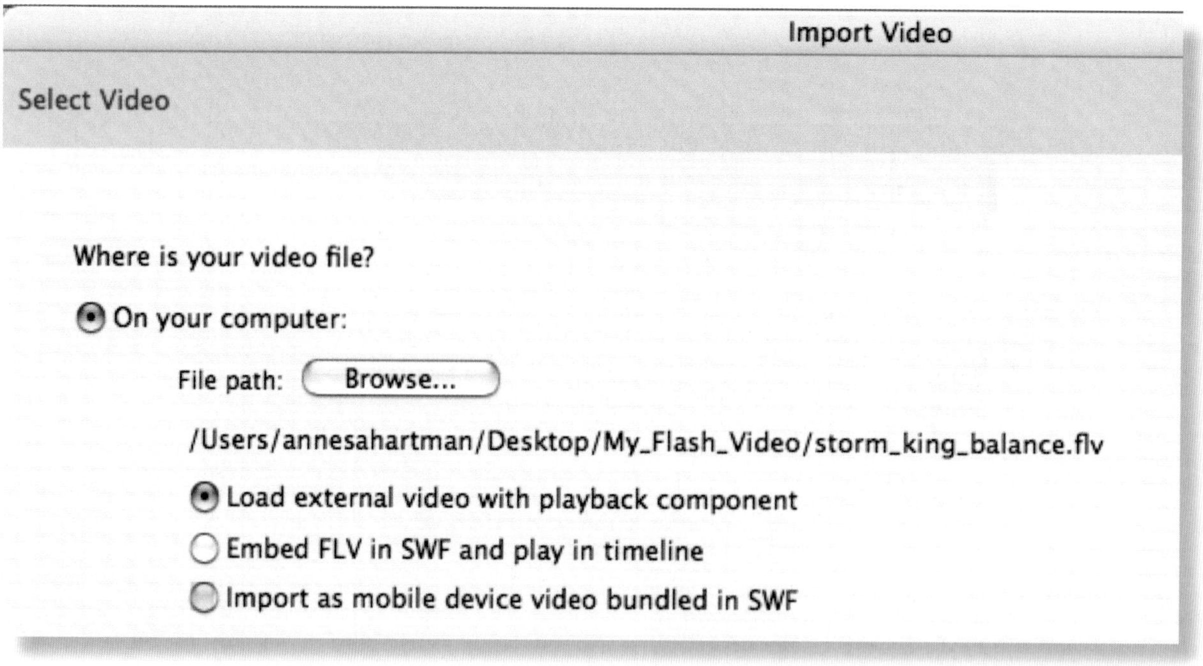

figure 10–21

Load external video with a playback component using the Import Video wizard.

4. Choose the Continue button.

5. Under the Skin option, choose the **SteelExternalAll.swf**. See Figure 10–22. A skin is a graphic element that contains the playback functionality of the video. Flash provides many premade skins. Some are placed over the video, and others are placed below the video element—feel free to check out the different skin options, and then settle on the **SteelExternalAll.swf** for this lesson.

6. Read the notes in the Skinning section of the wizard, and then choose the Continue button.

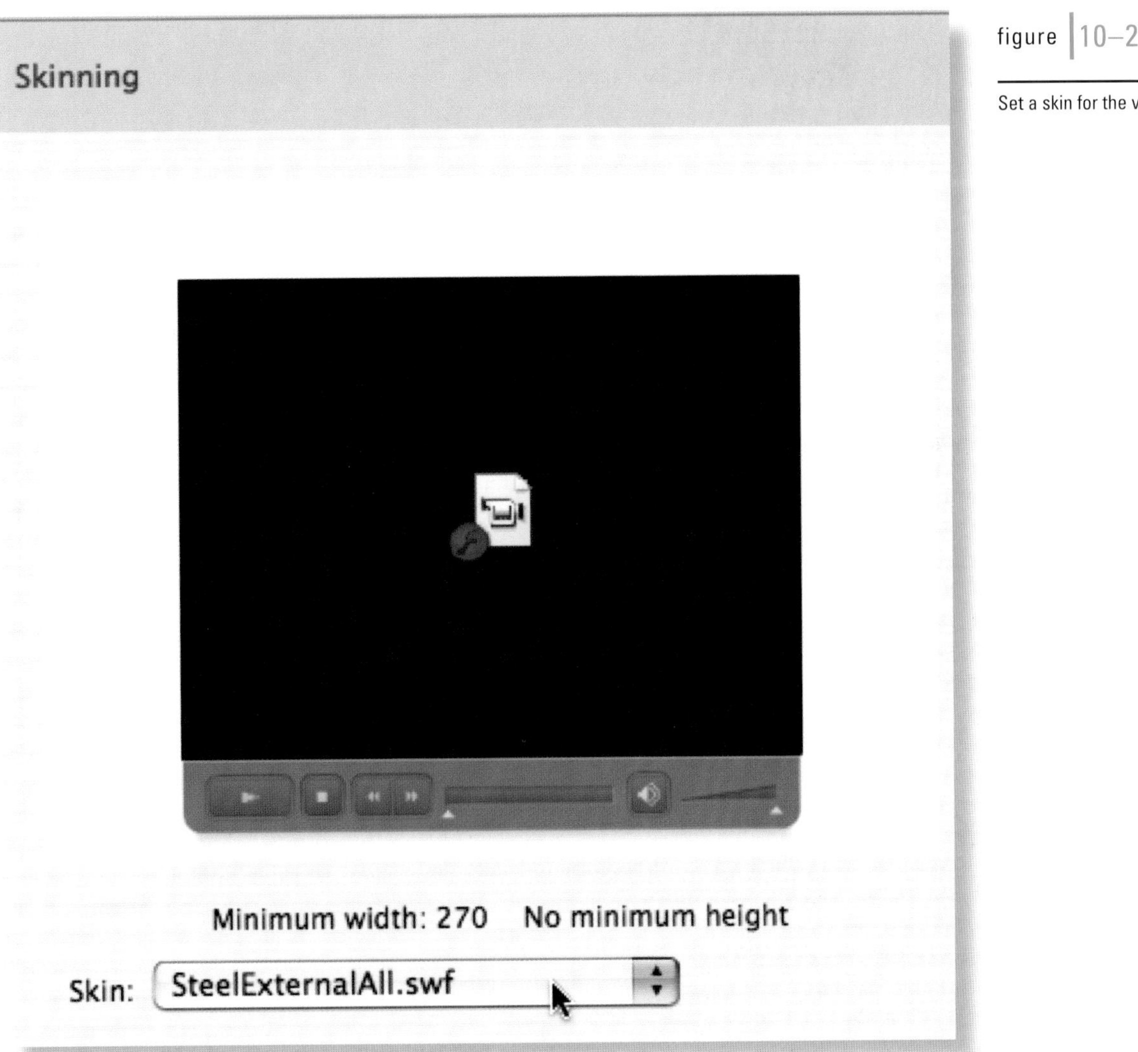

figure 10–22

Set a skin for the video.

7. Read carefully the information in the Finish Video Import section of the wizard. This information is provided as a reminder of how you will need to configure your file structure so that the video will play properly once loaded to a Web site. We won't load the content to a Web site, but it's good to know this information for when you eventually do! Select the Finish button.

8. The video appears on the Stage with the SteelExternalAll skin included. Choose Control > Test Movie to play the video and test out the controls. This video clip is a bit amateur, but it works—I recorded it at the Storm King Art Center, and then converted and optimized it for online delivery in iMovie. See Figure 10–23.

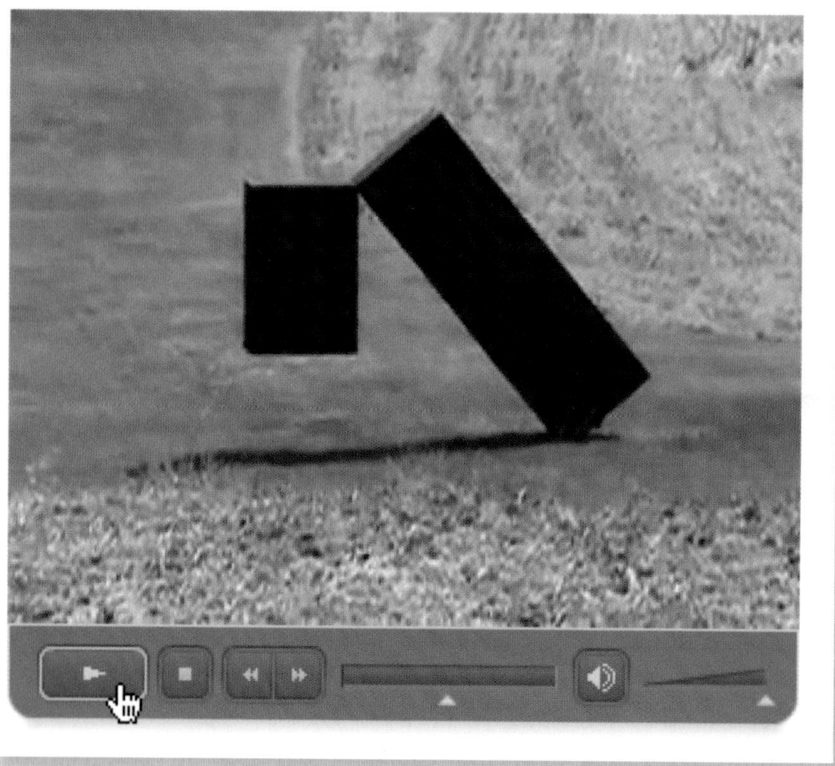

figure |10–23|

Explore the functionality of the video's playback.

9. Save your file.

Exploring the FLVPlayback Component

1. The functionality of this video is created automatically using the FLVPlayback Component—very swift! Open the Library panel to see the FLVPlayback Component in the Library.

2. Double-click on the FLVPlayback icon in the Library to open its Linkage Properties. Note that a unique identifier "FLVPlayback" has already been applied to the Component. See Figure 10–24. If you recall, you created identifiers for the sound files you explored in Chapter 9, which enabled you to call them properly into your FLA file and add interactivity. Same idea here. Close the Linkage Properties panel.

3. Select the video on the Stage and choose Window > Component Inspector. In the Parameters area, note the parameters that have already been defined for you. Especially, note the file name in the contentPath area—it indicates the location and the name of the video file. Let's try something; double-click on the file name **storm_king_balance.flv**, to open the Content Path window. See Figure 10–25.

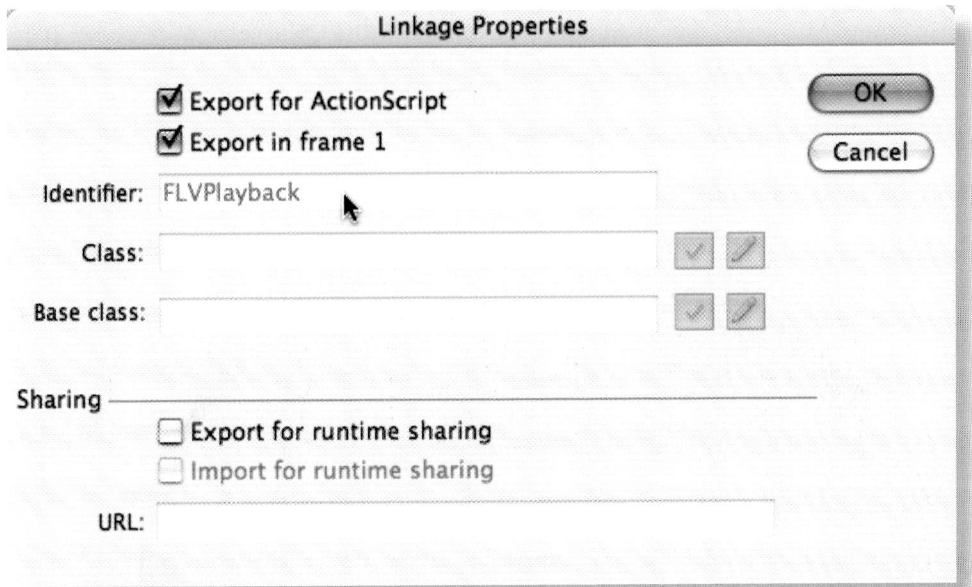

figure 10–24

The automatic functionality of the video uses the FLVPlayback Component. In the Linkage Properties of the video, a unique identifier is created in order for the Component to work properly.

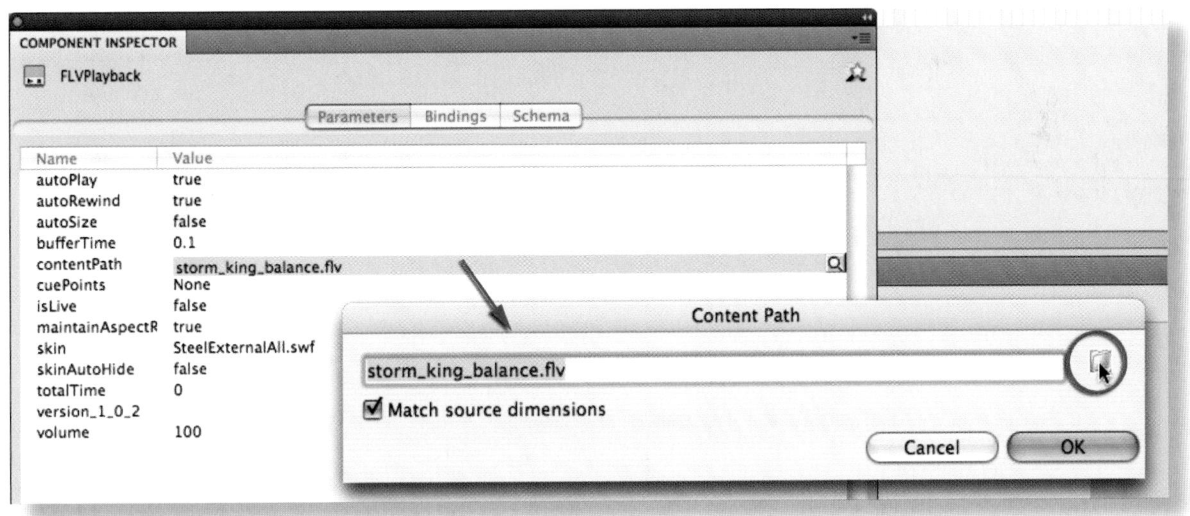

figure 10–25

Adjust the path for where the external video is located in the Component Inspector.

4. Change the video that is being called into the FLVPlayback Component—in the Content Path window, click on the folder to the right of the file name (refer to Figure 10–25 again) and browse for and select the file **storm_king_eye.flv** in your **My_Flash_Video** folder.

5. Choose OK in the Content Path window. The video is updated with the new one you imported.

6. Choose Control > Test Movie to test the new video. As you can see, the video presented in the Flash movie is explicitly linked to the video you select in the FLVPlayback parameters. If the video file is moved outside of the **My_Flash_Video** folder, the link will need to be updated to function properly.

7. One more thing to be aware of is to minimize Flash, and open your **My_Flash_Video** folder. Note that there is a new file that has been created in the folder along with the FLV video files and your **my_video_external.fla** and **swf—SteelExternalAll.swf**. The **SteelExternalAll.swf** is the video skin that makes the FLVPlayback Component work and is important to keep it intact with the rest of the items in your folder. See Figure 10–26.

> **Note:** The name of the skin file—in our lesson example, **SteelExternalAll.swf**—could change depending on the skin style you choose when first setting up an FLVPlayback Component.

8. Save your file. Well done!

figure 10–26

Be sure all the files necessary to make your Flash video presentation run effectively are located in one folder.

SUMMARY

Hopefully the Flash phenomenon has swept you up into its creative whirlwind. With the fundamentals of Flash now at your fingertips, no multimedia project—replete with graphics, animation, interactivity, audio, and video—is out of your reach. Go for the stars!

in review

1. What is a standard frame rate for playback of video via the Web?
2. What are some standard width and height pixel sizes for a Web video?
3. Define encoding.
4. What are FLV and F4V?
5. Explain the purpose of the AME.
6. Name at least two advantages of loading video externally into a SWF file rather than embedding?
7. What is a skin?
8. Why is it important to keep your file structure organized when working with an externally linked video?

exploring on your own

1. Looking for inspiration?
   - See Explorer Pages: James Couture after Chapter 9 for video examples and a personal account of working with Flash video.
   - Visit Adobe's Flash Developer Center for Flash video templates: *http://www.adobe.com/devnet/flash/video_templates.html*
2. Review some tips on preparing video for online delivery; visit: *http://videoeditingtips.net/* and/or do your own "video editing tips" search on the Web.

| *index* |

A

B

C

D

E

F

G

H

I

N

O

S

T

U

V

W

Z

IMPORTANT! READ CAREFULLY: This End User License Agreement ("Agreement") sets forth the conditions by which Cengage Learning will make electronic access to the Cengage Learning-owned licensed content and associated media, software, documentation, printed materials, and electronic documentation contained in this package and/or made available to you via this product (the "Licensed Content"), available to you (the "End User"). BY CLICKING THE "I ACCEPT" BUTTON AND/OR OPENING THIS PACKAGE, YOU ACKNOWLEDGE THAT YOU HAVE READ ALL OF THE TERMS AND CONDITIONS, AND THAT YOU AGREE TO BE BOUND BY ITS TERMS, CONDITIONS, AND ALL APPLICABLE LAWS AND REGULATIONS GOVERNING THE USE OF THE LICENSED CONTENT.

1.0 SCOPE OF LICENSE

1.1 Licensed Content. The Licensed Content may contain portions of modifiable content ("Modifiable Content") and content which may not be modified or otherwise altered by the End User ("Non-Modifiable Content"). For purposes of this Agreement, Modifiable Content and Non-Modifiable Content may be collectively referred to herein as the "Licensed Content." All Licensed Content shall be considered Non-Modifiable Content, unless such Licensed Content is presented to the End User in a modifiable format and it is clearly indicated that modification of the Licensed Content is permitted.

1.2 Subject to the End User's compliance with the terms and conditions of this Agreement, Cengage Learning hereby grants the End User, a nontransferable, nonexclusive, limited right to access and view a single copy of the Licensed Content on a single personal computer system for noncommercial, internal, personal use only. The End User shall not (i) reproduce, copy, modify (except in the case of Modifiable Content), distribute, display, transfer, sublicense, prepare derivative work(s) based on, sell, exchange, barter or transfer, rent, lease, loan, resell, or in any other manner exploit the Licensed Content; (ii) remove, obscure, or alter any notice of Cengage Learning's intellectual property rights present on or in the Licensed Content, including, but not limited to, copyright, trademark, and/or patent notices; or (iii) disassemble, decompile, translate, reverse engineer, or otherwise reduce the Licensed Content.

2.0 TERMINATION

1.1 Cengage Learning may at any time (without prejudice to its other rights or remedies) immediately terminate this Agreement and/or suspend access to some or all of the Licensed Content, in the event that the End User does not comply with any of the terms and conditions of this Agreement. In the event of such termination by Cengage Learning, the End User shall immediately return any and all copies of the Licensed Content to Cengage Learning.

3.0 PROPRIETARY RIGHTS

3.1 The End User acknowledges that Cengage Learning owns all rights, title and interest, including, but not limited to all copyright rights therein, in and to the Licensed Content, and that the End User shall not take any action inconsistent with such ownership. The Licensed Content is protected by U.S., Canadian and other applicable copyright laws and by international treaties, including the Berne Convention and the Universal Copyright Convention. Nothing contained in this Agreement shall be construed as granting the End User any ownership rights in or to the Licensed Content.

2.2 Cengage Learning reserves the right at any time to withdraw from the Licensed Content any item or part of an item for which it no longer retains the right to publish, or which it has reasonable grounds to believe infringes copyright or is defamatory, unlawful, or otherwise objectionable.

4.0 PROTECTION AND SECURITY

4.1 The End User shall use its best efforts and take all reasonable steps to safeguard its copy of the Licensed Content to ensure that no unauthorized reproduction, publication, disclosure, modification, or distribution of the Licensed Content, in whole or in part, is made. To the extent that the End User becomes aware of any such unauthorized use of the Licensed Content, the End User shall immediately notify Cengage Learning. Notification of such violations may be made by sending an e-mail to infringement@cengage.com.

5.0 MISUSE OF THE LICENSED PRODUCT

5.1 In the event that the End User uses the Licensed Content in violation of this Agreement, Cengage Learning shall have the option of electing liquidated damages, which shall include all profits generated by the End User's use of the Licensed Content plus interest computed at the maximum rate permitted by law and all legal fees and other expenses incurred by Cengage Learning in enforcing its rights, plus penalties.

6.0 FEDERAL GOVERNMENT CLIENTS

6.1 Except as expressly authorized by Cengage Learning, Federal Government clients obtain only the rights specified in this Agreement and no other rights. The Government acknowledges that (i) all software and related documentation incorporated in the Licensed Content is existing commercial computer software within the meaning of FAR 27.405(b)(2); and (2) all other data delivered in whatever form, is limited rights data within the meaning of FAR 27.401. The restrictions in this section are acceptable as consistent with the Government's need for software and other data under this Agreement.

7.0 DISCLAIMER OF WARRANTIES AND LIABILITIES

7.1 Although Cengage Learning believes the Licensed Content to be reliable, Cengage Learning does not guarantee or warrant (i) any information or materials contained in or produced by the Licensed Content, (ii) the accuracy, completeness or reliability of the Licensed Content, or (iii) that the Licensed Content is free from errors or other material defects. THE LICENSED PRODUCT IS PROVIDED "AS IS," WITHOUT ANY WARRANTY OF ANY KIND AND CENGAGE LEARNING DISCLAIMS ANY AND ALL WARRANTIES, EXPRESSED OR IMPLIED, INCLUDING, WITHOUT LIMITATION, WARRANTIES OF MERCHANTABILITY OR FITNESS FOR A PARTICULAR PURPOSE. IN NO EVENT SHALL CENGAGE LEARNING BE LIABLE FOR: INDIRECT, SPECIAL, PUNITIVE OR CONSEQUENTIAL DAMAGES INCLUDING FOR LOST PROFITS, LOST DATA, OR OTHERWISE. IN NO EVENT SHALL CENGAGE LEARNING'S AGGREGATE LIABILITY HEREUNDER, WHETHER ARISING IN CONTRACT, TORT, STRICT LIABILITY OR OTHERWISE, EXCEED THE AMOUNT OF FEES PAID BY THE END USER HEREUNDER FOR THE LICENSE OF THE LICENSED CONTENT.

8.0 GENERAL

8.1 Entire Agreement. This Agreement shall constitute the entire Agreement between the Parties and supercedes all prior Agreements and understandings oral or written relating to the subject matter hereof.

8.2 Enhancements/Modifications of Licensed Content. From time to time, and in Cengage Learning's sole discretion, Cengage Learning may advise the End User of updates, upgrades, enhancements and/or improvements to the Licensed Content, and may permit the End User to access and use, subject to the terms and conditions of this Agreement, such modifications, upon payment of prices as may be established by Cengage Learning.

8.3 No Export. The End User shall use the Licensed Content solely in the United States and shall not transfer or export, directly or indirectly, the Licensed Content outside the United States.

8.4 Severability. If any provision of this Agreement is invalid, illegal, or unenforceable under any applicable statute or rule of law, the provision shall be deemed omitted to the extent that it is invalid, illegal, or unenforceable. In such a case, the remainder of the Agreement shall be construed in a manner as to give greatest effect to the original intention of the parties hereto.

8.5 Waiver. The waiver of any right or failure of either party to exercise in any respect any right provided in this Agreement in any instance shall not be deemed to be a waiver of such right in the future or a waiver of any other right under this Agreement.

8.6 Choice of Law/Venue. This Agreement shall be interpreted, construed, and governed by and in accordance with the laws of the State of New York, applicable to contracts executed and to be wholly preformed therein, without regard to its principles governing conflicts of law. Each party agrees that any proceeding arising out of or relating to this Agreement or the breach or threatened breach of this Agreement may be commenced and prosecuted in a court in the State and County of New York. Each party consents and submits to the nonexclusive personal jurisdiction of any court in the State and County of New York in respect of any such proceeding.

8.7 Acknowledgment. By opening this package and/or by accessing the Licensed Content on this Web site, THE END USER ACKNOWLEDGES THAT IT HAS READ THIS AGREEMENT, UNDERSTANDS IT, AND AGREES TO BE BOUND BY ITS TERMS AND CONDITIONS. IF YOU DO NOT ACCEPT THESE TERMS AND CONDITIONS, YOU MUST NOT ACCESS THE LICENSED CONTENT AND RETURN THE LICENSED PRODUCT TO CENGAGE LEARNING (WITHIN 30 CALENDAR DAYS OF THE END USER'S PURCHASE) WITH PROOF OF PAYMENT ACCEPTABLE TO CENGAGE LEARNING, FOR A CREDIT OR A REFUND. Should the End User have any questions/comments regarding this Agreement, please contact Cengage Learning at Delmar.help@cengage.com.